SHAKESPEAREAN CRITICISM

Volume 10

CORIOLANUS

CORIOLANUS
Critical Essays

Edited by
DAVID WHEELER

Routledge
Taylor & Francis Group
LONDON AND NEW YORK

First published in 1995

This edition first published in 2015
by Routledge
2 Park Square, Milton Park, Abingdon, Oxon, OX14 4RN

and by Routledge
711 Third Avenue, New York, NY 10017

Routledge is an imprint of the Taylor & Francis Group, an informa business

© 1995 David Wheeler

All rights reserved. No part of this book may be reprinted or reproduced or utilised in any form or by any electronic, mechanical, or other means, now known or hereafter invented, including photocopying and recording, or in any information storage or retrieval system, without permission in writing from the publishers.

Trademark notice: Product or corporate names may be trademarks or registered trademarks, and are used only for identification and explanation without intent to infringe.

British Library Cataloguing in Publication Data
A catalogue record for this book is available from the British Library

ISBN: 978-1-138-84955-6 (Set)
eISBN: 978-1-315-72488-1 (Set)
ISBN: 978-1-138-85019-4 (Volume 10)
eISBN: 978-1-315-72486-7 (Volume 10)
Pb ISBN: 978-1-138-88773-2 (Volume 10)

Publisher's Note
The publisher has gone to great lengths to ensure the quality of this book but points out that some imperfections from the original may be apparent.

Disclaimer
The publisher has made every effort to trace copyright holders and would welcome correspondence from those they have been unable to trace.

CORIOLANUS
Critical Essays

Edited by
David Wheeler

GARLAND PUBLISHING, INC.
NEW YORK & LONDON / 1995

Copyright © 1995 David Wheeler
All rights reserved

Library of Congress Cataloging-in-Publication Data

Coriolanus : critical essays / edited by David Wheeler
p. cm. — (Shakespeare criticism ; vol. 11)
(Garland reference library of the humanities ; vol. 1646)
Includes bibliographical references.
ISBN 0-8153-1057-9
1. Shakespeare, William, 1564–1616. Coriolanus. 2. Coriolanus, Cnaeus Marcius—In literature. 3. Rome—In literature.
I. Shakespeare, William, 1564–1616. II. Wheeler, David, 1950–
III. Series. IV. Series: Shakespeare criticism ; vol. 11.
PR2805.C68 1995
822.3'3—dc20   94-30211

Printed on acid-free, 250-year-life paper
Manufactured in the United States of America

Contents

General Editor's Introduction	ix
Acknowledgments	xiii
Introduction *David Wheeler*	xv
"Dedication to *The Ingratitude of a Common-Wealth*," 1682 *Nahum Tate*	3
"The Argument of *Coriolanus*," 1710 *Charles Gildon*	7
"'Advertisement' to *Coriolanus*," 1755 *Thomas Sheridan*	11
"*Coriolanus*" (from *The Examiner*, 15 December 1816) *William Hazlitt*	15
From Lecture XXVI, "Criticisms on Shakespeare's Historical Dramas," 1846 *August Wilhelm von Schlegel*	21
From *A Study of Shakespeare*, 1880 *Algernon Charles Swinburne*	23
"*Coriolanus*" (British Academy Lecture, 1912) *A.C. Bradley*	25
"Shakespeare's Coriolanus: Elizabethan Soldier," 1949 *Paul A. Jorgensen*	47
"*Coriolanus*," 1965 *Tyrone Guthrie*	67

"*Coriolanus*: Wordless Meanings
and Meaningless Words," 1966
  James L. Calderwood   77

"Coriolanus: The Anxious Bridegroom," 1968
  Emmett Wilson, Jr.   93

"'Antony and Cleopatra' and 'Coriolanus,'
Shakespeare's Heroic Tragedies:
A Jacobean Adjustment," 1973
  J.L. Simmons   111

"*Coriolanus*," 1974
  Lawrence Danson   123

"'There is a world elsewhere':
Tragedy and History in *Coriolanus*," 1976
  Patricia K. Meszaros   143

"Coriolanus and Stavisky: The Interpenetration
of Art and Politics," 1986
  Felicia Hardison Londré   159

"Annihilating Intimacy in *Coriolanus*," 1986
  Madelon Sprengnether   179

"*Coriolanus*'s Stage Imagery on Stage,
1754–1901," 1987
  John Ripley   203

"*Coriolanus*: Body Politic and Private Parts," 1990
  Zvi Jagendorf   229

"Drama, Politics, and the Hero: *Coriolanus*,
Brecht, and Grass," 1990/91
  Martin Scofield   251

"To Their Own Purpose:
The Treatment of *Coriolanus* in the Restoration
and Eighteenth Century," 1994
  David Wheeler   273

"Shifting Masks, Roles, and Satiric Personae:
Suggestions for Exploring the Edge of Genre
in *Coriolanus*," 1994
  Karen Aubrey   299

Contents vii

"'On Both Sides More Respect':
A Very British *Coriolanus*," 1994
   S.K. Bedford   339

Illustrations   361

Reviews   369

1901 London Production with Sir Henry Irving
   The Athenaeum   371
   Saturday Review   373

1933 Paris Production
   The New York Times   375

1954 New York Production
   The Nation   377
   The New York Times   379
   The New York Times   383

1959 Stratford Production, with Laurence Olivier
   The New York Times   387

1965 New York Production
   The New York Times   389
   Shakespeare Quarterly   393
   Commonweal   397

1979 New York Production
   The Village Voice   403
   New York Magazine   407

1985 London Production
   Newsweek   409
   The New York Times   411

1988 New York Production
   Shakespeare Quarterly   415
   The New Republic   421
   The New York Review of Books   425
   The Nation   433

General Editor's Introduction

The continuing goal of the Garland Shakespeare Criticism Series is to provide the most influential historical criticism, the most significant contemporary interpretations, and reviews of the most influential productions. Each volume in the series, devoted to a Shakespearean play or poem (e.g., the sonnets, *Venus and Adonis*, the *Rape of Lucrece*), includes the most essential criticism and reviews of Shakespeare's work from the late seventeenth century to the present. The series thus provides, through individual volumes, a representative gathering of critical opinion of how a play or poem has been interpreted over the centuries.

A major feature of each volume in the series is the editor's introduction. Each volume editor provides a substantial essay identifying the main critical issues and problems the play (or poem) has raised, charting the critical trends in looking at the work over the centuries, and assessing the critical discourses that have linked the play or poem to various ideological concerns. In addition to examining the critical commentary in light of important historical and theatrical events, each introduction functions as a discursive bibliographic essay that cites and evaluates significant critical works—essays, journal articles, dissertations, books, theatre documents—and gives readers a guide to research on the particular play or poem.

After the introduction, each volume is organized chronologically, by date of publication of selections, into two sections: critical essays and theatre reviews/documents. The first section includes previously published journal articles and book chapters as well as original essays written for the collection. In selecting essays, editors have chosen works that are representative of a given age and critical approach. Striving for accurate historical representation, editors include earlier as well as contemporary criticism. Their goal is to include the widest possible range of critical approaches to the play or poem to demonstrate the multiplicity and complexity of critical response. In most instances, essays have been reprinted in their entirety, not butchered into snippets. The editors have also commissioned original essays (sometimes as many as five to ten) by leading Shakespearean scholars, thus offering the most contemporary, theoretically attentive analyses. Reflecting some recent critical approaches in Shakespearean studies, these new essays approach the play or poem from a multiplicity of perspectives, including feminist, Marxist, new historical, semiotic, mythic, performance/staging, cultural, and/or a combination of these and other methodologies. Some volumes in the series even include bibliographic analyses that have significant implications for criticism.

The second section of each volume in the series is devoted to the play in performance and, again, is organized chronologically by publication date, beginning with some of the earliest and most significant productions and proceeding to the most recent. This section, which ultimately provides a theatre history of the play, should not be regarded as different from or rigidly isolated from the critical essays in the first section. Shakespearean criticism has often been informed by or has significantly influenced productions. Shakespearean criticism over the last twenty years or so has usefully been labeled the "Age of Performance." Readers will find information in this section on major foreign productions of Shakespeare's plays as well as landmark productions in English. Consisting of more than reviews of specific productions, this section also contains a variety of theatre documents, including interpretations written for a particular volume by notable directors whose comments might be titled "The Director's Choice," histories of seminal productions (e.g., Peter Brook's *Titus Andronicus*) in 1955), and even interviews with directors and/or actors. Editors have also included photographs from productions around the world to help readers see and further appreciate the way a Shakespearean play has taken shape in the theatre.

General Editor's Introduction

Each volume in the Garland Shakespeare Criticism Series strives to give readers a balanced, representative collection of the best that has been thought and said about a Shakespearean play or poem. In essence, each volume supplies a careful survey of essential materials in the history of criticism for a Shakespearean play or poem. In offering readers complete, fulfilling, and in some instances very hard to locate materials, editors have made conveniently accessible the literary and theatrical criticism of Shakespeare's greatest legacy, his work.

Philip C. Kolin
University of Southern Mississippi

Acknowledgments

Obviously, in a project of this scope, I needed a great deal of help, and I received assistance from a variety of sources. I am grateful to the contributors and their publishers for allowing me to reprint their fine work. The periodicals, whose reviews of *Coriolanus* are reproduced in this volume, were generously cooperative in tracking down issues and authors and in granting permission to reprint the reviews. I am indebted to Karen Aubrey and Kristina Bedford for their contributions of important new essays. Thanks also to the photographers who graciously assisted in selecting photos and granted permission to reproduce them here.

Philip Kolin, general editor of the Shakespearean Criticism series, was invaluable in getting the project off the ground and in providing guidance and specific suggestions along the way. Many colleagues and administrators at the University of Southern Mississippi supported my work with their time, their expertise, and their money. Special thanks to Terry Harper, dean of the College of Liberal Arts, and to Karen Yarbrough, vice president for Research and Planning.

To my wife Marjorie Spruill Wheeler and my sons Scott and Jesse, I owe much more than a mere line of acknowledgment. They put up with my prolonged reclusion and constant babble about various interpretations and productions of a play that, once unknown to them, is now as familiar as *Gone With the Wind*.

Finally, there is my gratitude to and admiration for Cheryl Wagner, my research assistant. I would venture to say that Cheryl knows as much about *Coriolanus* as anyone alive. She assembled the most complete, indeed, the definitive worldwide production history of the play through her research and her correspondence with theatre companies around the globe. She read hundreds of books, essays, and reviews on *Coriolanus*, evaluating them, classifying them, summarizing them, drawing on her extraordinary comprehension of the play, of Shakespeare, and of competing critical methodologies. Thanks, Cheryl.

David Wheeler
Hattiesburg, MS 1994

Introduction

David Wheeler

When discussing Shakespeare's *Coriolanus*, I should probably begin where most writers begin: the play's unpopularity. And it is true that this, probably the last of the Shakespearean tragedies, has, through the centuries, been one of the least acted and least known of Shakespeare's plays. In itself, this fact is not startling; some of the plays have to be less popular than others, and we all agree that *Coriolanus* is no *Hamlet*. What is provocative (if not actually startling) is that generation after generation of critics have proclaimed for this play, as they have not for *Titus Andronicus*, *Pericles*, *Timon of Athens*, or *King John*, for instance, an essential greatness. Consequently, a great deal has been written about *Coriolanus*, and it is this conflict between the intellectual engagement the play offers those who study it, and the absence of emotional engagement for the general audiences who view it, that requires an explanation.

In 1972, Kenneth Muir offered a reason for *Coriolanus*'s ill success on the stage:

> *Coriolanus* is the least popular of the great tragedies and this is probably due to the character of the hero with whom modern audiences find it more difficult to sympathise than with those who commit murder or adultery.... His bad qualities seem a good deal worse because of one major difference between the Jacobean stage and ours. We profess to believe in democracy: they did not. The story of Coriolanus was nearly always told to illustrate the evils of the democratic form of government.[1]

Muir of course limits his explanation to account only for modern audiences, and we will hold off on the politics for the moment. But he is right to focus on character. Unlike comedies or history plays, which tend to be socially oriented, tragedies focus on individuals. Tragic plot structures record the rising and falling fortunes of the tragic figure. Traditionally (at least since Aristotle), we have tended to evaluate the power of a tragedy by the degree to which we can identify with the cause for the tragic fall and sympathize with the misfortune of the tragic hero(ine). And Muir is also right that we have more sympathy for the murderers Hamlet and Macbeth and the adulterer Antony than we have for Coriolanus. Why?

Some of the reasons here seem to be simple ones. First, the motivations for the precipitative actions of Shakespeare's more popular tragic heroes—and we can continue using Antony, Hamlet, and Macbeth as contrasting examples—are at once easier to understand and to identify with: simply put, they are more basic to human experience. Antony is driven by love (or lust) to his adultery. Ambition, a challenging wife, and encouraging prophesies propel Macbeth to murder and kingship and more murder. And Hamlet (a more difficult case, to be sure), is plagued by distraction, grief, love, and the commands by his father's ghost until he finally kills, and even then the murder of Polonius might be considered accidental. But Coriolanus does the things he does out of a sense of absolute moral righteousness, a righteousness he derives from privilege of birth. He is right simply because of who he is: a patrician, Rome's greatest military hero, Volumnia's son. While Shakespeare has frequently been praised for his universal subjects, for his "holding a mirror up to nature," it's rare to encounter someone like Coriolanus and much rarer, I would think, to feel the way he does. We do not understand his arrogance, and we do not like it.

Shakespeare, however, seems to stack the deck against Coriolanus in ways other than the depiction of his essential, unpleasant character. Whereas the plots of *Antony and Cleopatra*, *Hamlet*, and *Macbeth* all depict a continual decline in the fortunes of their title characters, *Coriolanus* is plotted differently: it's double-peaked as Coriolanus enjoys the great military victory over the Volscians, the triumphal procession into Rome, the

Introduction   xvii

actual election as Consul, then loses the Consulship and is exiled only to rise again in military victory and the bittersweet pleasure of revenge before his sudden and brutal murder. With such a plot, the audience misses the sustained and inevitable decline to death that it experiences with the other tragedies. Additionally, Antony, Hamlet, and Macbeth (as well as Lear and Richard II) all come privately to an understanding of what happened to them, and perhaps to a greater understanding of life in general; indeed, much of these plays' greatness might well be attributed to the profundity of these moments. In *Coriolanus*, however, Shakespeare grants his hero only one real soliloquy: IV.iv.11–26,[2] which comes at a moment pregnant with genuine dramatic potential. Coriolanus has been exiled, is alone in the city of his enemies, and is dressed "*in mean apparel*": an audience should be prepared to sympathize with him. His speech is about the world's "slippery turns," how friends can turn in a moment, seemingly by chance. Some readers have made much of this speech, arguing that here, the great man fallen correctly and tragically comprehends himself as victim to the fickle winds of history. But the speech ends with these lines:

> So with me:
> My birthplace hate I, and my love's upon
> This enemy town. I'll enter: if he slap me
> He does fair justice; if he give me way,
> I'll do his country service. (22–26)

Coriolanus here is not coming to grips with what happened to him; rather, he is explaining to the audience, and perhaps justifying to himself (if his self requires any justification), what he is going to do to Rome. He is explaining his offering his services to his erstwhile foe Aufidius. Thus, this soliloquy is not like the conscience-wrenching soliloquies in the other plays, but like a soliloquy in pre-Shakespearean (such as in the Tudor Interludes or as Marlowe uses soliloquy in *The Jew of Malta*) and early Shakespearean drama (e.g., Richard III's soliloquies) where a character reveals his/her intentions to the audience. (It should be noted that Shakespeare commonly employs this device for his Machiavellian villains: Richard III and Edmund in *King Lear*, for example.) In fact, Coriolanus never has a moment of self-examination or self-reflection. Shakespeare's other major tragic figures are thinkers and (more importantly) poets; Coriolanus is not. Whether he is incapable of thinking deeply and expressing his thoughts poetically or whether he is so certain of his rightness that there is no need for self-reflection, is debatable. In either case, audience identification and sympathy do not come easily.

Coriolanus has sometimes been charged with coldness,[3] but those charges are, I think, misplaced. He loves his family and is loved in return. And he is far from emotionless. Indeed, the Tribunes play his emotions like a fiddle in order to gain political advantage over him. His emotion, though, is not the emotion of Hamlet or Richard II or Lear; rather, it is the hot-blooded military passion of Hotspur, of Antony on occasion, and, of course, of Othello. But unlike Othello, Coriolanus's passion is never self-directed; his actions are unquestionably suicidal, but he would never kill himself. When his behavior is at odds with the world around him, he will attempt to destroy the world.

While the play contains the kinds of scenes that have rendered Shakespeare stageworthy for centuries—battles, confrontations, spectacle, a bloody finale—it must be said, finally, that audiences just do not like Coriolanus. Producers, directors, and writers (in Restoration England and pre-World War II France, for instance) have sometimes used *Coriolanus* to advance political causes, resulting in temporary popularity, sometimes wild and dangerous popularity, as we shall see, but the stage history of the play suffers prolonged gaps that must ultimately be blamed on the unattractiveness of the play's central character.

II

The unpopularity of *Coriolanus* on stage has not daunted critics. For historicists, political or economic critics (particularly Marxists), feminists, psychoanalytic critics, or linguistic-based critics, the play is rich with relevant material. Paul Jorgensen in 1949 simplified the critical scene only slightly in claiming that "the New Variorum *Coriolanus* offers ample evidence that criticism of this play has spent its force upon two sources of conflict: the relationship between the plebs and patricians and

Introduction

the relationship between Coriolanus and his mother."[4] Although critics have pursued other avenues (most notably language-based readings involving metaphor or Coriolanus's peculiar use of, or aversion to, language; source studies; and genre studies), it is the play's politics and Coriolanus's psycho-sexual relationship with Volumnia that have received most attention. Indeed, even Shakespeare's source for the play, North's translation of Plutarch's *Lives of Noble Grecians and Romanes* (1579), raises both issues in its first mention of Caius Martius (Coriolanus):

> *Caius Martius,* whose life we intend now to write, being left an orphan by his father, was brought up under his mother a widowe, who taught us by experience, that orphanage bringeth many discommodities to a childe, but doth not hinder him to become an honest man, and to excell in vertue above the common sorte: as they that are meanely borne, wrongfully doe complayne, that it is the occasion of their casting awaye, for that no man in their youth taketh any care of them to see them well brought up, and taught that were meete.[5]

Both of these topics, however, have expanded from Jorgensen's representation of them, and both of them have been revised by postmodern critical methodologies. Psychoanalytic critics have commented upon Coriolanus's arrested development (hence, Aufidius's taunting label "boy"); the triangular relationship between Volumnia, Coriolanus, and his wife Virgilia; replacement of the missing father by Menenius, the old patrician who refers to Coriolanus as "son"; or a homoerotic relationship between Coriolanus and his rival Aufidius. Political readings include not only studies of the obvious class conflict and its economic causes but also the basic issue of the best form of government: the dangers of democratic rule, the dangers of strong-man rule, and the dangers of an essentially militaristic regime in times of peace.[6]

As I demonstrate in another essay included in this volume, *Coriolanus* was produced several times from the 1680s until the mid-eighteenth century to illustrate the contemporary conflict between the English monarchy and the Parliament. Democratically elected officials were corrupt, incompetent, and unstable, vacillating in their views in accordance with the whims of a fickle electorate; single, hereditary rule inevitably resulted in favoritism for the ruling party and finally in tyranny. In the Restoration and eighteenth century, both sides used *Coriolanus* to advance their positions. While the nineteenth century spectacularized *Coriolanus* and showcased premier actors like John Philip Kemble, William Charles Macready, and Samuel Phelps, the twentieth century has witnessed a variety of productions set deliberately to point to contemporary politics. The best known perhaps is the 1933–34 production of *Coriolan* by La Comédie Française. The storm surrounding this production, chronicled ably by Felicia Hardison Londré in an essay reprinted here, produced riots and death, arguably contributing to the downfall of the government. As Martin Scofield describes in his essay, both Bertolt Brecht (playing upon social unrest in East Germany) and Gunter Grass (responding to Brecht and including a Brecht character—the Boss) adapted the play for post-World War II audiences. And in the United States companies have mounted black, Hispanic, and ethnically diverse productions. In 1993, at the University of Southern Mississippi, Aquila Productions of London staged a *Coriolanus* that looked to the political unrest in the former Soviet Bloc countries of Eastern Europe, countries trying to determine the direction of their governments. Director Peter Meineck referred to the character of Coriolanus as a "nuclear weapon," a nice thing to have around to threaten your enemies and useful in the event of an actual all-out war but extremely dangerous in peacetime. With the end of the Cold War and the downscaling of arsenals, a warrior-weapon like Coriolanus becomes obsolete.

"'Political,': there I said it," announces A.P. Rossiter in the *Coriolanus* essay from his well-known *Angel with Horns* (1961), "*Coriolanus* is about power: about State or *the State*; about order in society and the forces of disorder which threaten 'that integrity which should become' t' (III.i.159); about conflict, not in personal but political life; and—the aspect which catches our minds first—about the conflict of classes."[7] Rossiter is right: *Coriolanus* might well be Shakespeare's most overtly political play. It opens dramatically with a political meeting and a call for revolution:

Introduction xxi

> *First Cit.* We are accounted poor citizens, the patricians
> good. What authority surfeits on would relieve us. If they
> would yield us but the superfluity while it were whole-
> some, we might guess they relieved us humanely; but they
> think we are too dear: the leanness that afflicts us, the
> object of our misery, is as an inventory to particularise
> their abundance; our sufferance is a gain to them. Let us
> revenge this with our pikes, ere we become rakes. For the
> gods know, I speak this in hunger for bread, not in thirst
> for revenge. (I.i.14–24)

Shakespeare takes this class conflict issue from the Roman corn riots described in North's/Plutarch's life of Coriolanus, but Shakespeare moves the event from after the war with the Volscians to the beginning of the play, thereby increasing its importance and dramatically emphasizing the internal political conflict. As Philip Brockbank points out, however,

> although the corn-riots were taken by Shakespeare from
> Plutarch, he could not have been unaware of their
> closeness to his own time. Food shortages in the towns
> and peasant discontents in the country were commonplace
> both in Elizabeth's reign and James's, owing to the
> displacement of tillage by pasture and to the widespread
> enclosure of common land. Among the several insur-
> rections, particular attention has been drawn to the
> Oxfordshire rising of 1597 and the Midlands disturbances
> of 1607/8.[8]

(In our own times, playwright Edward Bond depicts in his play *Bingo* (1973) an elderly and decidedly conservative Shakespeare, retired in Stratford, siding with wealthy landowners against farmers involved in a similar class dispute.)

Offstage patricians compromise with the plebeian leaders by granting elected Tribunes participation in the government. Onstage, however, we find, in the play's most famous speech (I.i.126–54), Menenius disarming the rebels with the weapon of choice for the educated elite—rhetoric. In his "Fable of the Belly," Menenius's Belly declares,

> I receive the general food at first
> Which you do live upon; and fit it is,
> Because I am the store-house and the shop

> Of the whole body. But, if you do remember,
> I send it through the rivers of your blood
> Even to the court, the heart, to th'seat o'th'brain;
> And through the cranks and offices of man,
> The strongest nerves and small inferior veins
> From me receive that natural competency
> Whereby they live. And though that all at once,
> You, my good friends, . . .
>   Though all at once cannot
> See what I do deliver out to each,
> Yet I can make my audit up, that all
> From me do back receive the flour of all,
> And leave me but the bran. (130–45)

Menenius plays upon the common Renaissance metaphor of the body politic, with the Roman Senators as the belly and the people as the more or less distant body members. Though the belly does not labor, as do the hands, legs, back, and arms, in the production of food, it serves as a distribution center, determining allotment, by Menenius's standards, naturally. Menenius's final reference to the First Citizen as the assembly's "great toe," usually produces laughter on stage, bringing about a general goodwill that causes to go unnoticed the way the belly/Senate operates—invisible, secret, unaccountable.

Menenius's affable (but devious) relationship with the plebeians contrasts sharply with Coriolanus's contempt, which we witness almost immediately with his first appearance. Angry at the Senate's capitulation to the people's demands, Coriolanus, in a series of powerful speeches, calls the people "scabs," demoting them even further in the body's hierarchy of parts; derides their fickleness and inability to govern themselves; and finally dismisses them as "fragments" (I.i.221). This final label destroys at once Menenius's attempt (if only lip service) to incorporate the people into a unified body politic. In their analyses of the play reprinted below, both Patricia Meszaros and Zvi Jagendorf focus on the political body metaphor in *Coriolanus*. Meszaros's essay is essentially historicist, arguing that Shakespeare laments the passing of the traditional (and natural) English commonwealth into a more modern, impersonal "state." The Roman story allows him to glorify older values like honor and loyalty and to decry the inevitable political manipulations of

Introduction   *xxiii*

modern statecraft. Jagendorf, however, explores wholeness and fragmentation, presenting Coriolanus as a man striving to maintain the ideal of a self-sufficient whole, the final mutilation of his body vividly and visually illustrating his failure. Similarly, in his essay on the language of *Coriolanus*, Lawrence Danson provides evidence that the play's dominant rhetorical devices are metonymy and synecdoche, "figures of fragmentation and usurpation," rather than the more common, unifying figures of metaphor and simile.

In *Coriolanus*, Shakespeare concerns himself with both internal and external politics—both domestic and foreign affairs—and in doing so, confronts the relatively new force of nationalism. As Kenneth Burke points out,

> The Renaissance was particularly exercised by Machiavelli because he so accurately represented the transvaluation of values involved in the rise of nationalism. A transvaluation was called for, because *religion* aimed at *universal* virtues, whereas the virtues of *nationalism* would necessarily be *factional*, insofar as they pitted nation against nation. Conduct viewed as vice from the standpoint of universal religious values might readily be viewed as admirable if it helped some interests prevail over others.... But though (from the universal point of view) nations confront one another as factions, from the standpoint of any one nation factionalism is conceived in a narrower sense, with nationalism itself taking over the role of the universal.[9]

As the plot progresses, the fragmentation of social classes and political parties gives way to temporary nationalistic unification as Rome battles the invading Volscians. It is during times of war that Coriolanus is in his element. Coriolanus's military exploits exceed those of his Shakespearean counterparts—Antony and Othello, in particular—because they are represented onstage rather than merely related by other characters. Coriolanus's stature, consequently, becomes larger than life, legendary, a stature reinforced by the pageantry of his welcoming procession into Rome. But his lofty stature further removes him from the Roman people, and the walls of Atrium, where he prevailed with superhuman effort, are far removed from the Roman marketplace where political office is bought and sold with "voices."

Coriolanus believes that the Consulship is his by birthright, by military deed, by the Senate's desire. His unwillingness to display publicly his wounds to the people is usually attributed to his uncompromising pride, but his reason is also a political one. Such a presentation would acknowledge, would formalize the rights of the people to participate in Roman government, and Coriolanus refuses to recognize these rights. Volumnia, ambitious for her son in the way that Lady Macbeth is ambitious for her husband, urges Coriolanus to don the gown of humility and go through the motions of the political ritual; in this suggestion, she recalls Menenius in his clever lip service to political conciliation. After making a comparison to using "policy" in war, an analogue that she feels her son will understand, Volumnia explains why such posturing is necessary:

> Because that now it lies you on to speak
> To th'people; not by your own instruction,
> Nor by th'matter which your heart prompts you,
> But with such words that are but roted in
> Your tongue, though but bastards and syllables
> Of no allowance to your bosom's truth.
> Now, this no more dishonours you at all,
> Than to take in a town with gentle words
> Which else would put you to your fortune and
> The hazard of much blood.
> I would dissemble with my nature where
> My fortunes and my friends at stake requir'd
> I should do so in honour. I am in this
> Your wife, your son, these senators, the nobles;
> And you will rather show our general louts
> How you can frown, than spend a fawn upon'em
> For the inheritance of their loves and safeguard
> Of what that want might ruin. (III.ii.52–69)

While much is revealed in Volumnia's speech—the conflation of internal/external, of war and politics; the likening of the people to foreign enemies; and the need to dissemble to advance class/family interests—even more is revealed in Coriolanus's reply:

Introduction

> Well, I must do't.
> Away my disposition, and possess me
> Some harlot's spirit! My throat of war be turn'd,
> Which choired with my drum, into a pipe
> Small as an eunuch, or the virgin voice
> That babies lull asleep! The smiles of knaves
> Tent in my cheeks, and schoolboys' tears take up
> The glasses of my sight! A beggar's tongue
> Make motion through my lips, and my arm'd knees
> Who bow'd but in my stirrup, bend like his
> That hath receiv'd an alms! I will not do't,
> Lest I surcease to honour mine own truth,
> And by my body's action teach my mind
> A most inherent baseness. (III.ii.110–23)

But only a few lines later, he gives in: "Pray be content./Mother, I am going to the market-place:/Chide me no more" (130–32).

Several significant issues merge in this crucial scene. First, Coriolanus comprehends that his most important, indeed his essential, defining characteristic is his unfaltering and absolute loyalty to his "own truth," however misguided we may find that truth or that absolutism to be. Second, by giving in to his mother's request and to factionalist politics, he will fragment his body (essentially, his tongue and mouth, which will utter the false words) from his mind—or worse, corrupt that mind into "a most inherent baseness." And, finally, and most curiously, is the language—the images of childhood and acting—Coriolanus uses to describe the act he is asked to perform. Before an audience of the ruling class, Coriolanus, who just previously had been carried and cheered through the streets of Rome in triumph, finds himself being chided and instructed by his mother; very basically, his mother, like a mother with a reluctant child, manipulates him into doing something he doesn't want to do. Yet, she is his mother, and he cannot say "no."

He realizes that the act will emasculate him, prostitute him, reduce him to a schoolboy, a girl, a beggar, a "mountebank." Critics have seized upon these references to playing, to acting. For example, J.L. Simmons, in his "'Antony and Cleopatra' and 'Coriolanus,' Shakespeare's Heroic Tragedies: A Jacobean Adjustment," reprinted here, argues that Shakespeare is drawing upon the vulgar audiences of his own day and the polarizing class tensions of contemporary England. And James L. Calderwood, in "*Coriolanus*: Wordless Meanings and Meaningless Words," contends that in thus reducing the ceremony of the gown of humility to empty ritual, it becomes, like the fable of the belly, merely a sequence of words, devoid of common meaning, characteristic of a society that has lost its defining social values.

Succumbing to his mother's wishes leads Coriolanus to the disastrous confrontation with the Tribunes in the marketplace. His ultimate failure to "act" precipitates the charges of treason and his exile. In the play's final scene, of course, Coriolanus again gives in to his mother, this time when she begs him to spare his native city. As a Roman delegate, she appeals to his sense of patriotism, to his love for his family, and to his reputation; and last, as a mother, she accuses him of ingratitude:

> There's no man in the world
> More bound to's mother, yet here he lets me prate
> Like one i'th'stocks. Thou hast never in thy life
> Show'd thy dear mother any courtesy,
> When she, poor hen, fond of no second brood,
> Has cluck'd thee to the wars, and safely home,
> Loaden with honour. (V.iii.158–64)

Once again, Coriolanus capitulates:

> O mother, mother!
> What have you done? Behold, the heavens do ope,
> The gods look down, and this unnatural scene
> They laugh at. O my mother, mother! O!
> You have won a happy victory to Rome;
> But for your son, believe it, O, believe it,
> Most dangerously you have with him prevail'd,
> If not most mortal to him. (V.iii.182–89)

And once again Coriolanus is alert to the destructive impact succumbing to Volumnia is likely to have. As if immediately, if subconsciously, aware of the source of that destruction, a tearful Coriolanus, seeking validation, turns to Aufidius:

> Aufidius, though I cannot make true wars,
> I'll frame convenient peace. Now, good Aufidius,

Introduction

xxvii

> Were you in my stead, would you have heard
> A mother less? or granted less, Aufidius? (190–93)

In an aside, Aufidius makes it clear to us that he will play upon Coriolanus's honorable intention to secure for the Volscians a "convenient peace," an intention that requires his continued presence within Aufidius's grasp, to overleap his rival and secure for himself his former place as Volscian leader.

Both Aufidius and Volumnia are able to maneuver Coriolanus into carrying out their will because, at various moments in the play, he desires so much to please them. Psychoanalytic critics,[10] in their efforts to explain these complex relationships, have tended to focus on several pertinent passages in the play. The psycho-sexual nature of the Volumnia-Coriolanus relation-ship is perhaps best expressed in this oft-quoted speech spoken by Volumnia to Virgilia, who anxiously awaits her husband's return from the war:

> I pray you, daughter, sing, or express yourself in a more comfortable sort. If my son were my husband I should freelier rejoice in that absence wherein he won honour, than in the embracements of his bed, where he would show most love. When yet he was but tender-bodied, and the only son of my womb; when youth with comeliness plucked all gaze his way; when for a day of kings' entreaties, a mother should not sell him an hour from her beholding; I, considering how honour would become such a person—that it was no better than picture-like to hang by th'wall, if renown made it not stir—was pleased to let him seek danger where he was like to find fame. To a cruel war I sent him, from whence he returned, his brows bound with oak. I tell thee, daughter, I sprang not more in joy at first hearing he was a man-child, than now in first seeing he had proved himself a man. (I.iii.1–18)

Volumnia created him, raised him to be the honorable warrior, and the First Citizen is correct in saying of Coriolanus's deeds, "though soft-conscienced men can be content to say it was for his country, he did it to please his mother" (I.i.36–38). In her essay, "Annihilating Intimacy in *Coriolanus*," Madelon Sprengnether explores the theme of maternal destructiveness in the play, contrasting the effects of the hero's intimacy with a woman with those in plays—*Romeo and Juliet*, *Antony and Cleopatra*, and *Othello*—where similar destructiveness is present.

Analysis of the Coriolanus-Aufidius relationship centers upon Coriolanus's self-proclaimed identification with his rival:

> They have a leader,
> Tullus Aufidius, that will put you to't.
> I sin in envying his nobility;
> And were I anything but what I am,
> I would wish me only he . . .
> Were half to half the world by th'ears, and he
> Upon my party, I'd revolt to make
> Only my wars with him. He is a lion
> That I am proud to hunt. (I.i.227-35)

Aufidius is the male figure to whom Coriolanus turns after both capitulations to his mother, and, thus, has been sometimes interpreted as a father-figure. But, as Emmett Wilson demonstrates in "The Anxious Bridegroom," the relationship is ripe for homoerotic interpretations. When the exiled Coriolanus reveals his identity to Aufidius, the Volscian leader replies,

> Let me twine
> Mine arms about that body, where against
> My grained ash an hundred times hath broke,
> And scarr'd the moon with splinters. Here I clip
> The anvil of my sword, and do contest
> As hotly and as nobly with thy love
> As ever in ambitious strength I did
> Contend against thy valour. Know thou first,
> I lov'd the maid I married; never man
> Sigh'd truer breath; but that I see thee here,
> Thou noble thing, more dances my rapt heart
> Than when I first my wedded mistress saw
> Bestride my threshold. (IV.v.107-19)

Wilson suggests that castration and death are the prices Coriolanus pays for Aufidius's protection. In his essay on staging *Coriolanus*, Tyrone Guthrie, esteemed for his contributions to American theatre and for his productions of Shakespeare in particular, emphasizes that directors must be aware of the nature of the Coriolanus-Aufidius relationship. Exiled from family, friends, and native land, Coriolanus in

Introduction

Antium turns to his former rival for acceptance in what Guthrie refers to as a "love scene." Modern productions have occasionally played this theme. For instance, in a review of the 1984 BBC television production of *Coriolanus*, Roger Warren describes the staging:

> Coriolanus and Aufidius fought their duel virtually naked. After they had beaten the weapons out of each others' hands, they continued to grapple, their hands around one another's throats—but the stranglehold became almost an embrace: as they stared infatuated into each other's eyes, there was a cross-cut back to Rome. The effect was repeated when Coriolanus went to Antium. Aufidius took Coriolanus by the throat before embracing him and massaging his chest slowly and intently as he said that seeing Coriolanus there "more dances my rapt heart/Than when I first my wedded mistress saw/Beside my threshold." He and Aufidius were locked together once again during their final exchange, one sword held by both of them: as Aufidius turned the point toward him, Coriolanus seemed to accept it almost willingly, aware that by yielding to his mother and sparing Rome he had destroyed himself, in personal terms by being false to his "absolute" nature, in practical terms by placing himself in Aufidius' power. The conspirators were omitted, and their line "Kill, kill" was obsessively repeated by both Coriolanus and Aufidius, united to the end.[11]

In focusing their attention on the play's politics and the psycho-sexual nature of the relationships between characters, modern critics depart from the formal, structural studies and "great themes" approaches that characterize most traditional literary analysis of tragedies, in particular those of older critics such as H.N. Hudson, A.C. Bradley, Willard Farnham, and Eugene Waith.[12] In her provocative essay, "Shifting Masks, Roles, and Satiric Personae: Suggestions for Exploring the Edge of Genre in *Coriolanus*," written expressly for this volume, Karen Aubrey suggests that the failure of traditional critical approaches to explain the peculiar power of *Coriolanus* might well reside in a misunderstanding of the play's fundamental generic framework. Relying on theoretical formulations developed by Mikhail

Bakhtin, Aubrey offers a satiric reading, which accounts for the almost-continual undercutting of the central hero.

III

While this volume provides primarily a critical history of *Coriolanus*, it does not neglect the stage history of the play, and clearly productions can validate or at least expand critical readings. Though performances were scarce during the late seventeenth and eighteenth centuries, when *Coriolanus* was presented, it was often in adapted forms and often for political purposes. From the mid-eighteenth century until early in this century, the play showcased the lead actor and became a vehicle for stage spectacle, often introducing onstage hundreds of actors and, on occasion, live animals. In his 1987 *Coriolanus*'s Stage Imagery on Stage, 1754–1901," John Ripley offers a lively description of these productions, arguing persuasively that they depart radically from the minimalist power of the Shakespearean original. The full force of *Coriolanus* does not resurface, he maintains, until the twentieth century.

With the burgeoning proliferation of productions of Shakespeare in the second half of the twentieth century, *Coriolanus* has been performed with increasing regularity. While not enjoying the worldwide attention of Shakespeare's better-known works, the play has been staged successfully in Holland and Germany and, of course, particularly in the United States and Great Britain. The "Reviews" section records critics' reactions to prominent New York and British productions, with special attention to political interpretations, staging concerns, and the character of Coriolanus. Complementary to this section is S.K. Bedford's detailed account of London's 1984–85 National Theatre production, which was directed by Peter Hall and featured Ian McKellen in the title role. Bedford's own active participation as the director's assistant in the famous production provides a level of insight to the workings of a theatre company that is invaluable for students of Shakespeare, particularly literary ones.

Introduction

While certainly making no claims for comprehensiveness, this collection provides important and interesting critical essays on Shakespeare's *Coriolanus*. These essays are representative of both the time in which they were written and the critical approach from which they derive. Taken collectively, they identify those aspects of the play that have attracted critics of all ages and those critical directions from which the play has been examined. They provide any student of *Coriolanus*, consequently, a critical history of one of Shakespeare's most controversial plays and suggestions for avenues that might reward future exploration.

NOTES

1. Kenneth Muir, *Shakespeare's Tragic Sequence* (London, 1972; rpt., New York: Barnes and Noble, 1979), p. 172.

2. I refer throughout this introduction to the text of *Coriolanus* provided in the Arden Edition: *Coriolanus*, ed. by Philip Brockbank (London: Routledge, 1976).

3. See, for example, Huntington Brown, "Enter the Shakespearean Tragic Hero," *Essays in Criticism* 3 (1953), 285–302, and Carol Sicherman, "*Coriolanus*: the Failure of Words," *ELH* 39 (1972), 189–207.

4. Paul A. Jorgensen, "Shakespeare's Coriolanus: Elizabethan Soldier," *PMLA* 64 (1949), 221.

5. North's *Plutarch* is included as an appendix in the Arden *Coriolanus*, from which it is quoted here, pp. 313–14.

6. Notable political readings of *Coriolanus* that are not reprinted in this collection include: Hardin Craig, *An Interpretation of Shakespeare* (New York: Dryden Press, 1948), pp. 282–301; A.P. Rossiter, *Angel with Horns* (London: Longman's, 1961), pp. 235–52; Kenneth Muir, *Shakespeare's Tragic Sequence* (London, 1972; rpt., New York: Barnes and Noble, 1979), pp. 172–86; Stanley Cavell, "'Who does the wolf love?': Reading *Coriolanus*," *Representations* 1 (Summer 1983), 1–20; and A.D. Nuttall, *A New Mimesis: Shakespeare and the Representation of Reality* (London: Methuen, 1983).

7. A.P. Rossiter, "Coriolanus," in *Angel with Horns* (London, 1961; rpt. in *Twentieth-Century Interpretations of Coriolanus: A Collection of Critical Essays*, ed. James E. Phillips, Englewood Cliffs, NJ: Prentice-Hall, 1970), p. 62.

8. Philip Brockbank, in Arden *Coriolanus*, p. 26. For studies connecting the play to these peasant uprisings, see Geoffrey Bullough, *Narrative and Dramatic Sources of Shakespeare*, vol. 5, pp. 456–58, 553–58; and E.C. Pettet, "Coriolanus and the Midlands Insurrection of 1607," *Shakespeare Survey* 3 (1950), 34–42.

9. Kenneth Burke, "*Coriolanus*—and the Delights of Faction," *Hudson Review* 19 (1966), 196.

10. In addition to the critics adopting a psychoanalytic approach whose essays are reprinted below, see, for example, Coppélia Kahn, *Man's Estate* (Berkeley: U of California P, 1981), pp. 151–92 and Charles Hofling "An Interpretation of Shakespeare's *Coriolanus*," *American Imago* 14 (1957), 407–35.

11. Quoted in J.C. Bulman and H.R. Coursen, eds., *Shakespeare on Television: An Anthology of Essays and Reviews* (Hanover, NH: U P of New England, 1988), p. 305.

12. Bradley's essay is included here. For others see H.N. Hudson, *Shakespeare: His Life, Art, and Characters*, 2 vols., 4th ed. (Boston: Ginn and Company, 1872), 2, 490–518; Willard Farnham, *Shakespeare's Tragic Frontier: The World of His Final Tragedies* (Berkeley and Los Angeles: U of California P, 1950), pp. 207–64; and Eugene M. Waith, *The Herculean Hero in Marlowe, Chapman, Shakespeare and Dryden* (London: Chatto and Windus; New York: Columbia U P, 1962), pp. 121–43.

Coriolanus

1959 Royal Shakespeare Theatre Production, Stratford
Laurence Olivier as Coriolanus

Photograph by Angus McBean.
Reproduced by permission of the Harvard Theatre Collection.

Dedication to *The Ingratitude of A Common-Wealth*

Nahum Tate

TO
The Right Honourable
CHARL'S
Lord Herbert,
Eldest Son to the
Marquess of Worcester, &c.

My Lord,

    Your Lordship's favour for Learning in General, has encourag'd me to begg your Patronage of the following Sheets, which contain a remarkable piece of Roman History, though form'd into Play. I have yet another Plea for Pardon, since I impose not on your Lordship's Protection a work meerly of my own Compiling; having in this Adventure Launcht out in *Shakespear's* Bottom. Much of what is offered here, is Fruit that grew in the Richness of his Soil; and what ever the Superstructure prove, it was my good fortune to build upon a Rock. Upon a close view of this Story, there appear'd in some Passages, no small Resemblance with the busie *Faction* of our own time. And I confess, I chose rather to set the *Parallel* nearer to Sight, than to throw it off at further Distance. Yet there are none that can apply any Part (as Satyr) on themselves, whose Designs and Practises are not of the same Cast. What offence to any good Subject in Stygmatizing on the Stage, those *Troublers* of the State, that out of private Interest or Mallice, Seduce the

Multitude to *Ingratitude*, against Persons that are not only plac't in Rightful Power above them; but also the Heroes and Defenders of their Country.

Where is the harm of letting the People see what Miseries *Common-Wealths* have been involv'd in, by a blind Compliance with their popular Misleaders: Nor may it be altogether amiss, to give these Projectors themselves, examples how wretched their dependence is on the uncertain Crowd. Faction is a Monster that often makes the slaughter 'twas designed for; and as often turns its fury on those that hatcht it. The Moral therefore of these Scenes being to Recommend Submission and Adherence to Establisht Lawful Power, which in a word, is *Loyalty;* They have so far a natural Claim to your Lordship's Acceptance: This Virtue seeming Inheritance in Your Lordship, and deriv'd from your Ancestours with your Blood. We cannot cast an Eye on the sufferings of His late Majesty, but we find in broad Letters, the Allegiance and Services of Your Lordship's most honourable Grand-Father, who stopt at no Expence of Blood or Fortunes on His behalf; nor was Providence wanting to Crown his Singular worth with a Signal Glory.

> When Civil Discord thro' the Realm had Reign'd,
> And English Swords with English Blood were Stain'd,
> When out of Zeal Religion was expell'd,
> And Men for Conscience 'gainst their Prince Rebell'd,
> The best of Princes—When the Pow'r Divine,
> (On Purposes too deep for Reason's Line)
> Gave Rebell-Arms Success, and seem'd to bring
> Distress at once upon our Saint and King.
> Not *Jesse's* Son seem'd better form'd to Reign,
> Nor were his *Worthies* of a Nobler Strein!
> But what Relief can bravest Valour lend,
> When Heroes, not with Foes, but Fate Contend?
> The Age's Crimes for no less Curse did Call,
> And 'tis Decreed the Royal Cause must Fall!
> Of Conquest thus by Destiny Bereft,
> Our blasted War has yet one Garland Left.
> Alone the Foes united Strength to Fight,
> And Strike the last Fam'd Blow for Royal Right.
> This Honour to the Noble *Worcester* Fell,
> Who, always Brave, Himself did now Excel,
> His Friends, his Troops, his* House, his Cittadel!

Dedication to The Ingratitude of A Common-Wealth

> Here, tho' reduc'd to last Extreams He Lies,
> His cheerful Cannon still the Foe Defies;
> The more Distres't, the more his Virtue Shines,
> His Courage Rising as his Strength Declines:
> Oft from Unequal Force he Guards his Walls,
> Oft in fierce Sallyes on the Leaguer Falls.
> Thus while Expir'd the other Members Lye,
> *Worc'ster* Stirs Last the Heart of Loyalty.

Pardon my Lord this Start, for the Subject is scarce to be thought on without Transport. Nor has the same Fidelity to the Crown been wanting to compleat the Character of the present Marquess of *Worcester;* whose Eminent Virtues have rendred him an Ornament both of our Court and Age. What Expectations then the World conceives of Your Lordship is easily imagin'd, and what Instances of Noblest Qualifications Your Lordship has already given, the World needs no Information: Besides the Goodness of Your Lordship's Temper, and the Justice of your Principles; your Acquaintance with Books, and Judgment in Affairs, so far transcend Your Years, as would secure me from Flattery, though I should Launch into a Panegyrick. But I come to beg Protection, not to give Praise; My greatest Ambition being to Subscribe my Self,

Your Lordships
most Obedient
humble Servant,
N. Tate.

* Ragland Castle (the Marquess of *Worcester's* Seat) the last Garrison held out for the KING.

The Argument of *Coriolanus*

Charles Gildon

Caius Martins [sic] going to the Wars against the Volscians takes *Coriolus*, and beats *Tullus Aufidius*, and has the Glory of the War attributed to him by the Consul. On this he is to sue for the Consulship, which he disdains a great while, but at last submitting he does it aukerdly, and almost bursting with Disdain and Pride. This makes him lose the Consulship, and, on the Tribunes of the Peoples Words with him, rails so at the Commons and the Tribunes that he is accus'd as a Traytor, and at last Banish'd. He goes over to the *Volscians* and heads their Forces against *Rome* not yet prepar'd to receive him; *Cominius* first and *Menenius* next go to intreat him, but he proves inexorable till his Mother, Wife[,] Son, *Valeria*, &c. prevail, and he makes Peace betwixt the *Romans*, and *Volscians*. *Aufidius* on his return to *Antium* accuses him of Treason, and with the Conspirators stabs and kills him.

    The Character of *Martius* is truely Dramatic for his Manners are not only equal but necessary to his Misfortunes. His Pride and Rashness are what History gives him but his Modesty, and Aversion to Praise I cannot find in *Plutarch*, who makes him very well satisfy'd with the Praise given by *Cominius*. And indeed it seems something opposite to his Pride, which both in the Play and History was so signal in him. Our Poet seems fond to lay the Blame on the People, and every where is representing the Inconstancy of the People, but this is contrary to Truth; for the People have never discover'd that Changeableness which Princes have done. And *Plutarch* in the Life of *Pyrrhus* seems

7

sensible of this when he says—*Thus Kings have no Reason to Condemn the* People *for changing for their Interest, who in that do but imitate them, as the* great Teachers of Unfaithfulness *and Treachery, holding him the Bravest, who makes the least Account of being an honest Man.* And any one that will look over the *Roman* History will find such Inconstancy, and such a perpetual Changeableness in the Emperors, as cannot be parallel'd in the People of any Time or Country. What the *Greeks* or *Romans* have ever done against any of their fortunate or great Generals, is easily vindicated from a guilty Inconstancy, and Ingratitude. For the fault has always been in the great Men, who swelling in the Pride of their Success, have thought in deference to that, that they might and ought to do whatever they pleas'd; and so often attempted the Ruin of that Liberty themselves, for the Preservation of which their warlike Actions were only valuable. And so it was their changing their Manners, and not the People, that produc'd their Misfortunes; they lov'd them for Defending their Country and Liberties, but by the same Principle must hate them when they saught by their Ambition and Pride to subvert them, and this by a Constancy not variableness of Principle or Temper.

This is plain in the very Story of this Play for their Anger was just against *Coriolanus,* who thought so well of his own Actions as to believe, that ev'n the Rights, Customs, and Priviledges of his Country were his due for his Valour and Success. His turning a Traytor to his Country on his Disgrace is a Proof of his Principle. *Camillus* on the contrary banish'd on far less Occasion or Ground, brought his Country in Distress Relief against the *Gauls* so far was he from joining them.

This Contempt of the People often proceeds from an over Value of our selves, and that not for our superiour Knowledge, Virtue, Wisdom, &c. but for the good Fortune of our Birth, which is a Trifle no farther valuable in Truth, than it is join'd to Courage, Wisdom or Honour; yet what, when blindly valu'd by the Possessor, sets aside all Thoughts and endeavour to obtain those nobler Advantages.

Our English Poets indeed to flater Arbitrary Power have too often imitated *Shakespear* in this Particular, and preposterously brought the Mob on the Stage contrary to the Majesty of

The Argument of Coriolanus 9

Tragedy, and the Truth of the Fact. *Shakespear* has here represented, as in *Julius Caesar*, the Commons of *Rome*, as if they were the Rabble of an *Irish* Village, as senseless, ignorant, silly and cowardly, not remembering, that the Citizens of *Rome* were the Soldiers of the Common-wealth, by whom they Conquer'd the World; and who in *Julius Caesar*'s time were at least, as Polite, as our Citizens of *London*; and yet if he had but consulted them, he wou'd have found it a difficult Matter to have pick'd out such ignorant unlick'd Cubbs to have fill'd up his Rout.

It is no hard Matter to prove, that the People were never in the Wrong, but once, and then they were byass'd by the Priest to choose *Barabas* and cry out Crucify.

I have not room here to examine this Point with that Clearness, that I might; nor is it so much to our present Purpose; and yet I presume the Digression is not so foreign to the Matter as to deserve a judicious Censure.

The Character of *Martius* is generally preserv'd and that Love of their Country, which is almost peculiar to *Rome* and *Greece* shown in the principal Persons. The Scene of the Mother, Wife, and *Valeria*, is moving and noble there are a great many fine Lines in this Play, tho' the Expression or Diction is sometimes obscure and puffy. That of I *Citiz.* p. 1908. [of Rowe's ed.] is very just on all proud Men.

—*And cou'd be content to give him good Report for't but that he pays himself with being proud.* The Fable that *Menenius* tells the People, tho' in History is very well brought in here and express'd p. 1909 and 10.

Honour ill Founded upon the People.

He that depends upon your Favours, Swims with Fins of Lead, &c. p. 1912. you may look in the beginning of this Speech in the foregoing Page. The noble Spirit of *Volumnia* is well express'd in her Speech, p. 1916. and in all that Scene to p. 1919 where the Character is admirably distinguish'd from *Virgilia* and *Valeria*. The Speech of *Coriolanus* to the Soldiers. p. 1924 is good.

------------------*If any such be here*
(As it were Sin to doubt) that love this Painting, &c.

This Discourse betwixt the two Officers in the *Capitol*. p. 1937. is worth reading on the Head of *Popularity*.

Against Custom.

Custom calls me to it, &c. p. 1944.

In the Scene betwixt the *Tribunes* and *Martius* p. 1950, 51, 52. The haughty Pride, and insolent and virulent Temper of *Coriolanus* is justly painted.
Menenius is drawn an old humorous Senator, and indeed he talks like one. p. 1956 in Defence of the Pride and Outrage of his Friend. And the next page, when he asks what he has done against *Rome*, &c. when it is plain he was against the Rights of the Commons, as essential to the Government as the Nobles, perhaps more if that State be thoroughly consider'd. *Volumnias* Speech to her Son p. 1960. is not amiss. And that of *Coriolanus* p. 1961 and 2. is well Express'd—*Away my Disposition and possess me some Harlots Spirit*, &c. the Thoughts are not only pretty but very natural to his Pride on this Occasion.

On the turns of the World

Oh! World thy slippery Turns! Friends now fastsworn
Whose double Bosoms seem to wear on Heart, &c. p. 1972.

For the Life and Character of this Man you may read *Plutarchs, Lives,* and *Dyon: Hallicarn.*

"Advertisement" to *Coriolanus*

Thomas Sheridan

The person who undertook to alter, and adapt the following piece to the stage, did it with a view to preserve to the theatre two characters which seemed to be drawn in as masterly a manner as any that came from the pen of the inimitable *Shakespear*. These he found were likely to be admired in the closet only; for the play, in general, seemed but ill calculated for representation. Upon examining a play of *Thomson's* upon the same subject, tho' he saw great beauties in it, he could not but perceive that it was defective in some essential points, and must always appear tedious in the acting. From a closer view of both, he thought they might mutually assist one another, and each supply the other's wants. *Shakespear's* play was purely historical, and had little or no plot. *Thomson's* plot was regular, but too much of the epic kind, and wanted business. He thought, by blending these, a piece might be produced, which, tho' not perfect, might furnish great entertainment to, and keep up the attention of an audience. The success it has met with in both kingdoms (for it was first performed on the *Dublin* stage) has more than answered his expectation.

And he has good reason to hope that he has been the means of adding one play to the stock, which is likely to live in any company, where the characters of *Coriolanus* and *Veturia* [Volumnia] can be properly supported.

As the military entry in this play, representing a *Roman* Ovation, has been universally admired, it is judged not unnecessary, for the use of such as are not acquainted with the

Roman customs, to give the following account of that ceremony, together with the order of the procession, as it was exhibited at the Theatre-royal in *Covent-garden*.

Ovation was a lesser sort of triumph. It had its name from *ovis*, a sheep, which was sacrificed on this occasion, instead of a bull, used in the great triumph. The ovation was granted upon any extraordinary success against the enemy, in gaining a battle, taking a town, some remarkable exploit, or making an advantageous peace to *Rome*. But a triumph was never obtained, unless a kingdom was entirely subdued, and added to the *Roman* territories. They differed in form from each other principally in this, that in the Ovation all marched on foot, but in the triumph the victor was carried in a chariot drawn by horses, and followed by horse-men, which makes the representation of the latter, on the stage, impracticable.

Underneath is the order of the Ovation, as it was exhibited.

But, previous to that, there was a civil procession from the town, consisting of Priests, Flamens, Choiristers, Senators, Tribunes, Virgins, Matrons, and the Mother, Wife, and Child of *Coriolanus*. These walked to the sound of flutes and soft instruments, and lined the way to behold the military entry, and congratulate the victor. The Ovation was performed to the sound of drums, fifes and trumpets, in the following order.

The Order of the OVATION
Six Lictors.
One carrying a small Eagle.
Six Incense-bearers.
Four Souldiers.
Two Fifes.
One Drum.
Two Standard-bearers.
Ten Souldiers.
Two Fifes.
One Drum.
Two Standard-bearers.
Six Souldiers.
Two Standard-bearers.
Four Serpent Trumpets.
Four carrying a Bier with Gold and Silver Vases,

"Advertisement" to Coriolanus

Part of the Spoil.
Two Souldiers.
Two Standard-bearers.
Two Souldiers.
Four carrying another Bier with a large Urn and
 Four Vases.
Four Souldiers carrying a Bier loaden with Trophies,
 Armour, Ensigns, &c. taken from the Enemy.
Five Souldiers with mural and civick Crowns.
Four Captive Generals in Chains.
One carrying a small Eagle.
Twelve Lictors preceding the two Consuls.
M. MINUCIUS.

C. COMINIUS.
 CORIOLANUS.

A Standard-bearer, Another Standard-bearer,
with a Drawing of *Corioli*. with the name of *Corioli*
 wrote on the Banner.

Two carrying a large Eagle.
Four Standard-bearers.
Twelve Souldiers.

In the military Procession alone, independent of the Civil, there were an hundred and eighteen persons.

Coriolanus
(from *The Examiner*, 15 December 1816)

William Hazlitt

Coriolanus has of late been repeatedly acted at Covent-Garden Theatre. Shakespear has in this play shewn himself well versed in history and state-affairs. *Coriolanus* is a storehouse of political common-places. Any one who studies it may save himself the trouble of reading Burke's Reflections, or Paine's Rights of Man, or the Debates in both Houses of Parliament since the French Revolution or our own. The arguments for and against aristocracy, or democracy, on the privileges of the few and the claims of the many, on liberty and slavery, power and the abuse of it, peace and war, are here very ably handled, with the spirit of a poet, and the acuteness of a philosopher. Shakespear himself seems to have had a leaning to the arbitrary side of the question, perhaps from some feeling of contempt for his own origin; and to have spared no occasion of baiting the rabble. What he says of them is very true: what he says of their betters is also very true, though he dwells less upon it. The cause of the people is indeed but ill calculated as a subject for poetry: it admits of rhetoric, which goes into argument and explanation, but it presents no immediate or distinct images to the mind, "no jutting frieze, buttress, or coigne of vantage" for poetry "to make its pendant bed and procreant cradle in." The language of poetry naturally falls in with the language of power. The imagination is an exaggerating and exclusive faculty: it takes from one thing to add to another: it accumulates circumstances together to give the greatest possible effect to a favourite object. The understanding is a dividing and measuring faculty: it judges of things, not according to their immediate impression on the mind, but according to their relations to one another. The one is a monopolizing faculty, which seeks the greatest quantity of present excitement by inequality and disproportion; the other is a distributive faculty, which seeks the greatest quantity of ultimate good by justice and proportion. The one is an aristocratical, the other a republican faculty. The principle of poetry is a very anti-levelling principle. It aims at effect, it exists by contrast. It admits of no medium. It is every thing by excess. It rises above the ordinary standard of sufferings and crimes. It presents an imposing appearance. It shews its head turretted, crowned and crested. Its front is gilt and blood-stained. Before it, "it carries noise, and behind it, it leaves tears." It has its altars and its victims, sacrifices, human sacrifices. Kings, priests, nobles, are its train-bearers; tyrants and slaves its executioners— "Carnage is its daughter!" Poetry is right royal. It puts the individual for the species, the one above the infinite many, might before right. A lion hunting a flock of sheep or a herd of wild asses, is a more poetical object than they; and we even take part with the lordly beast, because our vanity, or some other feeling, makes us disposed to place ourselves in the situation of the strongest party. So we feel some concern for the poor citizens of Rome, when they meet together to compare their wants and grievances, till Coriolanus comes in, and, with blows and big words, drives this set of "poor rats," this rascal scum, to their homes and beggary, before him. There is nothing heroical in a multitude of miserable rogues not wishing to be starved, or complaining that they are like to be so; but when a single man comes forward to brave their cries, and to make them submit to the last indignities, from mere pride and self-will, our admiration of his prowess is immediately converted into contempt for their pusillanimity. The insolence of power is stronger than the plea of necessity. The tame submission to usurped authority, or even the natural resistance to it, has nothing to excite or flatter the imagination; it is the assumption of a right to insult or oppress others, that carries an imposing air of superiority with it. We had rather be the oppressor than the oppressed.

Coriolanus

The love of power in ourselves, and the admiration of it in others, are both natural to man; the one makes him a tyrant, the other a slave. Wrong, dressed out in pride, pomp, and circumstance, has more attraction than abstract right.— Coriolanus complains of the fickleness of the people: yet the instant he cannot gratify his pride and obstinacy at their expense, he turns his arms against his country. If his country was not worth defending, why did he build his pride on its defence? He is a conqueror and a hero; he conquers other countries, and makes this a plea for enslaving his own; and when he is prevented from doing so, he leagues with its enemies to destroy his country. He rates the people "as if he were a God to punish, and not a man of their infirmity." He scoffs at one of their tribunes for maintaining their rites and franchises: "Mark you his absolute *shall?*" not marking his own absolute *will* to take every thing from them; his impatience of the slightest opposition to his own pretensions being in proportion to their arrogance and absurdity. If the great and powerful had the beneficence and wisdom of gods, then all this would have been well: if with greater knowledge of what is good for the people, they had as great a care for their interest as they have for their own; if they were seated above the world, sympathising with their welfare, but not feeling the passions of men, receiving neither good nor hurt from them, but bestowing their benefits as free gifts on them, they might then rule over them like another Providence. But this is not the case. Coriolanus is unwilling that the Senate should shew their "cares" for the people, lest their "cares" should be construed into "fears," to the subversion of all due authority; and he is no sooner disappointed in his schemes to deprive the people not only of the cares of the state, but of all power to redress themselves, than Volumnia is made madly to exclaim,

> Now the red pestilence strike all trades in Rome,
> And occupations perish.

This is but natural: it is but natural for a mother to have more regard for her son than for a whole city: but then the city should be left to take some care of itself. The care of the state cannot, we here see, be safely entrusted to maternal affection, or to the domestic charities of high life. The great have private feelings of their own, to which the interests of humanity and justice must courtesy. Their interests are so far from being the same as those of the community, that they are in direct and necessary opposition to them; their power is at the expense of our weakness; their riches, of our poverty; their pride, of our degradation; their splendour, of our wretchedness; their tyranny of our servitude. If they had the superior intelligence ascribed to them (which they have not) it would only render them so much more formidable; and from gods would convert them into devils.

The whole dramatic moral of Coriolanus is, that those who have little shall have less, and that those who have much shall take all that others have left. The people are poor, therefore they ought to be starved. They are slaves, therefore they ought to be beaten. They work hard, therefore they ought to be treated like beasts of burden. They are ignorant, therefore they ought not to be allowed to feel that they want food, or clothing, or rest, that they are enslaved, oppressed, and miserable. This is the logic of the imagination and the passions; which seek to aggrandize what excites admiration, and to heap contempt on misery, to raise power into tyranny, and to make tyranny absolute; to thrust down that which is low still lower, and to make wretches desperate: to exalt magistrates into kings, kings into gods; to degrade subjects to the rank of slaves, and slaves to the condition of brutes. The history of mankind is a romance, a mask, a tragedy constructed upon the principles of *poetical justice;* it is a noble or royal hunt, in which what is sport to the few, is death to the many, and in which the spectators halloo and encourage the strong to set upon the weak, and cry havoc in the chase, though they do not share in the spoil. We may depend upon it, that what men delight to read in books, they will put in practice in reality.

Mr. Kemble in the part of Coriolanus was as great as ever. Miss O'Neill as Volumnia was not so great as Mrs. Siddons. There is a *fleshiness,* if we may so say, about her whole manner, voice, and person, which does not suit the character of the Roman Matron. One of the most amusing things in the representation of this play is the contrast between Kemble and little Simmons. The former seems as if he would gibbet the latter on his nose, he looks so lofty. The fidgeting, uneasy, insignificant gestures of Simmons are perhaps a little caricatured; and Kemble's supercilious airs and *nonchalance* remind one of the unaccountable abstracted air, the contracted eyebrows and suspended chin of a man who is just going to sneeze.

From Lecture XXVI
"Criticisms on Shakespeare's Historical Dramas"

August Wilhelm von Schlegel

The five tragedies of which I have just spoken are deservedly the most celebrated of all the works of Shakespeare. In the three last, more especially, we have a display of a loftiness of genius which may almost be said to surpass the powers of human nature: the mind is as much lost in the contemplation of all the heights and depths of these works as our feelings are overpowered by the first impression which they produce. Of his historical plays, however, some possess a high degree of tragical perfection, and all are distinguished by peculiar excellencies.

In the three Roman pieces, *Coriolanus, Julius Caesar,* and *Antony and Cleopatra,* the moderation with which Shakespeare excludes foreign appendages and arbitrary suppositions, and yet fully satisfies the wants of the stage, is particularly deserving of admiration. These plays are the very thing itself; and under the apparent artlessness of adhering closely to history as he found it, an uncommon degree of art is concealed. Of every historical transaction Shakespeare knows how to seize the true poetical point of view, and to give unity and rounding to a series of events detached from the immeasurable extent of history without in any degree changing them. The public life of ancient Rome is called up from its grave, and exhibited before our eyes with the utmost grandeur and freedom of the dramatic form, and the heroes of Plutarch are ennobled by the most eloquent poetry.

In *Coriolanus* we have more comic intermixture than in the others, as the many-headed multitude plays here a considerable part; and when Shakespeare portrays the blind movements of the people in a mass, he almost always gives himself up to his merry humour. To the plebeians, whose folly is certainly sufficiently conspicuous already, the original old satirist Menenius is added by way of abundance. Droll scenes arise of a description altogether peculiar, and which are compatible only with such a political drama; for instance, when Coriolanus, to obtain the consulate, must solicit the lower order of citizens whom he holds in contempt for their cowardice in war, but cannot so far master his haughty disposition as to assume the customary humility, and yet extorts from them their votes.

From *A Study of Shakespeare*

Algernon Charles Swinburne

I cannot but think that enough at least of time has been spent if not wasted by able and even by eminent men on examination of *Coriolanus* with regard to its political aspects or bearing upon social questions. It is from first to last, for all its turmoil of battle and clamour of contentious factions, rather a private and domestic than a public or historical tragedy. As in *Julius Caesar* the family had been so wholly subordinated to the state, and all personal interests so utterly dominated by the preponderance of national duties, that even the sweet and sublime figure of Portia passing in her "awful loveliness" was but as a profile half caught in the background of an episode, so here on the contrary the whole force of the final impression is not that of a conflict between patrician and plebeian, but solely that of a match of passions played out for life and death between a mother and a son. The partisans of oligarchic or democratic systems may wrangle at their will over the supposed evidence of Shakespeare's prejudice against this creed and prepossession in favour of that: a third bystander may rejoice in the proof thus established of his impartial indifference towards either: it is all nothing to the real point in hand. The subject of the whole play is not the exile's revolt, the rebel's repentance, or the traitor's reward, but above all it is the son's tragedy. The inscription on the plinth of this tragic statue is simply to Volumnia Victrix.

A loftier or a more perfect piece of man's work was never done in all the world than this tragedy of *Coriolanus*: the one fit and crowning epithet for its companion or successor is that bestowed by Coleridge—"the most wonderful." It would seem a sign or birthmark of only the greatest among poets that they should be sure to rise instantly for awhile above the very highest of their native height at the touch of a thought of Cleopatra. So was it, as we all know, with William Shakespeare. . . .

Coriolanus
(British Academy Lecture, 1912)

A.C. Bradley

Coriolanus[1] is beyond doubt among the latest of Shakespeare's tragedies: there is some reason for thinking it the last. Like all those that succeeded *Hamlet*, it is a tragedy of vehement passion; and in none of them are more striking revolutions of fortune displayed. It is full of power, and almost every one feels it to be a noble work. We may say of it, as of its hero, that, if not one of Shakespeare's greatest creations, it is certainly one of his biggest.

Nevertheless, it is scarcely popular. It is seldom acted, and perhaps no reader ever called it his favorite play. Indeed, except for educational purposes, it is probably, after *Timon*, the least generally read of the tragedies. Even the critic who feels bound to rank it above *Romeo and Juliet*, and even above *Julius Caesar*, may add that he prefers those dramas all the same; and if he ignores his personal preferences, still we do not find him asking whether it is not the equal of the four great tragedies. He may feel this doubt as to *Antony and Cleopatra*, but not as to *Coriolanus*.

The question why this should be so will at once tell us something about the drama. We cannot say that it shows any decline in Shakespeare's powers, though in parts it may show slackness in their use. It has defects, some of which are due to the historical material; but all the tragedies have defects, and the material of *Antony and Cleopatra* was even more troublesome. There is no love-story; but then there is none in *Macbeth*, and next to none in *King Lear*. Thanks in part to the badness of the Folio text, the reader is impeded by obscurities of language and irritated by the mangling of Shakespeare's meter; yet these annoyances would not much diminish the effect of *Othello*. It may seem a more serious obstacle that the hero's faults are repellent and chill our sympathy; but Macbeth, to say nothing of his murders, is a much less noble being than Coriolanus. All this doubtless goes for something; yet there must be some further reason why this drama stands apart from the four great tragedies and *Antony and Cleopatra*. And one main reason seems to be this. Shakespeare could construe the story he found only by conceiving the hero's character in a certain way; and he had to set the whole drama in tune with that conception. In this he was, no doubt, perfectly right; but he closed the door on certain effects, in the absence of which his whole power in tragedy could not be displayed. He had to be content with something less, or rather with something else; and so have we.

Most of the great tragedies leave a certain imaginative impression of the highest value, which I describe in terms intended merely to recall it. What we witness is not the passion and doom of mere individuals. The forces that meet in the tragedy stretch far beyond the little group of figures and the tiny tract of space and time in which they appear. The darkness that covers the scene, and the light that strikes across it, are more than our common night and day. The hero's fate is, in one sense, intelligible, for it follows from his character and the condition in which he is placed; and yet everything, character, conditions, and issue, is mystery. Now of this effect there is very little in *Coriolanus*. No doubt the story has a universal meaning, since the contending forces are permanent constituents of human nature; but that peculiar *imaginative* effect or atmosphere is hardly felt. And, thinking of the play, we notice that the means by which it is produced elsewhere are almost absent here. One of these means is the use of the supernatural; another a treatment of nature which makes her appear not merely as a background, nor even merely as a conscious witness of human feelings, sufferings, and deeds, but as a vaster fellow-actor and fellow-sufferer. Remove in fancy from *Hamlet*, *Lear*, and *Macbeth* all that appeals to imagination through these means, and you find them utterly changed, but brought nearer to *Coriolanus*. Here Shakespeare has deliberately withdrawn his hand from those engines. He found, of course, in Plutarch allusions to the gods, and some of these he used; but he does not make us feel that the gods take part in the story. He found also wonders in the firmament, portents, a strange vision seen by a slave, a statue that spoke. He found that the Romans in their extremity sent the priests, augurs, and soothsayers to plead with Coriolanus; and that the embassy of the women which saved Rome was due to a thought which came suddenly to Valeria, which she herself regarded as a divine inspiration, and on the nature of which Plutarch speculates. But the whole of this Shakespeare ignored. Nor would he use that other instrument I spoke of. Coriolanus was not the man to be terrified by twilight, or to feel that the stars or the wind took part against or with him. If Lear's thunderstorm had beat upon his head, he would merely have set his teeth. And not only is the mystery of nature absent; she is scarcely present even as a background. The hero's grim description of his abode in exile as "the city of kites and crows" (it is not in Plutarch) is almost all we have. In short, *Coriolanus* has scarcely more atmosphere, either supernatural or natural, than the average serious prose drama of today.

In Shakespeare's greatest tragedies there is a second source—in one or two the chief source—of supreme imaginative appeal, the exhibition of inward conflict, or of the outburst of one or another passion, terrible, heart-rending, or glorious to witness. At these moments the speaker becomes the greatest of poets; and yet, the dramatic convention admitted, he speaks in character. The hero in *Coriolanus* is never thus the greatest of poets, and he could not be so without a breach of more than dramatic convention. His nature is large, simple, passionate; but (except in one point, to which I will return, as it is irrelevant here) his nature is not, in any marked degree, imaginative. He feels all the rapture, but not, like Othello, all the poetry, of war. He covets honor no less than Hotspur, but he has not Hotspur's vision of honor. He meets with ingratitude, like Timon, but it does not transfigure all mankind for him. He is very eloquent, but his only free eloquence is that of vituperation and scorn. It is sometimes more than eloquence, it is splendid poetry; but it is never such magical poetry as we hear in the four greatest tragedies. Then, too, it lies in his nature that his deepest and most sacred feeling, that for his mother, is almost dumb. It governs his life and leads him uncomplaining towards death, but it cannot speak. And, finally, his inward conflicts are veiled from us. The change that came when he found himself alone and homeless in exile is not exhibited. The result is partly seen in the one soliloquy of this drama, but the process is hidden. Of the passion that possesses him when his triumph seems at hand we get a far more vivid idea from the words of Cominius than from any words of his own:

> I tell you he does sit in gold, his eye
> Red as 'twould burn Rome.

In the most famous scene, when his fate is being decided, only one short sentence reveals the gradual loosening of his purpose during his mother's speech. The actor's face and hands and bearing must show it, not the hero's voice; and his submission is announced in a few quiet words, deeply moving and impressive, but destitute of the effect we know elsewhere of a lightning flash that rends the darkness and discloses every cranny of the speaker's soul. All this we can see to be as it should be, but it does set limits to the flight of Shakespeare's imagination.

I have spoken of something that we miss in *Coriolanus*. Unfortunately there is something which a good many readers find, or think they find, and which makes it distasteful to them. A political conflict is never the center of interest in Shakespeare's plays, but in the historical plays it is an element more or less essential, and in this one it is very prominent. Here, too, since it may be plausibly described as a conflict between people and nobles, or democracy and aristocracy, the issue is felt to be still alive. And Shakespeare, it is thought, shows an animus, and sides against the people. A hundred years ago Hazlitt, dealing with this tragedy, wrote: "Shakespeare himself seems to have had a leaning to the arbitrary side of the question, perhaps from some feeling of contempt for his own origin; and to have spared no occasion of baiting the rabble. What he says of them is very true; what he says of their betters is also very true, though he dwells less upon it." This language is very tentative and mild compared with that of some later writers. According to one,

Shakespeare "loathed the common Englishman." He was a neuropath who could not endure the greasy aprons and noisome breath of mechanics, and a snob of the purest English water." According to another, he was probably afflicted for some years with an "enormous self-esteem." A hero similarly afflicted, and a nauseous mob—behold the play!

I do not propose to join this dance, or even to ask whether any reasonable conjecture as to Shakespeare's political views and feelings could be formed from the study of this play and of others. But it may be worthwhile to mention certain questions which should be weighed by anyone who makes the adventure. Are not the chief weaknesses and vices shown by the populace, or attributed to it by speakers, in these plays, those with which it had been habitually charged in antiquity and the Middle Ages; and did not Shakespeare find this common form, if nowhere else, in Plutarch? Again, if these traits and charges are heightened in his dramas, what else do we expect in drama, and especially in that of the Elizabethans? Granted, next, that in Shakespeare the people play a sorry political part, is that played by English nobles and Roman patricians much more glorious or beneficent? And if, in Hazlitt's phrase, Shakespeare says more of the faults of the people than of those of their betters, would we have him give to humble unlettered persons the powers of invective of lordly orators? Further, is abuse of the people ever dramatically inappropriate in Shakespeare; and is it given to Henry the Fifth, or Brutus (who had some cause for it), or, in short, to any of the most attractive characters? Is there not, besides, a great difference between his picture of the people taken as individuals, even when they talk politics, and his picture of them as a crowd or mob? Is not the former, however humorously critical, always kindly; and is a personal bias really needed to account for the latter? And, to end a catalogue easy to prolong, might not that talk, which is scarcely peculiar to Shakespeare, about greasy caps and offensive odors, have some other origin than his artistic nerves? He had, after all, some little gift of observation, and, when first he mixed with a class above his own, might he not resemble a son of the people now who, coming among his betters, observes with amusement the place held in their decalogue by the morning bath? I do not for a moment suggest that, by weighing such questions as these, we should be led to imagine Shakespeare as any more inclined to champion the populace than Spenser or Hooker or Bacon; but I think we should feel it extremely hazardous to ascribe to him any political feelings at all, and ridiculous to pretend to certainty on the subject.

Let us turn to the play. The representation of the people, whatever else it may be, is part of a dramatic design. This design is based on the main facts of the story, and these imply a certain character in the people and the hero. Since the issue is tragic, the conflict between them must be felt to be unavoidable and well-nigh hopeless. The necessity for dramatic sympathy with both sides demands that on both there should be some right and some wrong, both virtues and failings; and if the hero's monstrous purpose of destroying his native city is not to extinguish our sympathy, the provocation he receives must be great. This being so, the picture of the people is, surely, no darker than it had to be; the desired result would have been more easily secured by making it darker still. And one must go further. As regards the political situation, the total effect of the drama, it appears to me, is this. The conflict of hero and people is hopeless; but it is he alone who makes the conflict of patricians and plebeians, I do not say hopeless, but in any high degree dangerous. The people have bad faults, but no such faults as, in his absence, would prevent a constitutional development in their favor.

I will not try to describe their character, but I will illustrate this statement by comparing accusations of their opponents with the facts shown; for these we must accept, but the accusations we must judge for ourselves. In the first scene the people are called cowards, both by the hero and by their friendly critic Menenius. Now there is no sign that they possess the kind of courage expected of gentlemen, or feel the corresponding shame if their courage fails. But if they were cowards, how could Rome be standing where we see it stand? They are common soldiers of Rome. And when we see them in war, what do we find? One division, under Cominius, meets the Volscians in the field; the other, under Coriolanus, assaults Corioli. Both are beaten back. This is what Cominius says to his men:

> Breathe you, my friends: well fought: we are come off
> Like Romans, neither foolish in our stands,
> Nor cowardly in retire.

Nothing hints that the other division has not fought well or was cowardly in retire; but it was encouraged beforehand with threats, and, on its failure, with a torrent of curses and abuse. Nevertheless it advances again and forces the enemy to the gates, which Coriolanus enters, calling on his men to follow him.

> *First Sol.* Foolhardiness; not I.
> *Second Sol.* Nor I.
> *First Sol.* See, they have shut him in.
> *All.* To the pot, I warrant him.

Disgusting, no doubt; but the answer to threats and curses. They would not have served Cominius so; and indeed, when Lartius comes up and merely suggests to them to "fetch off" the reappearing hero, they respond at once and take the city. These men are not cowards; but their conduct depends on their leaders. The same thing is seen when Coriolanus himself appeals to the other division for volunteers to serve in the van. For once he appeals nobly, and the whole division volunteers.

Another charge he brings against the people is that they can neither rule nor be ruled. On this his policy of "thorough" is based. Now, judging from the drama, one would certainly say that they could not rule alone—that a pure democracy would lead to anarchy, and perhaps to foreign subjection. And one would say also that they probably could not be ruled by the patricians if all political rights were denied them. But to rule them, while granting them a place in the constitution, would seem quite feasible. They are, in fact, only too easy to guide. No doubt, collected into a mob, led by demagogues, and maddened by resentment and fear, they become wild and cruel. It is true, also, that, when their acts bear bitter fruit, they disclaim responsibility and turn on their leaders: "that we did, we did for the best; and though we willingly consented to his banishment, yet it was against our will." But they not only follow their tribunes like sheep; they receive abuse and direction submissively from anyone who shows goodwill. They are fundamentally good-natured, like the Englishmen they are, and have a humorous consciousness of their own weaknesses. They are, beyond doubt, mutable, and in that sense untrustworthy; but they are not by nature ungrateful, or slow to admire their bitterest enemy. False charges and mean imputations come from their leaders, not from them. If one of them blames Coriolanus for being proud, another says he cannot help his pride. They insist on the bare form of their right to name him consul, but all they want is the form, and not the whole even of that. When he asks one of them, "Well then, I pray, your price of the consulship?" the answer, "The price is to ask it kindly," ought to have melted him at once; yet when he asks it contemptuously it is still granted. Even later, when the arts of the tribunes have provoked him to such a storm of defiant and revolutionary speech that both the consulship and his life are in danger, one feels that another man might save both with no great trouble. Menenius tells him that the people

> have pardons, being ask'd, as free
> As words to little purpose.

His mother and friends urge him to deceive the people with false promises. But neither false promises nor apologies are needed; only a little humanity and some acknowledgment that the people are part of the state. He is capable of neither, and so the conflict is hopeless. But it is not so because the people, or even the tribunes, are what they are, but because he is what we call an "impossible" person.

The result is that all the force and nobility of Rome's greatest man have to be thrown away and wasted. That is tragic; and it is doubly so because it is not only his faults that make him impossible. There is bound up with them a nobleness of nature in which he surpasses everyone around him.

We see this if we consider, what is not always clear to the reader, his political position. It is not shared by any of the other patricians who appear in the drama. Critics have called him a Tory or an ultra-Tory; but the tribune who calls him a "traitorous innovator" is quite as near the mark. The people have been granted tribunes. The tribunate is a part of the constitution, and it is accepted, with whatever reluctance, by the other patricians. But Coriolanus would abolish it, and that not by law but by the sword. Nor would this content him. The right of the people to control the election of the consul is no new thing; it is an old traditional right; but it, too, he says, might well be taken away. The only constitution tolerable in his eyes is one where the patricians are the state, and the people a mere instrument to feed it and fight for it. It is this conviction that makes it so dangerous to appoint him consul, and also makes it impossible for him to give way. Even if he could ask pardon for his abuse of the people, he could not honestly promise to acknowledge their political rights.

Now the nobleness of his nature is at work here. He is not tyrannical; the charge brought against him of aiming at a tyranny is silly. He is an aristocrat. And Shakespeare has put decisively aside the statement of Plutarch that he was "churlish, uncivil, and altogether unfit for any man's conversation." Shakespeare's hero, though he feels his superiority to his fellow-patricians, always treats them as equals. He is never rude or overbearing. He speaks to them with the simple directness or the bluff familiarity of a comrade. He does not resent their advice, criticism, or reproof. He shows no trace of envy or jealousy, or even of satisfaction at having surpassed them. The suggestion of the tribunes that he is willing to serve under Cominius because failure in war will be credited to Cominius, and success in war to himself, shows only the littleness of their own minds. The patricians are his fellows in a community of virtue—of a courage, fidelity, and honor, which cannot fail them because they are "true-bred," though the bright ideal of such virtue become perfect still urges them on. But the plebeians, in his eyes, are destitute of this virtue, and therefore have no place in this community. All they care for is food in peace, looting in war, flattery from their demagogues; and they will not even clean their teeth. To ask anything of them is to insult not merely himself but the virtues that he worships. To give them a real share in citizenship is treason to Rome; for Rome means these virtues. They are not Romans, they are the rats of Rome.

He is very unjust to them, and his ideal, though high, is also narrow. But he is magnificently true to it, and even when he most repels us we feel this and glory in him. He is never more true to it than when he tries to be false; and this is the scene where his superiority in nobleness is most apparent. He, who had said of his enemy, "I hate him worse than a promise-breaker," is urged to save himself and his friends by promises that he means to break. To his mother's argument that he ought no more to mind deceiving the people than outwitting an enemy in war, he cannot give the obvious answer, for he does not really count the people his fellow-countrymen; but the proposal that *he* should descend to lying or flattering astounds him. He feels that if he does so he will never be himself again; that his mind will have taken on an inherent baseness and no mere simulated one. And he is sure, as we are, that he simply cannot do what is required of him. When at last he consents to try, it is solely because his mother bids him and he cannot resist her chiding. Often he reminds us of a huge boy; and here he acts like a boy whose sense of honor is finer than his mother's, but who is too simple and too noble to frame the thought.

Unfortunately he is altogether too simple and too ignorant of himself. Though he is the proudest man in Shakespeare, he seems to be unaware of his pride, and is hurt when his mother mentions it. It does not prevent him from being genuinely modest, for he never dreams that he has attained the ideal he worships; yet the sense of his own greatness is twisted round every strand of this worship. In almost all his words and deeds we are conscious of the tangle. I take a single illustration. He cannot endure to be praised. Even his mother, who has a charter to extol her blood, grieves him when she praises him. As for others,

> I had rather have one scratch my head i' the sun
> When the alarum were struck, than idly sit
> To hear my nothings monster'd.

His answer to the roar of the army hailing him "Coriolanus" is, "I will go wash." His wounds are "scratches with briars." In Plutarch he shows them to the people without demur; in Shakespeare he would rather lose the consulship. There is a greatness in all this that makes us exult. But who can assign the proportions of the elements that compose this impatience of praise: the feeling (which we are surprised to hear him express) that he, like hundreds more, has simply done what he could; the sense that it is nothing to what might be done; the want of human sympathy (for has not Shelley truly said that fame is love disguised?); the pride which makes him feel that he needs no recognition, that after all he himself could do ten times as much, and that to praise his achievement implies a limit to his power? If any one could solve this problem, Coriolanus certainly could not. To adapt a phrase in the play, he has no more introspection in him than a tiger. So he thinks that his loathing of the people is all disgust at worthlessness, and his resentment in exile all a just indignation. So too he fancies that he can stand

> As if a man were author of himself
> And knew no other kin,

while in fact public honor and home affections are the breath of his nostrils, and there is not a drop of stoic blood in his veins.

What follows on his exile depends on this self-ignorance. When he bids farewell to his mother and wife and friends he is still excited and exalted by conflict. He comforts them; he will take no companion; he will be loved when he is lacked, or at least he will be feared; while he remains alive, they shall always hear from him, and never aught but what is like him formerly. But the days go by, and no one, not even his mother, hears a word. When we see him next, he is entering Antium to offer his services against his country. If they are accepted, he knows what he will do; he will burn Rome.

As I have already remarked, Shakespeare does not exhibit to us the change of mind which issues in this frightful purpose; but from what we see and hear later we can tell how he imagined it; and the key lies in that idea of *burning* Rome. As time passes, and no suggestion of recall reaches Coriolanus, and he learns what it is to be a solitary homeless exile, his heart hardens, his pride swells to a mountainous bulk, and the wound in it becomes a fire. The fellow-patricians from whom he parted lovingly now appear to him ingrates and dastards, scarcely better than the loathsome mob. Somehow, he knows not how, even his mother and wife have deserted him. He has become nothing to Rome, and Rome shall hear nothing from him. Here in solitude he can find no relief in a storm of words; but gradually the blind intolerable chaos of resentment conceives and gives birth to a vision, not merely of battle and indiscriminate slaughter, but of the whole city one tower of flame. To see that with his bodily eyes would satisfy his soul; and the way to the sight is through the Volscians. If he is killed the moment they recognize him, he cares little: better a dead nothing than the living nothing Rome thinks him. But if he lives, she shall know what he is. He bears himself among the Volscians with something that resembles self-control; but what controls him is the vision that never leaves him and never changes, and his eye is red with its glare when he sits in his state before the doomed city.[2]

This is Shakespeare's idea, not Plutarch's. In Plutarch there is not a syllable about the burning of Rome. Coriolanus (to simplify a complicated story) intends to humiliate his country by forcing on it disgraceful terms of peace. And this, apart from its moral quality, is a reasonable design. The Romans, rather than yield to fear, decline to treat unless peace is first restored; and therefore it will be necessary to assault the city. In the play we find a single vague allusion to some unnamed conditions which, Coriolanus knows, cannot now be accepted; but everywhere, among both Romans and Volscians, we hear of the burning of Rome, and in the city there is no hope of successful resistance. What Shakespeare wanted was a simpler and more appalling situation than he found in Plutarch, and a hero enslaved by his passion and driven blindly forward. How blindly, we may judge, if we ask the questions: what will happen to the hero if he disappoints the expectation he has raised among the Volscians, when their leader is preparing to accuse him even if he fulfills it: and, if the hero executes his purpose, what will happen to his mother, wife, and child: and how can it be executed by a man whom we know in his home as the most human of men, a husband who is still the lover of his wife, and a son who regards his mother not merely with devoted affection but with something like religious awe? Very likely the audience in the theatre was not expected to ask these questions, but it *was* expected to see in the hero a man totally ignorant of himself, and stumbling to the destruction either of his life or of his soul.

In speaking of the famous scene where he is confronted with Volumnia and Valeria, Virgilia and her boy, and the issue is decided, I am obliged to repeat what I have said elsewhere in print;[3] and I must speak in the first person because I do not know how far others share my view. To me the scene is one in which the tragic feelings of fear and pity have little place. Such anxiety as I feel is not for the fate of the hero or of anyone else: it is, to use religious language, for the safety of his soul. And when he yields, though I know, as he divines, that his life is lost, the emotion I feel is not pity: he is above pity and above life. And the anxiety itself is but slight: it bears no resemblance to the hopes and fears that agitate us as we approach the end in *Othello* or *King Lear*. The whole scene affects me, to exaggerate a little, more as a majestic picture of stationary figures than as the fateful climax of an action speeding to its close. And the structure of the drama seems to confirm this view. Almost throughout the first three acts—that is, up to the banishment—we have incessant motion, excited and resounding speech, a violent oscillation of fortunes. But, after this, the dramatic tension is suddenly relaxed, and, though it increases again, it is never allowed to approach its previous height. If Shakespeare had wished it to do so in this scene, he had only to make us wait in dread of some interposition from Aufidius, at which the hero's passion might have burst into a fury fatal even to the influence of Volumnia. But our minds are crossed by no shadow of such dread. From the moment when he catches sight of the advancing figures, and the voice of nature—what he himself calls "great nature"—begins to speak in his heart long before it speaks aloud to his ear, we know the end. And all this is in harmony with that characteristic of the drama which we noticed at first—we feel but faintly, if at all, the presences of any mysterious or fateful agency. We are witnessing only the conquest of passion by simple human feelings, and *Coriolanus* is as much a drama of reconciliation as a tragedy. That is no defect in it, but it is a reason why it cannot leave the same impression as the supreme tragedies, and should be judged by its own standard.

A tragedy it is, for the passion is gigantic, and it leads to the hero's death. But the catastrophe scarcely diminishes the influence of the great scene. Since we know that his nature, though the good in it has conquered, remains unchanged, and since his rival's plan is concerted before our eyes, we wait with little suspense, almost indeed with tranquility, the certain end.

As it approaches it is felt to be the more inevitable because the steps which lead to it are made to repeat as exactly as possible the steps which lead to his exile. His task, as then, is to excuse himself, a task the most repugnant to his pride. Aufidius, like the tribunes then, knows how to render its fulfillment impossible. He hears a word of insult, the same that he heard then—"traitor." It is followed by a sneer at the most sacred tears he ever shed, and a lying description of their effect on the bystanders; and his pride, and his loathing of falsehood and meanness, explode, as before, in furious speech. For a moment he tries to check himself and appeals to the senators; but the effort seems only to treble his rage. Though no man, since Aufidius spoke, has said a word against him, he defies the whole nation, recalling the day of its shame and his own triumph, when alone, like an eagle, he fluttered the dovecotes in Corioli. The people, who had accompanied him to the marketplace, splitting the air with the noise of their enthusiasm, remember their kinfolk whom he slaughtered, change sides, and clamor for his death. As he turns on Aufidius, the conspirators rush upon him, and in a moment, before the vision of his glory has faded from his brain, he lies dead. The instantaneous cessation of enormous energy (which is like nothing else in Shakespeare) strikes us with awe, but not with pity. As I said, the effect of the preceding scene, where he conquered something stronger than all the Volscians and escaped something worse than death, is not reversed; it is only heightened by a renewed joy in his greatness. Roman and Volscian will have peace now, and in his native city patrician and plebeian will move along the way he barred. And they are in life, and he is not. But life has suddenly shrunk and dwindled, and become a home for pygmies and not for him.[4]

Dr. Johnson observed that "the tragedy of *Coriolanus* is one of the most amusing of our author's performances." By "amusing" he did not mean "mirth-provoking"; he meant that in *Coriolanus* a lively interest is excited and sustained by the variety of the events and characters; and this is true. But we may add that the play contains a good deal that is amusing in the current sense of the word—more of this, it has been observed, than do the other Roman tragedies. When the people appear as individuals they are frequently more or less comical. Shakespeare

Coriolanus

always enjoyed the inconsequence of the uneducated mind, and its tendency to express a sound meaning in an absurd form. Again, the talk of the servants with one another and with the muffled hero, and the conversation of the sentinels with Menenius, are amusing. There is a touch of comedy in the contrast between Volumnia and Virgilia when we see them on occasions not too serious. And then, not only at the beginning, as in Plutarch, but throughout the story, we meet with that pleasant and wise old gentlemen, Menenius, whose humor tells him how to keep the peace while he gains his point, and to say without offense what the hero cannot say without raising a storm. Perhaps no one else in the play is regarded from beginning to end with such unmingled approval, and this is not lessened when the failure of his embassy to Coriolanus makes him the subject as well as the author of mirth. If we regard the drama from this point of view we find that it differs from almost all the tragedies, though it has a certain likeness to *Antony and Cleopatra*. What is amusing in it is, for the most part, simply amusing, and has no tragic tinge. It is not like the gibes of Hamlet at Polonius, or the jokes of the clown who, we remember, is digging Ophelia's grave, or that humor of Iago which for us is full of menace; and who could dream of comparing it with the jesting of Lear's fool? Even that Shakespearean audacity, the interruption of Volumnia's speech by the hero's little son, makes one laugh almost without reserve. And all this helps to produce the characteristic tone of this tragedy.

The drawing of the character of Aufidius seems to me by far the weakest spot in the drama. At one place, where Aufidius moralizes on the banishment of the hero, Shakespeare, it appears to some critics, is himself delivering a speech which tells the audience nothing essential and ends in desperate obscurity.[5] Two other speeches have been criticized. In the first, Aufidius, after his defeat in the field, declares that, since he cannot overcome his rival in fair fight, he will do it in any way open to him, however dishonorable. The other is his lyrical cry of rapture when Coriolanus discloses himself in the house at Antium. The intention in both cases is clear. Aufidius is contrasted with the hero as a man of much slighter and less noble nature, whose lively impulses, good and bad, quickly give way before a new influence, and whose action is in the end determined by a permanent pressure of ambition and rivalry. But he is a man of straw. He was wanted merely for the plot, and in reading some passages in his talk, we seem to see Shakespeare yawning as he wrote. Besides, the unspeakable baseness of his sneer at the hero's tears is an injury to the final effect. Such an emotion as mere disgust is out of place in a tragic close; but I confess I feel nothing but disgust as Aufidius speaks the last words, except some indignation with the poet who allowed him to speak them, and an unregenerate desire to see the head and body of the speaker lying on opposite sides of the stage.

Though this play is by no means a drama of destiny, we might almost say that Volumnia is responsible for the hero's life and death. She trained him from the first to aim at honor in arms, to despise pain, and to

> forget that ever
> He heard the name of death;

to strive constantly to surpass himself, and to regard the populace with inhuman disdain as

> things created
> To buy and sell with groats.

Thus she led him to glory and to banishment. And it was she who, in the hour of trial, brought him to sacrifice his pride and his life.

Her sense of personal honor, we saw, was less keen than his; but she was much more patriotic. We feel this superiority even in the scene that reveals the defect; in her last scene we feel it alone. She has idolized her son; but whatever motive she may appeal to in her effort to move him, it is not of him she thinks; her eyes look past him and are set on Rome. When, in yielding, he tells her that she has won a happy victory for her country, but a victory most dangerous, if not most mortal, to her son, she answers nothing. And her silence is sublime.

These last words would be true of Plutarch's Volumnia. But in Plutarch, though we hear of the son's devotion, and how he did great deeds to delight his mother, neither his early passion for war not his attitude to the people is attributed to her influence, and she has no place in the action until she goes to plead with him. Hence she appears only in majesty, while Shakespeare's Volumnia has a more varied part to play. She cannot be majestic when we see her hurrying through the streets in wild exultation at the news of his triumph; and where, angrily conquering her tears, she rails at the authors of his banishment, she can hardly be called even dignified. What Shakespeare gains by her animation and vehemence in these scenes is not confined to them. He prepares for the final scene a sense of contrast which makes it doubly moving and impressive.

In Volumnia's great speech he is much indebted to Plutarch, and it is, on the whole, in the majestic parts that he keeps most close to his authority. The open appeal to affection is his own; and so are the touches of familiar language. It is his Volumnia who exclaims, "here he lets me prate like one i' the stocks," and who compares herself, as she once was, to a hen that clucks her chicken home. But then the conclusion, too, is pure Shakespeare; and if it has not majesty, it has something dramatically even more potent. Volumnia, abandoning or feigning to abandon hope, turns to her companions with the words:

> Come, let us go:
> This fellow had a Volscian to his mother;
> His wife is in Corioli, and his child
> Like him by chance. Yet give us our dispatch:
> I am hush'd until our city be a-fire,
> And then I'll speak a little.[6]

Her son's resolution has long been tottering, but now it falls at once. Throughout, it is not the substance of her appeals that moves him, but the bare fact that she appeals. And the culmination is that she ceases to appeal, and defies him. This has been observed by more than one critic. I do not know if it has been noticed[7] that on a lower level exactly the same thing happens when she tries to persuade him to go and deceive the people. The moment she stops, and says, in effect, "Well, then, follow your own will," his will gives way. Deliberately to set it against hers is beyond his power.

Ruskin, whose terms of praise and blame were never overcautious, wrote of Virgilia as "perhaps the loveliest of Shakespeare's female characters." Others have described her as a shrinking submissive being, afraid of the very name of a wound, and much given to tears. This description is true; and, I may remark in passing, it is pleasant to remember that the hero's letter to his mother contained a full account of his wounds, while his letter to wife did not mention them at all. But the description of these critics can hardly be the whole truth about a woman who inflexibly rejects the repeated invitations of her formidable mother-in-law and her charming friend to leave her house; who later does what she can to rival Volumnia in rating the tribunes; and who at last quietly seconds Volumnia's assurance that Coriolanus shall only enter Rome over her body. Still these added traits do not account for the indefinable impression which Ruskin received (if he did not rightly interpret it), and which thousands of readers share. It comes in part from that kind of muteness in which Virgilia resembles Cordelia, and which is made to suggest a world of feeling in reserve. And in part it comes from the words of her husband. His greeting when he returns from the war, and she stands speechless before him:

> My gracious silence, hail!
> Wouldst thou have laugh'd had I come coffin'd home,
> That weep'st to see me triumph? Ah, my dear,
> Such eyes the widows in Corioli wear,
> And mothers that lack sons.

His exclamation when he sees her approaching at their last meeting and speaks first of her and not of Volumnia:

> What is that curtsy worth, or those doves' eyes
> Which can make gods forsworn? I melt, and am not
> Of stronger earth than others;

these words envelop Virgilia in a radiance which is reflected back upon himself. And this is true also of his praise of Valeria in the lines perhaps most often quoted from this drama:

> The noble sister of Publicola,
> The moon of Rome, chaste as the icicle
> That's curdied by the frost from purest snow,
> And hangs on Dian's temple: dear Valeria!

I said that at one point the hero's nature *was* in a high degree imaginative; and it is here. In his huge violent heart there was a

Coriolanus

store, not only of tender affection, but of delicate and chivalrous poetry. And though Virgilia and Valeria evoke its expression we cannot limit its range. It extends to the widows and mothers in Corioli; and we feel that, however he might loathe and execrate the people, he was no more capable of injury or insult to a daughter of the people than Othello, or Chaucer's Knight, or Don Quixote himself.

Postscript

Professor Case, in the Introduction to his admirable Arden edition of *Coriolanus*, while approving the interpretation in this paragraph of the change in the hero's mind, withholds his assent to the stress laid in the paragraph on the particular idea of the *burning* of Rome. Instead of arguing the question I will simply describe the way in which the emphasis on that particular idea came to impress me.

When I was studying the play afresh with a view to this lecture, I noticed that, as the action approached its climax, the image of fire, not present to me before, became increasingly present, persistent and vivid; and at last, when Cominius, reporting his futile embassy to the hero, exclaims,

> I tell you he does sit in gold, his eye
> Red as 'twould burn Rome,

I said to myself, "Yes, *that* image of vengeance is what came to him in the solitude of his exile and has now become a possession." And, if I could have doubted this, doubt would have vanished when I reached Volumnia's speech (V.iii.131), and read the words, its *final* words,

> Yet give us our dispatch:
> I am hushed until our city be a-fire,
> And then I'll speak a little.

The "possession" is shattered, and the catastrophe sure—and welcome.

Dismissing imagination, I have now made a research, and some readers may be interested in the result.

Throughout the greater part of the play, though there is plenty of fighting and Corioles is taken, we hear, I think, nothing of any burning of towns or cities. There is a mention of fire at II.1.263–65, but it is the fire of contention between the hero and the people; and the "burning" and "fires" of III.ii.24 and III.iii.68 are those of hell; and even at IV.iii.20–25, where the image of fire is decidedly more vivid, this fire is that of the anger of the two parties in Rome. But in IV.vi.79, 83, 86, 116, 138, we have crowded and vivid references to the burning of the Roman territory by the army of Coriolanus, and to the prospect of his burning the city. And then, after a short scene, comes, at V.i.14, 17, 27, 32 (where Cominius makes the report of his interview and repeats the words of Coriolanus) fire-image after fire-image, the series culminating at 64 in that of the "eye red as 'twould burn Rome." In the next scene (7, 47, 72) the series, naturally, continues; but in V.iii where Volumnia is to appear, it ceases (for the hero is inwardly beginning to yield), until it reappears in her final words. And, after that, we have only the reference (V.v.3) to the "triumphant fires" in the saved city.

NOTES

1. Shakespeare's treatment of his subject is often best understood through comparison with his authority, Plutarch's *Life of Coriolanus* in North's translation, a translation most conveniently read in the volume edited by Prof. Skeat and entitled *Shakespeare's Plutarch*. For a full development of the comparison, and, generally, for a discussion of the play much more complete than mine could be, see Prof. MacCallum's book, *Shakespeare's Roman Plays and their Background* (1910), which is admirable both for its thoroughness and for the insight and justice of its criticism. I should perhaps add that, though I read the greater part of Prof. MacCallum's book when it appeared, I was prevented from going on to the chapters on *Coriolanus*, and did so only after writing my lecture. I left untouched in the lecture the many observations which this reading confirmed, but on one or two doubtful points I have added a Postscript.

Coriolanus

2. See Postscript.

3. *Shakespearean Tragedy*, p. 84.

4. I have tried to indicate the effect at which Shakespeare's imagination seems to have aimed. I do not say that the execution is altogether adequate. And some readers, I know, would like Coriolanus to die fighting. Shakespeare's idea is probably to be gathered from the hero's appeal to the senators to judge between Aufidius and him, and from the word "lawful" in the last speech:

> O that I had him,
> With six Aufidiuses, or more, his tribe,
> To use my lawful sword!

He is not before the people only, but before the senators, his fellow-patricians, though of another city. Besides—if I may so put it—if Coriolanus were allowed to fight at all, he would have to annihilate the whole assembly.

5. But Prof. MacCallum's defense of this passage is perhaps successful.

6. What she will utter, I imagine, is a mother's dying curse.

7. Yes, it is noticed by Prof. MacCallum.

Copyright the British Academy. Reproduced by permission from Proceedings of the British Academy 1912, *Vol. V.*

Shakespeare's Coriolanus: Elizabethan Soldier

Paul A. Jorgensen

The New Variorum *Coriolanus* offers ample evidence that criticism of this play has spent its force upon two sources of conflict: the relationship between the plebs and the patricians and the relationship between Coriolanus and his mother. These approaches have led to interesting speculation as to Shakespeare's own point of view. But the fact remains to be reckoned with that the two disastrous relationships which most have excited critics are also exciting in North's Plutarch and that Shakespeare's most important departures from his source are in another direction. In this paper I hope to show that Shakespeare drew principally upon the military situation of his own era and country in reshaping the Plutarchan story. In this reshaping, Coriolanus emerges as a soldier whose life comprises two significantly related phases: the soldier at war and the soldier in civil life. The Roman general's difficulty in adjusting himself to a nonmilitary career is of central importance because Shakespeare gave this problem a greater prominence and more clearly defined statement than did Plutarch. Nevertheless, Coriolanus' role in warfare is, in Shakespeare's design, basic to an understanding of his role in peace. What is more, the complexity of the former role has been underestimated by critics, most of whom esteem him an excellent warrior.[1]

We are of course made to feel the splendid strength of Coriolanus in battle, but eulogies of his generalship are consistently limited. His fellow commander, Titus Lartius, admires his "grim looks" and the "thunder-like percussion" of his sounds (I.iv.58–59).[2] The enemy leader, Titus Aufidius, observes that his antagonist "fights dragon-like" (IV.vii.22). And Volumnia, a careful student of her son's wars, envisions him plucking Aufidius "down by th' hair," stamping, and calling "Come on, you cowards!" (I.iii.33–36). These accounts suggest a lone, ardent fighter. Concerning wise leadership, the eulogies are silent. The limited nature of Coriolanus' military genius is dramatically evident in the battle scenes. His simple, ardent pugnacity is indicated when Aufidius' offensive makes him "sweat with wrath" (I.iv.27). When the Romans are beaten back to their trenches, "Enter *Marcius* cursing." And his most famous exploit, entering the gates of Corioles without support, befits an adventurer rather than a general. Plutarch's Coriolanus, in fact, does not enter the city alone. And it is not unlikely that in thus enhancing the daring of his hero, Shakespeare was recognizing and exploiting Coriolanus' resemblance to Elizabethan military adventurers.

Some such parallels were too close to have escaped any contemporary audience. Essex, a brilliant fighter and bad general, habitually led rather than directed the charge.[3] The audience might also have recalled Grenville's daring command of the *Revenge*. According to the Dutch Jan van Linschoten, who saw the battle, Grenville "went into the Spanish fleete, and shot among them, doing them great hurte, and thinking the rest would have followed: which they did not, but left him there and sayled away."[4] Grenville's fierce personality, moreover, would account not only for the desperateness of the attempt, but for his unpopularity as a leader. According to the nonpartisan Linschoten,

> he was a man very unquiet in his minde, and greatly affected to warre: . . . he had performed many valiant actes, and was greatly feared in these Islands, and knowne of every man, but of nature so severe, so that his owne people hated him for his fierceness, and spake verie hardly of him.[5]

Another commander, Edward Stanley, entered a breach by catching the head of a Spaniard's pike, trying to wrench it from his foe's grasp amidst the constant entertainment of pike thrusts

Shakespeare's Coriolanus: Elizabethan Soldier

and bullets, and then allowing himself to be hoisted over the parapet where he held off the enemy until he was joined by his fellows.[6] Coriolanus' single-handed entry into Corioles would have seemed to Shakespeare's audience no mere tale of legendary heroism.

Contemporary foreign accounts of the English soldier offer illuminating generalizations upon such examples of daring. Emanual van Meteren, a Hollander, said of the English: "The people are bold, courageous, ardent, and cruel in war, fiery in attack (*vyerlich int aegrijpen*), and having little fear of death; they are not vindictive, but very inconstant, rash, vainglorious."[7] Similar faint praise is accorded the English by John Barclay: "They contemne all dangers, and death it selfe, with more courage than judgement."[8] This reputation was not one of which thoughtful Elizabethans were proud. Numerous military tracts warned the people that generalship was more important than daring. The "plain shock and even play of battle" which had prevailed at Agincourt was no longer effective on the Continent, for Spaniards now excelled in the vital "subtil policie and martiall discipline."[9]

Especial attention was given in most contemporary military books to defining the qualities needed in a general. Stress is put upon traits making for pleasant relationships with the army, traits specifically lacking in Coriolanus. The general, according to a typical work, "would be courteous clement, and gentle. Nothing doth more please the common souldier.... Contrariwise, nothing doth more hurt sometimes, then the untimely rigour, and austerity of the Generall."[10] The general is also enjoined to prefer "the safety of his owne people before the killing of his enemies."[11] That such admonitions were necessary is attested by experiences in the Low Countries, where the policy of some of the "chief men of warre" had been "never to winne nor procure the love of their soldiers by anie affabilitie or favour shewed unto them, nor yet by anie care taking for their healthes and safeties." Soldiers, rather, were employed in "manie daungerous and vaine exploites and services, without any reason Militarie."[12] The common soldiers in the Corioles expedition are of course cowardly and are therefore partisan in charging their leader with foolhardiness. But it seems likely that

Shakespeare was aware of the newsworthy criticisms of Elizabethan commanders and that in the light of these he consciously represented Coriolanus as an inconsiderate general. It is certain that he departs from Plutarch in holding up Coriolanus for unfavorable contrast with Cominius, the Roman commander-in-chief. Contemptuous and brutal, Coriolanus alienates his army. Cominius does not curse his soldiers. And his battle techniques are both more humane and more versatile than Coriolanus', particularly in respect to retreats. "To give a brave charge," observed Captain Barnaby Rich, "is a thing proper to every ordinary souldiour, but to make a good retreat in time, & in order, therin consisteth the skill of the Captaine."[13] Some significance derives therefore from the episode introduced by the stage direction "Enter *Cominius* as it were in retire," an episode in clear contrast with the earlier scene in which Coriolanus enters cursing his retreating army. Cominius reassures his men:

> Breathe you, my friends. Well fought! We are come off
> Like Romans, neither foolish in our stands
> Nor cowardly in retire. (I.vi.1)

Elizabethans may not have thought Coriolanus' stand foolish, but many would have recalled an expression made axiomatic by military journalism: "Many mo fieldes have been lost for want of pollicy, than for want of strength."[14]

In turning from Coriolanus at war to Coriolanus in civil life, we view a conflict more central to the play. It has, however, been contended that the Roman is not seriously lacking in either department. According to MacCallum, Coriolanus is not merely a general with strategic skill; "he has the forethought and insight of a statesman, at any rate in matters of foreign and military policy."[15] And Hardin Craig has recently written: "Volumnia has brought up her son in a highly specialized way. She has quite definitely brought him up to be a soldier, a thing which means in chivalric opinion that he has been reared in pure nobility. . . . She chose to breed in him absolute knightliness and pure idealism."[16] MacCallum's praise, as will later appear, is deserved more by Plutarch's than by Shakespeare's hero. Professor Craig's remarks raise the important question of whether Coriolanus, brought up as a soldier, may serve as an example of "absolute knightliness."

For his limitations, whatever may have been Volumnia's efforts, are persuasively described by J.E. Phillips: "He is 'the arm our soldier.' There is no evidence . . . that his celebrated service to Rome was ever of anything but a military nature."[17] The "chivalric opinion" to which Professor Craig refers was at one time influential in English military life and had many reflections in dramatic literature. The gentleman-warrior, able in the arts of both war and peace, was exemplified in the persons of Sir Philip Sidney, a "well-letter'd warrior," and Fulke Greville, "Fair man at arms, the Muses' favourite."[18] On the stage were to be found knightly warriors like Lyly's Alexander, who states as his creed: ". . . joyning letters with launces, we endevor to be as good Philosophers as soldiers, knowing it no lesse praise to be wise, then commendable to be valiant."[19]

But by 1600, at the very latest, literature begins to feature less desirable representations of soldiers of all ranks.[20] Stage warriors take on traits of hardened fighters, traits given extreme delineation by Beaumont and Fletcher. Such warriors are wrathful, proud, indiscreet, profane. And it is not difficult to find evidence in actual life for such representations. John Norden, seeking to restore the ideal of gentleman-warrior, pays recognition to the real situation:

> But I have heard some of no small place in the warres affirme (with no lesse audacious insolencie, then hee ought to have sinceritie) that it is enough for the Ministrie to be masters of sinne, and that it beseemeth souldiers to live like souldiers, to sweare like souldiers, and to sinne like souldiers.[21]

Moral delinquency, as a source of dramatic conflict, was used mainly for purposes of comedy and limited to the lower military ranks. To noble commanders was assigned the loftier role of tragic incompatibility with peace-time society. In such representations the dramatists possibly relied upon popular knowledge of the unlucky civil careers of Elizabethan commanders, conspicuously Essex and his military friends, members of the "war party"[22]—men, to use Bacon's words, of a "military dependence." Essex did not closely resemble Coriolanus, but Bacon's letter of warning to the Earl might well, in large part, have been addressed to Shakespeare's hero. Essex is rebuked principally for being "of a nature not to be ruled." Another serious fault, carefully analyzed by Bacon, is

> that of a military dependence. Wherein I cannot sufficiently wonder at your Lordship's course; that you say, the wars are your occupation, and go on in that course; whereas, if I mought have advised your Lordship, you should have left that person at Plymouth; more than when in counsel ... it had been in season.[23]

Many other examples might be cited of military men who, like Coriolanus, move ungracefully from "th' casque to th' cushion" (IV.vii.43).[24] But more impressive than many examples is Lord Burghley's advice to his son:

> Neither by my consent shall thou train [thy sons] up to the wars. For he that setteth up his rest to live by that profession can hardly be an honest man or good Christian. ... Besides it is a science no longer in request than in use: soldiers in peace are like chimneys in summer.[25]

Equally cogent reasons against excessive devotion to warfare had been given influential expression by another authority on statecraft:

> They have ... many held, and doe hold in this opinion, that there is no maner of thing, which lesse agreeth the one with the other, nor that is so much unlike, as the civill life, to the Souldiours. Wherby it is often seene, that if any determin in the exercise of that kinde of service to prevaile, that incontinent he doth not onely chaunge in apparell, but also in custome and maner, in voyce, and from the fashion of all civill use, he doth alter.[26]

It should not be thought, however, that the "plain soldier" (to use a phrase made popular by Shakespeare's *Henry V*) in court or city was always viewed with disapproval. Otherwise it would be hard to explain the effect of Othello's forthright avowal (I.iii.81):

> Rude am I in my speech,
> And little graced with the soft phrase of peace;
> For since these arms of mine had seven years' pith
> Till now, some nine moons wasted, they have us'd

Their dearest action in the tented field,
And little of this great world can I speak
More than pertains to feats of broils and battle.

Many Elizabethan warriors, in both life and literature, had used similar words, and generally with no painful sense of self-deficiency. Most military writers of the time, though fluent as Barnaby Rich, refer complacently to the rudeness of their soldier-like lines and their fear of being indiscreet. Advocates of the civil state might frown, but the soldiers bow proudly, in recognition of their social disabilities. The conventionality of the apology for rudeness is amusingly shown in the attitude taken by Richard Peeke, a soldier who distinguished himself on the Essex expedition to Cadiz. Writing a literate account of his rash exploit, he takes the pose of repentant rudeness:

> I know not what the Court of a King meanes, nor what the fine Phrases of silken Courtiers are: A good Shippe I know, and a poore Cabbin, and the Language of a Cannon: And therefore, as my Breeding has bin Rough, (Scorning Delicacy:) And my Present Being consisteth altogether upon the Soldier, (blunt, plaine, and unpolished;) so must my writings be, proceeding from fingers fitter for the Pike than the Pen.[27]

There seems to have been considerable popular recognition of the worth of the "plain" warrior as opposed to courtly intriguers, and much of the credit for this recognition is due the soldier-authors who pleaded the cause of military men. Churchyard was typical in protesting the plight of those "that have followed the warres all their life daies, and knewe not how to flatter and faune, or crouch and coursie for commoditie," and this could apply not only to common soldiers but to "some of good birthe."[28] Entire books were dedicated to a defence of the military profession.[29] Most influential of all soldier-authors was probably Barnaby Rich, who throughout his many works pleads monotonously on behalf of the soldiers in England, "where I thinke of all other Countreys they are had in least estimation."[30] But Rich's ablest advocacy is presented not in his polemic tracts but in his popular[31] *Riche His Farewell to Militarie Profession* (1581). In "Sappho Duke of Manton," a story included in the *Farewell*, Rich makes fictional use of the tragic theme dear to him:

the vulnerability of a noble warrior in a corrupt society. Sappho was a "successful warrior . . . ; but the warres beying once finished and broughte to an ende, so that the empire remained in tranquilitie and peace, souldiors were forgotten, captaines were not cared for." Sappho's voice "served hym better to cheare his souldiors in the feeld, than either to fayne or syng ditties in a ladies chamber; his tongue had more used to speake simplie and plaine, then to dissemble with his freend, or to flatter with his foe."[32] As a result of his noble simplicity, the Duke became a victim of intrigue and was banished.

Shakespeare, too, gave more than one sympathetic representation of the soldier's plight. Hotspur is ill-used by the monarch for whom he had spent his blood. And Alcibiades, the rough captain in *Timon of Athens*, is interesting because of a resemblance to Coriolanus. *Timon* and *Coriolanus* were composed within one or two years of each other; and it is also noteworthy that Alcibiades and Coriolanus are parallel lives in Plutarch. Shakespeare's Alcibiades, denied a fair but boldly urged request by a corrupt senate, is banished. In conventional terms he marvels at this ingratitude for his services (III.v.109):

> Is this the balsam that the usuring Senate
> Pours into captains' wounds? Banishment!
> It comes not ill. I hate not to be banish'd.
> It is a cause worthy my spleen and fury,
> That I may strike at Athens.

Shakespeare's retrained sympathy is apparently with the captain, even in his successful military revenge on his country. Moreover, the structure of the play seems to imply a parallel between Timon's deserts as a philanthropist and Alcibiades' as a captain. But with Coriolanus the situation is different. Shakespeare gave careful attention to the welfare of the state in this play,[33] and although awareness is taken of Coriolanus' deserts as a soldier, the emphasis is plainly upon his limitations as a citizen.

These limitations become evident as soon as Coriolanus appears on the stage. Preceding his entry is the episode in which Menenius urges the rebellious citizens to take an enlarged view of their grievance. The old patrician employs the fable of the Belly and the Members in a careful explanation of the ideal state.

Then Coriolanus enters and falls to cursing the people. His proposal for remedying the grain shortage is to make a quarry

> With thousands of these quarter'd slaves as high
> As I could pick my lance. (I.i.202)

Coriolanus is a war-lover. And with the Elizabethans, as now, such an attitude was considered unsocial. Barnaby Rich, as usual echoing contemporary sentiment, remarked that "it is good to be a skilfull warriour, but ill againe to bee a great warre lover."[34] What is more, the humbler citizens of Shakespeare's audience would have recognized in Coriolanus' reason for welcoming the war a source of current grievance. The *Calendar of State Papers* (*Domestic*) bears evidence to an economic reason for military conscription. The shortage of grain, as acute in Elizabethan times as in Coriolanus', was a cause of social unrest and, with other economic maladjustments, produced malcontents. Military recruiting helped to rid the country of its restless elements,[35] the equivalent of Coriolanus' "musty superfluity." The ensuing warfare temporarily stills the domestic disturbance; but an added danger develops directly from Coriolanus' success in battle. The Volscian leader abandons hope of defeating his foe "true sword to sword," and resolves now to "potch at him some way,/Or wrath or craft may get him" (I.x.15). "He's the devil," acknowledges the soldier to whom Aufidius confides his sinister purpose. "Bolder, though not so subtle," is the general's significant comment. The audience is thus prepared for the fatal "policy" of the final episodes.[36]

Upon Coriolanus' return from the Volscian war, he begins his brief political career. It is with reluctance that he stands for consul, not because of any profound analysis of his own capabilities, but because of an intuitive distrust of any way of life other than his own—warfare. This distrust is partially responsible for his disinclination to deal intimately with the people and their problems. As he tells his mother (II.i.219),

> I had rather be their servant in my way
> Than sway with them in theirs.

The citizens, in turn, reluctantly acknowledge his deserts. "If," as one of them says, "he show us his wounds and tell us his deeds, we are to put our tongues into those wounds and speak for them" (II.iii.5). A more intelligent analysis is made by an officer in the Capitol (II.ii.27):

> He hath deserved worthily of his country; and his ascent is not by such easy degrees as those who, having been supple and courteous to the people, bonneted, without any further deed to have them at all into their estimation.

Notorious among those who have been "supple and courteous" are the tribunes Brutus and Sicinius. These men, like Aufidius developed by Shakespeare into crafty opposition to the warrior, shape circumstances so as to make them least compatible with his limited abilities. When Coriolanus assures Brutus: "Yet oft/When blows have made me stay, I fled from words" (II.ii.75), he is the victim of tragic irony, for the tribunes make his crisis one to be met with words, not blows.

The critical scenes of Coriolanus' candidacy and trial represent Shakespeare's most radical difference from Plutarch. The playwright, as MacCallum notes,[37] slights Plutarch's extensive economic and political background for Coriolanus' banishment. "The real center of the situation is Coriolanus' behavior when as candidate, and round this all else is grouped: and this behavior, it will be remembered, is altogether a fabrication on Shakespeare's part." A study of the material basis for this fabrication will disclose that Shakespeare depended significantly upon popular attitudes toward Elizabethan soldiers.

Plutarch's Coriolanus shows his wounds to the citizens as a matter of course. Shakespeare's hero mars his fortunes by his surly refusal to abide by what was for Plutarch's Coriolanus an honored Roman custom. Displaying one's wounds and boasting of military services bore an unusual stigma in Shakespeare's time, largely because of the shameless beggars and rogues who disgraced the military profession. Shakespeare possibly could not conceive of Coriolanus, a genuinely proud man, demeaning himself to the cheap displays of Ancient Pistol.[38] As a result of Coriolanus' rudeness when he seeks the citizens' "voices," a scuffle breaks out between gentry and populace. Coriolanus' friends beat the plebs back, but they have difficulty in persuading the general to retire until a reasonable conference is possible. He proposes to settle the dispute by force of arms: "On fair ground/I could beat forty of them" (III.i.242) is his illuminating comment. Cominius, the rational warrior, argues that "now 'tis odds beyond arithmetic,/And manhood is call'd foolery when it stands/Against a falling fabric" (III.i.245).

After Coriolanus is persuaded to depart, Menenius ascribes his friend's misfortune to traits not uncommon in Elizabethan commanders:

> His nature is too noble for this world.
> He would not flatter Neptune for his trident
> Or Jove for's power to thunder. His heart's his mouth:
> What his breast forges, that his tongue must vent,
> And being angry does forget that ever
> He heard the name of death. (III.i.255)

In his discerning, unorthodox interpretation of the play, O.J. Campbell maintains that Shakespeare did not intend this analysis as praise of his protagonist.[39] Certainly, as Campbell notes, it is a seriously common error to tear the first line of this speech from its context. Actually, Coriolanus is too noble for this world—the world of compromise, tact, and government—for reasons that the Elizabethans considered questionable virtues. Indeed, when Menenius must presently excuse to the tribunes his friend's behavior, he puts these same "noble" traits into a more realistic context (III.i.320):

> Consider this: he has been bred i' th' wars
> Since 'a could draw a sword, and is ill-school'd
> In bolted language; meal and bran together
> He throws without distinction.

"Too noble for this world" may please the nobility as a euphemism, but the canny Menenius knows that representatives of the people must have a candid explanation. And the clear implication of the more prosaic account is that Coriolanus, "bred i' th' wars," is socially uneducated. Menenius' explanation has its desired effect, for the general is granted a formal trial.

Only Volumnia can persuade Coriolanus to appear for this trial. Her influence is due partially to her understanding of his military temperament. Instead of rebuking his wrath, she tactfully explains that a brain can lead the "use of anger/To better vantage" (III.ii.30). She acknowledges the problem created by his most ardent antipathy (III.ii.90):

> I know thou hadst rather
> Follow thine enemy in a fiery gulf
> Than flatter him in a bower.

And—a stroke of genius—she not only gives him detailed directions for presenting himself in penitence, but she frames the apology for him in soldierly terms (III.ii.80):

> say to them
> Thou are their soldier, and, being bred in broils,
> Hast not the soft way which, thou doest confess,
> Were fit for thee to use, as they to claim,
> In asking their good loves.

The peculiar advantage of this speech for his purpose is that it had become conventionally less an humble apology than a complacent self-justification. Equally inspired is Volumnia's use of a military analogy in an attempt to convince her son that tact is desirable. "I have heard you say," she tells him,

> Honour and policy, like unsever'd friends,
> I' th' war do grow together. Grant that, and tell me,
> In peace what each of them by th' other lose,
> That they combine not there. (III.ii.41)

In spite of his unenthusiastic "Tush, tush," she pursues the argument, contending that this type of dissimulation is not less honorable "than to take in a town with gentle words" (III.ii.59).

An interesting feature of her reasoning is that Coriolanus, as Shakespeare conceived him, could scarcely have urged the use of policy in warfare and could never have captured a town with "gentle words," although these are practices enjoined upon a general by most Elizabethan military treatises. Volumnia's reminiscences seem to be an imperfect incorporation, in Elizabethan terminology, of material from Plutarch, whose Coriolanus employed policy on at least two occasions. In order to prick the Volsces on to war against Rome, he supposedly resorted to "craft and deceit" when he sent to the consuls in Rome "to accuse the Volsces falsely."[40] Again, heading the Volscian army, he employed a "fine device" to increase the dissension between Roman commonalty and Roman nobility and thus reduce opposition.[41] One can scarcely picture Shakespeare's soldier using a "fine device" or seeking to minimize resistance.

Plutarch's Coriolanus, though an aristocratic ruffian, is capable of "gentle words." He does not need his mother's help in devising the right utterance, and unlike Shakespeare's hero, he requires no urging to present himself for trial. He is credited with an "eloquent tongue," and for this reason Aufidius does not wish him to speak before the Volsces in his own defence.[42] And in persuading the Volsces to permit his service against the Romans, Coriolanus "spake so excellently in the presence of them all, that he was thought no less eloquent in tongue, than warlike in show: and declared himself both expert in wars, and wise with valiantness." Plutarch's hero thus reveals occasional characteristics which, to the Elizabethans, befitted a gentleman-warrior.

Shakespeare's Coriolanus, at any rate, succumbs more to his mother's importunity than to her argument and suddenly agrees to appear for trial. His speech of bitter acquiescence is, in large part, a farewell to war (III.ii.112):

> My throat of war be turn'd
> Which quier'd with my drum, into a pipe
> Small as a eunuch or the virgin voice
> That babies lulls asleep! . . . A beggar's tongue
> Make motion through my lips, and my arm'd knees,
> Which bow'd but in my stirrup, bend like his
> That hath receiv'd an alms!

Although not so grand as Othello's comparable utterance, these lines are an ardent statement of Coriolanus' pride in his military profession, certainly as intense as his devotion to the patrician class. When he appears for trial, a disastrous outcome is inevitable. Brutus' directions to his fellow tribune reveal a knowledge of Coriolanus' tragic potentialities:

> Put him to choler straight. He hath been us'd
> Ever to conquer, and to have his worth
> Of contradiction. Being once chaf'd, he cannot
> Be rein'd again to temperance. (III.iii.25)

To make matters worse, the general comes on the scene already "chaf'd." In mock deference to Menenius' "Calmly, I do beseech you," he prays the gods to

> plant love among's!
> Throng our large temples with the shows of peace
> And not our streets with war! (III.iii.35)

This ironic use of *peace* is stressed by its discordant echo throughout the scene, as in an O'Neill play. "Peace I say!" shouts the Aedile just before Coriolanus loudly demands to be heard. "Peace, ho!" proclaim the tribunes. And when the populace begins to riot, Sicinius cries "Peace!" The word is dramatically incongruous in a scene marked by outrage and leading to war.

It is in vain that Menenius reminds the plebs of his friend's deserts, "the warlike service he has done," "the wounds his body bears." Likewise futile is Menenius' employment of the conventional apology for the soldier who cannot behave civilly:

> Consider further,
> That when he speaks not like a citizen,
> You find him like a soldier. Do not take
> His rougher accents for malicious sounds,
> But, as I say, such as become a soldier
> Rather than envy you. (III.iii.52)

This is the very speech that Volumnia had instructed her son to make. But he can offer—and he does so promptly—only an instance of his "rougher accents" in asking why the citizens have divested him of his new honors. The tribunes then "put him to choler straight" and effect the sentence of banishment.

The scenes just reviewed—those of the candidacy and trial—reveal Shakespeare's detailed concern with his hero's military background and its consequences. The remainder of the play is more closely based on Plutarch. With some violence to consistency of character, Shakespeare forgets in two of the most emotional scenes that his hero characteristically speaks "like a soldier." The eloquent, persuasive words of Plutarch's aristocrat are put almost unchanged into the mouth of Shakespeare's warrior. But in large design, though not always in detail, Shakespeare reveals to the play's end his interest in Coriolanus as a soldier. One result of this interest is the emphasis—greater than Plutarch's—upon the citizens' guilt in rewarding their soldier with exile. Coriolanus himself is moved to complain of his "thankless country" to Aufidius (IV.v.74). Even the enemy general is stirred to sympathize with his ancient foe and resolves to pour war "into the bowels of ungrateful Rome" (IV.v.134).

Finally, Shakespeare altered the circumstances of Coriolanus' death so as to make the catastrophe result from his simple and violent nature. Plutarch's hero is slain before he has a chance to speak in his defence. In Shakespeare's version he is allowed to speak, and "gentle words" might have saved his life. But he is taunted by Aufidius so that by an outburst he will alienate popular sympathy. Once more Coriolanus is "chaf'd." Boastfully he recalls how, "like an eagle in a dovecote," he had "flutter'd your Volscians in Corioles." "Alone I did it," he roars, shortly before he is killed, longing at the very end for a chance to use his "lawful sword." There is thus a dramatic fitness in Shakespeare's conception of the way in which his hero should die.

It seems probable that Shakespeare benefited from current military convention in interpreting, though not always in devising, Coriolanus' behavior. He did so, of course, without discarding the Plutarchan conception of Coriolanus as a Roman patrician. The patrician merely became less eloquent, less tactful, less intelligent, less complex than Plutarch conceived him. This is not to depreciate either Shakespeare or his hero. The simplification was both deliberate and dramatically profitable. What is lost in subtlety of conception is compensated for by intensity of character and decisiveness of crisis.

The simplification of Plutarchan material is especially visible in the causes Shakespeare assigns for Coriolanus' tragic incompatibility with society. MacCallum voices the standard interpretation of the grounds for the tragedy in the first paragraph of his chapter "The Disasters of Coriolanus and Their Causes":

> Feeling for his country, feeling for his caste, feeling for his family, thus form the triple groundwork of Coriolanus' nobleness, but they fail to uphold it in the storm of temptation. As furnishing the foundation of conduct they

have dangers and defects, inherent in themselves, or incident to their combination, and these it is to which the guilt and ruin of Coriolanus are due.[43]

MacCallum's "triple groundwork" of noble flaws applies perfectly to Plutarch's Coriolanus, but will not suffice to explain the misfortunes of Shakespeare's hero. These are best accounted for by Aufidius as he runs through the possible reasons for his enemy's failure as a Roman citizen:

> First he was
> A noble servant to them [the Romans], but he could not
> Carry his honours even. Whether 'twas pride,
> Which out of daily fortune ever taints
> The happy man; whether defect of judgment,
> To fail in the disposing of those chances
> Which he was lord of; *or whether nature,*
> *Not to be other than one thing, not moving*
> *From th' casque to th' cushion, but commanding peace*
> *Even with the same austerity and garb*
> *As he controll'd the war.* (IV.vii.35)

The italicized explanation is probably the most important, for it is based upon Shakespeare's own shaping of the tragedy and has been offered several times before by Coriolanus' friends and hinted at by himself.

Probably in no other Shakespeare play is the hero's flaw so conveniently, so frequently, and so monotonously explained. The same misfortune befalls the general again and again, and it is explained repeatedly in one way: bred to the wars, Coriolanus bears himself awkwardly, and is ungratefully used, in time of peace. It is understandable why readers should feel greatest emotion during a scene which is not really calamitous and which, in Shakespeare's version, does not necessarily lead to tragedy—the intercession of Volumnia and the women. But in this careful labeling of Coriolanus and his flaw, Shakespeare secured, at the expense of some monotony, several scenes of sharp dramatic conflict, scenes which comprise the central portion of the play. And not of the least importance, he solicited the interest of his audience by minimizing the Roman issue of the plebeian-patrician battle over popular government and by stressing the simpler, more typically Elizabethan conflict between the soldier and an uncongenial society.

NOTES

1. Such is the verdict of three major 20th-century critics: Hardin Craig: "In the battles before Corioli Marcius is impeccable"—*An Interpretation of Shakespeare* (N.Y., 1948), p. 290; E.K. Chambers: "The first act shows us Coriolanus, on the whole, great; a great warrior, undaunted in danger, removed high above the greed and poltroonery of common man"—*Coriolanus* (N.Y., 1904), pp. xv-xvi; M.W. MacCallum: "He is . . . a general who once and again gives proof of his strategic skill"—*Shakespeare's Roman Plays and Their Background* (London, 1910), p. 373.

2. I have used the *Complete Works*, ed. Kittredge (Boston, 1936).

3. "My Lord of Essex was one of the first that got over the walls, followed by the souldiers as the place would give them leave"—*The Commentaries of Sir Francis Vere* (Cambridge, 1657), p. 39. Cf. p. 58.

4. "The Fight and Cyclone at Azores," *Arber's English Reprints* (London, 1871), p. 90.

5. *Ibid.*, pp. 91–92. Like Coriolanus (as seen by the tribunes), Grenville was a "man of intolerable pride and insatiable ambition"—Lane to Walsyngham, Sept. 8, 1585, *Cal. State Papers (Col.)*, I, 3.

6. J.W. Fortescue, *A History of the British Army* (London, 1910), I, 149–50.

7. *History of the Netherlands* (1599): in W.B. Rye, *England As Seen by Foreigners* (London, 1865), p. 70.

8. *Icon Animorum* (1614); Englished by Thomas May (1633), p. 81: quoted in Willard Farnham, "The Tragic Prodigality of Life," *Essays in Criticism, Second Series* (Berkeley, 1934), p. 189. Cf. Languet's letter to Sidney (Feb. 15, 1578): "In our countries we can scarcely find a veteran commander and this owing simply to our recklessness. The Spaniards alone are free from this species of madness and therefore they possess generals of the utmost experience in the art of war, who effect far more by genius than by strength."

9. Robert Barret, *The Theorike and Practike of Moderne Warres* (London, 1598), p. 8.

10. Matthew Sutcliffe, *The Practice, Proceedings, and Lawes of Armes* (London, 1593), pp. 42–43. Cf. Barnaby Rich, *The Fruites of Long Experience* (London, 1604), pp. 29–30.

11. Rich, *A Path-way to Military Practise* (London, 1587), sig. C1^v.

12. *Certain Discourses, Written by Sir John Smythe, Knight* (London, 1590), "Proeme Dedicatorie."

13. *Pathway*, sig. C3. Sir John Norris engineered a famous retreat in 1592, "then the which," wrote Bacon, "there hath not been an Exploit of Warre more celebrated. For in the true judgement of Men of Warre, honourable Retreats are no wayes inferiour to brave Charges; As having less of Fortune, more of Discipline, and as much of Valour"— *Considerations Touching a Warre with Spaine* (London, 1629), p. 38.

14. Rich, *A Right Exelent and Pleasaunt Dialogue* (London, 1574), sig. C5.

15. MacCallum, p. 373.

16. Craig, p. 289.

17. *The State in Shakespeare's Greek and Roman Plays* (N.Y., 1940), p. 162.

18. George Peele, "Polyhymnia," *Works*, ed. Dyce (London, 1829–39), II, 204.

19. *Campaspe*, I, i, 82–84, *Works*, ed. Bond (Oxford, 1902). Shakespeare's earlier plays stress this ideal. Cf. Talbot's eulogy of Bedford (*1 Henry VI*, III,ii,134):

> A braver soldier never couched lance,
> A gentler heart did never sway in court

and the idealization of the Black Prince in *Richard II*, II.i.173.

20. The definitions of Character writers, though oversimplified, are an index to the change in public opinion. See especially Overbury's "A Souldier," a creature of wrath and impulsiveness, in *The Overburian Characters*, ed. Paylor (Oxford, 1936), p. 24, and the Character drawn by Shakespeare's Jaques, *As You Like It*, II.vii.149.

21. *The Mirror of Honor* (London, 1597), p. 33.

22. The dramatic importance of this party is proved by R.B. Sharpe, *The Real War of the Theaters* (Boston, 1935). A suggestive statement of the plight of Elizabethan "war men" is to be found in *An Apologie of the Earle of Essex, against those which jealously and maliciously,*

tax him to be the hinderer of the peace and quiet of his country (London, 1603). See especially sigs. A2ᵛ, C1, and C1ᵛ.

23. Oct. 4, 1596. James Spedding, *The Letters and the Life of Francis Bacon* (London, 1862), II. 413.

24. For example, the account by Sir Francis Vere, most astute of Elizabethan generals, of his indiscretions at court, *The Commentaries of Sir Francis Vere*, pp. 26, 46–47, 66, 68. Also illuminating is the behavior of Christopher St. Lawrence at the Council table, where he spoke "pasionat as a Soldier," *Letters and Memorials of State*, ed. Collins (London, 1746), II, 137–38.

25. *Annals of the Reformation*, ed. Strype (Oxford, 1824), IV, 477.

26. *The Arte of Warre, Written in Italian by Nicholas Machiavel, and set foorth in English by Peter Withorne* (London, 1588), sig. A1.

27. *Three to One: Being an English-Spanish Combat, Performed by a Westerne Gentleman, of Tavystoke in Devonshire with an English Quarter-Staffe, against Three Spanish Rapiers and Poniards . . .* (London, 1625), sig. A4. For evidence that this kind of apology had already reached the status of a Character, see Nicholas Breton, "The Scholler and the Souldiour," *The Wil of Wit* (London, 1597), sig. I4ᵛ.

28. Thomas Churchyard, *A Generall Rehearsall of Warres* (London, 1579), sigs. M3ᵛ, O1ᵛ, and O2.

29. Geffrey Gates, *The Defence of Militarie Profession* (London, 1579); Thomas Trussell, *The Souldier Pleading His Owne Cause* (London, 1619).

30. *A Right Exelent and Pleasaunt Dialogue*, sig. C2.

31. Shakespeare assuredly knew the work. *Twelfth Night*, according to Chambers, is probably indebted to the *Farewell's* "Appolonius and Sylla," and another tale, "Of Two Brethren and Their Wives," has recently been suggested as a source for *The Merry Wives*. See Dorothy H. Bruce, "*The Merry Wives* and *Two Brethren*," *SP*, 39 (1942).

32. *Farewell*, ed. Collier (London, 1846), pp. 22–23.

33. See the chapter on *Coriolanus* in J.E. Phillips, *op. cit.*

34. *Fruites of Long Experience*, p. 5.

35. Cf. C.G. Cruickshank, *Elizabeth's Army* (Oxford, 1946), pp. 9–10.

36. This sinister "policy" is not found in Plutarch's Aufidius. Shakespeare thus points the soldier-intriguer antithesis.

37. MacCallum, p. 510.

38. Cf. *Henry V*, V.i.93–94.

39. *Shakespeare's Satire* (Oxford Univ. Press, 1943), p. 209.

40. *Shakespeare's Plutarch*, ed. Tucker Brooke (London, 1909), II, 183.
41. *Ibid.*, p. 185.
42. *Ibid.*, p. 206.
43. MacCallum, p. 598.

Reprinted by permission of the Modern Language Association of America from Paul A. Jorgensen, "Shakespeare's Coriolanus: Elizabethan Soldier," PMLA 64 (1949), 221–35. Copyright, 1949 by the Modern Language Association of America.

Coriolanus

Tyrone Guthrie

Coriolanus is not often produced.
Why is this?
It has a splendid leading part, in which the extrovert brilliance of an important actor can be brilliantly deployed. It has a magnificent part for a senior lady, quite as good as Juliet's Nurse, better than Paulina in *Winter's Tale*, Katherine of Aragon or The Countess Roussillon in *All's Well That Ends Well*. It is one of Shakespeare's least untidily constructed plays (though this author can never expect high marks for neatness) as well as one of his most vigorously theatrical. What is the deterrent?

I personally am always a little put off by Roman dress. It may be becoming—I guess it is—to those of perfect physique, but the ordinary mortal does not look well with skinny arms and legs thrusting out of a metal corselet. Greaves and armlets do not conceal but accentuate muscular shortcomings, and if, instead of armor, togas are worn, everyone seems to be scurrying about on Ladies' Night at the Turkish Bath. Yet Roman dress seems no deterrent to the production of *Julius Caesar*, one of the most frequently performed of Shakespeare's plays; and anyway, it is not necessary to play *Coriolanus* in Roman dress. It could, in my opinion, perfectly well be given in Elizabethan or in modern dress, or, even better, as in a splendid production by Michael Langham at Stratford, Ontario, in the period of Napoleon Bonaparte.

I think a likelier reason for the play's neglect is the fact that none of its chief characters are very "sympathetic." There is a theory in the modern theatre, and particularly in New York, that an audience expects to "identify with"—a barbarous phrase—certain aspects of the characters in a play or novel. In *Coriolanus* there is no one with whom right-minded members of either sex would normally wish to identify. Coriolanus is far too big for his breeches, and eventually turns out to be a bad egg too. Menenius is a fuddy-duddy, a nice enough old person but there is nothing in him with which anyone under a hundred and eleven years old could identify. The Tribunes? well, after all the scandal about the Teamsters Union, let's face it! no one much wants to identify with a Tribune. Of the ladies, Volumnia is a battle-axe, Virgilia the most colorless of namby-pambies, and Valeria so small a part as not to appear in the identification parade.

For my part I do not subscribe to the notion that audiences want to identify. I do not believe that to enjoy *Hamlet* you have to undergo the absurd delusion that *you*, a necktie salesman, just wild about your stamp collection and a brunette named Shirley with cute hips, or *you*, a Presbyterian minister's widow in a small apartment in Flatbush . . . that either of you is under the absurd delusion that *you* are Hamlet. I do not believe that, to succeed, a play or story must be peopled with sympathetic characters. Becky Sharp is not sympathetic, but she is interesting, and that makes her better company than that goody-goody bore Amelia Sedley, with whom Thackeray intended his female readers to identify. Macbeth and Lady Macbeth are not sympathetic, nor is Peer Gynt, nor Harpagon in *The Miser*. Regina, in *The Little Foxes*, is not sympathetic. Yet the lack of sympathetic central characters has not come between any of these plays and their audience.

Can the difficulty be that the play's politics are unacceptable? Shakespeare, as always, takes no side in the controversy which he presents. The better educated upper-classes put their case more eloquently, and in the case of Menenius with humor; but the Tribunes speak up clearly and well and are allowed dignity in their final scenes of defeat, when, with Coriolanus at the gates, their enmity to him seems to have brought disaster upon Rome.

I suspect that since the re-emergence of Shakespeare as an important and successful dramatist—namely since about the 1700s—the excessive arrogance of Coriolanus may have seemed less credible and more unsympathetic than it did to Shakespeare's contemporaries a hundred years before. Audiences have become more and more politically inclined towards the tribunes' views, more and more unsympathetic toward the patricians. With the passing of more years this will become even more the case. Audiences are better at feeling than thinking. They are also creatures of habit. Plays and novels have for centuries been expected to have heroes and heroines—the selfsame people with whom the twentieth century has been trying to identify. Therefore, in *Coriolanus*, it is disconcerting to find that the central character, the handsomest and bravest fellow around, the center of the sex interest, such as it is—and this we shall discuss later—is really rather horrid. In most plays and stories, the upper-classes are "good," and though there are members of the Good Poor (Cardinal Newman's phrase)—mostly old nurses, coachmen, and retainers of the upper orders—as a whole it is a well-established convention that the lower orders must be either comic or composed of dangerous and undesirable elements. So it is disconcerting in *Coriolanus* to find ourselves unable to identify with either the patricians or the plebeians. No one could say that the Tribunes were Good Poor; neither are they comic. One doesn't know which side to be on.

Today Liberty, Equality, and Fraternity are beginning to seem over simple and over esteemed ideas. Now we are beginning to rumble our Tribunes of the People. They are no longer dear little Jack-the-Giant-Killers wrestling on our behalf with the Giant of Capitalism. They are themselves capitalists: rich, powerful, and tyrannical. Furthermore, the figure of Coriolanus, the upper-class militarist, hungry for political power and supported by powerful connections, though still conceivable, has ceased to be a menace. Such a political simpleton, however well-connected with The Establishment, would not last five minutes in modern public life.

And yet, is this true? Coriolanus would have made a fabulous television personality. Handsome as Apollo, a stunning military hero, he would appear, naturally, in uniform, his splendid chest loaded with the glittering testaments of his valor, his brusque no-nonsense manner, his obvious sincerity, the well-known fact of his devotion to wife, baby son and, above all, to his widowed mom.... Why, the sheer novelty of a candidate who did not promise to give the voters more of everything they might be likely to want, who did not skate lightly and ambiguously over the thin ice of race equality or religious difference, who did not try to flatter the common man by creating himself anew in the common usage, but, on the contrary, insisted upon the difference between himself and the herd and promised only blood, sweat, and tears...! A cinch. The electorate would be knocked flat on its collective back and vote him a legislative blank check.

So, perhaps, *Coriolanus* may be due to make a comeback in the theatre, not as the almost clinical examination of the character whom Shakespeare imagined, but rather as a passionate political affirmation of the public need for an Almighty Father. A spanking, blockbusting *Heldentenor* could be wafted to theatrical triumph on the wings of political enthusiasm. And if you ask how the *Heldentenor* could achieve the desertion to the Volsces and the betrayal of Rome without losing sympathy, then you do not know anything at all about the magic of *Heldentenoren* when they fire off rhetorical tirades of high caliber, and about the blind gullibility of an audience in the grip of powerful prejudice.

But none of this has much to do with *Coriolanus* as evidenced by Shakespeare's text. Shakespeare was not concerned to glorify a hero, still less, cheaply, to debunk him—although he was, I think, concerned to debunk certain upper-class conceptions about honor. He was intending rather to examine the human being, weak, fallible, like all of us, and, again like all of us, lost without the love and approval of those whose approval and love were the sun and moon of his private world.

It is interesting to compare Shakespeare's treatment with Plutarch's *Life of Coriolanus*, from which he derived the story. Plutarch allows us to feel that the plebeians have a better case than Shakespeare grants them. Plutarch's Coriolanus, therefore, appears even more unreasonable and intractable than Shakespeare's. But, broadly speaking, the political picture is similar. What Shakespeare has done is to suggest more plausible and interesting reasons for the shocking treachery of Coriolanus

Coriolanus

after he has been banished from Rome. Plutarch assumes that he was motivated solely by outraged pride. Plutarch, with his strong democratic and liberal bias, implies that Coriolanus's conduct is no more than the reverse of that medal whose obverse is an upper-class, military notion of honor.

Shakespeare, too, takes some pretty shrewd cracks at this kind of honor. Volumnia, particularly, is allowed some scarifying remarks of a kind which are only too familiar in the mouths of elderly females of military caste. Her very first speech whacks home the satiric point, and lets us understand that the fatherless, only son of such a widow had no alternative but to try to be the kind of man his mother had determined to make him. Side by side with Volumnia, Shakespeare places two other figures of great significance in the explanation of Coriolanus: Menenius (a charming humorous aristocrat, an old friend of the family, and a father-figure to Coriolanus) and Tullus Aufidius.

In Plutarch, Aufidius is no more than the protagonist of the Volscian politico-military theme. Shakespeare makes him far more important. As early as the second scene of the play he is introduced for no other purpose than to show him to the audience and to establish from the start that he is an important figure: he is shown dominating a meeting of the Volscian senate. The matter of the debate could easily have been conveyed to the audience in the preceding scene, and indeed most of it is. But Shakespeare considers it important that we should see and hear Aufidius and get an impression of him as one of the dominant elements in his scheme of the play.

He has already been described in the dialogue of the opening scene as the chief military rival of Coriolanus:

> Were half to half the world by th'ears, and he
> Upon my party, I'd revolt, to make
> Only my wars with him: he is a lion
> That I am proud to hunt.

Later, at the start of the battle sequence in and around Corioli (Act I, Scene 4) he is once more planted as the adversary whom Caius Marcius (not yet created Coriolanus) longs to meet. And again in Scene 5: "There is the man of my soul's hate, Aufidius." Throughout Scene 6 this theme is repeated, and finally, in Scene 8, the two meet in single combat. This is one of those scenes which an inattentive or inexperienced reader might lightly slip over, since the lines convey no more than the commonplaces of formal defiance. But in a well-ordered production, this is the crisis toward which the preceding sequence has been building.

In Shakespeare, these single combats are always of symbolic importance. Compare, for instance, Hamlet versus Laertes, Macbeth versus Macduff, Richard III versus Richmond. They represent the resolution in action of an antagonism which has already been implied in the dialogue and which is crucial to the whole meaning of the play. Nowadays in the theatre they tend to be skimpy and perfunctory—a few stylized whacks and innocuous bangs. This is all wrong. They are intended, like the great passages of rhetoric, not merely to jet-propel the meaning of the story, but to thrill the audience with a display of virtuosity and, because of that, to be "high-spots," quite apart from their contribution to the plot. In this instance, the single combat is interrupted: *"Certain Volsces come in the aid of Aufidius. Marcius fights till they be driven in breathless."* The interruption serves two purposes: it shows Marcius as a superman, able to cope with a whole group of adversaries, and it plants the eventual assassination at the hands of Aufidius's confederates. This time, Aufidius chides them for their "officious" assistance. (It seems to me a nice point whether or not the actor should be really angry with them or merely accuse them of officiousness for the benefit of bystanders and because their intervention has failed.) Two scenes later, again emphatically placed—a quiet low-keyed scene after a long, rowdy, bustling sequence—Aufidius, in a speech of formidable rhetorical power, voices his passionate hatred of Coriolanus.

Now the play moves on to the political business of creating Coriolanus Consul—business which, though interesting and full of good theatrical effects, does not, as far as I can see, add much to our insight into the principal characters. The rather reasonable objection of the Tribunes to Coriolanus as Consul is his intransigent arrogance, his true-blue, dyed-in-the-wool conservatism. It does not seem to me, any more than it did to the Tribunes, a good idea to appoint a man to high political office just because he is a national hero.

Coriolanus

In the fourteenth scene of the play (Act III, Scene 1) the theme of the Volscian war is briefly interpolated into that of the consular election. The defeated Volscians are said to have rallied and to be ready once more to attack Rome. But the threat of war is not taken seriously. Instead, concentration is centered upon the personal antagonism between Coriolanus and Aufidius. Aufidius's remark is reported to Coriolanus, "That of all things upon the earth he [hates] Your person most; that he would pawn his fortunes To hopeless restitution, so he might Be call'd your vanquisher." And Coriolanus wishes he could "oppose his hatred fully."

The play then returns to the business of consular election. The Tribunes forbid Coriolanus to assume office. He rounds on them furiously, refuses to be pacified by his patrician friends and warns them of the dangers of yielding to democracy. The Tribunes put him under public arrest; a scuffle ensues in which the plebeian party is forced to withdraw, and the situation now holds a serious threat of civil war. In the face of this, Menenius promises the Tribunes that he will bring Coriolanus before the people to apologize.

The action then moves into the home of Coriolanus. It is Volumnia, his mother, who finally prevails on him to meet the people, in a long, interesting, psychological scene, the more notable because it is a quiet interim between preceding and subsequent scenes of noisy, agitated bustle. This section of the play comes to its peak with the banishment of Coriolanus, followed by a brief coda, when he bids farewell to his friends at the gates of Rome. The tone is heavily ironical, and the scene ends on his assurance to the family:

> Bid me farewell, and smile . . .
> While I remain above the ground you shall
> Hear from me still; and never of me aught
> But what is like me formerly.

They hear nothing of him whatever, until he appears before Rome at the head of a Volscian army which threatens to destroy the city and all its people.

The audience, however, now sees Coriolanus, "*in mean apparel, disguised and muffled,*" at Antium, the stronghold of the Volsces, where dwells Aufidius. Now, for the first time in the play (Act IV, Scene 4), Shakespeare makes use of soliloquy—a device which he always uses partly to reveal the real, as opposed to simulated, feelings of a character, and partly for particular emphasis. In this case the soliloquy takes the form of a little meditation, on the part of an otherwise completely unmeditative person, upon the interchangeable nature of love and hate. It is the perfect preparation for what follows—the *scène à faire*, the confrontation of the play's protagonists.

It should be recalled that these two meet three times in the play: their single combat, interrupted by the Volscian supporters of Aufidius, this scene (Scene 5), and the final scene, where, before Coriolanus can defend himself against the furious and jealous accusations of Aufidius, he is butchered by the selfsame Volscian supporters.

The scene which we are now considering cannot be truly regarded as other than a love scene. The soliloquy indicates this: the language and imagery of Aufidius's speech (Act IV, Scene 5, lines 108–141 in the Yale and Oxford Editions) make it unmistakable. Were I to direct the scene, I would suggest that at the end of Coriolanus's speech (line 107) the audience should be unable to tell from the expression of Aufidius what the effect on him of this speech has been. The suspense should be sustained until, after a long pause, he begins to speak very gently and emotionally. Coriolanus should be moved, but not surprised by this gentleness, but not till the end of the phrase, "I'd not believe them more Than thee, all-noble Marcius" (line 112) should his emotion express itself in tears. He should cry like a child—the pent-up tears which he could not shed before the Romans—and be clasped in the arms of Aufidius like a child by his father. The scene explains the otherwise incredible and shocking treachery of Coriolanus. Shakespeare has rejected Plutarch's simpler explanation, that he simply betrayed Rome out of pique, like a spoiled child.

The spoiled child, the dominating widow's only son, is shown; the inadequacy of the wife and the father-substitute are shown; but side by side with these there has been built up the important figure of the hated rival. Rome—an image of mother—has rejected him; and, be it noted, the rejection was precipitated because, against his better judgment, he yielded to his real mother's advice that he should confront the Tribunes and the people. In his mind, she was responsible for, and therefore guilty of, the brutal rejection. The wounded animal, homeless, has to seek shelter somewhere. The hated/loved rival, the Laertes to his Hamlet, the Macduff to his Macbeth, the Creon to his Oedipus, is sought.

I am aware that I have ventured into the domain of psychoanalysis and I do so with humility. But I think it is clear that Shakespeare is again and again concerned to show that people under great stress act in a grossly unconventional, and apparently illogical, manner, and that the explanation of such action is what his tragedies, and to a considerable extent his comedies, are really about. Those of us whose business it is to prepare his plays for the stage are constantly brought face to face with our inadequacy to interpret the most interesting and mysterious aspects of his work. The scholars have signally failed here. They have wrought nobly to untangle knots which an intelligent application to the *text* can solve. Again and again, however, it is apparent that the text alone is only a limited guide. "Over and above," and "between the lines," not in them, lies the real meaning. Moreover, when it comes to the meaning of a scene, character, a crucial moment, the scholars take refuge behind a barricade of textual pedantry; a fusillade is fired of cross-references, suggested commas, interpolated colons and dashes, but no attempt is made to capture the fugitive meaning.

What I am trying to say is that, ill-equipped as I know myself to be, I must try to give the psychological explanation as I see it.

Rome and his mother have jointly cast out Coriolanus. The image of the career-rival now presents itself as a possible father or elder brother, something which has always been missing in his life. Hate turns to love—a surprising transition, to make us accept which is the purpose of the soliloquy. In a relationship somewhere between a son and a lover he throws himself on the mercy of Aufidius.

The attitude of the latter is ambiguous. In this scene, he embraces Coriolanus and shows to him a tenderness which is at least fatherly, or brotherly. Later, he becomes jealous, and finally, violently hostile.

Is his attitude in this love scene sincere?

I think so. As with Coriolanus, his protestations of hatred have been suspect in their violence. It is an ambivalent love-hate. In the tenderness and, let us not forget, the surprise of the moment, he embraces Coriolanus in all sincerity and promotes him to a position and power which he afterward, in cold blood, regrets.

The final scenes of the play are of superb and thrilling mastery, but they present no new twists or surprises of character. It should be noted, however, that the chilling and killing rejection by Coriolanus of Menenius's plea to have mercy on Rome corresponds to the classic pattern of the murder of the father-figure by the protagonist—a pattern which Freud found so significant in the Oedipus legend, and which he claimed is repeated to greater or lesser degree in every human life. Menenius is to Coriolanus what Laius is to Oedipus, Duncan to Macbeth, Caesar to Brutus, or Polonius to Hamlet.

Reprinted with the permission of Macmillan Publishing Company from In Various Directions: A View of the Theatre *by Tyrone Guthrie. Copyright 1955 by Wharton Productions, Ltd., renewed 1983 by Ulster Bank Dublin Trust Company.*

Coriolanus: Wordless Meanings and Meaningless Words

James L. Calderwood

Standing inspection before the plebeians as a candidate for the consulship, Coriolanus asks himself why he is compelled to endure what is to him a degrading experience, and answers,

> Custom calls me to'it.
> What custom wills, in all things should we do't.
> The dust on antique time would lie unswept,
> And mountainous error be too highly heapt
> For truth to o'er-peer. Rather than fool it so,
> Let the high office and the honor go
> To one that would do thus. (II.iii.124–130)[1]

Coriolanus's indictment of "custom" as the means through which society perpetuates error and obscures truth expresses verbally what is visually evident to the audience, for in the present situation "error" is equivalent to the gown of humility which Coriolanus wears over the truth of a proud and unbending spirit. In the world of *Coriolanus* there is no traffic between "custom" and "truth." The sense of community needed for the ritual custom of inspection to be "truth"—for the ritual to stand as a reference point of values shared by both Coriolanus and the plebeians—simply does not exist. The ritual form, which should be a symbol of social order and harmony, has become meaningless because it is invested with false content. And in becoming meaningless in this fashion the ritual ironically becomes a true symbol of the social and political disorder into which Rome has fallen.

It is not only customs or rituals that have become meaningless symbols in Rome; symbols themselves have become meaningless, and, most important, words have become meaningless. As Sigurd Burckhardt has argued,[2] it is the logical corollary of the dissolution of a stable order that language should become flaccid, words semantically irresolute, and truth itself hard to come by. The bond between what is meant and what is understood by words, the common ground between speaker and listener which makes dialogue possible, is the whole social structure from which language issues. If this structure breaks down, as it does in *Coriolanus*, language breaks down with it. In what follows I shall suggest that examining the breakdown of language in *Coriolanus* will provide us with a useful and, hopefully, an illuminating perspective from which to view the play. In particular, we will find in Coriolanus's attempts to defend himself against linguistic chaos a reflection of his more general problem of establishing a sense of personal identity and worth in terms of the concept of honor.

The play opens with the cacophony of the plebeians' speech, all of them speaking at once. We quickly learn that the plebeians have no good words for Coriolanus, that they will not "give him good report" for his actions in the field since he "pays himself with being proud" (I.i.32–34). "In hunger for bread," the plebeians have mutinied in hopes of obtaining a more equitable distribution of grain. But when they encounter Menenius, instead of bread or grain they are given a banquet of words, the Fable of the Belly. "What say you to'it?" Menenius asks complacently, referring to the belly's answer to the complaining members of the body, and Second Citizen replies tersely, "It was an answer"—a string of words in response to another but, so far as the citizen is concerned, devoid of substance and bearing no recognizable relation to the present case. Voicing vituperations as he enters, Coriolanus replies to Second Citizen's sarcastic "We have ever your good word" with "He that will give good words to thee will flatter/Beneath abhorring" (I.i.170–72). There are, it becomes evident, no "good" words available, in the sense of arising from a common ground of values and facts, and hence

Coriolanus: *Wordless Meanings and Meaningless Words*

having a generally acknowledged meaning. To the plebeians "hunger" is a word filled with meaning and force—"They said... That hunger broke stone walls" (209–210)—but to Coriolanus all the plebeians' words of complaint are merely "shreds" of air "vented" through the vulgar mouth (212–213). The rebellion itself, as he and Menenius perceive, is mostly verbal, full of sound and fury but lacking the substance of firm intent and action, "For though abundantly they lack discretion,/ Yet are they passing cowardly" (206–207). And so far as Coriolanus is concerned, the plebeians themselves are like so many unreliable words: "He that trusts to you,/Where he should find you lions, finds you hares;/Where foxes, geese" (174–76). They will not answer to the right names nor mean what they should.

Lacking a common set of values, feelings, allegiances, principles, and knowledge, and hence lacking a viable language, Coriolanus and the plebeians can have no real dialogue. It is not that Shakespeare is making out a case against either of them in the interests of a political philosophy; perhaps too much has been made of that. But he is—while presenting the issue in a spirit of "negative capability," distributing good and ill to both parties without aspiring to the dubious exactitude of right or wrong, true or false—he is, among other things, exploring what happens to language when mere "opinion" encroaches upon authority. At the opening of the play the plebeians have already been given the tribunes, the "tongues o' th' common mouth" (III.i.22). With the addition of a tongue the common mouth acquires a voice; but it is an unreliable voice. William Rosen has argued convincingly that the plebeians are presented in the play as the embodiment of unstable "opinion"[3]—phonic chameleons echoing the words of the tribunes, a "multitudinous tongue" (III.i.156) giving voice now to one thing, now to another. Fickle, vacillating, mutable, constant only in capriciousness, the plebeians exercise a corrosive influence upon language. "With every minute," Coriolanus says to them, "you do change a mind,/And call him noble that was now your hate,/Him vile that was your garland" (I.i.186–88). Used thus language falls apart. The symbol "noble" as applied to a man is emptied of meaning, in the sense of having an identifiable referent, if the same referent is in the next instant symbolized by "hateful." Words lose their substance, drift free of meanings, and become merely noises or breath. Full of sound, the plebeians' words have no stable point of reference, cannot be relied upon at any given moment to mean what they literally say, and hence come dangerously close to signifying nothing.

If the popular language is unacceptable, its words corrupt, its relation to truth shifting and elusive, then one must, or at least Coriolanus must, create a language of his own in which the validity and reliability of words are restored. And in his ruthless devotion to his own conception of truth we may see an attempt on Coriolanus's part to fashion a private language whose words, unlike those of the plebeians, are cemented to their meanings and incapable of distortion. He invests his words with meaning in one sense by being "constant" to his word, to his promise (I.i.242-43). Again, when given the name "Coriolanus" he dedicates himself to keeping the meaning of the word intact and unambiguous, intending, as he tells Cominius "at all times/To undercrest your good addition/To th' fairness of my power" (I.ix.71-73). The name and the thing united inseparably, "Coriolanus" will have one meaning only, at all times and in all situations, and so in his person it does. This singleness and unchangeableness of meaning that he aspires to is suggested again in the same scene. Cominius has had the drums and trumpets sounded in honor of Coriolanus's achievements in battle. Coriolanus responds with adolescent truculence, speaking of the instruments as though of misused words:

> May these instruments, which you profane,
> Never sound more! When drums and trumpets shall
> I' th' field prove flatterers let courts and cities be
> Made all of false-fac'd soothing! (I.ix.41-44)

We shall return to this scene later, but for the moment it is enough to observe that drums and trumpets have for him one use only, the military use that is now being "profaned," just as words have, or should have, he feels, one meaning only. Divorced from its use or meaning, each becomes corrupt, its truth falsified.

Compared with that of the plebeians, Coriolanus's is a stereotyped language—even, in its emphasis upon the exactness

Coriolanus: *Wordless Meanings and Meaningless Words* 81

and reliability of meanings for all occasions, a form of scientific language; and insofar as this can be suggested by the language of poetic drama, his speech reflects such a conception of language. In the first place, Coriolanus is highly distrustful of speech generally, preferring to use, instead of words, the unambiguous expressive power of his sword—"When blows have made me stay, I fled from words" (II.ii.76). Lacking the verbal resources and the confidence in language required for effective argument, he remains taciturn whenever possible, and in the two major scenes where his family appeals to him (III.ii and V.iii) he locks himself in silence, neither acknowledging nor attempting to refute the arguments pressed upon him. Insensitive to the tone or connotative qualities of words, he is, as Menenius says, "ill-school'd/In bolted language; meal and bran together/He throws without distinction" (III.i.321-23). If for him language is not subject to modification by the requirements of different social situations, not flexible enough to respond in tone and style to the demands of decorum—if it is not a social instrument, neither is it an instrument with which to probe and express the workings of the consciousness. Coriolanus has only three, rather abbreviated soliloquies in the play (II.ii.119-31, IV.iv.12-26, V.iii.22-37), and in none of them does he turn the focus of language upon himself. Thus it is characteristic that the most penetrating exploration of what may lie within him must come from the outside, in the speech by Aufidius at the end of Act IV. In line with his general distrust of words, there is very little of the lyric in his speech. His address to Valeria in V.iii, for instance—

> The noble sister of Publicola,
> The moon of Rome, chaste as the icicle
> That's curded by the frost from purest snow
> And hang's on Dian's temple (64-67)

—stands in unexpected contrast with the "meal and bran" of his typical language. He rarely calls upon the full evocative power of language; there is none of the richness and depth of expression in his speech that we take for granted in Hamlet's, and none of the "Othello music." Nor does he engage in wordplay: of all Shakespeare's tragic heroes, he must be the least given to punning. In short, then, he is preoccupied with the meanings of words rather than with words themselves, and though Shakespeare speaks superb poetry through him, Coriolanus is not, as Richard II is usually said to be, a poet himself.

We might even argue that Coriolanus's general imperceptiveness—his rigidity of mind, his lack of self-awareness, his failure to see issues of people in their full reality (his inability, for instance, to view the plebeians in a way that does justice to their mixed character)—owes something to the inflexibility of his language and to his indifference to nuances of meaning governed by tone and style. Devoted to truth, he cannot grasp the full truth about either himself or others because truth, especially in qualitative matters of human values or character, will not yield itself fully to a language oriented to exact but blunt meanings. In his single-minded concern that words mean precisely what they say, for example, he is unable to distinguish between "false-fac'd soothing" and genuine admiration, and hence he misses the truth of Cominius's feelings when he rejects his praise after Corioli: "Too modest are you," Cominius admonishes him, "More cruel to your good report than grateful/ To us that give you truly" (I.ix.53–55). Shakespeare elsewhere pointedly relates Coriolanus's use of language to his cast of mind. In the passage cited earlier, Menenius says that Coriolanus is "ill-school'd/In bolted language; meal and bran together/He throws without distinction" (II.i.321–23). Later, when Coriolanus has led the Volscian army to the gates of Rome and is preparing to burn the city, Cominius reports on the ill success of his attempt to intercede with Coriolanus:

> I offered to awaken his regard
> For's private friends; his answer to me was,
> He could not stay to pick them in a pile
> Of noisome musty chaff. He said 'twas folly,
> For one poor grain or two, to leave unburnt
> And still to nose th' offence. (V.i.23–28)

An insensitivity to distinctions in words, it would seem, reflects, and perhaps helps create, a general insensitivity of feeling and a lack of discrimination in matters of human worth. The man who in some degree brutalizes language may well come to brutalize justice. However, to avoid adopting Coriolanus's own pseudo-precise, black or white view of things, we should observe that his devotion to meaning is a source of strength as well as of weakness in him. It is to his credit, for instance, that he is ultimately unable to divorce language from meaning in the way Volumnia advocates when she asks him

> to speak
> To th' people; not by your own instruction,
> Nor by the matter which your heart prompts you,
> But with such words that are but roted in
> Your tongue, though but bastards and syllables
> Of no allowance to your bosom's truth. (III.ii.52–57)

The Machiavellian technique with words that Volumnia argues for here is no less destructive of the stability of language than the plebeians' verbal capriciousness. When words are "but roted in" in tongue, when they are no longer a reliable bridge between purport and understanding, they become truly "bastards and syllables of no allowance."

II

In an unstable society whose verbal currency is fluctuating back and forth between inflationary and deflationary levels, one can never know at any time what words are worth. Coriolanus's response is to revert to a private verbal standard in which he gives his own value to words and, refusing to accept outside currency, good or bad, "pays himself with being proud" (I.i.33–34). Dismissing the plebeians' words as illegal tender, he will neither take payment from them nor give any to them. "Answer to us," Sicinius says, and Coriolanus replies that "'tis true, I ought so" (III.iii.61–62); but he cannot answer as Volumnia, the patricians, and the plebeians want—can reply only in his own language because his "heart's his mouth" (III.i.257) and "Being once chaf'd . . . he speaks what's in his heart" (III.iii.27–29). But to construct a "private language" is of course a futile venture since language, to be language, must be public. Hence no genuine verbal transactions are possible between him and the plebeians. In accord with Gresham's Law of verbal currency, the plebeians' bad words have driven out of circulation Coriolanus's good words—"good" in terms of his own verbal standard. Unless he can be forced to put his words back into circulation, he must be held a menace to society—and he cannot be so forced:

> Let them pronounce the steep Tarpeian death,
> Vagabond exile, flaying, pent to linger
> But with a grain a day, I would not buy
> Their mercy at the price of one fair word. (III.iii.88-91)

Thus the people banish him, though he defiantly insists upon giving the word his own meaning: "I banish you!" (III.iii.123).

The difficulties Coriolanus encounters with language are closely related to those he encounters in forming a sense of personal identity and worth. As he distrusts words in general and is preoccupied with the private meanings he invests them with, so he distrusts public estimations of himself and is preoccupied with his own inner integrity, his nobility. To be fully authentic, inner worth or nobility needs to be based upon personal convictions firmly held but also identified with something external to self—God, office, cause, social class, political movement, etc. In the Renaissance concept of honor, for instance, authentic honor involved a harmonious merger of self-esteem and public esteem, inner nobility publicly recognized as such. On this view, self-worth does not fully exist until it has achieved a station in the public consciousness as represented by fame, glory, good name, reputation. Thus Volumnia tells Virgilia that when Coriolanus was still a comely and promising youth she, "considering how honour would become such a person, that it [i.e., his noble person] was not better than picture-like to hang by th' wall, if renown made it not stir, was pleas'd to let him seek danger where he was like to find fame" (I.iii.10-14). However, if the social order has become corrupt and there is nothing external to self with which nobility can be identified, then nobility itself becomes susceptible to corruption. It may turn into the blind idealism of Troilus or the misanthropy of Timon, or, in trying to sustain itself in isolation, it may petrify into pride, as it does in Coriolanus. For although Brutus may say that Coriolanus seeks "fame" (I.i.28ff.), Coriolanus himself seems only too aware that fame is meaningless unless it is received from a society worthy of rendering it. The value of the plebeians' "good report" is as dubious as the value of their words in general, for, as he says,

Coriolanus: Wordless Meanings and Meaningless Words 85

"With every minute you do change a mind,/And call him noble that was now your hate,/Him vile that was your garland" (I.i.186–88). If the identity and value of the self are made dependent upon public interpretations, then the whole structure of the self is in danger of collapsing as the social order collapses. Coriolanus's response to this problem is to render himself independent of public judgment by withdrawing into the fortress of his own nobility where he can be himself alone, as within the walls of Corioli "He is himself alone,/To answer all the city" (I.iv.51–52). He will answer the Volscians with his sword, but he refuses to be answerable to the plebeians', and ultimately to Rome's, judgments of him. It is not that he rejects unfavorable views of himself only; he rejects favorable views as well. For to accept praise would be to relinquish his right to total self-definition by acknowledging that his nobility is at least partly dependent upon the interpretations of others, even his mother (I.ix.13–15). Thus his pseudo-modesty is prompted less by self-effacing than by self-aggrandizing motives; it is actually an assertion of the autonomy of self.

Coriolanus's attitudes towards both words and nobility come into dramatic focus in terms of the motif of "name." In I.ix he both receives a name and forgets one. For his accomplishments at Corioli he is honored with the name "Coriolanus." It is a public honor, a symbol of the repute in which he is held, and the value of the name is supplied by the good opinion which prompts its bestowal. However, as we have said, Coriolanus is reluctant to accept others' judgments of him, even when the judgment is favorable. He accepts the name here and says that he will keep it meaningful, that he intends "at all times/To undercrest your good addition/To th' fairness of my power" (I.ix.71–73), which should mean that he will so conduct himself that "Coriolanus" remains publicly accepted as a symbol of nobility. But as his subsequent conduct reveals, he has not accepted an obligation to the public so much as an obligation to self. He invests the name with his own private meaning and remains true to that, to his own conception of nobility, despite the fact that as he does so "Coriolanus" becomes increasingly a public symbol of pride instead of nobility. The name as public symbol, as a negotiable word, is of less importance to him than the meaning which he himself injects into it. This leads to difficulties, of course, and in the same scene (I.ix) Shakespeare forecasts these difficulties when he has Coriolanus forget the name of the poor man of Corioli who had treated him hospitably.

In this minor incident with the man from Corioli, what Shakespeare is doing, it seems evident, is illustrating the futility of private meanings that cannot be translated into a public language. To Cominius and the others, the man from Corioli is meaningless, an anonymous Volscian prisoner; but to Coriolanus the man has a private significance that distinguishes him from all the other Volscian prisoners and makes him worthy of release. However, the private meaning of the man cannot be expressed by a publicly recognized symbol, the name Coriolanus has forgotten, and hence the kindness Coriolanus would do him cannot be effected. Unless meanings find their way into the public language and become subjects of general agreement, they are as doomed to anonymity as the Volscian prisoner.[4] Coriolanus could be well instructed by the plight of the man from Corioli, since he refuses to allow his private identity, his "meaning," to enter and conform to, or in any way to be affected by, the mainstream of public opinion. Typically, however, he learns nothing from the incident, and hence, he, like the Volscian, is finally banished into obscurity—"I' th' people's name" (III.iii.104)—losing his "good name" publicly though for him it remains privately and unalterably "good."

Thus we may see in the conflict between Coriolanus and the plebeians a conflict between a stationary meaning and drifting words, between private meanings incapable of fitting into a public language and a public language that has become meaningless, or, as we have said in our title, between wordless meanings and meaningless words. Isolated from one another in this fashion, both meanings and words become self-destructive as well as destructive of language generally. It is one of the major ironies of the play that Coriolanus, resolute, unyielding, shackled to his own verbal and moral integrity, becomes by virtue of these qualities every bit as manipulable by the tribunes as are the plebeians by virtue of their fickle irresolution (see, e.g., II.i.269-75, II.iii.266-68). Until the stable meaning can be linked reliably to the right word, language in Rome remains as chaotic as Rome's social and political order.

After his banishment from Rome Coriolanus appears without warning in Antium, where he seeks Aufidius. His situation when he faces Aufidius in IV.v is analogous to that of the man of Corioli earlier. "Whence com'st thou?" Aufidius asks him, "What wouldst thou? Thy name? Why speak'st not? Speak, man: what's thy name?" (58–59). Coriolanus's reluctance to give his name can hardly be attributed to fear of consequences; fear, and most of all fear of physical punishment, is simply alien to him. Rather it would seem that he is attempting to impose his private identity upon Aufidius, his own individual "meaning" apart from his public name, as though despite the "mean apparel" he wears and the fact that his face is muffled the force of his unique nature could make him recognizable. Hence he then unmuffles himself, saying, "If Tullus, not yet thou know'st me, and, seeing me, dost not think me the man I am, necessity commands me name myself." That Aufidius must ask for the name five times is a measure of Coriolanus's commitment to his private identity, to "the man I am" as distinct from the man he is publicly regarded as being. But at the same time, Aufidius's inability to identify him without the name reveals the futility of so exclusive a commitment to private meaning. For without name, honor, a public identity, Coriolanus becomes, not the autonomous individual he has striven to be, but a blank. Unable to acquire recognition on his own terms—"Know'st thou me yet?" he asks, and Aufidius replies "I know thee not. Thy name?" (69–70)—he is commanded by necessity to name himself:

> My name is Caius Marcius, who hath done
> To thee particularly and to all the Volsces
> Great hurt and mischief; thereto witness may
> My surname, Coriolanus. The painful service,
> The extreme dangers, and the drops of blood
> Shed for my thankless country are requited
> But with that surname; a good memory
> And witness of the malice and displeasure
> Which thou shouldst bear me. Only that name remains.
> (IV.v.71–79)

His private identity unrecognizable without the name, Coriolanus seems here for the first time to realize that his public identity is gone too, and that it matters. "Only that name remains": but the honorable surname has become merely breath, a word from which Rome has siphoned all meaning. Deprived of private and public meaning, and with little else to lose, Coriolanus can thus offer himself to Aufidius: "then, in a word, I also am/Longer to live most weary, and present/My throat to thee and to thy ancient malice" (100–102). It is not too farfetched to suggest that the phrase "in a word" here should be read literally. To live only "in a word," a sound void of significance, which is what "Coriolanus" has become, is worse than death.

By shifting his allegiance to the Volscians, Coriolanus trades in his identity as "Coriolanus." "Coriolanus" is no symbol of honor in Corioli—Aufidius accepts him, not as "Coriolanus," but as "Marcius" (IV.v.107, 112, 132, 153); nor is it any longer a symbol of honor in Rome, where "Coriolanus" has reverted to "Marcius" (IV.vi.29, 43, 65, 70, 75). Its reserves of good opinion depleted, the name has become mere breath, an inadmissible sound; and Coriolanus has become "a kind of nothing" operating only on the borrowed capital of hatred. Reporting upon his attempt to intercede with Coriolanus, Cominius says:

> Yet one time he did call me by my name,
> I urg'd our old acquaintance, and the drops
> That we have bled together. Coriolanus
> He would not answer to; forbade all names;
> He was a kind of nothing, titleless
> Till he had forg'd himself a name o' th' fire
> Of burning Rome. (V.i.9–15)

If Coriolanus has himself become nothing, he now has the power to reduce Rome to nothing also, and in the process to forge for himself a new identity. When he was in Rome, the name of the people was dominant, and his own private meaning could find no adequate expression in their "voices" or language. Now he is the controller of language, and Rome must come to him to discover its own identity and meaning, whether it will remain "Rome" or be reduced to rubble. Roman words no longer have any power of definition. Thus when Menenius makes his bid for Coriolanus's mercy, he is told by the watchman, "The virtue of your name/Is not here passable" (V.ii.12–13); is silenced by Coriolanus, "Another word, Menenius,/I will not hear thee speak" (V.ii.97–98); and is mocked by the watchman again as he leaves: "Now, sir, is your name Menenius?"—"'Tis a spell, you see, of much power" (V.ii.101–103).

However, if Coriolanus has cashed in his identity as "Coriolanus" by becoming the Volscians' general, he seems at some level of awareness to realize that a new identity forged in the fires of burning Rome is no more admissible than "Coriolanus" in Corioli. Though his conduct as Volscian general looks good on the surface, Aufidius observes, "yet he hath left undone/That which shall break his neck or hazard mine/ Whene'er we come to our account" (IV.vii.24–26). He has given his "word" to the Volscians that he will serve their cause, but this verbal commitment is not backed by a full psychic commitment, as Aufidius perceives. Thus his nascent identity as Volscian general collapses when in V.iii his family bring their combined verbal and emotional pressures to bear upon him. The name that he would forge in the fires of burning Rome is revealed in its true nature for him by Volumnia:

> . . . if thou conquer Rome, the benefit
> Which thou shalt thereby reap is such a name
> Whose repetition will be dogg'd with curses,
> Whose chronicle thus writ: "The man was noble,
> But with his last attempt he wip'd it out,
> Destroy'd his country, and his name remains
> To th' ensuing age abhorr'd." (V.iii.142–48)

That name and the meaning that goes with it he rejects. As a result, "Coriolanus" becomes again a symbol of honor in Rome, and Coriolanus himself regains in the consciousness of the Romans his former identity: "Unshout the noise that banish'd Marcius!" one of the senators cries as Volumnia and the others make their triumphant entrance to Rome, "Repeal him with the welcome of his mother" (V.v.4–5).

Coriolanus, however, returns, not to Rome, but to Corioli, knowing perfectly well what the cost of his betrayal will be: "Most dangerously you have with [your son] prevail'd," he tells Volumnia, "If not most mortal to him," adding, however, "But let it come" (V.iii.188–89). In a speech hopelessly out of character with his former self (V.v.71–84), he attempts to reinstate himself with the Volscians, defending himself in his public role as Volscian general. But Aufidius, in attacking him as Volscian general, also attacks him personally as "Marcius" and "boy." "'Marcius!'" Coriolanus repeats angrily. "Ay, Marcius, Caius Marcius! Dost thou think/I'll grace thee with that robbery, thy stol'n name,/Coriolanus, in Corioli?" (88–90). Coriolanus's violent repetition, "'Marcius!'" indicates that he is now identifying himself with "Coriolanus." But what does "Coriolanus" mean to him now? Does he realize that by saving Rome he has earned the right to "Coriolanus" again, that the word has again become a symbol of honor in Rome, and that in accepting the name for himself he is asserting not merely an individual identity but also his public identity as a Roman? If so, then it would seem that the wordless meaning and the meaningless word have finally achieved the synthesis required for language to be viable. However, if such a synthesis is suggested, it is so only briefly, as though Shakespeare momentarily flashed into view an ideal possibility which must remain dramatically unrealized. For in his last assertion of identity it is not an image of himself as Rome's soldier that Coriolanus capitalizes upon:

> Cut me to pieces, Volsces; men and lads,
> Stain all your edges on me. "Boy!" False hound!
> If you have writ your annals true, 'tis there
> That, like and eagle in a dove-cote, I
> Flutter'd your Volscians in Corioli;
> Alone I did it. "Boy!"

He is attempting of course to create an image of self superior to the occasion, invoking death not for the man who saved Rome and betrayed the Volscians, but for the man who stormed Corioli single-handed. There is a certain limited grandeur in his assertion of a self transcendently isolated and autonomous, answerable to nothing but its own conception of nobility; it has a meaning and force, but it is still the old meaning, unmodified by experience, untouched by understanding. Coriolanus never learns what Aufidius knows, that "our virtues/Lie in th' interpretation of the time" (IV.vii.49–50), that the private meaning becomes fully meaningful only when it submits to the discipline of language. Yet he does impose his meaning upon language, or, perhaps more accurately, language and the "interpretation of the time" are sufficiently flexible at the end to accept the Coriolanus meaning under the head of "noble"—"Yet he shall have a noble memory" (155)—although the last word of the play, "Assist," suggests a relation between meanings and words, and between individuals and societies, that he could never grasp.

NOTES

1. All references are to the text in *The Complete Plays and Poems of William Shakespeare*, ed. William A. Neilson and Charles J. Hill (Cambridge, Mass.: Harvard University Press, 1942).

2. Sigurd Burckhardt, "The King's Language: Shakespeare's Drama as Social Discovery," *Antioch Review*, 21 (1961), 369–87.

3. William Rosen, *Shakespeare's Craft of Tragedy* (Cambridge, Mass.: Harvard Univ. Press, 1960), pp. 167–71.

4. Coriolanus's inability to give a name to the "meaning" of the man from Corioli here parallels Bottom's difficulties in *AMND* when he awakens in Act IV, Scene i. The fairy reality experienced by fools like Bottom evaporates into "airy nothing," becoming a wordless "dream past the wit of man to say what dream it was," because Bottom lacks not only the wit but also the power over language to "say what dream it was." See "A Midsummer Night's Dream: The Illusion of Drama," *MLQ*, 26 (1965), 506–22.

Reprinted by permission from James L. Calderwood, "Coriolanus: Wordless Meanings and Meaningless Words," Studies in English Literature 6 (1966), 211–24. Copyright 1966 by Studies in English Literature.

Coriolanus: The Anxious Bridegroom

Emmett Wilson, Jr.

In *Coriolanus*, Shakespeare adapted a plot from North's translation of *Plutarch's Lives* into an intensive exploration of a pathological mother-son relationship. It is the story of a son who attempts to rebel against his mother, to whom he has been inordinately attached. The son is ultimately destroyed when he renounces his rebellion and submits to his mother. In this paper, I wish to examine certain aspects of the play for the unconscious fantasies which may have determined the handling of the narrative material from which Shakespeare worked. In particular, I suggest that an examination of the wedding night references in the play is essential for an understanding of the work on a psychoanalytical level.

The play has sometimes been cited as peculiar among Shakespeare's works. Critics discern a "slackness" in Shakespeare's dramatic power (2,3,8). This slackness is supposed to be reflected in the way in which Shakespeare handled his source material. If we compare Shakespeare's adaptation with the original in North's translation, we find at several points an almost slavish closeness to the source. This dependence on North is so extensive that at first reading, the play seems little more than a simple dramatization of the plot from North (4,11,13,14). Editors have been able to make emendations and fill textual lacunae in the play by referring to North, so faithfully has Shakespeare followed his source. The later acts of the play, especially, show a marked increase in borrowing, and tend to rely almost exclusively on North. Shakespeare might, of course, have been under some merely temporal pressure to complete the play, but this marked change in the processing of the material could also have been due to the conflictual nature of the subject matter. At any rate, Shakespeare seems to have adhered doggedly to his source in order to finish his task.

Yet, the earlier acts and the characters introduced there involve a good deal of revision and reworking of the material. Shakespeare has developed certain characters and added others, and has elaborated on the relationship of Coriolanus to the various individuals who are significant to him. Further, Shakespeare's particular choices of expression in the play are striking. The language has been called harsh (4). The poetry seems at times to disguise only slightly some rather grotesque ideas. As an example of the grossness of thought, consider Coriolanus' rebuke to the tribunes for their failure to control the mob: "You being their mouths, why rule you not their teeth?" (3.1.36).* These additions by Shakespeare to his source material are important for a psychological understanding of the play.

Imagery

The peculiar imagery Shakespeare has chosen tends to support the view that the theme of the play was one to which the playwright was psychologically sensitive. The images tend to fall within a narrow range. Caroline Spurgeon found these to be concerned largely with bodily functions, sickness, and loss of diseased bodily parts (17, pp. 347–49). Blood, and things made bloody, are constantly mentioned. Stoller (18) calls attention to the numerous staves, pikes, rakes, swords, and other phallic equivalents. There are many references to wounds and to parts of the body, or simply to parts. Coriolanus shouts angrily to the mob, "Go get you home, you fragments!" (1.1.211).

    Combat and sexuality are often linked. Battles are described in sexual images, or talk of battle provides the opportunity for a reference to sexual activity. Cominius, the Roman commander-in-chief, proudly describes some teenage battle exploit of Coriolanus as occurring at an age when he might

Coriolanus: The Anxious Bridegroom

have acted "the woman in the scene" (2.2.92). Peace is a "great maker of cuckolds" (4.5.225). Coriolanus threatens to beat the Volscians "to their wives" (1.4.41). Volumnia, his mother, says of Coriolanus' impetuous attitude toward the mob,

> ... I know thou hadst rather
> Follow thine enemy in a fiery gulf
> Than flatter him in a bower. (3.2.90–92)

Curiously, while Coriolanus is in battle in Act I, Volumnia and her friend go to visit a lady lying in (1.3.72).

Another significant group of images is oral. In this play of a mother-child relationship, there are frequent allusions to food, nourishment, ingestion, hunger, biting, or devouring. To note one important instance: Some servingmen are speaking of the personal rivalry between Coriolanus and his Volscian opponent, Aufidius. They recall the battle of Corioli:

> *First Serv.* Before Corioli he [Coriolanus] scotched him and notched him like a carbonado [meat cut up for cooking].
> *Second Serv.* And he had been cannibally given, he might have boiled and eaten him too. (4.5.186–89)

In some images, aggressive impulses are characteristically directed towards the interior of the body. Coriolanus' attacks on Rome are said to be "pouring war/Into the bowels of ungrateful Rome" (4.5.129). When Volumnia entreats Coriolanus to cease warring on Rome, he is said to want to tread upon his mother's womb (5.3.124). He is charged with

> Making the mother, wife and child, to see
> The son, the husband and the father, tearing
> His country's bowels out. (5.3.101–03)

This juxtaposition of aggression with the family relationships is striking, and provides unambiguous evidence of the symbolic character of the attack on Rome as an attack on those objects whom previously Coriolanus had loved. The repetition of this sort of imagery is impressive, and indicates the extent and strength of certain unconscious fantasies: the fear of being eaten, and the rage against the mother's engulfing body.

The Wedding Night

In the midst of these grotesque images of blood, aggression, and bodily destruction, there is a scene in which Coriolanus rises to intense lyric expression. In the battle at Corioli, he expresses the joy of victory, and greets his general, Cominius with

> O, let me clip ye
> In arms as sound as when I wooed; in heart
> As merry as when our nuptial day was done,
> And tapers burned to bedward! (1.6.29–32)

Here, we find an obvious reference to a specific sexual event, and an unconscious reference in the phallic burning tapers. The significance of the image is further heightened by one other reference to a wedding night. When Coriolanus joins Aufidius as an ally against Rome, Aufidius expresses *his* joy by referring to his bride on her first crossing the threshold, and he declares that he is even more rapt by Coriolanus than he was by his bride:

> Know thou first,
> I loved the maid I married: never man
> Sighed truer breath; but that I see thee here,
> Thou noble thing, more dances my rapt heart
> Than when I first my wedded mistress saw
> Bestride my threshold. (4.5.112–17)

Commentators have noted these two references to the wedding night (1,9,11). Perhaps the most insightful is Rank's brief discussion (15, p. 215f.). However, the meaning of these two passages in *Coriolanus* has not been sufficiently explored. Further examination of these passages is important, for the wedding night images condense several major themes of the play.

To understand Coriolanus' reference to his wedding night, we need to examine the scene in which the reference occurs. Preceding Coriolanus' lyric recall of this event, there is a series of scenes of the battle before Corioli, in which Coriolanus is especially in danger of being deserted by his men and closed up within the gates of the enemy town. Coriolanus exhorts his soldiers to charge the Volscians when the battle first begins at the gates of Corioli. In particular, he threatens any stragglers with

Coriolanus: The Anxious Bridegroom

his "edge" (1.4.29). This threat proves insufficient. As Coriolanus follows the Volscians to the gates of their city, he still needs to urge the Roman soldiers to enter the gates with him:

> So, now the gates are ope. Now prove good seconds.
> 'Tis for the followers fortune widens them,
> Not for the fliers. Mark me, and do the like. (1.4.43–45)

Yet precisely before the open gates, he is deserted. The Roman response to his exhortation is:

> *First Sol.:* Foolhardiness. Not I.
> *Second Sol.:* Nor I.
> *First Sol.:* See, they have shut him in. (1.4.46–47)

In Plutarch, when Coriolanus stormed the gates, others were with him (16, p. 308). The complete abandonment is stressed by the soldiers: "He is himself alone,/To answer all the city" (1.4.52–53). They immediately suppose that he is dead, that he is gone "to th' pot" (1.4.48). In view of the recurrent theme of being eaten, it is very likely that those commentators are correct who suppose that the pot here is a cooking pot, and that the line means that Coriolanus has been cut to pieces (8, pp. 110–11).

The battle is carried by the Romans as their commander, Cominius, arrives. Coriolanus reappears, covered with blood. He sees Cominius and asks, "Come I too late?" Cominius replies, "Ay, if you come not in the blood of others,/But mantled in your own" (1.6.27–29). Coriolanus responds to the question whether he is wounded by saying that his arms are as sound as before he married, and then refers to his wedding night in an effusion of joy and enthusiasm. Curiously, Coriolanus does not give a direct answer to Cominius' question until he boasts later to Aufidius: "'Tis not my blood/Wherein thou seest me masked" (1.8.9–10).

In these scenes at Corioli, we have a battle in which the important elements are the opening and penetration of the enemy's defenses with the resulting danger of destruction to the attacker. Following the battle, there is a specific reference to the first sexual union between Coriolanus and his bride. As if to underscore the allusion to defloration, Cominius immediately after the wedding night memory, addresses Coriolanus as "Flower of warriors" (1.6.32). There is, I suggest, a symbolic parallel between the battle at Corioli and unconscious fantasies concerning the experience of the wedding night. The battle is, as it were, a symbolic re-enactment of the anxiety provoking sexual event, defloration. The battle scene at Corioli expresses the unconscious equation of coitus with a violent, damaging assault, an equation which we noted earlier in the imagery of the play. Castration anxieties aroused by coitus are heightened by the actual accompaniment of the sexual act by bleeding and a change in the female's bodily status (6,19). In the unconscious, defloration is equated with the castration of the sexual partner, and there is an associated dread of a mutilating retaliation. The feared punishment, castration, is symbolized in the battle by the danger of becoming entrapped within the gates, to be cut up and devoured. In the memory of defloration which follows the battle scenes, Coriolanus may well be attempting to deal with his terrifying discovery that he had created a sexual difference in his bride, by making her into a woman, i.e., a person who had been deprived of the phallus. Ultimately, the punishment that is dreaded for this act is a revenge by his mother on her son for having entertained these notions of assault against her body and, of course, on a deeper level, the woman who is castrated in the sexual act would be the phallic mother, Volumnia (19).

If I am correct in this analysis of the battle at Corioli, then the award of the name, "Coriolanus," for exploits in that battle may also be of psychological importance. For this, however, we must turn to a passage in North which has not been transferred to the play, but which may very well have influenced Shakespeare in his conception of the battle scenes. In the play, the hero receives his *agnomen*, "Coriolanus," as an honorary "trophy" for the events of the battle. The unconscious meaning of such a trophy is familiar to us as signifying the castration of the enemy and the sadistic wish to rob him of his penis (5). But from North's translation of Plutarch's *Life of Coriolanus*, we learn that the name could also have been given to signify, and to compensate for, an injury which the bearer of the name had received. In North, a lengthy discussion occurs on the Roman habit of according such names. In this passage North states:

> Sometimes also [the Romans] give surnames derived of some mark of misfortune of the body. As Sylla, to say, "crooked-nose"; Niger, "black"; Rufus, "red"; Caecus,

"blind"; Claudus, "lame." They did wisely in this thing to accustom men to think that neither the loss of sight nor other such misfortunes as may chance to men are any shame or disgrace unto them; but the manner was to answer boldly to such names, as if they were called by their proper names (16, p. 314).

In view of this comment from North on the secondary meaning of an *agnomen* as commemorative of mutilation, there is a significant parallel to be noted between the attempt to master the psychological sequellae of mutilation by the award of a compensatory *agnomen*, and the use Shakespeare makes of the scene before Corioli as a repetition in symbolic form of an experience involving an intense fear of bodily mutilation in retaliation for forbidden sexual wishes. The same psychological mechanism would seem to be operative in the *agnomen* and in the repetition of the traumatic scene—the attempt to master a traumatic event by some compensatory maneuver after the fact. Coriolanus was wounded at Corioli, and when he stands for the consulship, Coriolanus must display the scars from the battle at Corioli, scars which mark him as having distinguished himself in the service of Rome just as much as his *agnomen* and other honors do. When Coriolanus rejects the subservient position which he had maintained to Volumnia in the first half of the play, he vehemently rejects his *agnomen* at the same time, and wants to forge another in the "fire of burning Rome" (5.1.14). There are thus some indications of a reversal of the significance of the name received at Corioli to represent Coriolanus' continued subservience to Volumnia, and his acquiescence in the role that she demanded of him.

The wound motif continues and further develops the fantasy which appears in the battle scenes at Corioli. The question of these wounds comes to dominate the scenes subsequent to the battle, and provides us with important information on the relationship between Coriolanus and his mother. The phallic castrating mother rejoices in his wounds for the purpose of going before the people: "O, he is wounded: I thank the gods for't" (2.1.107) because "there will be large cicatrices to show the people when he shall stand for his place" (2.1.132). It was a traditional requirement that all aspirants to the consulship stand before the populace and display battle wounds. Coriolanus, however, finds this custom ignominious and objectionable. The mob has from the first been presented as a cannibalistic threat to Coriolanus (1.1), and it has been suggested that the mob stands for the aggressive and dangerous aspects of the mother (1). Coriolanus' reluctance to display his wounds to the mob is Shakespeare's modification of his source, for in Plutarch the problem does not arise at all. Moreover, standing for the consulship is Volumnia's idea, and Coriolanus can be prevailed upon to go to the people with his wounds only at his mother's insistent cajoling and threats. Volumnia's wish to see her son as a consul, and her role in forcing him to submit to the people, give evidence of the way in which Shakespeare has adapted the plot to strengthen the dominating influence which Volumnia has over her son. Just as she had rejoiced in his wounds, the mob is to see in these same wounds evidence that Coriolanus loves and will faithfully serve Rome. Volumnia thus forces Coriolanus into a position of pleasing and placating the aggressive aspects of herself which the mob symbolizes. Coriolanus can flatter the mob only if he shows his wounds, i.e., if he shows those symbols of castration which were needed to continue in his mother's favor. The sexual nature of the display of his body to the populace is suggested when Volumnia says that it is to "flatter [his enemy] in a bower" (3.2.92). Menenius excuses Coriolanus' insolence by "He loves your people,/But tie him not to be their bedfellow" (2.2.60–61). But it is clear that this is a sexual submission, not a conquest. At the moment of capitulation to Volumnia's urgings, Coriolanus launches a torrent of petulant language showing that his position is not only ignominious but also a threat to his masculinity. To submit will make his voice "Small as an eunuch . . ." (3.2.114). Finally he begins to speak as a little boy:

> Mother, I am going to the market place:
> Chide me no more . . . Look, I am going. (3.2.131–2, 134)

Rebellion against the Phallic Mother

I have so far explored *Coriolanus* in those sections which express the fantasies associated with the active phase of the Oedipus complex and the expected castration by the phallic mother for entertaining aggressive impulses toward her. I now turn to the episodes in which Coriolanus rebels against the phallic mother and seeks an alternative expression of his oedipal striving. Coriolanus abandons Rome and his mother, and turns traitor to the Romans, joining with their traditional enemies, the Volscians.

Rebellion is introduced in the opening scene, in which the Roman mob is about to turn against established authority. The mob is quieted, by means of a tale of another rebellion, that of the body's members against the belly (1.1). This theme of betrayal is sustained throughout the play. In certain passages, a sexual betrayal is clearly suggested. In the scene immediately preceding Coriolanus' suit to join Aufidius and betray the Romans, a Roman traitor and a Volscian spy meet to exchange information and the following comment is made:

> I have heard it said the fittest time to corrupt a
> man's wife is when she's fallen out with her husband
> (4.3.26–28)

These frequent allusions to treachery and betrayal provide a background for the behavior of Coriolanus, who is at first falsely, and later with some justification, labelled a traitor. It is the false charge of treason that provokes Coriolanus and provides him with the excuse to become a traitor in fact by leading an attack on Rome at the head of the Volscian forces. When Coriolanus capitulates to his mother's entreaties in Act V and leaves off his attack on Rome, he is in the awkward position of betraying the Volscian cause which he had joined. Aufidius can justifiably charge him with treason and demand his death.

There are, in addition, some clear indications of Coriolanus' extreme ambivalence toward his libidinal objects. This ambivalence is expressed in a total repudiation and withdrawal when negative feelings have been aroused. In changing allegiance from Rome to the Volscians, Coriolanus plots the total destruction of Rome. When Coriolanus left Rome in Act IV, he was still friendly with his party in Rome, and was ready to acknowledge and express his affection for his mother and his family. In Act V, he rejects all overtures from these friends. In Plutarch, Coriolanus is milder and shrewder. He spares the goods and estates of the nobles in his war on Rome, thereby spreading party dissension in Rome. Revenge on Rome in the form of a humiliating surrender would have been satisfactory for Plutarch's Coriolanus. In Shakespeare, nothing short of the destruction and burning of Rome itself will do. Coriolanus rejects Menenius, his mother Volumnia, and his wife. At the moment that Volumnia's embassy arrives at the Volscian camp, Coriolanus resolves to "stand/As if a man were author of himself/And knew no other kin" (5.3.35–37). He had made the same resolve to Menenius earlier: "Wife, mother, child, I know not. My affairs/Are servanted to others" (5.2.75–76). This insistence on a complete rejection is characteristic of Shakespeare's Coriolanus, who seems unable to tolerate any ambiguity in situations which involve his emotional commitment.

In addition, Coriolanus views any struggle for power with extreme anxiety. He resents the newly established office of tribune. Where, in North's version, Coriolanus' objection is restrained, in Shakespeare, Coriolanus objects to the Tribuneship because

> It makes the consuls base! and my soul aches
> To know, when two authorities are up,
> Neither supreme, how soon confusion
> May enter 'twixt the gap of both and take
> The one by th'other. (3.1.108–12)

It is reasonable to suppose that the prototypes in the unconscious of these two warring authorities are to be found in the original family situation, with parental roles presumably confused and conflicting, providing the opportunity to exploit and intensify the difficulties between the parents, and to play one off against the other.

In his soliloquy just before he goes over to the Volscians as an enemy of Rome, Coriolanus also expresses the theme of ambivalence and his concern with the struggle for supremacy:

> O world, thy slippery turns! Friends now fast sworn,
> Whose double bosoms seems to wear one heart,
> Whose hours, whose bed, whose meal and exercise
> Are still together, who twin, as 'twere, in love
> Unseparable, shall within this hour,
> On a dissension of a doit, break out
> To bitterest enmity. So, fellest foes,
> Whose passions and whose plots have broke their sleep
> To take the one the other, by some chance,
> Some trick not worth an egg, shall grow dear friends
> And interjoin their issues. So with me:
> My birthplace hate I, and my love's upon
> This enemy town. (4.4.12-24)

Here, Coriolanus anticipates the intensely homoerotic relationship into which he is about to move, when Aufidius will want to "twine" his arms around him (4.5.105). Yet he also anticipates the outcome of the trust he is about to place in Aufidius, for a moment after this extended comment on the transiency of human relationships, we see Coriolanus embraced as a bosom friend, and welcomed with greater joy than the welcome accorded a new bride, by the man who will shortly bring about his death.

Quest for a Surrogate Father

I will now examine the aspects of the play which indicate Coriolanus' attempt to institute a satisfactory expression of the passive phase of the Oedipus complex, in which he aspires to be loved by a powerful father, displacing his mother as his father's primary object.

Coriolanus' biological father remains vague in both North and Shakespeare. Yet two figures in the play serve as psychological representatives of a father to Coriolanus. One of these is the old family friend, Menenius. The other is Aufidius, who becomes an idealized father after the rejection of Volumnia.

Menenius is an apt psychological symbol for the weak and conquered father appropriate to Coriolanus' wishes in the active phase of the Oedipus complex in which Volumnia is in the ascendancy as Coriolanus' object. Shakespeare developed the charming and complex character of Menenius almost independently of North, who gives only a few hints concerning a gentle old man who was loved by the people, and was a good choice to carry the Senate's message to a rebellious populace. But Menenius remains a weak person, especially in comparison with the stalwart Volumnia. He fawns over a letter which Coriolanus had written him, in a fashion virtually indistinguishable from the responses of the women who have also received letters (2.1). Perhaps the most masterly touch in the contrast of Volumnia and Menenius is in their parting exchange after Coriolanus has been accompanied to the gates of Rome as he goes into exile. Menenius' response to this day of emotional trials is to note that he is hungry and to arrange for dinner. Not so for Volumnia:

> Men: You'll sup with me?
> Vol: Anger's my meat: I sup upon myself
> And so shall starve with feeding. (4.2.49–51)

Many passages explicitly refer to Menenius as Coriolanus' father. In his embassy to save Rome, Menenius declares confidently to a guard who is preventing him from seeing Coriolanus, "You shall perceive that a Jack guardant cannot office me from my son Coriolanus" (5.2.59). It is also apparent that the relationship is erotically tinged. Menenius in his frustration shouts at the guard, "I tell thee, fellow,/Thy general is my lover" (5.2.13–14), and Coriolanus, after sending the disappointed old man away, says: "This man, Aufidius,/Was my beloved in Rome" (5.2.85–86). It would seem that Menenius adulated Coriolanus too much to be an ideal substitute for the missing father. Menenius boasts, for example, "I have been/The book of his good acts" (5.2.13–14). Also, Menenius often acts as Volumnia's agent, i.e., as a person who can appeal to Coriolanus and affect his behavior only through Coriolanus' respect and awe for his mother. As Coriolanus' anger against the mob is beginning to get out of control, Menenius attempts to restrain Coriolanus with: "Is this the promise that you made to your mother?" (3.3.87).

In opposition to the quasi-familial situation of the earlier scenes of the play in which a strong mother dominates both Coriolanus and his weak, defeated, and castrated father, there is

Coriolanus: The Anxious Bridegroom

later the alternative oedipal solution in which Coriolanus repudiates his mother, and all her symbolic representatives, to seek out the strong, masculine father. The awesome figure of Aufidius, a marked contrast to Menenius, provides the second father symbol in the play.

The turn to Aufidius involves an intense and passive homoerotic relationship, for which we have been prepared. Even while Coriolanus and Aufidius are still enemies, Aufidius was admired. Coriolanus tells us in Act I:

> I sin in envying his nobility;
> And were I anything but what I am,
> I would wish me only he. (1.1.219–221)

Passive homosexual yearnings which Coriolanus had felt for a strong father now find expression in the renunciation of Volumnia in favor of a loving relationship with the virile Aufidius. The second allusion to a wedding night occurs in Act IV, when Aufidius welcomes Coriolanus as an ally. This time, however, it is Aufidius who thinks of his wedding night. Coriolanus is clearly supplanting Aufidius' previous erotic attachment to a woman. This new and strong father is eager to accept Coriolanus, and he looks on Coriolanus as on a bride crossing the threshold, even preferring his present happiness with Coriolanus to his wedding night.

The sexual character of this turning from Volumnia to Aufidius is also shown in the banter with the servingmen in this scene:

> Serv: How, Sir! Do you meddle with my master?
> Cor: Ay, 'tis an honester service than to meddle with
> thy mistress. (4.5.45–46)

A servingman later says that Aufidius now loves Coriolanus as a woman: "Our general himself makes a mistress of him..." (4.5.194).

Earlier, Coriolanus was able to express his memory of defloration anxieties as he embraced Cominius, that is, when he is protected in a homoerotic embrace he can recall the threatening heterosexual experience. Another such embrace occurs between Aufidius and Coriolanus. In both scenes containing the wedding night allusions, the same word is used for this embrace, *viz.*, "clip." Coriolanus had turned to Cominius with the words: "O, let me clip ye/In arms as sound as when I wooed . . ." (1.6.29–30). In his welcome to Coriolanus, Aufidius uses this word also:

> Auf: Here I clip
> The anvil of my sword, and do contest
> As hotly and as nobly with thy love
> As ever in ambitious strength I did
> Contend against thy valor. Know thou first,
> I loved the maid I married. . . .
> (4.5.108–113)

In Elizabethan English, "clip" would have meant both "to embrace" and "to cut off." In this repeated word, we thus have an unconscious continuation of the theme of castration which links the two wedding night allusions.

The embrace with Aufidius involves, on the unconscious level, the necessity for undergoing castration as a precondition of the father's love. To gain the love of Aufidius, Coriolanus must reject his city, his family, his mother, he must hate his birthplace, and turn his love onto the man who had previously been his rival. It is precisely the question of what further price must be paid to be loved by Aufidius that leads to difficulties in the new role as Aufidius' minion. Earlier, we saw that Coriolanus had feared castration as a retaliation for what he had wished to do to his mother. Now he expects that he must give up his masculinity in order to be loved by the strong and virile father.

Coriolanus attempts to meet this condition, on a symbolic level. In his soliloquy he had anticipated an eventual rivalry and falling out with Aufidius (4.4.12). Passages in the play indicate Coriolanus' self-destructive tendencies which will cause his own downfall. The tribunes had recognized this self-destructive trait and used it to their advantage. Brutus hoped to make Coriolanus angry because

> then he speaks
> What's in his heart; and that is there which looks
> With us to break his neck. (3.3.28–30)

Aufidius' jealousy is aroused when Coriolanus becomes haughty by the honors bestowed on him by the Volscians. When

Coriolanus: The Anxious Bridegroom

Volumnia's pleas prevail and the attack against Rome is called off, Coriolanus has in effect given Aufidius sufficient reason for anger. Coriolanus sees his own downfall, although he feels helpless to control or modify the events:

> O my mother, mother! O!
> You have won a happy victory to Rome;
> But, for your son, believe it, O, believe it,
> Most dangerously you have with him prevailed,
> If not most mortal to him. But let it come.
> Aufidius.... (5.3.185–90)

He has betrayed the Volscians, and it is with this that Aufidius charges him, and justifies killing him.

The relationship with Aufidius is incomplete until he has made an attack on Coriolanus' body. On a deeper level, Coriolanus' death at the hands of Aufidius is also a love-union with Aufidius, which has been achieved by giving up his masculinity. By the equation of death and castration, Coriolanus has obtained the longed-for union with his father. At the moment of this attack, Coriolanus is denied his *agnomen* and condescendingly called "boy" instead. Almost the last breath Coriolanus takes is expended in his anger at this name of "boy." He boasts of his exploits at Corioli:

> 'tis there
> That, like an eagle in a dovecote, I
> Fluttered your Volscians in Corioli
> Alone I did it. "Boy!" (5.6.114–17)

In his anger, Coriolanus recalls his role at Corioli, an episode which symbolized a mutilating attack on the mother's body. This memory occurs precisely at the moment when he is to succumb to a mutilating attack by the strong father to whom he had offered himself as a love object. His identification with his mother is now complete, for he is about to be attacked and loved by his father in her stead, just as he had once desired to love her.

In summary: We may regard the earlier portions of *Coriolanus* as an articulation of the conflict found in those family constellations in which the father abdicates his function as a masculine figure for the son to identify with and to form an ego ideal (10). Menenius fulfilled this role symbolically in the initial situation. There is a splitting of the unconscious elements, with the defeat and castration of the father pushed into the past as an historical death, while certain aspects of the father are displaced on to Menenius in the present. In the place of a strong father, there is the ineffectual Menenius, whom Coriolanus may disregard as a feared rival for his mother.

However, Coriolanus' incestuous strivings are constantly stimulated and intensified by Volumnia in her erotization of the relationship. Coriolanus fears being engulfed by Volumnia in her ambitious designs to use him for her own goals. He is to function as her penile projection, by winning victories which will make her proud and give her opportunity to extol her blood. She would prefer military exploits to any show of tenderness:

> If my son were my husband, I should freelier rejoice in that absence wherein he won honor than in the embracements of his bed where he would show most love.
> (1.3.2-4)

The ego boundaries between mother and son are vague and indistinct. Coriolanus feels undifferentiated from his mother who is inimical to his development as an individual distinct from her. Coriolanus' view of his male role is thus markedly disturbed.

The sexualized attachment to Volumnia is uncomfortable because of the awareness of his hostility toward her, and of his aggressive impulses directed toward her body. Coriolanus has to deal not only with his own aggression and hatred, but also with the tendency to project this aggression on to its object in the form of anticipated retaliation for these angry and hostile feelings. Coriolanus is operating on the phallic dichotomy of "having a penis" vs. "being castrated" (7). These were precisely the themes involved in the wedding night reference in Act I, *viz.*, the belief that in intercourse violence is done to the woman's body, and the expectation of castrating punishment for this violence. The symbolic representation of this engulfment and destruction takes place in the battle when Coriolanus is closed off within the enemy gates and supposed dead.

Along with the fears of being castrated by the phallic mother, Coriolanus has feminine, passive wishes to submit to a strong father, even if the price is castration as a precondition for the father's love. The later portions of the play articulate this intense wish for a virile, loving father. Coriolanus joins with Aufidius to war against the mother's body, pouring war into her bowels, and treading upon her womb. Aggression towards Volumnia, which had in the earlier sections of the play been symbolically channeled on to the mob as representative of the mother, is now expressed by the massive rejection of Rome, birthplace, and mother. Aufidius and Coriolanus unite in love for one another and in mutual hatred for Rome and mother. Yet this solution is not completely successful until Aufidius is provoked to attack Coriolanus' own body, and Coriolanus achieves a love-death at the hands of the father for whom he had so ardently yearned.

NOTE

* The edition used is John Munro, *The London Shakespeare*, New York: Simon and Schuster, 1958, Vol. 6; Eyre and Spottiswoode Ltd., 1957.

BIBLIOGRAPHY

1. Barron, David. "Coriolanus: Portrait of the Artist as Infant," *The American Imago*, 19 (1962), 171–93.
2. Bradley, A.C. *Coriolanus*. British Academy, Annual Shakespeare Lecture. Oxford Univ. Press, 1912.
3. Brooke, Stropford A. *On Ten Plays of Shakespeare*. London: Constable, 1905.
4. Evans, B. Ifor. *The Language of Shakespeare's Plays*. London: Methuen, 1952.

5. Fenichel, Otto. "Trophy and Triumph," in *Collected Papers, Second Series*, Fenichel and Rapaport, eds. New York: Norton, 1954, pp. 141–62.
6. Freud, S. "The Taboo of Virginity," *Standard Edition*, Vol. 11, pp. 193–208.
7. ———. "Some Psychical Consequences of the Anatomical Distinction Between the Sexes," *Standard Edition*, Vol. 19, pp. 238–58.
8. Furness, H.H. *A New Variorum Edition of Shakespeare: The Tragedie of Coriolanus*. Philadelphia: Lippincott, 1928.
9. Granville-Barker, Harley. *Prefaces to Shakespeare*. Princeton Univ. Pres, 1946, Vol. 2.
10. Lidz, T., Fleck, S., and Cornelison, A.R. *Schizophrenia and The Family*. New York: International Universities Press, 1965.
11. MacCullum, M.W. *Shakespeare's Roman Plays and their Background*. London: Macmillan, 1910.
12. Munro, John. *The London Shakespeare*. New York: Simon and Schuster, 1958, Vol. 6.
13. Muir, Kenneth. *Shakespeare's Sources*, I. London: Methuen, 1961.
14. Putney, Rufus. "Coriolanus and His Mother," *The Psychoanalytic Quarterly*, 31 (1962), 364–81.
15. Rank, Otto. *Das Inzest-Motiv in Dichtung und Sage*. Leipzig and Wien: Franz Deuticke, 1926.
16. Spencer, T.J.B. *Shakespeare's Plutarch*. Harmondsworth: Penguin, 1964.
17. Spurgeon, Caroline. *Shakespeare's Imagery*. Cambridge Univ. Press, 1935.
18. Stoller, Robert J. "Shakespearean Tragedy: Coriolanus," *The Psychoanalytic Quarterly*, 35 (1966), 263–74.
19. Yates, Sybille L. "An Investigation of the Psychological Factors in Virginity and Ritual Defloration," *International Journal of Psycho-Analysis*, 11 (1930), 167–84.

Reprinted with permission from Emmett Wilson, Jr., "Coriolanus: The Anxious Bridegroom," *American Imago* 25 (1968), 224–41. Copyright 1968 by The Johns Hopkins University Press.

"Antony and Cleopatra" and "Coriolanus," Shakespeare's Heroic Tragedies: A Jacobean Adjustment

J.L. Simmons

Shakespeare wrote many plays about heroes, but only *Antony and Cleopatra* and *Coriolanus* are distinguished by heroic appeals that are exclusively and definitively aristocratic. Coriolanus and Cleopatra make strange bedfellows; yet despite their different life styles they share an unyielding horror of being scrutinized and judged by a vulgar audience. When the Queen of Egypt contemplates her dishonor at the hands of Octavius, her most terrifying thought is the vulgarization of her nobility in a dramatic representation for a popular Roman audience:

> *Cleopatra.* Now, Iras, what think'st thou?
> Thou an Egyptian puppet shall be shown
> In Rome as well as I. Mechanic slaves,
> With greasy aprons, rules, and hammers, shall
> Uplift us to the view; in their thick breaths,
> Rank of gross diet, shall we be enclouded,
> And forc'd to drink their vapour.
> *Iras.* The gods forbid!
> *Cleopatra.* Nay, 'tis most certain, Iras. Saucy lictors
> Will catch at us like strumpets, and scald rhymers
> Ballad us out o' tune; the quick comedians
> Extemporally will stage us, and present
> Our Alexandrian revels; Antony
> Shall be brought drunken forth, and I shall see

Some squeaking Cleopatra boy my greatness
I' th' posture of a whore. (V.ii.206-20)[1]

Cleopatra dazzlingly holds up a mirror to the world of the Globe playhouse. Her speculation about a Roman play reflects the actual dramatic event of Shakespeare's Roman play: the Roman populace looks exactly like the London populace crowded around her upon stage; Cleopatra is in fact being boyed by some incredibly young master and often, no doubt, in the exaggerated posture of a whore; the Alexandrian revels have already generated the laughter to encloud the Globe with the vapor of garlic. In other words, the heroic couple have already been exposed to the dramatic humiliation which the noble Cleopatra dreads; and they have deserved it to the extent that their aspiration has been punctuated comically by the reality.

But Cleopatra's mirror image is, of course, one-dimensional. The Roman performance will merely be grotesque caricature rendered with crude dramaturgical techniques and inspired by an even cruder moralism. Such a play might well have been in the popular repertory of the 1580s, something like a Roman *Famous Victories*. The appeal to the Roman populace, Cleopatra insists, will obliterate the dignity of heroic tragedy and the glory of heroic love. Shakespeare's Cleopatra, by implication, thus denies the varletry of censuring London a simplistic moral response to her tragedy: *Antony and Cleopatra* is obviously so much more than Cleopatra's projected Roman play, more than what the Roman populace could appreciate. At the same time, her trepidation—her dramatic vulnerability—points to the lovers' failure to realize their heroic vision in action. Those mechanic slaves with their rules represent a legitimate measurement which Shakespeare's comprehensive point of view incorporates.

It is very difficult to analyze the efficacy of such dramatic moments which bring the play into the world of the audience and at the same time, paradoxically, reinforce the audience's participation in the imaginative world of the play. This process of what Maynard Mack calls engagement and detachment manipulates not only the individual response of the playgoer but also, in some ritualistic way, the corporate response wherein individuals, with wits as diversely colored as their heads, become an audience.[2] My purpose is not to investigate how this mystery works in the theater; I only want to show that Shakespeare in these latest Jacobean tragedies—and particularly in *Coriolanus*—was manipulating his audience in a new way and that this new way implies a different kind of audience, one which cannot optimistically be expected to make a corporate response.

The famous passage in *Antony and Cleopatra* anticipates precisely the crucial dramatic scene in *Coriolanus*. In both cases the image of public display—Cleopatra exhibited as the prize of Caesar's triumph, Coriolanus standing for election in the marketplace—dissolves effortlessly into the image of a demeaning theatrical performance: "It is a part/That I shall blush in acting" (*Coriolanus*, II.ii.142–43). More insidiously, the breath of the people, which Coriolanus despises as much as Cleopatra, has the power to determine the value of his performance, his moral worth and his fame.

In *Coriolanus* Shakespeare creates out of the political situation a play within a play. For his performance Coriolanus will be assigned costume, lines, and action. Although the stage directions of the folio give us no instructions, he would also probably require a simple bench or trestle stage assembled for the occasion—such a construction as had proved effective in the production of *Volpone* in 1605/6. The King's Men owned Jonson's play and therefore the stage property needed for Volpone's performance as mountebank (II.i). Perhaps Jonson's great work reinforced upon Shakespeare's mind the pejorative implications of role-playing, particularly that Italianate role-playing which inspired Shakespeare's original formation of "mountebank" as a verb (*OED*):

> Mother, I am going to the market-place;
> Chide me no more. I'll mountebank their loves,
> Cog their hearts from them, and come home belov'd
> Of all the trades in Rome. (III.ii.131–34)

Coriolanus is literally to approach the people with his platform, in the process emblematizing himself as the most corrupt and dishonest of actors.

Shakespeare thus dramatizes, as the crux of his final tragedy, a theatrical relationship between aristocratic actor and popular audience, the very image which appalled Cleopatra. What completes the image in *Coriolanus* is that the vulgar "audience" breathing on the hero has another audience breathing on it. The judicious breath of the real audience is bated on both the hero and his witnessing mob. It is not by any means the first time that Shakespeare has identified the act of moral judgment with the theatrical judgment of an audience. In *King John*, for example, at the moral and military stalemate between France and England, the citizens of Angiers, unable to choose between Arthur and John, "stand securely on their battlements/ As in a theatre" (II.i.374–75). Shakespeare develops the moral enigma of Julius Caesar by characterizing him as an actor performing for that "stinking breath" which offstage all but overpowers Casca and Caesar himself. In the funeral scene Brutus and Antony, on a constructed pulpit-stage, perform for the uncertain plaudits of two audiences, one onstage and one in the yard.

What differentiates those earlier plays is that the ambivalences they dramatize do not directly involve any relationship with social class. As Ernest Schanzer observed in connection with *Julius Caesar*, the Renaissance equivalents of John Dover Wilson and Sir Mark Hunter—pro- and anti-Caesarians—might well have been in the audience;[3] but two such men could easily have been sitting, or even standing, side by side. *Coriolanus*, however, intentionally and inevitably strikes a social division within the audience. It is perhaps not a division exact enough to be marked by whether one stands or sits. But the sensibilities and prejudices which *Coriolanus* brings into exacerbating play are unquestionably those largely determined by one's social class, and it seems to me that criticism has, by and large, been too engaged in the partisan business of defending or attacking Coriolanus to recognize and accommodate Shakespeare's obvious dramatic strategy.

The ingredients of this class opposition certainly are not new in *Coriolanus*. The mob has been treated in earlier plays with all of its moral, intellectual, political, and hygienic liabilities. Coriolanus' charges against the people and his arguments for absolute authority are the most common of Shakespearian commonplaces. But *Coriolanus* is nevertheless distinctive, as critical discomfort with the play reveals. The groundling watching *Coriolanus* in 1608 would probably be prepared, as he surely was in the 1590s, to assent to the prejudices against the mob, as in fact the Third Citizen does within the play. But these commonplaces do not appear incidentally as a congenially orthodox support for the English royalty and hierarchy. The social opposition in *Coriolanus* serves as basis for the imagery, theme, and structure; it determines the hero's tragedy. Coriolanus evokes these prejudices not in the spirit of political didacticism but in his visionary loathing.

Explicitly Shakespeare brings aristocratic and heroic appeals into tension with a popular and unheroic world. The noblest Roman of them all does not wish to perform for the breath of those who, because they are not themselves noble, have no understanding of nobility. The people's imagistic association with materialism stigmatizes them as opposed to the Roman ideal of virtue and honor:

> See here these movers that do prize their hours
> At a crack'd drachma! Cushions, leaden spoons,
> Irons of a doit, doublets that hangmen would
> Bury with those that wore them, these base slaves,
> Ere yet the fight be done, pack up. (I.v.4–8)

In response to this action Coriolanus scathingly refers to "the common file" as "our gentlemen," and thematically his sarcasm is apt. The people's identification with money and trade hopelessly vulgarizes them. Volumnia has instilled in her son the aristocratic Roman (and English) attitude toward "woollen vassals, things created/To buy and sell with groats" (III.ii.9–10). When these vassals reject Coriolanus, they confirm the aristocratic prejudice against their unsavory breath, as abhorrent to patrician sensibilities as an association with trade:

> You have made good work,
> You and your apron men; you that stood so much
> Upon the voice of occupation and
> The breath of garlic-eaters! (IV.vi.96–99)

The objection against the mob's breath, so commonly charged in the popular drama, here transcends fastidiousness and represents a desire to protect noble ideals from enclouding "opinion." It is the same desire which provokes Cleopatra's horror of "thick breaths,/Rank of gross diet."

Of course one can easily oversimplify the stratification of English society, as historians have notably cautioned us. No doubt the audience was made up of many, both reputable and disreputable, who identified with neither patricians nor plebeians—or with both. Nevertheless, the social appeals in *Coriolanus*, both positive and negative, clearly distinguish the aristocracy and the gentry from the vulgar who are "defiled" by trade, craft, money, and gross diet. Since the play allows no middle ground between the extremes, the mob encompasses more than the poor rabble in *2 Henry VI*, more than the usual unruly apprentices. From Coriolanus' perspective "the voice of occupation" incorporates what would be the entire citizen class of London, the City as distinct from Court and Country. After Coriolanus is exiled, the temporary respite—with "tradesmen singing in their shops" (IV.vi.8)—suggests nothing so strongly as a Roman holiday for complacent shoemakers; the City world of Simon Eyre emerges, without Dekker's romanticizing, totally at odds with the classical glory of Rome.

Shakespeare juxtaposes two incompatible images of Rome—one idealistic and heroic, the other realistic and antiheroic. Thus the play offers the paradox of a city at once the destined glory of the world and a common bickering village. The glory that was Rome, historically perceived, stands out all the more convincingly in that it struggles against political liabilities endemic to all earthly cities. By Englishing the citizens, Shakespeare ironically gives Rome historical immediacy. At the same time, the patrician ideal of Rome in its startling contrast appeals all the more in its aura of antiquity: it is so decidedly ancient history. The scenic effect of the costuming would likely have encouraged this division between the grand and the common. As John Dover Wilson deduced from the Henry Peacham sketch of *Titus Andronicus*, "the lower classes [were] played apparently in 'modern dress,' whereas every effort was obviously made, contrary to the assumptions of our theatrical historians, to attain accuracy in the attire worn by patricians."[4]

In confronting the aristocratic ideal of Rome with a contemporaneous antagonistic City, *Coriolanus* more than incidentally reflects the social and political turmoil of Jacobean England. E.C. Pettet has argued a topical connection between the uprisings in the play and the Midlands Insurrection of 1607, both fomented in part by scarcity of corn and by hostility toward the gentry.[5] And W. Gordon Zeeveld has demonstrated that Jacobean royalists made allusions to the *tribuni plebis* to impugn the activists struggling for the initiative in James's first Parliament (1604–10).[6] But Shakespeare's experimentation with antagonistic appeals and points of view was perhaps most directly inspired by an instinctive awareness that the audience had been affected by the social and political divisiveness surrounding the playhouse. As Gerald Bentley observes, "In the years immediately before and after 1608, the London theatre audience was developing the social cleavage which is such a marked characteristic of the Jacobean and Caroline drama and stage.[7] Bentley is referring, in his important essay, to the year in which the King's Men took over the lease to the Blackfriars after James had evicted the children's company; but the year is also the date most frequently urged for *Coriolanus*. Precise dating, however, is not necessary; for whether it was first performed just before or just after 9 August 1608 when the King's Men arranged for the lease of the private theater, *Coriolanus* grows out of a period when Shakespeare as both playwright and shareholder was having to reckon with new dramatic fashions, new audiences, and even a new playhouse. The play reveals the strain as well as the genius of Shakespeare adjusting to a theatrical environment marked by Jacobean fragmentation, particularly by the growing alienation of that important segment of the London audience typically associated with trade and increasingly characterized as sectarian in spirit. The bonds of national unity which Elizabeth had maintained over religious, economic, and political factions had dissolved; and no area of English life responded to the loss more sensitively than the theater.

One hesitates to urge a predominance of external influences on that creativity which gave us *Antony and Cleopatra* and *Coriolanus*, but out of the bombardment of internal and external stimuli came two distinctly heroic tragedies which for the first time in Shakespeare's career treat aristocratic appeals that are definitively and insistently exclusive. The common people of Rome, Cleopatra knows, cannot respond to heroic love because they are not capable of such passion; they are not heroes.[8] No more are they capable of appreciating Coriolanus' *virtus*; they are not virtuous. Antony and Coriolanus, as Eugene M. Waith has argued, are generically Herculean; they tower heroically above the common rout in their aspirations, actions, and passions.[9] They strive for an excellence to distinguish them from both the bestial and the vulgar:

> Kingdoms are clay; our dungy earth alike
> Feeds beast as man. The nobleness of life
> Is to do thus . . . (I.i.35–37)

Although Antony's "thus" is assuredly not Coriolanus', both Herculean heroes attempt to achieve a greatness triumphantly beyond the level of clay. They cannot, however, ultimately succeed:

> Here I am Antony;
> Yet cannot hold this visible shape . . . (IV.xiv.13–14)

> I melt, and am not
> Of stronger earth than others. (*Coriolanus*, V.iii.28–9)

But while the ultimate failure asserts the hubris of the protagonists, the heroic attempt is substantial enough to affirm their tragic nobility.

The greatness of Shakespeare's two heroic tragedies (and here I disagree with Professor Waith) lies in the fact that the heroes and the heroics within the imaginative world of the plays have moral relevance to the real world of the audience. Shakespeare does not, that is to say, significantly urge special judgments for Antony and Coriolanus or suggest that in their greatness they rise above morality or create one of their own. Shakespeare is concerned with the moral status of heroes, and he renders Antony and Coriolanus critically from first to last. In fact, the irony frequently crowds both Antony and Coriolanus to the brink of the comic, even the satiric.[10] Shakespeare quite grants that heroes, in an unheroic world, are all but unendurable. The horror of Cleopatra and Coriolanus in contemplating their representation before a vulgar crowd implies that the capacity to be heroic is absurd without the select audience to appreciate heroism.

After *I Henry IV, Julius Caesar, Hamlet,* and *Troilus and Cressida* one would expect Shakespeare to bring the idea of the hero under moral scrutiny; heroism, like honor, receives definition and qualification rather early in Shakespeare's career. But only in *Antony and Cleopatra* and *Coriolanus* does Shakespeare treat heroism and honor in restrictively aristocratic manifestations, and this new subject-matter clearly reflects the trend of theatrical fashion. The heroic tragedies to follow—from the plays associated with Beaumont and Fletcher to the Caroline decadence—prove the taste of an increasingly exclusive audience for extravagant treatments of heroic virtue and love. These plays appeal to a concept of honor that becomes more rarified as it receives less definition and qualification. Shakespeare, however, chose to create heroic drama, necessarily exclusive in its moral appeals, for what was still a popular audience, although an increasingly unsettled one. But how was the dramatist to satisfy such an audience, the social fragmentation of which involved moral fragmentation? The same question can be posed in terms of Shakespeare's artistic integrity: how was Shakespeare to write such drama, with its special focus, without losing the all-encompassing vision which was his genius?

In resolving the problem, Shakespeare acknowledges once again that all the world's a stage and proceeds to dramatize the problem. By his very nature Coriolanus is inescapably as divisive a figure for the members of the real audience as for their social and political counterparts on the stage. Daringly, the conflict extends topically from the stage into the audience's immediate frame of reference as spectators of a play, as members of their own social classes, and as citizens of their own earthly city. If the experiment is brilliant, it has the air of a valedictory success; one can understand why Shakespeare wrote no more tragedies. Of the many historical presentiments to be discovered in Shakespeare's work, none is more profound than the demonstration in *Coriolanus* of the inevitable effect of social divisiveness upon the most public of art forms. Within a few decades following 1608, that effect would involve the closing of the theaters, but not before the loss of national unity had made the drama all but irrelevant.[11]

As Alfred Harbage insists in his *Shakespeare and the Rival Traditions*, Shakespeare remains a dramatist for the popular, not the coterie, theater; but the appeals in these last two tragedies and the audience which those appeals imply suggest distinctions not made in Professor Harbage's general survey.[12] The evidence presented in his study will nevertheless confirm that *Antony and Cleopatra* and *Coriolanus* differ signally from characteristic plays in the popular repertory, plays which appeal beyond antagonistic differences to common social, political, and ethical values. Professor Harbage cites these two works with suspicious infrequency, given their importance; and those few citations overlook the opposing characteristics which make the plays so problematic and provocative. The vision of the absolute aristocratic state no less than that of heroical love rejects—and is rejected by—bourgeois values. The prudent craftsmen and tradesmen are no more inclined to Coriolanus' martial virtue than they are to Antony and Cleopatra's heroic passion. The two plays, in fact, suggest the absurdity of juxtaposing the conflicting points of view much as does *The Knight of the Burning Pestle*, a play of the same period (c. 1608). Like the Citizen and his wife who are the jarring and unsympathetic audience for Beaumont's City comedy, the Roman tradesmen will either miss the point or morally disapprove of it. Whereas Beaumont generates comedy, Shakespeare generates tragedy out of the social disharmony within an audience.

Shakespeare, however, uses his unsympathetic audience positively as well as negatively in regarding and evaluating his heroic characters. While Coriolanus' vision is granted its validity, the physical world of the trade and working class offers a system of checks more profound than the hero understands. The moral vision of Shakespeare's two heroic tragedies incorporates the popular, didactic morality of the people: Antony and Cleopatra are certainly overthrown by lust; Coriolanus is indeed a victim of his own pride. But Shakespeare also creates a heroic aspiration beyond that moralism even while aware that the greatness of his tragic Romans must be a limited and qualified one. Cleopatra's theatrical fears, therefore, are symptomatic of a moral comprehensiveness achieved by a playwright manipulating a diverse audience with diverse points of view. And Shakespeare finally, I believe, transcends the diversity.

NOTES

1. *William Shakespeare: The Complete Works*, ed. Peter Alexander (Glasgow, 1951). This text is cited throughout.

2. "Engagement and Detachment in Shakespeare's Plays," in *Essays on Shakespeare and Elizabethan Drama in Honor of Hardin Craig*, ed. Richard Hosley (Columbia, MO, 1962), pp. 275–96.

3. *The Problem Plays of Shakespeare* (London, 1963), p. 33.

4. "*Titus Andronicus* on the Stage in 1595," *Shakespeare Survey* 1 (Cambridge, 1948), p. 21.

5. "*Coriolanus* and the Midlands Insurrection of 1607," *Shakespeare Survey* 3 (Cambridge, 1950), pp. 34–42.

6. "*Coriolanus* and Jacobean Politics," *MLR* 57 (1962), 321–34.

7. "Shakespeare and the Blackfriars Theatre," *Shakespeare Survey* 1 (Cambridge, 1948), p. 45: "The gentry, the court, the professional classes, and the Inns of Court men went to the Blackfriars, the Phoenix, and later to the Salisbury Court; the London masses went to the larger and noisier Red Bull and Fortune and Globe. This new state of affairs was just developing when the King's men had their conferences about the Blackfriars in 1608."

8. For the semantic confusion behind "heroical love," a confusion which encouraged the belief that only the great are subject to this overwhelming passion, see John L. Lowes, "The Loveres Maladye of Hereos," *Modern Philology* 11 (1914), 491–546.

9. *The Herculean Hero in Marlowe, Chapman, Shakespeare, and Dryden* (New York, 1962), passim.

10. See R.A. Foakes, *Shakespeare: the Dark Comedies to the Last Plays: From Satire to Celebration* (Charlottesville, VA, 1971), pp. 85–93. Foakes discusses the "distancing" in these plays as Shakespeare's response to

the drama of the decade, particularly Marston's and the repertory of the children's companies.

11. See David M. Bevington, *Tudor Drama and Politics* (Cambridge, MA, 1968), p. 297.

12. *Shakespeare and the Rival Traditions* (New York, 1952).

Reprinted with the permission of Cambridge University Press from J.L. Simmons, "'Antony and Cleopatra' and 'Coriolanus', Shakespeare's Heroic Tragedies: A Jacobean Adjustment," Shakespeare Survey 26 (1973), 95–101. *Copyright 1973 by Cambridge University Press.*

Coriolanus

Lawrence Danson

In *Othello* and *Macbeth* we saw language used imaginatively but also perversely. In *Othello*, we looked at the relationship between a lying fable and the fable that tells essential truth; in *Macbeth*, at the unnaturalness of evil as it is embodied in a language of inversions and paradox. Now, in examining *Coriolanus*, it may seem that we are turning away from the imaginative use of language in almost any form: the peculiar stylistic barrenness (compared to the poetic richness of the previous plays), the narrowness of its "range of tone and feeling,"[1] is one of the most frequently remarked characteristics of *Coriolanus*. And the hero of the play may also seem out of place in this study: I have located as a primary impetus for tragic action a man's need to achieve self-expression; however, Coriolanus is not only the least eloquent of Shakespeare's tragic figures but one who (as we shall see) specifically rejects that humanizing speech sought by Titus or Hamlet.

Coriolanus is in these ways exceptional. In another way, however, it is perfectly Shakespearean, for in this play, as much as in *Macbeth*, style and theme (those handy abstractions we use for discursive analysis) are inextricably united. The almost hallucinatory metaphoric richness of *Macbeth* is the linguistic embodiment of its action; the apparently bare style of *Coriolanus* is, similarly, the fitting language for its quite different action. And as we can trace the action of *Macbeth* through an examination of its peculiar rhetoric, so we can trace the action of *Coriolanus*—only here we can be more specific about the particular rhetorical device at issue. The stylistic peculiarity of *Coriolanus* comes very largely from the unusual prominence given to metonymy and synecdoche—modes of expression directly related to the nature of the thing to be expressed.[2]

To say that metonymy and synecdoche, rather than the more customary metaphor and simile, are the most prominent rhetorical figures in *Coriolanus* is not, I am aware, the most exciting of all possible observations. But there is reason to believe that the distinction between metonymy and metaphor is of more fundamental significance than might at first appear, and shortly I will be offering evidence to support the claim. The distinction is of importance to theories of poetry in general, but here I will be concerned only with its significance for *Coriolanus*. And as a first step in relating the figure of metonymy to the themes of the play, we may note that metonymy and synecdoche are figures of fragmentation and usurpation—of parts representng the whole and of the whole absorbing its parts; and that *Coriolanus* is a play about the relationship of the individual to the community, of the community to its constituent members, and of the association of man with man, and of man with the elements that compound him.

Coriolanus is a world of "fragments" (the epithet is directed by Caius Marcius Coriolanus at the common people of Rome), populated not by men but by parts of men. A "great toe" is bid to address an assembly of "scabs" (I.i.153, 164), a youthful warrior's "Amazonian chin" drives "the bristled lips before him" (II.ii.89), the tribunes of the people are "the tongues o' th' common mouth" (III.i.22). Repeatedly, parts or functions of men are made to stand for the whole: men give their "voices" (that is, their votes); but also they *are* merely voices, disembodied, autonomous, grotesque. (But the returning hero hails his wife as his "gracious silence" [II.i.166].) The epithet *voices* comes quite naturally; the word had, in Elizabethan usage, the technical meaning of "votes," and was so used by North in translating Plutarch.[3] But in Act II, scene 3, where Coriolanus must humble himself before the people and sue to them for their "voices," the act and the actor are made contemptuously synonymous. The people's role in the state, according to Coriolanus, is merely to give their voices as they are directed (although when they overstep themselves they do clamor hungrily for other oral gratifications), and so they become no more than gaping mouths and noisy voices; they are, as Coriolanus mockingly accuses them, "most sweet voices," "worthy voices!" (109, 134). Such frequently repeated reductive images as these create in the play a grotesquerie of partial beings distorted into impossible positions: a warrior, for instance, must display himself by displaying his wounds, and the grateful people "are to put [their] tongues into those wounds and speak for them" (II.iii.6).

In a play so rich in vituperation as *Coriolanus*, it is not surprising to find these reductive images, but for their frequently metonymic character some explanation is necessary. And one is not far to seek: the play's numerous and striking metonymies are conditioned—in effect called into being—by Menenius's fable of the body and the belly. There is, I think, no other play in which Shakespeare so clearly allows a single image to dominate. The fable, slowly and amusingly developed by the garrulous patrician in Act I, scene 1, largely determines the nature of the succeeding imagery, and determines it in the direction of metonymy.

Menenius's "pretty tale" is, as he is content to remark, hardly new. The state is like a man: in both state and man, health depends upon the cooperation of all the members and organs, each of which must perform its allotted task. Thus the smiling belly of Menenius's fable reminds "th' discontented members, the mutinous parts" (I.i.109) of the body that, although he receives "the general food at first," he does so only to distribute it to his "incorporate friends" (128–29). (And thus the well-fed patricians are supposed to do for the hungry plebeians.) The very commonplace nature of this little moral tale is all to Shakespeare's purpose; it is only a special application of the universally known correspondence of microcosm and macrocosm—a correspondence so simple (yet inclusive) that, once established by Menenius thus early in the play, it can continue to preside over the play's imagery till the end.

We are, in a sense, imprisoned within the limits of vision the fable establishes; we remain within its frame of reference, where, whether our attention is directed to the individual man or to the world at large, we see before us the human body, its parts at war one with the other. The dominance of the image gains for the play a simplifying clarity, but loses the complicating expansiveness characteristic of metaphor. For Menenius's fable is not a metaphor but an extended metonymy; it is, indeed, an instance of what Kenneth Burke (in his somewhat specialized vocabulary) describes as "the 'noblest synecdoche,' the perfect paradigm or prototype of all lesser usages, [which] is found in metaphysical doctrines proclaiming the identity of 'microcosm' and 'macrocosm.' In such doctrines," writes Burke, "where the individual is seen as a replica of the universe, and vice versa, we have the ideal synecdoche, since microcosm is related to macrocosm as part to whole, and either the whole can represent the part or the part can represent the whole."[4] In *Coriolanus*, once Menenius has established his version of this prototypic metonymy, defining for us the macrocosm of Rome both in its present dissentient reality and in its unrealized ideal of order, the microcosmic metonymies follow inevitably: finishing his tale, Menenius turns to the First Citizen and asks, "What do you think,/You, the great toe of this assembly?" (I.i.152).

In the midst of Rome's fragmentary citizens, its mere parts of men loudly demanding the rights of whole men, stands Coriolanus—indivisibly whole, heroically complete, refusing (but, as we shall see, in vain) any division of his essence. With monolithic integrity Coriolanus denies in himself those contradictions (or, from another point of view, complexities) which mark lesser mortals. Over and over, this distinction is drawn between Coriolanus and the self-divided rabble which surrounds him: the people "can yield [their voices] now/And straight disclaim their tongues" (III.i.34); they have bodies without hearts and tongues which "cry/Against the rectorship of judgment" (II.iii.201); the tribunes have "ears and eyes for th' time,/But hearts for the event" (II.i.259)—but Caius Marcius is the man whose "heart's his mouth;/What his breast forges, that his tongue must vent" (III.i.257). Unlike his enemies, Coriolanus is integrated, all-of-a-piece; heart, mouth, breast, and tongue work together to one end—an end, it may be noted, of almost inhuman simplicity.

Coriolanus's insistence upon singular wholeness sets him apart even from his fondest allies. Indeed, it is his mother Volumnia, in Act III (as once again, and fatally, she will do in Act V), who most effectively condemns her son's impossible ideal. Coriolanus cannot understand why Volumnia would have him act other than as his heart bids: "Why did you wish me milder? Would you have me/False to my nature? Rather say I play/The man I am" (III.ii.14). To follow Volumnia's politic advice would be to accept in himself that state of fragmentation he despises in others:

> Must I go show them my unbarb'd sconce? Must I
> With my base tongue give to my noble heart
> A lie that it must bear?
>
> . . . .
>
> I will not do't
> Lest I surcease to honour mine own truth,
> And by my body's action teach my mind
> A most inherent baseness. (III.ii.99–101, 120–123)

But such indeed is Volumnia's advice, and she will herself provide the example:

> Pray be counsel'd;
> I have a heart as little apt as yours,
> But yet a brain that leads my use of anger
> To better vantage. (III.ii.28–31)

With heart thus divided from brain, Coriolanus must force himself to speak "such words that are but roted in /Your tongue, though but bastards and syllables/Of no allowance to your bosom's truth" (55).

We may question the ultimate moral value of Volumnia's counsel, but her urging does redress, if only too humanly, the inhumanity of Coriolanus's posture. Inhuman, for Coriolanus's demands, upon himself and others, go beyond even the ideal of harmony defined in Menenius's fable. By the logic of the Microcosm-macrocosm analogy, the individual as well as the state is made up of disparate parts: the parts may, at best, work in easy cooperation, but to deny (as Coriolanus would do) one's essentially fragmentary nature is to deny one's humanness.

The body-synecdoches which describe the common people would never do to describe Coriolanus, and indeed there come to be attached to him metonymies of another sort that turn him from a human being into (in G. Wilson Knight's apt phrase) "a slaying machine of mechanic excellence."[5] Before Corioli, "from face to foot/He was a thing of blood, whose every motion/Was tim'd with dying cries" (II.ii.106). The whole man is fused so immediately with his function that he is not merely a warrior but the embodied shape of war itself: "Death, that dark spirit, in's nervy arm doth lie,/Which, being advanc'd, declines, and then men die" (II.i.151). His obsessive drive for simple wholeness of being is most perfectly expressed when his jubilant soldiers, shouting and waving their caps, "take him up in their arms," and Coriolanus cries with the ecstacy of fulfillment, "O; me alone! Make you a sword of me?" (I.vi.76).

What Coriolanus denies in himself, he despises in the state and would extirpate—its fragmentary, representative nature, its at least partial democracy of functions. Thus far he is faithful to Menenius's analogy: he is a totalitarian both of the emotions and of the body politic. On the political level, it may be noted, Rome's very form of government is a type of metonymy; again, the general observation is Kenneth Burke's:

> A ... synecdochic form is present in all theories of political representation, where some part of the social body (either traditionally established, or elected, or coming into authority by revolution) is held to be "representative" of the society as a whole. . . . [I]n a complex civilization any act of representation automatically implies a synecdochic relationship (insofar as the act is, or is held to be, "truly representative").[6]

But Coriolanus, who despises the man whose mouth speaks other than as his heart prompts, whose every function is not knit into one machine-perfect instrument for achievement, cannot brook such synecdochic representation—in Rome, a synecdoche that leaves the "voice" grotesquely dominant over the whole. He cannot brook it, at any rate, unless he is the part that stands for the whole. The quarrel between Coriolanus and the people is thus made fully irreconcilable precisely over the question of a synecdoche: "Where is this viper/That would depopulate the

Coriolanus

city and/Be every man himself?" demands the tribune Sicinius (III.i.263) and: "What is the city but the people?"—to which the people's answer comes, "True,/The people are the city" (III.i.199). And Coriolanus's response is as clear and consistent: one man alone, he turns upon his assembled judges and cries, "I banish you" (III.iii.125).

Perhaps the oddest, certainly one of the most revealing, aspects of Coriolanus's demand for wholeness of being is his distrust of words, and indeed of all the conventional symbolic means (verbal and gestural) that men have for expressing themselves. For all his vituperation, it is the refusal to speak—to exhort his men kindly, to acknowledge their praise, to show his wounds (a sort of silent speech), to answer Aufidius's accusations—which is most characteristic of him. In fact, the disastrous refusal to show his wounds to the people also suggests the reason for Coriolanus's antipathy to the conventional arts of language: it is a refusal to allow parts to speak for his whole.

And so with all language, and especially the language of explanation and self-definition: the very words and gestures by which men make their meanings apparent, which *stand for* us, are implicated in that self-divisiveness against which Coriolanus struggles, are things (as Coriolanus sees it) apart from us that come, basely, to represent us. Coriolanus, we know, cannot flatter or hear flattery spoken of him—but beyond that we are left with the impression that he simply cannot speak; for to accept words in place of the whole man is to be like the common people, "the wisdom of [whose] choice is rather to have my hat than my heart" (II.iii.97). Cominius describes the only mode of communication, of mediation between himself and the world, which Coriolanus can approve: Coriolanus, he says, "rewards/ His deeds with doing them, and is content/To spend the time to end it" (II.ii.125). No discursive substitute or memorial ceremony, but only the man in action, the thing itself, can suffice. Only in the instant when man and deed are totally united in the act that defines the man is he adequately expressed; only when Coriolanus *is* his sword is Coriolanus wholly manifested.

Coriolanus's uneasiness over the arts of language is in a way reminiscent of Hamlet's struggle with the problem of self-expression. Hamlet, in Act I, finding himself in a world of seeming, disdains (like Coriolanus) all the "actions that a man might play," and therefore is deprived of "all forms, moods, shapes of grief" that could denote him truly. His whole allegiance is, initially, to "that within which passes show." And Coriolanus too, like Hamlet, relates hypocrisy to the histrionic: "Would you have me/False to my nature?" we have heard him demand of Volumnia; "rather say I play/The man I am." His protest against "playing" is buttressed by the venerable platonic charge that the feigning of drama or poetry may lead to a blurring of the lines between role and reality, or to an outright usurpation of the one by the other. Coriolanus will not play any part but "the man I am," "Lest I surcease to honour mine own truth,/And by my body's action teach my mind/A most inherent baseness."

But these similarities between Hamlet and Coriolanus cannot be more than superficial. For Hamlet, under the exigencies of his situation and with the aid of a troop of professional actors, discovers a way to unite histrionic action with the action that is immediate being. Coriolanus, on the other hand, never unites the two senses of acting. Instead, we find him confronted with a paradox he is quite incapable of resolving, that the actions he undertakes in order to be most true to "the man I am" lead him to a baseness least like his ideal of selfhood.

In proper names, that class of words whose special function it is to represent us, we find the paradox most clearly revealed. Cominius (who, though a soldier, is as easy with language as Coriolanus is uneasy with it) seems to have found an acceptable formula: the one appropriate gesture the army can offer its hero is to bestow upon him a name which most nearly identifies the doer with his deeds:

> and from this time,
> For what he did before Corioli, call him
> With all th' applause and clamour of the host,
> Caius Marcius Coriolanus.
> Bear th' addition nobly ever! (I.ix.62)

The name is informed immediately with its occasion and is close enough to the wordless integrity Coriolanus would prefer. But still it is only words, still a synecdoche standing inadequately for the whole man. And the history of Coriolanus's name, its acquisition and its loss, is a history that reveals the impossible nature of its bearer's quest to be heroically self-constituted.

For the bestowing of a name, especially one so intrinsically related to its bearer as "Coriolanus," is a social act, defining relationships, going outside of whatever purely inner integrity we can conceive. Now everything Coriolanus does is done to be true to himself, but everything he does after his break with Rome—the Rome which named him and so largely defines his being—proves him a traitor not only to Rome but to himself. He believes he is true to himself even in making his alliance with Aufidius; that is, given the man Caius Marcius Coriolanus, this new alliance is the one he must make: but that name remains to show that in being thus true to "himself," he is being false to another self who is a son, a husband, a father, a Roman.

The new alliance makes his name an anomaly, and as early as his first appearance before Aufidius it is held to be an embarrassing impediment; to Aufidius's repeated demand, "Speak, man. What's thy name?" he at last replies:

> If, Tullus,
> Not yet thou know'st me, and, seeing me, dost not
> Think me for the man I am, necessity
> Commands me name myself. (IV.v.54)

The name remains, but not its meaning; the relationships of honor and of enmity that it implied are being overturned:

> My name is Caius Marcius, who hath done
> To thee particularly, and to all the Volsces,
> Great hurt and mischief; thereto witness may
> My surname, Coriolanus. The painful service,
> The extreme dangers, and the drops of blood
> Shed for my thankless country, are requited
> But with that surname—a good memory
> And witness of the malice and displeasure
> Which thou shouldst bear me. Only that name remains.
> (IV.v.65)

The name that once defined him as closely as a name can do, has now become a measure of the distance its bearer has traveled from himself, from his own identity. It is a state which cannot be allowed to endure, and shortly we have Cominius's report:

> "Coriolanus"
> He would not answer to; forbad all names;
> He was a kind of nothing, titleless,
> Till he had forg'd himself a name i' th' fire
> Of burning Rome. (V.i.11)

The loss of his name in the pursuit of an ideal of integrity reveals the full irony of Coriolanus's career. Now he must remain "a kind of nothing, titleless," or else forge a new name in a new social relationship—but one that makes him a traitor to the man he was.

The question of selfhood I have been discussing is not one, it must be admitted, which Coriolanus, the least introspective of Shakespearean heroes, thinks much about. To him, rather, the question appears to be one more appropriate to soldiers, the question of manhood. And it is therefore curious, but also appropriate, that we learn more about the *childhood* of this insistently heroic man than we do about the childhood of any other of Shakespeare's tragic heroes. The play's domestic emphasis is vastly important: it leads directly to Aufidius's taunt, "Boy!" and to Coriolanus's destruction. Volumnia is, of course, the person most responsible for her son's striving toward heroic manhood (and it is a large part of the play's irony that, as the First Citizen astutely recognizes, much of Coriolanus's drive for self-sufficiency results from his need "to please his mother" [I.i.38]); Volumnia, who, when her young son came home wounded from battle, "sprang not more in joy at first hearing he was a man-child than now in first seeing he had proved himself a man" (I.iii.18). And hearing Volumnia, and seeing the results of her training in her ferocious son, we are forced to recognize how the desire to prove oneself a man can imply, in fact, the desire to be less than—or at least other than—a fully sentient human being. When Macduff hears how Macbeth has slaughtered his family, he is told to bear it like a man. He replies that he must also *feel* it like a man: that is a sort of manhood Coriolanus knows nothing about.

To be a man, as Coriolanus understands it, is to be sufficient and whole in a way no man in fact can be. But to be a

Coriolanus 133

"boy" is eminently human: the boy's very incompleteness implies the contingency of a human state. And in *Coriolanus* the boy is always present before us, contained in, or superimposed upon, the man he has become. Presenting young Marcius to his father, Volumnia says, "This is a poor epitome of yours,/Which by th' interpretation of full time/May show like all yourself" (V.iii.68); this is another instance of microcosm and macrocosm, and the reflection works both ways: in the man Coriolanus we see the boy Caius Marcius.

And we have seen him from the start: "O' my word, the father's son" (I.iii.57), Valeria declares, as she describes how young Marcius "mammock'd" a butterfly; and that childish image is never far away as we watch the grown man in his rage, mammocking his human enemies. The two sets of images—boy and butterfly, man and enemy—come together in Cominius's description of Coriolanus: the Volscian soldiers, he says, "follow him/Against us brats with no less confidence/Than boys pursuing summer butterflies" (IV.vi.93). And at the beginning of Act V, scene 4 the image, subtly varied now, makes a last appearance. The subject under discussion is Coriolanus's inflexible enmity to Rome: "Is't possible that so short a time can alter the condition of a man?" asks Sicinius. And Menenius replies: "There is differency between a grub and a butterfly; yet your butterfly was a grub. This Marcius is grown from man to dragon; he has wings, he's more than a creeping thing."

Here the image is used to demonstrate Coriolanus's emergence as the mature destroyer of Rome, but again we cannot help recalling the boy who "mammock'd" a butterfly. Only now, by a remarkable compression of the image, Coriolanus *is* the butterfly—and a butterfly who has been a grub; the image reminds us that Coriolanus was a boy (a "grub"), has grown, did change, must change. Menenius continues his frightening description of Coriolanus, who "moves like an engine," who "is able to pierce a corslet with his eye, talks like a knell, and his hum is a battery"—but this is scene 4, and in scene 3 we have already watched the mechanical monster weeping before his mother.

Coriolanus in the pride of his manhood is himself, then, only a "fragment": he has taken his manhood for the whole, but it is still merely a part, representative of something much more complex. In Act V, scene 3, where Volumnia appears before him with his wife, son, and friend, that buried complexity is brought irresistibly home to Coriolanus. He tries, as he has tried all along, to "stand/As if a man were author of himself/And knew no other kin" (35); for only autogenous man could withstand Volumnia's appeal. But his own words show the futility of his effort:

> My wife comes foremost, then the honour'd mould
> Wherein this trunk was fram'd, and in her hand
> The grandchild to her blood. (22)

Coriolanus is not his own man, he cannot be: "Thou art my warrior;/I holp to frame thee," Volumnia declares (62). Earlier, Coriolanus had protested that he would only "play the man I am"; here his cue is indeed to act sternly, but he finds that, "Like a dull actor now/I have forgot my part and I am out,/Even to a full disgrace" (40). Coriolanus collapses before Volumnia's show of relationships; it is the return of the repressed, as that part of himself which he has tried to deny—the part which is still humanly contingent and still therefore a "boy"—demands recognition.

I have tried thus far to show the importance of metonymy and synecdoche to the overall scheme of *Coriolanus*, have called attention to the way in which Menenius's prototypic metonymy (his fable of the body and the belly) controls much of the play's imagery, and have shown how the figure of metonymy is related to Coriolanus's quest for simple integrity of being. There is more still which must be said about the play—but here I want to return to a question that has been left hanging: whether there is indeed a fundamental distinction to be made between metonymy and synecdoche (on the one hand) and metaphor and simile (on the other), and whether that distinction can help us to understand not only the thematic but also the stylistic nature of *Coriolanus*.

And stylistically *Coriolanus* is an oddity—a work of Shakespeare's maturity which lacks precisely those qualities of poetic expansiveness and suggestiveness characteristic of the mature Shakespeare, a work whose undeniable power is even, in part, the result of that notable lack. There is a narrowness about *Coriolanus*, but it is also a concentration, a forcefulness. "The play's style is bare," writes Wilson Knight, who goes on to describe it (with perhaps more poetic color than is appropriate) "there is here a swift channeling, an eddying, twisting, and forthward-flowing stream; ice-cold, intellectual, cold as a mountain torrent and holding something of its iron taste."[7] This unusually frigid style raises problems for critics who admire quite different qualities in Shakespeare, problems implicit in A.C. Bradley's almost querulous comment (to which many other critics have given assent), "No doubt the story has a universal meaning, since the contending forces are permanent constituents of human nature; but that peculiar *imaginative* effect or atmosphere [which one associates with Shakespearean tragedy] is hardly felt."[8]

There have been various attempts to account for this lack of "atmosphere," not the least successful of which is Bradley's own: he points out that there is virtually nothing of the supernatural in the play and that there is an uncharacteristically sparse use of the pathetic fallacy. But the most rewarding analysis is by Maurice Charney, who observes that none of the characters except Menenius use "figurative language fully and naturally," and that Coriolanus himself, in his aversion to eloquence, refuses to use "language as an exploration of consciousness." The result, writes Charney is that

> When Coriolanus does use figures of speech, he inclines to similes rather than metaphors, since they provide a simpler and more explicit form of expression. Both the vehicle and the tenor of the image are very carefully balanced and limited, usually by the connective "like" or "as" (I count ninety-three similes in the play, fifty-seven with "as" and thirty-six with "like"). The similes do not suggest new areas of meaning, but give points already stated an added force and vividness. Their function is illustrative rather than expressive.[9]

Now I have not provided a statistical analysis of the play's metonymies and synecdoches: for one thing, distinguishing these rhetorical figures is a far more subjective exercise than distinguishing similes; and for another, I am less interested in raw numbers than in relative prominence of effect. (Menenius's elaborately developed fable, for instance, might count as a single instance of metonymy, but its importance to the entire scheme of the play would hardly emerge from such a count.) But if I have been at all successful in showing the relevance of metonymy to the play's theme, it will not be superfluous to suggest that, despite the excellence of Charney's analysis, it is not only the prominence of simile (that narrower metaphor), but also of metonymy and synecdoche which most strikingly accounts for the play's unusual concentration of effect.

According to René Wellek and Austin Warren, "we may divide the tropes of poetry most relevantly into figures of contiguity [i.e., metonymy and synecdoche] and figures of similarity"; and Wellek and Warren go on to report "the notion that metonymy and metaphor may be the characterizing structures of poetic types—poetry of association by contiguity, of movement within a single world of discourse, and poetry of association by comparison, joining a plurality of worlds."[10] It does not particularly matter whether we think of synecdoche as a special case of metonymy or (as Kenneth Burke suggests) of metonymy "as a special application of synecdoche." What is important is that both metonymy and synecdoche, the figures of contiguity, are confined to "movement within a single world of discourse"—in *Coriolanus*, as we have seen, the single world defined by Menenius's prototypic metonymy; while both metaphor and simile, the figures of comparison, bring together worlds ordinarily not joined, performing the work of fusion which, especially in a post-Romantic age, is more popularly considered "poetic." If this distinction is valid, the prominence of metonymy in *Coriolanus* will help us to account for the peculiarly narrow effect of the play; for whereas metaphor reaches out to broaden a play's poetic world through the addition of other worlds to it, metonymy separates, parses, even diminishes, but also clarifies, the elements of *Coriolanus*'s world.

The "notion" (as Wellek and Warren describe it) of the fundamental distinction between metonymy and metaphor has been impressively substantiated by Roman Jakobson. In his *Fundamentals of Language,* Jakobson discusses, from the linguist's point of view, the significance of various clinical investigations of aphasia, the disease characterized by loss of speech. Jakobson concludes that, although "The varieties of aphasia are numerous and diverse . . . all of them oscillate between . . . two polar types. . . . Every form of aphasic disturbance consists in some impairment, more or less severe, either of the faculty for selection and substitution or for combination and contexture."[11] In one polar type, in which the "relation of similarity" is lost, the aphasic has in effect lost the ability to use metaphor; in the other type, which affects "the relation of contiguity," the aphasic has lost the ability to use metonymy. The study of the loss of language thus reveals "the bipolar structure of language." Jakobson writes:

> The development of a discourse may take place along two different semantic lines: one topic may lead to another either through their similarity or through their contiguity. The *metaphoric* way would be the most appropriate term for the first case and the *metonymic* way for the second, since they find their most condensed expression in metaphor and metonymy respectively. . . . In normal verbal behavior both processes are continually operative, but careful observation will reveal that under the influence of a cultural pattern, personality, or verbal style, a preference is given to one of the processes over the other.[12]

In *Coriolanus* both processes are of course operative, and it need hardly be said that, in general, Shakespeare's tendency is to favor the metaphoric way; but the metonymic process is strikingly prominent in *Coriolanus*, and its prominence does much to account for the uneasiness critics have felt with the play. Shakespeare is for us Coleridge's myriad-minded Shakespeare, the master of the esemplastic imagination, of the metaphoric process. Critics at home with the products of romanticism and symbolism—literary schools based, as Jakobson observes, on "the primacy of the metaphoric process"—are equally comfortable with Shakespeare. But *Coriolanus* is different; it has, as Bradley (among others) complains, "scarcely more atmosphere" than the realistic drama of Bradley's day, and realism is a method which follows "the path of contiguous relationships," of metonymy.

Shakespeare's tragedies build to a culminating ritual which contains at least the possibility that it will be a device for wonder in times to come. In this matter, too, *Coriolanus* manages to be anomalous while still bearing clearly the Shakespearean stamp. The final scene of the play, with which I will conclude this discussion, is one of the most powerful yet also one of the most disconcerting scenes in any of the plays. What disconcerts, I think, is not just the sheer brutality of Coriolanus's death, but the question of worth it raises. Is there anything in the death of Coriolanus that can make us feel that sense of an end attained, an expression perfected, which is felt in the ritualized deaths of other Shakespearean tragedies? Or does the play's lack of "imaginative effect" extend to its concluding actions, where peevishness suddenly escalates to the level of brute, irredeemable horror?

Despite its heroic panoply, Coriolanus's final entry upon the stage, "marching with drum and colours; the Commoners being with him," is in the bitterly ironic mode of *Troilus and Cressida*. It is ironic, first of all, because this procession is in Corioli instead of Rome. It is ironic, too, because (like a similar moment of stage pageantry in *Troilus*) it follows not a battle but the unexpected postponement of a battle. However relieved we may be that Coriolanus has spared Rome, there is still, dramatically, a sense of anticlimax. And it is most bitterly ironic because we have just heard the plans of Aufidius and his conspirators, and we know that this hero marching in triumph is in fact only a victim being readied for the slaughter. Under the circumstances, the cheering commoners may sound to us more like a mocking satiric chorus than a great man's deserved retinue.

It would not require a Machiavellian genius to rouse the irascible Coriolanus to a pitch where an enemy might, with some show of justification, turn violently on him. But the way in which Aufidius goes to work shows a knowledge of his man born of careful observation, and we may notice that the relationship between these two men has always had about it something of that irresolute, quasi-sexual love-hate we observed in the combatants of *Troilus and Cressida*. Aufidius looses three perfectly aimed taunts; in effect, he sums up in three

Coriolanus

dramatically spaced words the history, as we have seen it, of Coriolanus's self-defeating career. "Traitor" is the first thrust; immediately comes Coriolanus's uncomprehending protest, "Traitor! How now?"—and Aufidius answers with his next taunt:

> *Auf.* Ay, traitor, *Marcius!*
> *Cor.* Marcius!
> *Auf.* Ay, Marcius, Caius Marcius! dost thou think
> I'll grace thee with that robbery, thy stol'n name
> Coriolanus, in Corioli? (V.vi.87; emphasis added)

The third taunt is withheld while Aufidius provides a travestied description of how Coriolanus, "For certain drops of salt," betrayed the Volscians:

> at his nurse's tears
> He whin'd and roar'd away your victory,
> That pages blush'd at him, and men of heart
> Look'd wond'ring each at others. (97)

Again, it is Coriolanus's protest which brings the next, and crowning, insult:

> *Cor.* Hears't thou, Mars?
> *Auf.* Name not the god, thou *boy* of tears! (100; emphasis added)

This quick *agon* is as tersely, perfectly managed as anything I know in Shakespeare. But what is, for our purposes, most remarkable about it—and about what follows it—is the departure it makes from the more typical tragic finales. For here it is the antagonist, Aufidius, who in his taunting recapitulation of the play's action comes closest to making (for whatever vile reasons) an effort at understanding, while Coriolanus's stuttering replies and bursts of rage prove him as essentially uncomprehending as he has been throughout the play. He does, it is true, briefly manifest a concern that his story be told aright; for one instant, at any rate, it sounds as if we are to have something structurally comparable to Hamlet's "Absent thee from felicity" or Othello's "Soft you, a word or two before you go":

> Cut me to pieces, Volsces; men and lads,
> Stain all your edges on me. "Boy"! False hound!
> If you have writ your annals true, 'tis there
> That, like an eagle in a dove-cote, I
> Flutter'd your Volscians in Corioli.
> Alone I did it. "Boy"! (112)

But how sadly incomplete would be those annals Coriolanus wishes to be preserved! The image of the eagle in a dovecote is magnificent—but it shows no gain in insight, no development beyond the limited self-awareness Coriolanus has always shown. At the crucial instant, Coriolanus shows himself still incapable of any understanding of relationship; still he must maintain his aloneness, still reject the epithet "boy," and still, therefore, remain something less than a full man.

And if the ending of *Coriolanus* leaves us with an uneasy sense of waste, the reason lies, I think, largely in this; for in this play, suffering does not bring to the sufferer any new understanding. The hero who from the outset would not demean himself with words still will not make that exploration of consciousness which might result in an expression to denote him truly. And what of those left behind?—for, as we have seen, the epitaphs spoken at the end contribute much to that sense of ritualized fulfillment we normally experience in Shakespeare's tragedies. The penultimate tableau—"*Draw both the Conspirators, and kils Martius, who falles, Auffidius stands on him*" (Folio reading)—is disturbing enough; but Aufidius's concluding speech is, to my mind, worse still:

> My rage is gone,
> And I am struck with sorrow. Take him up.
> Help, three o' th' chiefest soldiers; I'll be one.
> Beat thou the drum, that it speak mournfully;
> Trail your steel pikes. Though in this city he
> Hath widowed and unchilded many a one,
> Which to this hour bewail the injury,
> Yet he shall have a noble memory.
> Assist.

We could believe in Antony's "This was the noblest Roman of them all," spoken over Brutus; but Aufidius's sudden, inexplicable remorse is so hollow that it seems to me only to add insult to mortal injury. The final speech serves the practical need of clearing the stage, but its content is unearned and, like the cheers of the commoners which began the scene, is depressingly ironic. The effect is, I think, intentional, and however unusual for Shakespeare, right. For a part of the essential tragic experience is the effort to wrest an alphabet which will speak to men the wonder of life and death: Coriolanus refuses to make that effort; and though the "noble memory" the play leaves in the mind of its audience is real enough, it is (like the play's metonymic rhetoric) less conducive to imaginative expansion than the memory left by *Hamlet* or *King Lear*.

NOTES

1. D.J. Enright, "*Coriolanus:* Tragedy or Debate," *Essays in Criticism* 4 (1954), 4.

2. I take "metonymy" (the use of the name of one thing to represent another thing with which it is associated) as the general term, reserving "synecdoche" (the part for the whole, the species for the genus, etc.) for more specialized cases. Examples of "the thing contained for the container" are rare, but notable is the contribution James Thurber made in his studies with Miss Groby: "If a woman were to grab up a bottle of Grade A and say to her husband, 'Get away from me or I'll hit you with the milk,' that would be a Thing Contained for the Container" (*The Thurber Carnival* [New York, 1945], p. 53). Thanks to Prof. A. Walter Litz for recalling it to my attention.

3. Several writers have commented on the use of *voice* in the play: see especially Leonard F. Dean, "Voice and Deed in *Coriolanus*," *University of Kansas City Review* 21 (1955), 177–84; Norman Rabkin, *Shakespeare and the Common Understanding* (New York, 1967), pp. 134–35. (According to Dean, *voice* occurs forty-six times in the play; according to Rabkin, forty-one; Martin Spevak, *A Complete and Systematic Concordance to the Works of Shakespeare*, Vol. 3 [Hildesheim, 1968], gives twelve instances of *voice* and thirty-six of *voices*.)

4. "Appendix D: Four Master Tropes," *A Grammar of Motives* (1945; republished together with *A Rhetoric of Motives*, Cleveland, 1962), p. 508.

5. *The Imperial Theme* (London, 1931), p. 168.

6. *Grammar of Motives*, p. 508.

7. *Imperial Theme*, p. 155.

8. *A Miscellany* (London, 1929), p. 77. For similar comments about the play's style, see M. St. Clare Byrne, "Classical Coriolanus," *The National Review* 96 (1931), 426–30; Peter Alexander, *Shakespeare's Life and Art* (London, 1939), p. 179; H.J. Oliver, "Coriolanus as Tragic Hero," *Shakespeare Quarterly* 10 (1959), 53–60. Both Byrne and Oliver stress the "realism" of the play.

9. *Shakespeare's Roman Plays* (Cambridge, MA, 1961), pp. 31–32.

10. *Theory of Literature*, 2nd ed. (New York, 1956), pp. 183–85.

11. "Two Aspects of Language and Two Types of Aphasic Disturbance," in *Fundamentals of Language* (with Morris Halle) (The Hague, 1956), p. 76.

12. Ibid.

Reprinted by permission of Yale University Press from Lawrence Danson, Tragic Alphabet: Shakespeare's Drama of Language *(New Haven: Yale University Press, 1974), pp. 142–62. Copyright 1974 by Yale University Press.*

"There is a world elsewhere": Tragedy and History in *Coriolanus*

Patricia K. Meszaros

No other Shakespearean play has been so controversial and so variously interpreted as *Coriolanus*, but it may be said without too much oversimplification that criticism of it has generally taken one of four approaches. For a long time, discussion focused on the supposed aristocratic or democratic sympathies of the playwright. Perhaps in reaction to this overriding concern with politics, another group of commentators beginning with Swinburne has insisted that *Coriolanus* is the private, personal tragedy of a noble hero flawed by pride, immaturity, lack of self-knowledge, or an uncontrollable temper. A third group, more sophisticated than the first, sees neither fascist nor democratic leanings in the playwright, but nevertheless finds his treatment of politics very "modern"—i.e., unheroic, unidealistic, and unpleasant. They must usually conclude that the play's mode is unrelieved irony, if not satire. But illuminating studies of the "Elizabethan world picture" as the background of the English history plays have led other critics to view the Roman history from the same perspective. Seen in this light, *Coriolanus* becomes a "political tragedy," warning against revolt or violation of degree and order in the commonwealth. More recently, however, several critics have recognized that the background of the play is not Elizabethan but Jacobean, and that interpretation of its politics must be adjusted to a different world view.[1]

Because most of these approaches are not mutually incompatible, eclectic reading yields insights into almost every scene in *Coriolanus*. Yet it does not, I think, yield a very satisfying description of the nature of the play's tragic effect. The difficulty seems to lie in the necessity of reconciling tragic form, historical content, and a frequently ironic tone, without creating a genre that might have been named by Polonius.

In *Fools of Time: Studies in Shakespearean Tragedy* (Toronto, 1967), Northrop Frye makes some observations about tragedy and irony that make wonderful sense when applied to *Coriolanus*:

> The basis of the tragic vision is being in time, the sense of the one-directional quality of life, where everything happens once and for all, where every act brings unavoidable and fateful consequences.... Death is what defines the individual, and marks him off from the continuity of life that flows indefinitely between the past and the future (p.3).
>
> Being in time is not the whole of the tragic vision: it is, in itself, the ironic vision. Because it is the basis of the tragic vision, the ironic and the tragic are often confused or identified (pp. 3–4).
>
> What makes tragedy tragic, and not simply ironic, is the presence in it of a counter-movement of being that we call the heroic, a capacity for action or passion, for doing or suffering, which is above ordinary human experience (pp. 4–5).

The action of *Coriolanus* involves two related movements: the steady onward roll of history seen in the progress of the Roman state through a period of transition in its government, and the heroic curve of the life of Caius Marcius played out within it. The first movement is ironic, the second tragic.

A late and apparently experimental play, *Coriolanus* may have been Shakespeare's attempt to translate a sense of momentous political change in England into dramatic terms, following the Renaissance habit of using the past both to illuminate the present and to distance it for objective consideration. What the play reflects, in my view, is Shakespeare's peculiarly acute vision of the way in which political history—the fate of the *polis*—and tragedy—the fate of the individual—are interrelated in such a period of momentous change.

To support and develop this interpretation, I want to reemphasize the importance of the Jacobean context of *Coriolanus* and briefly describe certain of its aspects, in order to show how the classical story was molded to the form and pressure of the time.

As W.G. Zeeveld has shown, the specific political context of *Coriolanus* was the struggle for sovereignty in Parliament,[2] but the broader movement within which that struggle took place was the general weakening of belief in a universal natural law, with the Augustinian notion that all power is of God being replaced by the theory and practice of "politics" as an autonomous, secular activity. The Roman state in the play is not the medieval *respublica* or the body politic of the familiar "Elizabethan world picture," but the political entity described by Machiavelli and openly accepted as reality by Bacon. Shakespeare's play is perhaps the first great work of imaginative literature to portray the triumph of this new, essentially modern political and historical outlook over the old, essentially medieval one, and to examine the destiny of a noble human being caught in the historical process, the passing of an era.

For a thousand years European man had been able to see himself not only as a member of a body politic, the subject of a king, but also as a member of the larger and greater society of Christendom. The duties and privileges of the subject and the prince, the unquestionable moral and social framework reflecting "natural law," had been built into the divinely ordered commonwealth existing within the divinely ordered *respublica Christiana* within the divinely ordered universe. But the decentralization of Christendom and the rise of secular nations shattered this unified picture, and required a re-orientation of values toward the smaller, more immediate political entity, the state. In England, the re-orientation was fairly complete at the accession of James. The break with Rome followed by the long struggle for sovereignty between Crown and Parliament had brought about an increasing loss of faith in the concept of a permanently ordered commonwealth, and as the credibility of the concept diminished, so the word itself, "commonwealth," came gradually to be replaced by the word "state," with its more impersonal, mechanistic connotations. According to Philip Styles, the change took place within Shakespeare's lifetime, and he suggests that it can be traced through the plays.[3]

Indeed, a close analysis aided by the new Spevack *Concordance* and the *Oxford English Dictionary* reveals a striking fact: "state" in the sense of *OED* meaning 29 ("the political organization which is the basis of civil government . . . hence, the supreme civil power vested in a country or nation") appears in *Coriolanus* eighteen times by my count, or in about twice as many instances as in any of Shakespeare's other plays.[4] In contrast, "commonwealth," which appears eight times in *2 Henry VI*, occurs in *Coriolanus* only once (at IV.vi.14), unless we also count the rather attenuated circumlocutions "weal o' th' common" (I.i.146), and "body of the weal" (II.iii.176).[5]

What was the semantic value of "state" for Shakespeare and his Jacobean audience? I suggest that the word had come to stand for "commonwealth" emptied of its theological content, to signify a body politic subject to temporary secular control rather than to the working of eternal divine law. J.H. Hexter has shown that Machiavelli used the term *lo stato* with remarkable consistency to denote the object of exploitative control by the prince.[6] For Machiavelli, he says, the state was not a "matrix of values," but "the mechanism the prince uses to get what he wants" (p. 134). The chief concern of the prince (and of *The Prince*) was "come mantenere lo stato," or, as Garrett Mattingly puts it, "How to keep the government running and how to keep running the government."[7] Although it is unlikely that Shakespeare and his contemporaries could have used the word with Machiavelli's precision, it is nevertheless clear that Rome in *Coriolanus* is a state which everyone in the play except Caius Marcius wants, for different reasons and to varying degrees, to control, to exploit, to "maintain."

No hero in Shakespeare is so isolated as Caius Marcius. He takes Corioli alone, stands alone before the people in his gown of humility, suffers banishment alone, and finally dies alone in a foreign city, alienated from Roman and Volscian alike. This much the playwright found in his source. But he has constructed his play so that Marcius confides in no one (Cominius, who might have been a Horatio, is never permitted his function), and speaks only one soliloquy (IV.iv.12–26), which is more expository and formal than revelatory and personal. Moreover, the play lacks a commentator; neither a scurrilous Thersites nor a wise Fool offers a perspective on the hero's behavior. All these factors contribute to an opacity in his characterization. But although Granville-Barker is correct in pointing out that the introspection of a Hamlet or a Macbeth would be inappropriate for this man of action,[8] it also seems to me that Shakespeare has deliberately sacrificed perspicuousness in his hero in order to make clearer the nature of his tragedy. Coriolanus understands no one in the play and is understood by no one because he alone adheres to a world view which has ceased to be valid either for the other characters or for the play's Jacobean audience. He is "distanced" aesthetically because what he believes in and stands for is a remote and outmoded ideal. Marcius lives by a system in which human nature is an integral part of a Great Nature encompassing both *polis* and *cosmos;* the other characters live by a system which makes of politics a science answerable only to the necessity of maintaining the state and concerned with human qualities only as they are relevant to that end.

Indeed, the opening scene of *Coriolanus* raises the question whether individual "nature" and the common good are inevitably compatible. The people, who are incensed at their "chief enemy," Caius Marcius, because they hold him personally responsible for their famished condition, argue that his services to the country in war count for nothing, for he has always served his own pride and his mother's, not the country's good. Only one citizen protests: "What he cannot help in his nature, you account a vice in him" (I.i.38–39). We are reminded, though not very strongly, of the traditional view that since the individual and the body politic are parts of one harmonious Great Nature, what is good for the one must be good for the other. According to this view, Marcius' aristocratic pride is natural, just as it is natural that the body politic should have aristocrats to serve as its head.

Although the patrician Menenius ostensibly explains and justifies this very position, I think misunderstanding of this scene and its famous belly fable has been a major difficulty in criticism of the play. Some critics have accepted the fable as another statement of the Tudor political ideal, like Canterbury's beehive speech in *Henry V*, supposing it to be a standard against which subsequent behavior in the play is to be measured. For instance, J.E. Phillips writes, "Shakespeare examines the conduct of Coriolanus and the plebeians and shows how in each case failure to observe fundamental principles of political action set forth in the first scene [i.e., by Menenius] threatens to destroy the social organism designed by nature for the welfare of all."[9] Examined closely, however, the speech is ambiguous, the speaker suspect. Menenius is old, pleasure-loving, full of humours—hardly an ideal spokesman. The fable itself is introduced as a "pretty tale" (I.i.85), stale with frequent telling. Thus the importance of the fable is undercut while its political orthodoxy is made to seem at best old-fashioned, or at worst, if we accept M.M. Reese's interpretation, "a spurious conception of 'order' that ... represents the determination of the propertied classes to preserve the existing structure of society in their own interest."[10] Even the speech introducing the fable (I.i.61–74) is capable of ironic interpretation. Menenius asks the people to have faith in the "charitable care" of the patricians, "who care for you like fathers," since, in any case, they can do nothing to change the *status quo*. The "Roman state, whose course will on/The way it takes," appears to be not so much an instrument of benevolent natural law as a powerful juggernaut rolling over the helpless citizens. Far from providing a *locus classicus* for the play's political philosophy, the scene establishes Menenius as a "politic" man in the pejorative sense the word had already acquired in Shakespeare's time. Too complacent to be interested in controlling the state himself, he is at least bent on maintaining control of it for his class. He succeeds temporarily by voicing comfortable platitudes.

Sicinius and Brutus are far less subtle politicians, yet they know what they are about. Although they reveal the true nature of their concern when they speak to the people of Marcius as one who must be prevented from arriving at "a place of potency and sway o' the *state*," they remember to flatter the plebeians by mentioning "Your liberties and charters that you bear/I' the *body of the weal*" (II.iii.172–77; italics mine). The Tribunes pay lip service in this rather oblique phrase to the *commonwealth*, but when they think of power, they speak of the *state*. Later, at the scene of his banishment, they cynically describe Coriolanus as "a foe to th' public weal" (III.i.175). But their last reference to the body politic is charged with unconscious dramatic irony; they are in power, Coriolanus is banished, and Sicinius taunts Menenius:

> Your Coriolanus
> Is not much missed, but with his friends.
> The commonwealth doth stand, and so would do,
> Were he more angry at it. (IV.vi.12–15)

We know, of course, that Rome is in imminent danger of destruction.

For the Tribunes, then, as for Menenius, the commonwealth is a convenient fiction, not a vital reality. Because they see the state merely as a source of power, they have no end in view for Rome itself, but have constantly to shape their policy to meet the exigencies of the moment, now manipulating the people, now appeasing the senators (as when they allow Coriolanus' sentence to be mitigated from death to banishment), but always serving the immediate end of maintaining their political control. They do not understand Marcius because they can conceive of no position *vis à vis* the state but their own, and therefore wrongly attribute to him motives similar to theirs. From the beginning they have feared his consulship because it would weaken the power of the Tribunate. They see their conflict with Coriolanus quite simply as a power struggle. When they first hear that the banished Marcius is leading the Volscian forces to the gates of Rome, both Tribunes interpret the news as a rumor, another move in a political chess game:

> Sic.   This is most likely!
> Bru. Raised only, that the weaker sort may wish
>   Good Marcius home again.
> Sic.   The very trick on't. (IV.vi.69–71)

When they find that Marcius does indeed intend to burn the city, they are completely shattered. With rumors, machinations calculated to raise a faction for Coriolanus in the city, they could cope; the possibility that the city may be destroyed around them leaves them baffled, for this is not a "politic" move and so has never been dreamt of in their philosophy.

Menenius wants control of the state for his class, the Tribunes want it for themselves, but Volumnia wants it for her son, and she sees his martial success as a means to it. Archetypal Roman matron though she seems to be, Volumnia's views are as modern as Machiavelli's. For her, power is honor, and honor is power. She wants Coriolanus to use his honor (synonymous in her mind with glory) won in battle to gain political control. Instead, he loses honor in her eyes by failing to grasp power when it is within his reach.

Clearly, Marcius is isolated from his class, the governors of his city, and his family, for the representatives of all three live in a world whose existence he cannot or will not admit. *His* Rome is a commonwealth whose welfare and glory are inseparable from his own. It is not conceit, but his profound sense of the eternal fitness of things that leads him to answer honestly when the plebeians ask his reason for requesting the consulship: "Mine own desert," but "not mine own desire" (II.iii.63,65). Because "politics" does not exist for him, he can recognize neither the need to assure his control of the state by accommodating himself to the expectations of the populace, nor the need to handle Brutus and Sicinius with circumspection and out-maneuver them in their bid for power. When he speaks of the Roman "state," he does not use the word in the modern sense. He envisions a body politic in which plebeians and patricians, citizens and senators, are bound by inherent duties and prerogatives, as his most impassioned political speech makes clear:

> Therefore, beseech you,—
> You that will be less fearful than discreet;
> That love the fundamental part of *state*
> More than you doubt the change on 't; that prefer
> A noble life before a long, and wish
> To jump a body with a dangerous physic
> That's sure of death without it—at once pluck out
> The multitudinous tongue; let them not lick
> The sweet which is their poison. (III.i.149–57)

"There is a world elsewhere"

He uses "state" here in the sense of "the rulers, nobles, or great men of a realm" (*OED* meaning 26, now obsolete), urging the senators who love their fundamental right to govern to apply strong physic to a body politic in danger of death. Ironically, this highly conservative speech is interrupted by the Tribunes' cry of "traitorous innovator" (III.i.174)

Marcius' reaction to the absurdity of what follows, his sentence of banishment, is to reverse its terms. Rome has been the mirror reflecting his ideas of honor and order; now it shows him a distorted, fragmented image. *He* has remained constant, but his commonwealth has turned traitor to itself. "*I* banish *you!*" he cries, "There is a world elsewhere" (III.iii.124,136).

From his point of view, therefore, Marcius' alliance with the Volscians is not treachery. As he takes leave of this friends and family in Rome, he says,

> While I remain above the ground, you shall
> Hear from me still, and never of me aught
> But what is like me formerly. (IV.i.51–53)

I see no reason to doubt his self-knowledge, nor to posit a change of heart before he appears at the gate of Antium. If Marcius' beliefs can indeed be identified with that system of values now labeled medieval, it is possible that his search for a "world elsewhere" is for another part of what might be called in a play not distanced by a classical Roman setting the *respublica Christiana*. He seeks the return of an order he believes to be universal.

It is possible, too, that contemporary theatrical conditions would have supported this interpretation. When Aufidius' servant asks him where he dwells, Coriolanus answers, "Under the canopy" (IV.v.38), rejecting a specific nationality and referring to his home beneath the heavens—the painted underside of the roof over the playhouse stage. And just as the same painted stars shone on Rome and Antium alike, so the tiring-house facade, by serving as both the gates of Rome and the gates of Antium (not to mention those of Corioli), underscored the idea that individual cities are microcosms fulfilling similar functions within the macrocosm, rather than unique, autonomous entities.[11]

Understandably, Coriolanus seeks the "world elsewhere" in the city of his former enemy, Aufidius, since he sees the Volscian general almost as an *alter ego*: "And were I any thing but what I am," he has said, "I would wish me only he" (I.i.226–27). Because he identifies with Aufidius as a warrior, Marcius assumes that he will find his own values reflected in the Volscian and his state. His tragic error is therefore one of judgment, not of principle; Coriolanus fails to recognize that Aufidius is as "politic" and concerned with winning and holding power as the Roman Tribunes are. Unlike Brutus and Sicinius, though, Aufidius is capable of reflecting upon the nature of power rather than just calculating his next move. In a long monologue spoken to his lieutenant (IV.vii.28–57), he articulates the new assumptions against which Marcius has been blindly struggling. Our virtues, he says,

> Lie in th' interpretation of the time;
> And power, unto itself most commendable,
> Hath not a tomb so evident as a chair
> T' extol what it hath done. (IV.vii.50–53)

Whereas Coriolanus believes that his natural superiority gives him an absolute right to rule, Aufidius knows that excellence itself is relative, and that nothing insures its recognition so much as a seat of power from which to display it. For the present, Coriolanus has virtues which Aufidius himself can use, but only temporarily: "When, Caius, Rome is thine,/Thou art poor'st of all; then shortly art thou mine" (IV.vii.56–57). It is interesting, though, that while Aufidius claims that Marcius' virtue has a purely relative and temporary value, to be used as a means to an end, he also says,

> I think he'll be to Rome
> As is the osprey to the fish, who takes it
> By sovereignty of nature. (IV.vii.33–35)

This seems to be a remnant of the old belief in a hierarchical order of nature—the belief which motivates all of Coriolanus' actions. For Aufidius, though, it is no more than a metaphor. Even if Coriolanus were to take Rome by "sovereignty of nature," Aufidius, who recognizes such superiority only as another weapon in his arsenal, would be standing behind him, ready to take over and maintain control of the state.

"Sovereignty of nature" is no longer efficacious in itself, in a world where men like Aufidius and the Tribunes are willing to pay lip service to it to gain their private ends. Only one person in the play has yet to learn this lesson. Until confronted by his wife, his son, and his mother as supplicants, Coriolanus has believed that his personal honor and natural sovereignty are inseparably linked in the order of things, that personal and political morality are one. Then, in a blinding flash the world he has been inhabiting without understanding breaks upon his consciousness, and he sees that by persisting in a system of beliefs and values long since abandoned by those around him, he has created a situation in which the demands of "nature" are fragmented and conflicting.

In order to yield to his natural impulse to save his family, Coriolanus must not only betray his new allies, but also recognize as treachery his adoption of their cause. At first, in an attempt to salvage some of his honor and to avoid labeling himself a double traitor, he would have "All bond and privilege of nature, break!" (V.iii.25). Like Shakespeare's great villains, Iago and Edmund, he would stand "As if a man were author of himself/And knew no other kin" (V.iii.36–37). But recognizing even in the midst of this resolve that his mother and son have claims on him which "Great Nature cries, 'Deny not!'" (V.iii.33), he finally chooses to remain true to a system of belief which even he now sees to be no longer viable. A man like Coriolanus, self-defined by interlocking loyalties to family, class, and commonwealth, and by his belief in a Great Nature under which all loyalties are subsumed, cannot be "author of himself." When he yields to Volumnia and "holds her by the hand, silent," he is truly tragic; understanding the true nature of his fate, he has chosen and accepted it:

> O mother, mother!
> What have you done? Behold, the heavens do ope,
> The gods look down, and this unnatural scene
> They laugh at. (V.iii.182–85)

The scene is "unnatural" for many reasons, but partly because Volumnia has done what Coriolanus himself could not do—she has sacrificed her son for the state:

> O my mother, mother! O!
> You have won a happy victory to Rome;
> But for your son—believe it, O believe it!—
> Most dangerously you have with him prevailed,
> If not most mortal to him. But let it come. (V.iii.185–89)

The Roman matron's triumph is as bitter as her son's sacrifice. Rome's salvation is obviously only temporary, for it is the nature of policy to win ephemeral victories that must be guarded and preserved by its continued exercise. Aufidius, after all, still has his troops ready, and Rome has lost the great warrior who saved her before. Back in Antium, Aufidius takes stock of his situation: he must get rid of Marcius, but not before he knows the mood of the people (V.vi.12–16). Assured of their discontent, he accuses Coriolanus of treachery in a scene that closely parallels the earlier accusation by the Tribunes. This time, there are no sympathetic patricians to intervene, and when the mob finally parts we see an emblematic tableau: the politic Aufidius stands on the body of the noble Coriolanus.

The politician survives, the play says, because it is his business to do so. It also says that the man who will not bend his principles to policy, who will not admit that the supposedly immutable laws by which the commonwealth is governed are really subject to control by men, is doomed to destruction. At the same time, it looks closely at one of those men, and celebrates the absolute value, the stark dignity, of a life dedicated to honor and true to a faith in divine order. Northrop Frye's description of the effect of the tragic experience fits *Coriolanus* perfectly: we feel that "the heroic and the infinite have been; the human and finite are" (*Fools of Time*, p. 6).

Some critics, attempting to explain the relationship of tragedy and history in *Coriolanus,* have identified Rome itself as the play's protagonist.[12] Zeeveld sees the fall of Caius Marcius as a personal tragedy "involving and precipitating a larger political tragedy" (p. 321). But the fate of Rome (and of England) is *history*, not tragedy. The state is not involved in the fall of Caius Marcius; there is no "cease of majesty" here. Indeed, in

Coriolanus alone of all Shakespeare's great tragedies (I discount *Timon*), the only death is that of the hero.[13] He dies alone, surrounded by the enemy, with no Horatio to tell his story, no Malcolm or Albany to restore order to the commonwealth, no Antony to praise him as "the noblest Roman of them all." The city and its people go on without him, even as they had chosen to do when they exiled him. From the beginning of the play it has been clear that Rome is not a commonwealth but a state, autonomous and amoral; and since no moral rottenness can be purged by the death of Coriolanus, the state cannot participate in his moral triumph. It is exempt from both the tragic suffering and the tragic exaltation of the hero. It is subject only to history.

It is history, then, that involves and precipitates the personal tragedy of Caius Marcius Coriolanus. He is the victim of political, historical forces outside his control and beyond his understanding. As a time-bound human being, he is destroyed because he resists the inexorable force which would move him along in the stream of history. As a tragic hero adhering to what he takes to be absolute values, he triumphs, even in defeat, over those forces. Thus Shakespeare has given us in *Coriolanus* a double vision of man as victim of historical forces and man as victor over them. He has placed the tragic movement of the individual life within the larger, ironic movement of history. But the tragic vision prevails.

Notes

1. It is impracticable to list here all the critical discussions of *Coriolanus* falling into one or more of these categories, and a selection would be invidious. Recent criticism that I have found particularly helpful for a study of the play in its Jacobean context includes Kenneth Burke, "*Coriolanus*—and the Delights of Faction," *Hudson Review*, 19 (1966), 185–202; David G. Hale, "*Coriolanus:* The Death of a Political Metaphor," *Shakespeare Quarterly* 22 (1971), 197–202 [on the inadequacy of the belly fable as an analogy for the body politic]; and Clifford C. Huffman, *Coriolanus in Context* (Lewisburg, 1972), a very thorough

study of "mixed government" as the background of the play, which appeared as this essay was being written. My argument parallels Huffman's at certain points; however, both our approaches and our conclusions are different (though I think complementary).

2. "*Coriolanus* and Jacobean Politics," *MLR*, 57 (1962), 321–34. E.C. Pettet, "*Coriolanus* and the Midlands Insurrection of 1607," *Shakespeare Survey* 3 (1950), 34–42, suggests that specific current events may have influenced Shakespeare's treatment of Plutarch's narrative.

3. "The Commonwealth," *Shakespeare Survey* 17 (1964), 113.

4. *The Merchant of Venice* has nine instances, *Henry VIII* between seven and ten (the number is approximate because some instances are ambiguous). Although *Merchant* is a comparatively early play, its setting in the great Renaissance republic may account for the frequent appearance of "state" in the play, as G.N. Clark suggests. In *The Birth of the Dutch Republic* (London 1946), Clark argues for a direct connection between the rise of independent states in the Netherlands and the use of "state" in the modern sense in English. He mentions Shakespeare's use of the word, but seems to have overlooked *Coriolanus*, since he finds "state' commoner in *The Merchant of Venice* "than in any of his other plays" (pp. 27–29).

5. All quotations and line references are taken from Harry Levin's edition of *Coriolanus* for *The Complete Pelican Shakespeare*, gen. ed. Alfred Harbage (Baltimore, 1969).

6. "*Il principe* and *lo stato*," *SR* 4 (1957), 113–38.

7. "Changing Attitudes towards the State during the Renaissance," in William H. Werkmeister, ed., *Facets of the Renaissance* (New York, 1963), p. 29. Unable to make use of Hexter's work, which appeared between the delivery of this lecture and its publication, Mattingly refers to it in a footnote as "brilliant and persuasive" (p. 39, note 32).

8. *Prefaces to Shakespeare* (Princeton, 1946), III, 99–100.

9. *The State in Shakespeare's Greek and Roman Plays* (New York, 1940), p. 10. In his edition of *Coriolanus* for the New Cambridge Shakespeare (Cambridge, 1960), J. Dover Wilson says that the belly fable was intended to set forth "the point of view of all right-minded persons in [Shakespeare's] audience" (p. xx), and W. Gordon Zeeveld describes it, in *The Temper of Shakespeare's Thought* (New Haven, 1974), as "axiomatic to his audience and to Shakespeare, a self-evident defense of commonwealth" (p. 102).

10. *The Cease of Majesty* (New York, 1961), p. 141.

11. For an interesting discussion of the emblematic significance of the tiring house facade, see George R. Kernodle, "The Open Stage: Elizabethan or Existentialist?" *Shakespeare Survey* 12 (1959), 1–7.

12. Donald A. Stauffer writes in *Shakespeare's World of Images* (New York, 1949), "The state is more important than any of its members," and "Rome . . . is the hero of this play" (pp. 249, 252). According to D.J. Enright, "The tragedy is the tragedy of Rome: its sickness is traced to a pronounced lack of self-understanding both in its people and in Coriolanus." See "*Coriolanus:* Tragedy or Debate?" *Essays in Criticism* 4 (1954), 15. In *Shakespearean Tragedy: Its Art and Its Christian Premises* (Bloomington, IN, 1969), Roy W. Battenhouse offers an extended reading of *Coriolanus* from "an Augustinian perspective" ("The Reshaped Meaning of *Coriolanus*," pp. 303–74). Augustine's "definition of Rome's tragic flaw" (p. 308), he argues, supplied Shakespeare with a historical perspective unavailable to Plutarch, enabling him to shape a "symbolic statement of pagan deficiencies" (p. 374). Thus the story of Coriolanus "becomes under Shakespeare's revision the tragedy of an ethos" (p. 310).

13. Frye remarks, "The more ironic the tragedy, the fewer the central characters who die" (*Fools of Time,* p. 6).

Reprinted by permission from Patricia K. Meszaros, "'There is a world elsewhere': Tragedy and History in Coriolanus," Studies in English Literature 16 (1976), 273–85. Copyright 1976 by Studies in English Literature.

Coriolanus and Stavisky: The Interpenetration of Art and Politics

Felicia Hardison Londré

Repeatedly throughout French theatre history two subjects have aroused the passions of the French theatregoer: art and politics. The famous opening-night riots at *Le Cid* in 1636, *Hernani* in 1830, and *Ubu roi* in 1896 all resulted in the overthrow of stale artistic conventions by the new art that each of these works represented. Examples of productions that had political repercussions are abundant—like the historical dramas of Marie-Joseph Chénier that did so much to promote the French Revolution (until his *Caius Gracchus* in 1792 caused a backlash demonstration), or the 1943 Comédie-Française production of Claudel's mystico-religious *Soulier de satin* that was gleefully interpreted by the French in German-occupied Paris as "resistance theatre." One noteworthy theatrical event that succeeded in arousing both artistic and political passions was not even a French play—nor was it contemporary, although the most often-repeated comment about it was: "It seems to have been written just yesterday."[1] This was a production of Shakespeare's *Coriolanus* at the Comédie-Française in the 1933–34 season, just at the time when the Third Republic was nearly toppled by the public's response to press revelations of the Stavisky scandal.

Sacha Stavisky's name was unknown to all but a few people when *Coriolan* opened on 9 December 1933 to an enthusiastic audience and rave reviews. Three weeks into the play's run (in repertory), newspapers began carrying stories of "the Stavisky affair," which soon grew into a *cause célèbre*. The implication that this rogue and swindler was intimate with and protected by elected officials, including two Cabinet members, shattered the French people's confidence in their government,[2] and helped to foment the tragic street demonstrations of 6 February 1934 that left fifteen dead and 1,326 wounded. The public—already discontented by economic tribulations and demoralized by the low level of international esteem to which France had clearly fallen at the Geneva Conference of October 1933—found an outlet for its sense of rage and frustration at performances of *Coriolan*. In these disturbances, the rumble of revolution came from the right. Royalists, feeling vindicated by mounting evidence that parliamentary government was not working, cheered the lines of dialogue that characterized the Plebeians as a fickle, unthinking mob. But even moderates found Shakespeare's text uncannily apt in its expression of sentiments that many felt toward the left-wing government then in power. In this line, for example, Coriolanus seemed to refer directly to the government corruption revealed by the Stavisky scandal:

> Your dishonour
> Mangles true judgment and bereaves the state
> Of that integrity which should become't,
> Not having the power to do the good it would,
> For th'ill which doth control't. (III,i)

The French translation of those lines was: "Votre douceur nous perd, elle nous déshonore. Semblable politique ôte au gouvernement l'unité hors laquelle il n'est pas de gouvernement. Vous désirez le bien, et vous ne pouvez plus faire le bien, car vous vous soumettez au contrôle du mal."[3]

Thus we might say that the patrician, self-contained Coriolanus and the charming but unscrupulous Stavisky—one fictional and one real-life figure—emerged as prototypes of the public's perception of the political right and left respectively. The intermingling of art and politics represented by these two figures takes many interesting forms. Stavisky himself was attracted to the theatre, and two of his earliest swindles were theatre-related;[4] eventually he took over the Empire Music Hall, which offered one of the best shows of the 1932 Paris season.[5] Not only did Coriolanus and Stavisky both envisage themselves at the apex of an Empire, but both adored their wives, both had only

Coriolanus and Stavisky

sons, and both acquired new names at critical junctures in their careers. Coriolanus, formerly Caius Martius, earned his name by conquering the city of Corioli. Sacha Stavisky assumed the new identity of Serge Alexandre in 1927 when, after his release from prison, he began undertaking ever more grandiose schemes and upgraded his lifestyle accordingly.[6] There is even a kind of serendipity in Stavisky's choice of the name Alexandre; in the Comédie-Française production, Coriolanus was played by an actor who used the single name Alexandre! Although Stavisky was accepted among the smart set at Deauville and elsewhere, he remained essentially "a gentlemen among gangsters, a gangster among gentlemen."[7] Although Menenius says of Coriolanus, "his nature is too noble for the world" (III. i), Frank Kermode comments that if "nobility " "consists in the licensed rage of war, [Coriolanus] is noble enough to be a god; if it is the conduct of a man in civil society, he is a beast."[8] One final parallel between these two opposing figures is the manner of their deaths. Coriolanus is killed by those whom he had made his allies, the Volscians, whom he had successfully led in battle. Stavisky's death, in the first week of January 1934, in a hilltop villa at Chamonix, was reported as a suicide, but circumstances suggested that he was killed by his former protectors, the police, who had profited from his schemes, but found it necessary to get rid of him because he knew too much.

That background provides an interesting context for examining various aspects of the 1933–34 Comédie-Française production of *Coriolan*. At the time, some of the blame for the demonstrations in the theatre was placed on the translation by René-Louis Piachaud, a Swiss journalist, poet, and critic, who had previously translated *Othello*, *A Midsummer Night's Dream*, and *The Merry Wives of Windsor*. According to *The Times* (20 February 1934), "M. Piachaud, who lives in Geneva and emerges as seldom as possible from the seventeenth century, was suspected to have been summoned to Paris as a dangerous reactionary engaged in political propaganda under cover of an apparently harmless devotion to ancient texts. With most of the reputable critics of France and his distinguished services to literature behind him, M. Piachaud made short work of his detractors."[9] For one thing, Piachaud had begun work on the translation as early as 1929, a more stable moment in France; and it was apparently done at the suggestion of an actor, Léon Bernard, who coveted the role of Menenius, which he did get to play and for which he won unanimous praise from the critics. Piachaud submitted his translation to Lugné-Poe, who in turn recommended it to M. de Monzie, Ministre de l'Education nationale. With the double recommendation of de Monzie and M. Mistler, sous-secrétaire d'Etat aux Beaux-Arts, the manuscript went to the Comité de Lecture of the Comédie-Française and was unanimously accepted on 30 May 1932. When the theatre's chief administrator Emile Fabre returned from a trip and read the manuscript, he was worried about certain passages that he saw as possibly provocative, given the average Fenchman's readiness to fulminate against elected representatives, regardless of their party affiliation. Fabre made his apprehensions known to de Monzie, who then submitted the text for review by two noted Anglicists, Louis Gillet and M. l'inspecteur général Garnier.[10] Their verdict was that Piachaud "avait suivi scrupuleusement le texte de Shakespeare et que certaines expressions, loin de dépasser la pensée du génial dramaturge anglais, se trouvaient plutôt adoucies par notre langage."[11] Thus sanctioned, Fabre decided to direct the play himself, since the staging of crowd scenes was a particular specialty of his. Fabre's precautions are significant in the light of his later dismissal from his post.

On the other hand, after examining both the Comédie-Française promptbook and the published text of Piachaud's translation, Ruby Cohn has shown that there are a few instances in which the adaptation betrays "Piachaud's anti-Plebeian sentiment."[12] Her strongest example comes at the end of a scene in which the tribunes, Brutus and Sicinius, stir up Plebeian sentiment against Coriolanus (II.iii); there Piachaud gave them added exit lines, as if to underscore the tribunes' hypocrisy:

> Brutus: Les tribuns n'ont rien fait!
> Sicinius: Les tribuns n'ont rien vu!
> Brutus: Les tribuns n'ont rien su!

Another instance occurs in Coriolanus's stirring speech to the Plebeians after they have banished him (III.iii). Cohn implies that Piachaud invented the line, "Romains dégénérés, vos pires ennemis, c'est vous-mêmes,"[13] but reference to Shakespeare's original suggests that this is actually an example of the aforementioned "softening" of the text, which might also be called "gross simplification." This is Shakespeare's original from which Piachaud distilled "Degenerate Romans, you are your own worst enemies":

> Have the power still
> To banish your defenders, till at length
> Your ignorance (which finds not till it feels,
> Making but reservations of yourselves,
> Still your own foes) deliver you as most
> Abated captives to some nation
> That won you without blows!

Certainly, Piachaud cut Shakespeare's fourth longest play "afin que *Coriolan* pût être joué entre 8h.15 et minuit"[14] but also to stress Coriolanus's heroism and downplay his treason. Fabre's stage compositions set Coriolanus apart from all the other characters, his solitary splendour in the crowd scenes emphasizing the great gulf between him and the Plebeian masses portrayed by over one hundred extras.[15]

With hindsight, two factors allow us to conclude that the perceived pro-Fascist slant of the production "was in the times rather than the text."[16] First, the translation was revived at the Comédie-Française in 1956 in a theatricalist production that "sparked no controversies, nor even much enthusiasm."[17] Second, theatre audiences in the early months of 1934 were reacting vociferously to isolated lines in even quite innocuous plays like Musset's *Un Caprice*, written in 1837. One line in this charming little domestic comedy elicited an anti-democratic uproar: "Ce sont de drôles d'auberges que ce minstères. On y entre et on en sort sans savoir pourquoi. C'est une procession de marionnettes." One reviewer recalled having seen a production of *Un Caprice* forty years earlier, starring Mounet-Sully, and even then the line was greeted with laughter and applause. He commented that the audience really ought instead to cry out: "C'est faux! Les ministères ne sont pas de drôle d'auberges. On s'y installe, on y demeure. On ne s'en laisse pas déloger." This same theatre reviewer ventured further that "les manifestations de la Comédie-Française sont un signe des temps. Des fautes persistantes affaiblissent le régime et compromettent son existence. Les régimes défunts n'ont pas été tués; ils se sont tués. Il est temps que notre parlementarisme démocratique fasse un effort pour reconquérir l'affection du pays s'il tient à éviter un sort semblable."[18] At a performance of Victor Hugo's *Ruy Blas*, the invocation "O! ministres intègres..." brought catcalls from the audience. *La Carcasse*, a contemporary comedy by Denys Amiel and André Obey, perceived as insulting to the French Army, occasioned an uproar in the house, challenges hurled at the Chambre des députés, and riots in the square outside the theatre.[19] The unreasonableness of these demonstrations was pointed out by a number of theatre critics. Most were able to distinguish between the genuine artistic merit of the production of *Coriolan* and the spurious appropriation of some aphorisms by political factions. A reviewer who attended the performance on 3 January noted that most of the applause for lines deriding elections and extolling the power of central authority emanated from the cheapest seats, but then he went on to comment: "Que nos luttes actuelles aient de l'écho dans la salle de la rue Richelieu les soirs qu'on joue *Coriolan* et que les adversaires de nos institutions démocratiques et parlementaires se placent sous le patronage de Shakespeare, c'est, je crois, une fâcheuse absurdité.[20]

Coriolan was a clear artistic triumph when it opened on 9 December 1933. It was welcomed all the more enthusiastically because French theatre was at a low ebb just then. Only a year before, the Manchester *Guardian*'s Paris correspondent had detailed his diagnosis that the "French stage of to-day" was "not in the best of health."[21] The world economic crisis was hurting theatre in general, and the state subsidy of the Comédie-Française in particular was far from adequate. Fabre, however, spared no expense in mounting *Coriolan*. André Boll's elaborate sets were at once stylized and archaeologically accurate:

> Quant aux décors que M. André Boll a su styliser, tout en respectant la vérité archéologique, ils accomplissent ce miracle de nous restituer une Rome étrangement vivante, grandiose san doute, mais "habitable." Elle s'oppose avec adresse à la Coriole des Volsques aux demeures plus simples, encore un peu barbares. La vision du Capitole, avec ses gradins, ses escaliers couverts d'une foule

grouillante, la vision surtout de Rome vue du haut du Palatin, alors que le soleil joue sur les toits plats, les terrasses à l'italienne, est une des meilleures réussites scéniques qu'ils nous ait été donné de voir depuis longtemps au théâtre, non seulement en France, mais dans le monde.[22]

Many reviewers praised Fabre's blocking of the Roman Plebeians "avec tout son pittoresque, ses violences, sa perpétuelle diversité."[23] Their 285 costumes designed by M. Bétout were all different from one another but unified by the use of various neutral hues.[24] Raymond Charpentier's original music evocatively underscored the play's many moods: military heroism, savagery, lyric tendresse, lamentation.[25] Critical praise for individual performances[26] tended to be as effusive as André Antoine's overall assessment in *L'Information* (12 December 1933): "Au point de vue de l'interprétation, il y a longtemps que nous n'avions eu, rue Richelieu, un aussi heureux ensemble."[27]

The enthusiasm that greeted *Coriolan* is further exemplified by the title of the leading article in *Comœdia* (9 December 1933): "La répétition générale est une grande date du Théâtre." That preview performance on 8 December had culminated in twenty curtain calls and enraptured cries of "Vive Fabre!" directed toward the administrator's box. The critic Gabriel Boissy added: "C'est peut-être aussi une grande journée pour la France. Chaque fois que notre pays se trouve à la croisée des chemins, qu'il hésite et qu'il ne sait trop d'ou s'élève la vérité, on a vu soit de la littérature, soit du théâtre paraître un de ces appels qui orientent les esprits timides ou incertains."[28]

The striking contemporary applicability of so many lines in the play was recognized by the public even from the opening performances. At performances in December 1933, that recognition was manifested by enthusiastic applause for the stirring long speeches. The fact that France had seen two changes of government since October (Daladier replaced by Sarraut in October, Sarraut replaced by Chautemps in November) gave special significance to the lines spoken by Coriolanus in III.i:

> This double worship,
> Where one part does disdain with cause, the other
> Insult without all reason; where gentry, title, wisdom

Cannot conclude but by the yea or no
Of general ignorance—it must omit
Real necessities, and give way the while
To unstable slightness.

Piachaud's rendering of those lines reads: "Partout, quand le pouvoir se trouve divisé, partout quand le savoir, le rang, et la noblesse voient leurs décisions dépendre, en fin de compte, ou d'un 'oui' ou d'un 'non' de la foule imbécile, je dis que là, fatalement, la faiblesse est chez elle, et le désordre règne."[29]

The new Premier Ministre, Camille Chautemps, understood the uneasiness about the rapid changes of government and, more practically, he succeeded in stabilizing France's financial situation. He came under attack, however, from the right-wing newspaper *Action Française,* which had long served as a vehicle for the reactionary ideas of Charles Maurras and Léon Daudet. *Action Française* gave its name to a militant right-wing movement that probably numbered about 60,000 adherents in the early 1930s.[30] Its criticism of Chautemps was based on nothing more serious than the fact that Chautemps's government was merely another Radical (left-wing) Party government that was more narrowly based than the Radical government it had just replaced. An unforeseeable series of events fortuitously gave credence to *Action Française'*s seemingly "prophetic" anti-Parliamentary campaign.[31] On 23 December, the Paris-Strasbourg express crashed into the Paris-Nancy commuter train at Lagny, only ten miles from Paris. 219 people, including many children going home for the Christmas holidays, were killed. The disaster was magnified by the fact that railway authorities were slow to notify the police, and medical services were delayed for many hours, so that—in addition to those who were killed—over 350 wounded men, women, and children lay on a railway embankment most of the night in temperatures below freezing. A public clamour arose against "the directors of the railway, who were Duputies and financiers, the friends and supporters of Ministers."[32] 23 December also happened to be the date of the arrest of Tissier, the manager of the Bayonne *Crédit Municipal,* which served as the front for Stavisky's Bayonne Bonds swindle,[33] and that was the date that Stavisky, alias Serge

Alexandre, disappeared, supposedly "with connivance of the authorities."[34]

The facts about Stavisky's life and career came out in the press during the first week in January 1934. The public learned that this underworld "king of Paris" had been granted "liberté provisoire" through nineteen postponements of his trial during the six years since his 1927 release from prison. It seemed clear that Stavisky could not have got away with six years of financial adventurism without the protection of the judiciary, some highly placed goverment officials, and the police. On 3 January, *Action Française* published two letters that had been written by the Minister of Labour, Dalimier, in June and September 1932, promoting the sale of Bayonne Bonds. This shook the credibility of the government in the eyes of the whole country, not just the Royalists.[35] Newspapers across the entire political spectrum took up the issue, led by *Action Française*, which headlined "A bas les voleurs!" The 7 January issue contains these inflammatory words: "There is no law and no justice in a country where magistrates and the police are the accomplices of criminals. The honest people of France who want to protect their own interests, and who care for the cleanliness of public life, are forced to take the law into their own hands."[36] Chautemps did not grasp the intensity of public sentiment and blundered terribly in rejecting a proposed parliamentary Commission d'enquête into the Stavisky affair. To make matters worse for Chautemps, it was his own brother-in-law, M. Pressard, the chief public prosecutor of Paris, who had been responsible for many of the nineteen postponements of Stavisky's prosecution. According to Alexander Werth, "the public naturally wondered whether that did not account for M. Chautemps's opposition to the formation of a committee of inquiry. In France two and two always make four."[37] The Chautemps government fell on 27 January.

It is not surprising that the disturbances at performances of *Coriolan* intensified during those weeks in January 1934. The whole audience reacted appreciatively when a joker in the top gallery called out, at the entrance of the tribunes Brutus and Sicinius: "Eh! visez-les! V'là Léon Blum et Paul Boncour." (Léon Blum was the leader of the Socialist Party in the Chambre des députés, and Paul Boncour was the Foreign Minister under

Chautemps.) The entrance of the Lictors clearing the way for the Tribunes in II.ii, was often greeted with some smart remark in the house; "Police! police!," cried a good-humoured wag one evening to the delight of his fellow spectators.[38] The Left occasionally made its feelings known at performances. On 17 January the occupant of a first-gallery box began whistling to disrupt the performance. Finally, an irritated audience member stood up and called out, "Monsieur est sans doute député?" The whistling continued, unperturbed. It was then noted that the heckler occupied the box reserved for the Conseil municipal. He was not himself a city councillor, but a guest. The leftist had obtained his seat courtesy of an elected official of the right![39] At another performance, reported on 27 January, the usual enthusiasm that followed Coriolanus's stirring Act III, scene ii, anti-Republican speech was countered by a strident whistle from one of the galleries. Chaos ensued. Here is the report published in the *Œil de Paris*:

> Ce fut un désordre indescriptible. Dans le tumulte, on entendait: "Vive la République! Hou! A la porte les siffleurs!" Et même: "Bravo, Hitler!"
>
> Devant tout ce bruit les gardes municipaux étaient impuissants et ne savaient où cueillir l'initiateur du scandale. Tout au plus purent-ils séparer deux quidams à l'orchestre, qui commençaient à se prendre aux cheveux.
>
> Sur scène, c'était le désarroi complet. Les comédiens continuaient à dire leur texte personne n'écoutait, et M. Léon Bernard dut recommencer trois fois la même phrase, avant qu'un de ses camarades lui répondit. Certains acteurs crièrent au semainier qui, dans un coin, levait les bras vers les cintres! "Baissez le rideau!" Mais le brave homme affolé, ne savait que faire.
>
> C'est un électricien qui, de lui-même, rendit la lumière à la salle, dans la pensée sans doute qu'on allait interrompre la représentation. Là-dessus, le bruit cessa comme par enchantement. De tous côtés on entendit: "Chut! chut!" et M. Alexandre enchaîna.[40]

Edouard Daladier succeeded Chautemps as Premier Ministre, and this brought several days of calm. The streets became even quieter after 1 February, when the Paris taxi drivers went on strike to protest against a new petrol tax. Then Daladier made two great blunders, one political and one artistic. On 3 February, in a blatant play for Socialist support in the formation of his new government, Daladier dismissed Jean Chiappe from his post as prefect of the Paris police. (Chiappe—whose personal involvement with Stavisky was never precisely determined—was noted for his harsh treatment of Communists in contrast to his leniency toward Royalist street demonstrators.) Many segments of the public were infuriated by the sacking of Chiappe, who was a popular figure. Since obtaining his post in 1927 he had drastically cut down street prostitution and reduced Paris traffic fatalities by thirty per cent through his introduction of "passages cloûtés." Daladier's other foolish move was to dismiss Emile Fabre from his post as Administrateur général of the Comédie-Française. Fabre was told that he was being dismissed so that the post could go to Georges Thomé, directeur de la Sûreté général. According to Alexander Werth: "When Emile Fabre was asked to resign it was naturally said that he was now being punished for having provided the Royalists with an opportunity of displaying their anti-Republican sentiments and of hailing Shakespeare as an ally of [Léon] Daudet and Charles Maurras. The idea of putting a policeman at the head of the House of Molière was met with loud but angry laughter. The fact that M. Thomé had missed his vocation by entering the police service—he was, indeed, a man of literary tastes, and he even wore a *cravate Lavallière*—seemed neither here nor there."[41]

The news of both dismissals became public on Sunday, 4 February. *Coriolan* was on the bill that night at the Comédie-Française, and that performance marked the peak of intensity of audience demonstrations. An observer behind the scenes reported that just before curtain time the cast and crew were still discussing the event "avec cette ardeur combative qui est, sans doute, l'une des plus belles vertus des gens de théâtre."[42] And in the sold-out auditorium, passions were running equally high. At the end of the first scene, the audience began chanting, "Vive Fabre," and took up the cry again after each successive scene. The interval was an occasion for both hostile harangues against the government's action and eager acclaim for the popular theatre administrator. The final curtain was twenty-five minutes later than usual due to the interruptions, and some twenty curtain calls did not quell the shouts and gestures, which continued outside the theatre. M. Fabre himself departed under a hail of "vivas."[43] On 5 February, newspapers carried a long open letter to Thomé. The following sentences will suggest the tone of the whole:

> Voyons, Monsieur, notre République n'est pas si athénienne que les subtilités dont elle pare ses démarches ne soient facilement intelligibles.... Paris ne vous accepte pas et on vous a sévèrement prévenu hier que les Comédiens français repoussaient avec indignation une présence qu'ils considèrent à bon droit comme injurieuse.... Laissez la Comédie-Française à ceux dont c'est le métier de la servir, à ceux qui l'ont apprise, et, dans le serein repos que vous vous serez ainsi conquis, vous ne nous aurez donné peut-être qu'un spectacle mais quel spectacle!"[44]

Daladier received his share of harsh language. Under the single-word headline "Coriolan," the *Echo de la Loire* ran a story that included the following invective:

> Et vous pensez si le bruit de ces applaudissements entrait douloureusement dans les délicates oreilles de nos tyrans ridicules. Ils ne pouvaient se venger sur Shakespeare. Ils se sont rattrapés sur M. Emile Fabre.... Que par cet incident burlesque mais odieux et significatif la psychologie d'un Daladier nous soit révélée. Ce prétendu homme de bronze n'est qu'une baudruche emportée au souffle du vent qui passe."[45]

As a result of the public uproar, Fabre was reinstated as Administrateur général about forty-eight hours after his dismissal. As one critic expressed it: "Nous sommes au pay de La Fontaine. Il y eut une belle morale à cette histoire. Ce fut M. Fabre qui revint et le gouvernement qui partit."[46]

The fall of the Daladier government resulted from the tragic aftermath of the other dismissal, that of Jean Chiappe as préfet de police. Coming on top of the Stavisky affair, Chiappe's dismissal was the last straw for many hitherto moderate Parisians. Between the 4 February announcement of it and the next session of the Chambre des députés on Tuesday, 6 February, there was a two-day interval that afforded time to amass support for a demonstration. No conspiracy or plan of action uniting the various right-wing Leagues has ever been proved.[47] They were simply borrowing "a tradition of the Left, for ever since 1791 it had been the customary procedure of demonstrators to invade the Chamber."[48] The Députés met at 3 P.M., and Daladier delivered his Ministerial Declaration, which was punctuated with unprecedented catcalls from the Right. However, by 9 P.M. Daladier had won his majority, including the Socialist votes he had bought with Chiappe's dismissal. Meanwhile, across the bridge from the Chambre des députés, on the Place de la Concorde, a crowd assembled. There may have been as many as 20,000 demonstrators, plus another 800,000 bystanders who came out of curiosity.[49] Mounted guards set up barriers on the bridge. Rioters began tearing up paving stones and metal fence-railings with which to attack the police. The police in turn used their sabres. A city bus was captured and set afire by the rioters. At around 7 P.M. the first shots were fired. Numerous witnesses later confirmed that the rioters fired first. The total casualties of the seven-hour battle were fourteen rioters, one guard, and one woman at a second-floor window of the Hôtel de Crillon, who was hit by a stray bullet. The seriously wounded numbered 555 rioters and spectators, and 770 policemen. Daladier's govern-ment resigned the next day, 7 February.

Performances of *Coriolan* had been announced for that day as well as for 9 and 11 February, but the government closed all the subsidized theatres for a national day of mourning on 7 February. On 9 February newspapers carried the announcement that all performances of *Coriolan* would be suspended indefinitely.[50] *Action Française* reported that this was done by order of "le ministre de l'Instruction et des Beaux Arts Berthod ... dans le ministère des assassins."[51] According to *Le Matin*, however, "à aucun moment, il n'avait été dans les intentions du gouvernement d'interdire les représentaions d'une œuvre qui, sans être l'une des meilleures du théâtre shakespearien, n'en est pas moins le plus grand succès de ces dernières années à la Comédie-Française."[52] Since the financially-beleaguered theatre had taken 30,267 francs at the box office for the last performance (4 February) of *Coriolan* despite the taxi drivers' strike, there was considerable pressure to re-open the production. The economic dimensions of the situation become apparent when one compares the receipts for *Coriolan* with those for the theatre's other productions that week; the 5 February performance of *Rodogune* and *Le Médecin malgré lui*, for example, brought only 6461 francs.[53] According to sociétaires of the House of Molière, the absence of *Coriolan* from the repertory for the rest of the season could have meant a loss of a million francs. The government finally saw the light on 3 March when, only a few hours after having telephoned Fabre to advise him that "the time was not yet right" for bringing back *Coriolan*, Berthod recalled Fabre to countermand his earlier advice and tell him that he was free to offer *Coriolan* again whenever he liked.[54] The deciding factor, apparently, was the press announcement that the play's translator Piachaud had received a very tempting offer for the play from a big commercial boulevard theatre, free of the kind of government controls that hampered the state-subsidized Comédie-Française. The thought of all those box-office receipts going to a commercial theatre was too much for Berthod, but he cautioned Fabre that "le public devra ... se tenir sage et éviter d'appaudir trop énergiquement les impertinentes critiques shakespeariennes de la démocratie..."[55]

Performances of *Coriolan* resumed at the Comédie-Française on 11 March. Passions had cooled after a new government was formed in the Chambre des députés by Gaston Doumergue, a former Président de la République called out of retirement to serve as Premier Ministre of a National (centrist) government. His Cabinet included representatives of every party in the Chambre except the Socialists and the Communists; even the much-discredited Radicals got six of the twenty Cabinet posts. That cooperative spirit was reflected in a speech made before the curtain by Denis D'Inès to the audience that packed the house for *Coriolan* on 11 March:

> Mesdames, Messieurs,
> Vous savez dans quelles conditions les représentations de *Coriolan* avaient été interrompues. Nous les reprenons ce soir dans une atmosphère de sérénité. Il y a peu de vraisemblance, d'ailleurs, qu'une pièce écrite il ya trois

siècles, jouée avec succès à chaque saison sur tous les théâtes d'Europe et à Paris même, il y a vingt ans, puisse être un sujet actuel de querelles entre les citoyens français. En montant *Coriolan*, la Comédie-Française n'a songé qu'à présenter au public un chef-d'œuvre littéraire. Nous vous demandons d'honorer avec nous ce soir, dans le calme et hors de toute arrière-pensée, la mémoire de Shakespeare, hôte illustre et magnifque de la Maison de Molière.[56]

Coriolan remained in the repertoire during the autumn season, playing to large audiences, without further incident; it achieved a run of fifty-two performances on 30 November 1934.[57]

In 1936 the Popular Front came to power, headed by the Socialist Léon Blum. After less than three months in office Premier Ministre Blum summoned Fabre to his office and told him that "plusieurs députés se refuseront à donner de nouveaux moyens à la Comédie tant qu'il sera en place." Fabre immediately resigned.[58] Harold Hobson's account of this episode is amusing: "The Popular Front Government deposed the Administrator, Emile Fabre, and put in his place Edouard Bourdet, a skilful dramatist who had written an excellent play (*La Prisonnière*) about lesbianism. A striking and paradoxical change immediately took place. Whereas under Fabre the sparse audiences had been shabbily dressed, under Bourdet, the nominee of a left-wing Governement, they became a practical exhibition of *la haute couture*."[59]

The intermingling of art and politics is clearly a perennial characteristic of French theatre. The political passions aroused by the 1934 *Coriolan* are amply documented, but I have claimed that the production had artistic repercussions as well. It was the bellwether for a number of important French plays on Greek and Roman subjects written in the 1930s and 40s, including Giraudoux's 1937 *Électre,* Cocteau's 1940 *La Machine infernale,* Sartre's 1942 *Les Mouches,* and Anouilh's 1944 *Antigone.* The controversy aroused by *Coriolan* may also have prompted Giraudoux's abandonment of a play entitled *Brutus,* which he had announced in June 1934. Instead, he wrote *La Guerre de Troie n'aura pas lieu* (1935), a less politically tendentious choice of classical subject than the potentially "troublesome" *Brutus*.[60] When a classical authority figure in the mould of Coriolanus—an Orestes, or an Oedipus, or a Creon—strode on stage, audiences sat up and looked for political implications. We might say, too, that *Coriolan* finally won the battle for Shakespeare in the French theatregoer's longstanding love-hate relationship with the Bard—a vacillation that can be traced all the way back to Voltaire. By either standard, then, political or artistic, *Coriolan* was a landmark production in French theatre history.

NOTES

1. Gabriel Reuillard, "Quand le public manifeste aux représentations de 'Coriolan' à la Comédie-Française," *Excelsior* (28 January 1934).
2. An Observer, "The Stavisky Scandal," *The Atlantic Monthly* 15 (March 1934), p. 358.
3. René-Louis Piachaud, "La Tragédie de Coriolan," *La Petite Illustration*, No. 661 (10 February 1934), p. 22.
4. Richard Seaver, "Introduction," *Stavisky: the Script* (New York, 1974), pp. xi–xii.
5. Alexander Werth, *France in Ferment* (New York, 1935), p. 84.
6. Seaver, p. xv.
7. Werth, p. 80.
8. Frank Kermode, "Coriolanus," *The Riverside Shakespeare* (Boston, 1974), p. 1394.
9. John Palmer, "Coriolanus and M. Stavisky," *The Times* (20 February 1934), p. 12.
10. Edouard Champion, *La Comédie-Française: anées 1933 et 1934* (Paris, 1935), pp. 163–64.
11. Ibid., p. 164.
12. Ruby Cohn, *Modern Shakespeare Offshoots* (Princeton, 1976), p. 13.
13. Ibid., p. 14.
14. "La Quinzaine théâtrale," *Le Courier du Centre* (Limoges, 10 January 1934).

15. Champion, pp. 177–81. The extras (205 men, 20 women, and 6 children) were cast as follows: 92 common people, 30 Roman soldiers, 10 Roman lictors, 4 standard-bearers, 40 senators, 3 high priests, 10 Volscian soldiers, 3 Volscian officers, 3 Volscian nobles, 4 young women in white, 10 ladies-in-waiting to Volumnia, 6 women of the people, 6 children.

16. Daniel J. Watermeier, "Coriolanus," *Notable International Shakespeare Revivals: The Post-War Years* (Greenwood Press, 1986).

17. Ibid.

18. Louis Perie, "La Politique au théâtre," *Marseille Soir* (2 January 1934).

19. Sylvie Chevalley, *La Comédie-Française hier et aujourd'hui* (Paris, 1970), p. 57.

20. "La Quinzaine théâtrale."

21. "Pessimism on the French Stage," *Literary Digest* 114 (10 December 1932), p. 13.

22. "La Théâtre à Paris," undocumented clipping from the Bibliotèque-Musée de la Comédie-Française.

23. Gabriel Boissy, "Coriolan: Le plus beau spectacle actuel," *Comœdia illustré* (6 January 1934).

24. Champion, p. 179.

25. Marc Semenoff, "Théâtre de la Comédie-Française," *Rampe* (1 January 1934).

26. The following were cast in the major roles: Léon Bernard (Menenius Agrippa), Alexandre (Caius Marcius/Coriolan), Denis d'Inès (Sicinius Velutus), Charles Granval (Brutus), Jean Hervé (Tullius Aufidius), André Bacqué (Cominius), Pierre Dux (Un Serviteur), Colonna Romano (Volumnie), Vera Korène (Virgilie).

27. Champion, p. 172.

28. Ibid., p. 167.

29. Piachaud, p. 22.

30. Wilfred Knapp, *France: Partial Eclipse* (New York, 1972), p. 30.

31. Werth, p. 76.

32. Anonymous, "The Paris Riots: The Story of an Eyewitness," *Harper's Magazine* 168 (May, 1934), p. 707.

33. Werth, pp. 86–87.

34. Anonymous, p. 708.

35. Werth, pp. 86–90.

36. Ibid., p. 91.

37. Alexander Werth, "The Stavisky Tragi-Comedy," *The New Statesman and Nation* 7 (14 April 1934), p. 538.

38. Reuillard.

39. Ibid.; see also Champion, pp. 101, 183.

40. "Coups d'œil en coulisse," *Œil de Paris* (27 January 1934).

41. Werth, *France in Ferment*, p. 127.

42. "La Représentation mouvementée de 'Corilan'" (dateline 5 February), undocumented clipping from the Bibliothèque-Musée de la Comédie-Française.

43. Ibid.

44. Dateline Paris, 5 February 1934, undocumented clipping from the Bibliothèque-Musée de la Comédia-Française.

45. "Coriolan," *Écho de la Loire* (7 February 1934).

46. Jean Barreyre, "Coriolan (Comédie-Française)," *Ric et Rac* (3 March 1934).

47. Werth, *France in Ferment*, p. 142.

48. Knapp, pp. 21–23.

49. Anonymous, p. 710.

50. Champion, p. 183.

51. "Shakespeare interdit à la Comédie-Française," *Action Française* (4 March 1934).

52. *Le Matin* (4 March 1934).

53. Champion, p. 102.

54. *Le Matin*.

55. "On jouera 'Coriolan' à la Comédie-Française," *Action Française* (5 March 1934).

56. Champion, p. 185.

57. Ibid.

58. Jacques Lorcey, *La Comédie-Française* (Paris, 1981), p. 89.

59. Harold Hobson, *French Theatre since 1830* (London, 1979), p. 166.

60. Laurent Lesage, *Jean Giraudoux: His Life and Work* (University Park, 1979), p. 72.

Reprinted by permission from Theatre Research International *11 (Summer 1986), pp. 119–32. Copyright 1986 by* Theatre Research International.

Annihilating Intimacy in *Coriolanus*

Madelon Sprengnether

Whatever else they are about, Shakespeare's tragedies demonstrate, with a terrible consistency, the ways in which love kills. My argument here concerns the structures of homoerotic and heteroerotic bonding that constitute the primary forms of relationship in the tragedies, the assumptions regarding femininity they entail, and the manner in which they combine, with particular deadliness, in the late tragedy *Coriolanus*. In this play, which reveals a deep fantasy of maternal destructiveness, one can see elements of a preoedipal plot that underlies the other plays, though less explicably articulated in them. In this plot, the hero both desires and fears the annihilation of his identity that intimacy with a woman either threatens or requires. This is, in effect, a matriarchal plot, in which union with the body of a mother/lover is fatal to the hero. In order to demonstrate the relevance of this argument to *Coriolanus* I will first discuss preoedipal object-relations theory as it illuminates the gender structures of patriarchal culture; next I will review the patterns that gender relationships assume in Shakespearean tragedy, emphasizing the unique ways in which these patterns combine in *Coriolanus*; and I will conclude by considering some implications of these structures for both psychoanalytic and Shakespearean discourse.

Object-relations theory, on which several recent studies of Shakespeare rely, proposes a modern psychoanalytic myth: that the infant must undergo a process of separation and individuation from its mother with whom its first experience is one of union.[1] Robert Stoller articulates most clearly the assumptions concerning the development of masculinity contained in the idea of mother-infant symbiosis. He states that in

> the whole process of becoming masculine in the little boy from the day of birth on, his still-to-be-created masculinity is endangered by the primary, profound, primeval oneness with mother, a blissful experience that serves, buried but active in the core of one's identity, as a focus which, throughout life, can attract one to regress back to that primitive oneness. That is the threat lying latent in masculinity, and I suggest that the need to fight it off is what energizes some of what we are familiar with when we call a piece of behavior "masculine." So—something I never quite articulated before—in one sense, the process of the development of core gender identity is not the same in males and in females. There is a conflict that females are spared; core gender identity in males is not, as I have mistakenly said, quite so immutable. It carries in it the urge to regress to an original oneness with mother.[2]

This hypothesis seems at once to undermine and to revise classical oedipal theory, with its focus on male rivalry and female castration. Femininity, from the point of view of Stoller (and object-relations theory generally) is primary, while masculine identity is something achieved rather than given and always at risk of becoming lost or diffused back into the original feminine matrix.[3] On another level, one could say that preoedipal theory supplements oedipal theory, making explicit the competing set of assumptions concerning the representatives of masculinity (the father) and femininity (the mother) that inform and motivate patriarchal culture. In this view, the structure of patriarchal control manifest in Freud's description of the son's accession to the position of the father (through successful negotiation of the oedipal and castration complexes) is continually threatened with subversion by an equally powerful matriarchal influence. Looked at this way, as aspects of one another, which, taken together, provide a working description of the psychological underpinnings of patriarchal culture, oedipal and preoedipal theory may be seen to illuminate the gender

Annihilating Intimacy in Coriolanus

conflicts typical of such a social structure. More specifically, these two theories, locked in tension with one another, possess rival claims of authority embodied respectively in the figures of father and mother. It is Shakespeare's engagement with this latter figure, and with the undertow of femininity she represents that I propose to explore in *Coriolanus*.[4] First, however, I want to summarize some of the developments in Shakespeare's other tragedies that cast light on the particular horror of Coriolanus' death. In my conclusion, I shall return to the questions raised in this study concerning the figure of the mother as she is represented in oedipal/preoedipal theory.

Femininity in Shakespeare's tragedies, as I have argued elsewhere, provides the ground against which the tragic action is dramatized.[5] Ambivalence on the part of the hero towards that which he considers feminine (whether in the context of homoerotic or heterosexual bonding) structures his relationships, just as it necessitates his death. The manner of the hero's death varies, however, according to his desire either for merger with a woman, as Richard Wheeler describes it, or for a form of homoerotic bonding that occurs in the context of a pursuit of heroic masculinity.[6] While the former finds its characteristic expression in the love-death of the romantic tragedies, the latter focuses on the exaggerated violence of relationships among men based on the exclusion of femininity. The desire for merger with a woman, which predominates in *Romeo and Juliet, Othello, Antony and Cleopatra,* and in variant form in *King Lear,* can only be accomplished through the destruction of both partners.[7] The flight from women, on the other hand, and the pursuit of heroic masculinity in the form of erotically charged male rivalries, which structure the history plays as well as the tragedies *Julius Caesar, Hamlet,* and *Macbeth,* lead to the spectacle of male competitors locked in fatal combat.

The tragic hero oscillates between heterosexual and homoerotic impulses, as does his counterpart in the comedies, with the difference that the violence so often threatened or symbolically enacted in the plays culminating in heterosexual marriage erupts in the tragedies in the context of both heterosexual and homoerotic embrace. In both instances the position feared by the hero is that which he considers to be feminine, and the tragic irony proceeds from the fact that it is this position that opens to him the full range of his own emotions and commands his ultimate surrender.

The heroes of *Romeo and Juliet, Othello,* and *Antony and Cleopatra* retreat from their initial gestures towards heterosexual union to a world of masculine loyalties embodied in a companion who disdains or avoids the love of women and who bases his identity on his definition of himself as a fighter or a soldier. Mercutio challenges Romeo's allegiance to Juliet by seducing him into the feud, thereby spoiling the potentially comic movement of the play. With Mercutio's taunt of "vile submission" in his ears, Romeo chooses to set aside his love for Juliet in order to avenge the death of his friend. At this crucial moment, he perceives heterosexual love as dangerously effeminate, corroborating the estimation of Mercutio, who understands Romeo's passion as a defection. Ironically, Romeo's choice of the "manly" role of avenger leads to the ruin of his love, placing him more securely in the position of victim of passion that he seeks momentarily to avoid. An act of violence not only precedes the moment of sexual consummation in this play, but it also becomes its prevailing metaphor, as the rhetoric of death as love and love as death indicates. Romeo's fears regarding heterosexual encounter are finally realized literally in the double suicide with which the play concludes.

Othello provides a more complex instance of this pattern. Here, the hero's swerve away from the pursuit of heterosexual love takes place through the intervention of Iago, a character who disparages women and whose ruinous designs seem motivated in part by his anger at having been displaced in the affections of his master. This play presents two patterns of erotic destructiveness neatly intertwined, one involving the relationship between Iago and Othello, the other between Othello and Desdemona. As I have argued elsewhere, the form taken by Iago's disappointed love for Othello binds him to his master, as witnessed in the exchange of vows in the middle of the play, at the same time that it relentlessly destroys Othello.[8] This structure exhibits some of the features of erotically charged male rivalry that appear with varying degrees of intensity in other plays. In particular, it reveals the hierarchical ordering characteristic of

Annihilating Intimacy in Coriolanus

these relationships, the fundamental assumption that in each pair one must dominate, the other submit, and in extreme cases that one at least must die.

For Othello, in whom heterosexual passion has awakened a terrifying sense of dependence ("and when I love thee not/Chaos is come again" III.iii.91-92), the retreat from union with Desdemona into the world of doubt and suspicion created by Iago offers a paradoxical security in the midst of his anguish.[9] Unable to accept the position of emotional risk in which he has placed himself by his marriage to Desdemona, he falls prey to the misogynist inventions of Iago, whose honesty he steadfastly upholds over that of his wife. In attempting to defend himself against a fantasied betrayal, Othello reveals the extent to which he fears and mistrusts Desdemona and perhaps women in general.[10] Othello's ambivalence regarding heterosexual passion, while more intricately portrayed than that of Romeo, similarly engenders a tragic conclusion. The fusion of love and violence that characterizes both the action and the rhetoric of the end of the play serves as an apt expression of Othello's divided impulses.

In *Antony and Cleopatra*, the hero's movement away from Cleopatra and toward Octavius and the world of male alliance in the beginning of the play, though justified by external events, is also fueled by his ambivalence. Antony's alternating views of Cleopatra as vile seductress and enchanting queen reflect his alternating impulses of fear and desire. The specific danger felt by Antony in Egypt—the danger expressed in the Roman censure of Antony's relationship with Cleopatra, hinted at in the playful exchange of garments described by Cleopatra, and explicitly detailed by Enobarbus in his disapproval of Cleopatra's participation in battle—is loss of military identity, which he equates with feminization.

In the beginning of the play, Antony leaves Egypt altogether in order to recover his masculine sense of himself. Later, having returned to Egypt and lost his first battle with Octavius, he attempts to recover his identity through repeated military encounters. This strategy fails when, in his moment of deepest despair, he, like the poet of the sonnets, believes himself to have been doubly betrayed by a dark lady and a boy in one another's arms: "Triple-turn'd whore! 'tis thou/Hast sold me to this novice, and my heart/Makes only wars on thee" (IV.xii.13–15). In the end, the anxiety and rage occasioned in him by Cleopatra's behavior give way, as they do for Othello, to a desire for union with his lover in death. Antony's suicide enacts both aspects of his relation to Cleopatra: his wish to submit to her and his conviction that she will destroy him.

King Lear, which ends in another kind of love-death, reveals a variation on this pattern. While the romantic tragedies focus specifically on the heterosexual love relationship, *King Lear*, in which the hero's passionate love for his daughter Cordelia engenders a desire for a role reversal in which he would take the position of a son toward a nurturing mother, touches another and perhaps stronger chord. Lear's rage and pain at being denied protection suggest the helplessness of an infant in relation to an all-powerful mother. For Lear to acknowledge his feelings, moreover, in the beginning of the play, threatens his sense of manhood. Anger, curses, and threats of banishment serve Lear as a means of repressing the grief, hysteria and eventual madness that he associates with a feminine loss of control. In these early strategies of denial he more nearly resembles the inflexible Coriolanus than the heroes of the romantic tragedies. In the manner of his breakdown, however, he resembles Romeo, Othello, and Antony, all of whom undergo an emotional transformation through their experience of vulnerability in relation to a woman. For Lear this transformation involves first a recognition of his dependence on his non-nurturing daughters, which leads to his misogynist vision of all women as centaurs, then to a submission to his helpless love for his one nurturing daughter. This submission, like that of Romeo, Othello, and Antony, effectively requires his death. Realizing that he is indirectly responsible for the death of Cordelia, he cannot then bear to be separate from her. Here, as in the romantic tragedies, love kills: through his fear and resistance, the hero ironically engages the very forces that bring about his destruction.

The assumption shared by the plays *Romeo and Juliet*, *Othello*, *Antony and Cleopatra*, and *Lear* may be stated in the following way: the hero experiences intense feeling for a woman

Annihilating Intimacy in Coriolanus

as feminizing, an awareness that he attempts to escape or repress, and that in turn creates the condition of union in destruction that comprises both the conclusion of the play and the actualization of a basic fantasy about heterosexual relations. In these plays, a literal loss of self is the price the hero pays for his union with a woman.

In the other significant group of plays, including *Hamlet, Julius Caesar,* and *Macbeth,* the hero's recoil from heterosexual passion and his corresponding repudiation of femininity engage him in a pursuit of heroic masculinity through the defeat of one or more male rivals. In this structure of encounter (homoerotic rather than heterosexually oriented), it is the submissive or feminine posture that the hero seeks to avoid but ultimately embraces, as does his counterpart in the romantic tragedies.

For Hamlet, the confirmation of manhood involves the killing of a rival, a condition imposed by his father. The task of avenging his father's death, however, sets him directly in opposition to his mother, and by extension, to Ophelia. Hamlet's rage against what he considers the deceptiveness of women resembles that of Othello, Antony, and Lear in their moments of greatest anxiety about betrayal. His impulses, however, more evenly divided than theirs between the desire for feminine protection and for the refuge of masculine solidarity, more effectively paralyze him for most of the play. Finally, laboring under his father's injunction, he will choose the honesty of Horatio over that of Ophelia, displacing his passion for her into an intimate rivalry with her brother, which kills them both.

While Hamlet oscillates between conflicting allegiances to women and to men, tipping the balance finally on the side of paternal authority, Brutus and Macbeth pursue a more rigidly defined ideal of masculinity in which male rivalries predominate. These plays, structured by the assumption that masculine identity consists primarily in inflicting wounds on one's rival, inevitably turn the sword, in a castrating or self-castrating gesture, against the hero himself. *Julius Caesar* and *Macbeth,* like *Coriolanus,* exhibit a terrible logic in which the roles of wounder and wounded and their corresponding relations of dominance and submission are reversed.

In *Julius Caesar* it is a woman who, oddly enough, articulates the fundamental masculine ethic of the play by voluntarily wounding herself to demonstrate her capacity for stoic endurance and to win her husband's confidence. In a play obsessed with wounds—with the spectacle of Caesar's hacked and bleeding body and the ritually self-inflicted wounds of the conspirators Cassius and Brutus—Portia's gesture is far from gratuitous. In her zeal to prove her masculine trustworthiness, she reveals the underlying paradox of the play, which equates manliness with injury, so that the sign of masculinity becomes the wound.

There is, moreover, an inverse relationship in *Julius Caesar*, as in *Macbeth* and *Coriolanus*, between the degree of anxiety concerning femininity and the amount of surface violence. Caesar's death results, in an immediate sense, from his fear of appearing foolish or womanly by attending seriously to Calpurnia's dream. Similarly, Brutus' splitting of consciousness in his rational consideration of murder blinds him to its emotional consequences, causing him, like Macbeth, to fall victim to hallucinations where he more nearly confronts the truth of his experience. In denying or suppressing the kind of non-rational awareness expressed in superstition, dream, or simply in tender consideration, the protagonists initiate a cycle of violence, extraordinary in its emphasis on physical mutilation, which ultimately consumes them.

Both Brutus and Cassius, who choose a manner of death consistent with their sense of honor and masculinity, die in the arms of friends in a parody of erotic embrace, turning the sword used against Caesar against themselves. While Cassius instructs Pindarus "with this good sword/That ran through Caesar's bowels, search this bosom" (V.iii.41–42), Brutus in his own death invokes the spirit of the man he both loved and murdered: "Caesar, now be still/I kill'd not thee with half so good a will" (V.v.50–51). The relationships among men in *Julius Caesar*, based in part on a repudiation of femininity, reveal a pattern of erotic destructiveness.[11] The attempt to construct an ideal masculinity, to demonstrate absolute sexual difference, collapses into an odd parody of femininity in which it is men, not women, who bleed.

In *Macbeth*, the flight from femininity is at once more obvious and more gruesome in its particular manifestations and conclusion. As many readers have observed, the idea proposed by Lady Macbeth and embraced by her husband in his relentless eradication of his enemies is based on the exclusion of reactions and emotions considered feminine and hence weak. Not to be all male in this distorted formulation is to become vulnerable, even disturbingly female, as Lady Macbeth implies in her attempts to shake Macbeth from his distraction at the banquet: "Are you a man?" (III.iv.57); "What? quite unmann'd in folly?" (III.iv.73); "O, these flaws and starts/(Impostors to a true fear) would well become/A woman's story at a winter's fire" (III.iv.62–65). The dissociation of sensibility necessitated by Macbeth's course of action, one which requires a divorce between eye and hand, between consciousness and deed, is both more severe than that of Brutus and more deadening. It feeds, moreover, on a fantasy of total invulnerability, of a condition of perfect maleness, in which only a man similarly uncontaminated by femininity—"not of woman born"—can harm the hero.

Macbeth's fantasy of invulnerability coincides with an actual diminishment of stature and an increasing subjection to feminine powers, which appear in the guise of the witches. This terrible femininity, the nightmare counterpart of Macbeth's rapacious masculinity, ultimately claims him, though true to his violent course he dies at the hands of a male rival. In a final humiliation, moreover, he is beheaded, an act of physical mutilation (read psychoanalytically as castration) that emphasizes the vulnerability he has desperately sought to deny.

Both structures of action I have so briefly outlined portray the tragic consequences of the hero's ambivalences regarding femininity. If heterosexual passion does not actually feminize him, it makes him vulnerable to the woman's power to abandon or betray him, a position in which he loses mastery. On the other hand, seeking confirmation of his masculinity in more or less exclusive relationships with men, the hero finds only an illusion of selfhood that easily fragments in the high-pressured sphere of male competition. Both strategies of relationship place him in the posture of submission that he resists and fears. Both incite him to violence, and both implicate or unite him in death with the object of his violence.

Coriolanus, as a late tragedy, not only repeats the major preoccupations of the preceding plays, it also combines the two competing structures of relationship I have described in a particularly excruciating way. While Coriolanus, like Hamlet, Brutus, and Macbeth, dies as a soldier, the manner of his death, like that of Romeo, Othello, and Antony, involves submission to a woman. The conjunction of these two structures, as in a deadlock or stalemate, seems to deprive each of its distinctive gratification. Coriolanus dies with neither the dignity of a warrior nor with the luxury of the illusion of union in death. Instead he is mutilated by his enemy Aufidius and survived by his mother, the woman who has most compelled his love. This play portrays the futility of both tragic structures at the same time that it exposes the inexorable logic behind them. The hero's flight from femininity, the undertow of which he feels most critically in relation to his mother, implicates him in cycles of eroticized violence that shatter his body as well as his identity. In the deep fantasy of this play, femininity, as represented by the figure of the mother, is both powerful and primary, and hence (as in Stoller's view) subversive of masculine identity.[12] More disturbingly, Shakespeare explores in this play a fantasy that underlies the other tragedies though less clearly articulated in them—a fantasy of maternal omnipotence in which a mother seeks the death of her son.[13] What *Coriolanus* demonstrates, I believe, is that the barriers to intimacy in Shakespeare's tragedies stem from the hero's anxieties regarding the figure of a mother/lover who threatens the annihilation of his identity, a condition he both desires and fears.

Volumnia, who maintains, like Portia, the paradoxical equation of wounds with masculinity, seems to thrust her son towards death. Claiming that "blood becomes a man," she states:

> The breasts of Hecuba,
> When she did suckle Hector, look'd not lovelier
> Than Hector's forehead when it spit forth blood
> At Grecian sword, [contemning]. (I.iii.40–43)

Annihilating Intimacy in Coriolanus

On hearing of her son's exploits at Corioli, she exclaims, "O, he is wounded, I thank the gods for't," (II.i.121). She later delights in dwelling on his wounds. When asked by Menenius how he has been hurt, she replies:

> I' th' shoulder and i' th' left arm. There will be large cicatrices to show the people, when he shall stand for his place. He receiv'd in the repulse of Tarquin seven hurts i' th' body. (II.i.147–50)

In another complex and revealing statement, Volumnia explains to Virgilia why men should make war not love:

> If my son were my husband, I should freelier rejoice in that absence wherein he won honor than in the embracements of his bed where he would show most love. When yet he was but tender-bodied and the only son of my womb; when youth with comeliness pluck'd all gaze his way; when for a day of kings' entreaties a mother should not sell him an hour from her beholding; I, considering how honor would become such a person, that it was no better than picture-like to hang by th' wall, if renown made it not stir, was pleas'd to let him seek danger where he was like to find fame. To a cruel war I sent him, from whence he return'd, his brows bound with oak. I tell thee, daughter, I sprang not more in joy at first hearing he was a man-child than now in first seeing he had prov'd himself a man. (I.iii.2–17)

Love and war are so intertwined in Volumnia's imagination that eroticized violence becomes the mark of her relationship with her son. To be a man and to love his mother, Coriolanus must be wounded, a condition he more than fulfills in the course of the play, until his mutilated body becomes the visible emblem of his destiny.

Coriolanus himself eroticizes violence, though this is most evident in his relationship with Aufidius, which seems initially to confirm rather than to undermine his manliness. Like other Shakespearean heroes, Coriolanus associates fighting and the kind of male bonding offered in battle with manhood, so that he fully endorses the equation of wounds with masculinity offered by his mother. The appeal of the battlefield, as Cominius describes it, seems to reside in its function as a place of ritual disidentification from femininity.[14] Cominius suggests, in the following passage, that until he proved himself a man Coriolanus was more like a girl, or, like the young man of the sonnets, "for a woman first created":

> Our then dictator,
> Whom with all praise I point at, saw him fight,
> When with his Amazonian [chin] he drove
> The bristled lips before him. . . .
> In that day's feats,
> When he might act the woman in the scene,
> He prov'd best man i' th' field, and for his meed
> Was brow-bound with the oak. His pupil age
> Man-ent'red thus, he waxed like a sea,
> And in the brunt of seventeen battles since
> He lurch'd all swords of the garland. (II.ii.89–101)

In battle, Coriolanus defines himself as separate from his powerful mother—as not female.

Displaying a notable lack of interest in his marriage and the affairs of women, Coriolanus pursues instead a male rival whom he can love on the battlefield. Only in this context, which provides a superficial support for his masculine self-definition, can he express vulnerability. Exhausted and bleeding from his conquest of Corioli, for instance, he insists on revealing himself to Aufidius:

> The blood I drop is rather physical
> Than dangerous to me. To Aufidius thus
> I will appear, and fight. (I.v.18–20)

The intensity of Coriolanus' attachment to his rival expresses itself through opposition:

> Were half to half the world by th' ears, and he
> Upon my party, I'd revolt, to make
> Only my wars with him. He is a lion
> That I am proud to hunt. (I.i.233–35)

That Coriolanus reserves his language of tenderness for situations of mortal danger involving men is indicated by the following passage addressed to Cominius:

> O! let me clip ye
> In my arms as sound as when I woo'd, in heart
> As merry as when our nuptial day was done
> And tapers burnt to bedward! (I.vi.29–32)

This passage, of course, anticipates Aufidius' greeting of Coriolanus late in the play:

> Know thou first,
> I lov'd the maid I married; never man
> Sigh'd truer breath; but that I see thee here,
> Thou noble thing, more dances my rapt heart
> Than when I first my wedded mistress saw
> Bestride my threshold. (IV.v.113–18)

Both men use the rhetoric of heterosexual passion to express intensity of feeling for another man. Because Coriolanus, in the beginning of the play, assumes mastery on the battlefield, whether in relation to Cominius or Aufidius, such a rhetoric does not threaten his masculinity. By the time he joins forces with Aufidius, however, his situation has become significantly more complex.

While Coriolanus can accept his mother's demand that he be wounded on the battlefield, he cannot accept her request that he reveal his wounds in public. While the former supports his fragile self-definition, the latter subverts it by revealing the contradiction at its heart. For Coriolanus to show his wounds is to expose his incompleteness, his implicitly castrated condition. Hoping to avoid this humiliation, he first pleads,

> Let me o'erleap that custom; for I cannot
> Put on the gown, stand naked, and entreat them
> For my wounds' sake to give their suffrage. (II.ii.136–38)

When he actually appears before the people, he only alludes to his wounds, promising to show them in private. He takes refuge from the indignity of his position, moreover, in his rigid concept of verbal integrity.[15] Words, for Coriolanus, appear to be as subversive as wounds. Like Othello, who prides himself on his rudeness of speech as confirmation of his honesty, Coriolanus claims, "When blows have made me stay, I fled from words" (II.ii.72). Menenius, not without criticism, later describes the basis of Coriolanus' relationship to language.

> He would not flatter Neptune for his trident,
> Or Jove for power to thunder. His heart's his mouth;
> What his breast forges, that his tongue must vent,
> And, being angry, does forget that ever
> He heard the name of death. (III.i.255-59)

Anything less than an absolute correspondence between words and feelings (in this case any emotion other than anger) undermines Coriolanus' sense of himself. Specifically, he cannot tolerate any evidence of a split between seeming and being. Sensing his mother's disapproval of his contemptuous dismissal of the demands of the plebeians, he justifies himself saying, "Would you have me/False to my nature? Rather say, I play/The man I am" (III.ii.14-16). When, on the contrary, Volumnia urges him to dissemble, Coriolanus responds,

> Must I
> With my base tongue give to my noble heart
> A lie that it must bear? Well, I will do't;
> Yet, were there but this single plot to lose,
> This mould of Martius, they to dust should grind it
> And throw't against the wind. To th' market-place!
> You have put me now to such a part which never
> I shall discharge to th' life. (III.ii.99-106)

Here Coriolanus imagines total physical disintegration as preferable to acting, the threat of which he characterizes more explicitly in the following passage:

> Away, my disposition, and possess me
> Some harlot's spirit! My throat of war be turn'd,
> Which quier'd with my drum, into a pipe
> Small as an eunuch, or the virgin voice
> That babies lulls asleep! The smiles of knaves
> Tent in my cheeks, and schoolboys' tears take up
> The glasses of my sight! (III.ii.111-17)

The ultimate humiliation for Coriolanus, and the one from which he flees into the arms of Aufidius, is to be female. What is most interesting about this passage, however, is the way it reverberates throughout Shakespeare's plays, touching as it does on the sensitive issue of language in relation to acting. Coriolanus' association of acting with harlots, eunuchs, virgins, and schoolboys evokes a complex figure that appears through-

Annihilating Intimacy in Coriolanus

out Shakespeare's plays and is central to his art—that of the boy actor, the vehicle of an extraordinary range of verbal ingenuity and at the same time a figure of ambiguous sexual identity.

Generally speaking, the characters in Shakespeare's plays with the most complex kinds of awareness are the ones who are most at home with the possibilities of multiple meaning generated by lies, puns, riddles, and the condition of disguise.[16] What these features of language and identity share is a kind of split between appearance and reality which itself resembles the art of acting. The discrepancy between appearance and reality is made explicit in the figure of the boy actor who plays the part of a woman, and becomes self-consciously artful when the heroine he is portraying in turn disguises herself as a boy. While the comedies playfully exploit the possibilities of this convention, the tragedies on the whole, in their references to acting, reveal a more anxious relation to it. The heroes of the tragedies who associate deception and betrayal with women also regard verbal facility as dangerously feminine. The more they distrust language, the more rigid they become in their self-awareness and the more brittle in their masculine identity. Coriolanus' professed inability to play a part is directly related to his anxieties concerning his maleness; the inflexibility of his language is a reaction against the image of blurred sexual identity represented by the figure of the boy actor in a woman's role.[17]

Rejecting the ambiguous sexual identity of the boy actor who would "act the woman in the scene," Coriolanus becomes instead a "thing of blood." Turning towards Aufidius, after his banishment, he attempts to recover himself through his earlier strategy of making war on the object of his affections—this time Rome. "My birthplace [hate] I, and my love's upon/This enemy town" (IV.iv.23–24). Whereas making war in the beginning of the play provides Coriolanus with a gratifying form of self-definition, here he merely situates himself precariously between two enemies, between his old rival Aufidius and his new rival Rome, the two forces that combine to destroy him. Coriolanus' awareness of the danger of his position in relation to Aufidius appears in the casual reference to his death which accompanies his decision ("If he slay me,/He does fair justice" [IV.iv.24–25]) and in the suicidal challenge he offers to his enemy

> I also am
> Longer to live the most weary, and present
> My throat to thee and to thy ancient malice;
> Which not to cut would show thee but a fool,
> Since I have ever followed thee with hate,
> Drawn tuns of blood out of thy country's breast,
> And cannot live but to thy shame, unless
> It be to do thee service. (IV.v.94–101)

Even though war in this instance deprives Coriolanus of the position of dominance so necessary to his self-esteem, he finds it preferable to the kind of exposure (and threat of feminization) recommended by his mother for political gain. By offering to serve Aufidius, moreover, Coriolanus achieves another end—that of severing himself from his mother, "as if a man were author of himself"—at the same time that he turns in matricidal fury against her:

> Making the mother, wife, and child to see
> The son, the husband, and the father tearing
> His country's bowels out. (V.iii.101–3)

The futility of Coriolanus' situation manifests itself long before the end of the play. If Rome doesn't kill him, Aufidius will. Movement in either direction for Coriolanus is deadly. By embodying so explicitly the structures of eroticized violence in homoerotic and heterosexual bonding that alternately predominate in the other tragedies, and by locating himself at the intersection of these two structures, Coriolanus reveals the tragic paradox that animates them both. In his anxieties about femininity (either in relations with women where he fears a loss of masculinity, or in relations with men where he wounds himself to prove his manhood) the hero can seek only his own destruction.

The play in one sense concludes with Coriolanus' realization that he "cannot make true wars," that both his mother's injunctions (that he be wounded and that he expose his wounds) involve him in contradictions that undermine the simple military identity he has sought and prized. He dies the

Annihilating Intimacy in Coriolanus

unhappy victim of this truth. Having yielded to the "woman's tenderness" he has discovered within himself, he nevertheless becomes so enraged by Aufidius' taunt, "thou boy of tears," that, in defiance, he invites his own dismemberment:[18] "Cut me to pieces, Volsces, men and lads,/Stain all your edges on me" (V.vi.111–12). At the end, Coriolanus is metaphorically unmanned and literally mutilated, making his death singularly brutal and devoid of emotional gratification.[19]

Though Volumnia's role in Coriolanus' downfall has generated much negative commentary, the lessons to be drawn from it do not concern bad mothering *per se*.[20] Volumnia and Coriolanus are complementary partners in a fantasy structure that circulates, in less explicit form, through Shakespeare's tragedies. What is unusual about *Coriolanus* is the specific asymmetry of its conclusion: the two characters most responsible for the hero's death outlive him. This play is unique among the tragedies, moreover, in allowing a central female figure to survive. While Gertrude, Desdemona, Emilia, Goneril, Regan, Cordelia, and even Lady Macbeth all die within moments of the hero, Volumnia does not. Even Juliet and Cleopatra choose to join their lovers in death. If the image of a mother mourning the death of her son recalls that of the Pietà (in a Christian context), it also evokes that of the mother goddesses of the older fertility cults.[21] In the pagan rituals and myths the lover of the goddess is also sometimes regarded as a son. What characterizes all of these stories is the primacy of the mother and the inevitable death of her son/lover.[22] For Coriolanus, the moment of his submission to his mother signals his death.

> O my mother, mother! O!
> You have won a happy victory to Rome;
> But, for your son, believe it—O, believe it—
> Most dangerously you have with him prevail'd,
> If not most mortal to him. But let it come. (V.iii.185–89)

In the deep fantasy of this play, a son is sacrificed to his mother in a perverse fertility rite that benefits no one.[23] At the same time, there is no escape in the logic of Shakespeare's tragedies from such a conclusion. Union with a woman throughout this sequence of plays is dangerous, if not fatal, while those who flee women to pursue a counter-fantasy of ideal masculinity succumb to the contradiction inherent in the attempt to author oneself. The best death is reserved for the hero who accepts what Freud describes in *Beyond the Pleasure Principle* as the impulse ultimately to return to an undifferentiated (maternal) source.[24]

The reading I have just offered poses some theoretical questions I want to discuss (if not to resolve) that transcend the study of Shakespeare's plays. Most critics who read Shakespeare through the medium of psychoanalytic theory regard the theory itself (whether oedipal or preoedipal) as a fairly accurate model of human psychology. Volumnia, in such a reading, must appear as a terrible mother, a perversion of an implicit maternal norm of care and protectiveness. If, however, as I suspect, the figure of the mother as she is represented in preoedipal theory is a product of the oedipally organized patriarchal imagination, then other possibilities of interpretation emerge.

Freud's emphasis on the boy's oedipal struggle toward maturity, accompanied by his insistence on female castration, desubjectifies the mother (as the object of the boy's desire) at the same time that it confers on her the power and the fascination of an undifferentiated subjectivity—the power of Nature as opposed to Culture traditionally ascribed to women. Preoedipal theory, which entails a shift of focus from the father to the mother, in other ways supplements this view. The mother, still portrayed from the child's perspective as lacking subjectivity, appears as the matrix out of which his or her individuality is formed. In the ideal version of such a process, the mother, or her body, offers a paradisal state of oneness or plenitude from which the child suffers a gentle, though inevitable, Fall. This figure finds expression in countless variations on the theme of the Virgin Mother. Such an image of maternity, however, ideally nurturant and nonsexual, engenders its own dark twin. The sexual mother (sometimes termed "phallic") is as threatening in aspect as her counterpart is benign. She appears as a witch or whore. The inseparability of the two figures (good mother/bad mother) becomes apparent, however, if one considers the full implications of the concept of mother/infant symbiosis. In this concept the mother's body becomes the locus of fantasies of both union and separation, the mother herself the representative of

Annihilating Intimacy in Coriolanus

both plenitude and loss. Stated thus, preoedipal theory constitutes the most recent attempt to locate the origins of human consciousness and history with the agency of a woman and her transgression—Eve.

If, as I am suggesting, preoedipal theory in its construction of the figure of mother complements oedipal theory by offering a rival, though suppressed claim to authority, it also reveals the ambivalences encoded in patriarchal culture towards the figure who embodies this authority. That she should appear then in the guise of Volumnia is not surprising. That the shape of Shakespeare's tragedies should be defined by the male hero's responses to such a figure and the subversion of his masculinity that she represents is occasion for pity as well as terror.

Notes

This essay was presented, in earlier drafts, at the Humanities Institute, Stanford University, 1982, the annual meeting of the Shakespeare Association of America, 1983, and at The Newberry Library conference on Changing Perspectives on Women in the Renaissance, 1983. It was first published in *Women in the Middle Ages and the Renaissance*, ed. Mary Beth Rose (Syracuse University Press, 1986), pp. 89–111, and is reprinted here by permission of the author and Mary Beth Rose. Copyright 1986, Mary Beth Rose.

1. See Coppélia Kahn, *Man's Estate* (Berkeley: Univ. of California Press, 1981), and Richard Wheeler, *Shakespeare's Development and the Problem Comedies* (Berkeley: Univ. of California Press, 1981). Many of the essays in *Representing Shakespeare: New Psychoanalytic Essays*, eds. Murray M. Schwartz and Coppélia Kahn (Baltimore: Johns Hopkins Univ. Press, 1980) are also informed by this point of view. See in particular Janet Adelman's brilliant essay "'Anger's My Meat': Feeding, Dependency, and Aggression in *Coriolanus*," pp. 129–49. My own reading of femininity in Shakespeare, though different in important respects from the views of these critics, owes much to their work.

2. Robert Stoller, "Facts and Fancies: An Examination of Freud's Concept of Bisexuality," in *Women and Analysis*, ed. Jean Strouse (New York: Grossman Publishers, 1974), p. 358.

3. For Robert Stoller, there is no question that femininity (for both boys and girls), based on the infant's first identification with its mother, is primary. See "The Sense of Femaleness," and "The 'Bedrock' of Masculinity and Femininity: Bisexuality," in *Psychoanalysis and Women*, ed. Jean Baker Miller (Baltimore: Penguin Books, 1973), pp. 260–72 and 273–84. In his article "Facts and Fancies: An Examination of Freud's Concept of Bisexuality," Stoller also refers to biological evidence that "human tissue starts as female in fetal life, regardless of the chromosomal sex," so that "contrary to what Freud found psychologically and then extrapolated as if it were a biological fact, a clitoris is not a little penis; rather, anatomically, a penis as an androgenized clitoris," *Women and Analysis*, p. 345. Leaving the question of fetal development aside, the assumption of an original mother-infant symbiosis would seem logically to support the notion of a primary femininity. Nancy Chodorow, in *The Reproduction of Mothering: Psychoanalysis and the Sociology of Gender* (Berkeley: Univ. of California Press, 1978) explores in detail the implication of mother-infant symbiosis for masculine and feminine development.

4. Of all the readings of *Coriolanus* I have encountered, Janet Adelman's is surely the most compelling. She sees "the image of the mother who has not fed her children enough" at the center of the play, interpreting Coriolanus' rigid masculinity as a "defense against acknowledgment of his neediness." See *Representing Shakespeare*, pp. 129–49, pp. 130, 132.

5. See "'I wooed thee with my sword': Shakespeare's Tragic Paradigms," in *Representing Shakespeare*, pp. 170–87; "'All that is spoke is marred': Language and Consciousness in *Othello*," in *Women's Studies*, eds. Gayle Greene and Carolyn Ruth Swift, 9 (1982): 157–76; and "'And when I love thee not': Women and the Psychic Integrity of the Tragic Hero," *Hebrew University Studies in Literature* (Spring 1980): 44–65. These articles were published under the name Madelon Gohlke.

6. Richard Wheeler divides the tragedies into two groups, each of which exhibits a characteristic movement: towards trust/merger or towards autonomy/isolation. In the first group he includes *Hamlet, Othello, King Lear,* and *Antony and Cleopatra*, while the second consists of *Troilus and Cressida, Macbeth, Timon of Athens,* and *Coriolanus*. While these polar categories are instructive in describing the dominant movements of the plays, they obscure to some extent the shared ground in the hero's anxious relation to femininity and the extent to which

homoerotic bonding appears both as an alternative to the more obvious danger of heterosexual passion and as an affirmation of the hero's heroic masculinity. See "'Since first we were dissevered': Trust and Autonomy in Shakespearean Tragedy and Romance," in *Representing Shakespeare*, pp. 150–69.

7. Charles Forker points out that "stories of disastrous love could explore the ambivalent relations between attraction and repulsion, commitment and doubt, freedom and bondage, elation and despair; they could address the contradictory needs for intimacy and separateness, for self-discovery and self-annihilation," "The Love-Death Nexus in Elizabethan Renaissance Tragedy," *Shakespeare Studies* 8 (1975): 211–30.

8. See "All that is spoke is marred': Language and Consciousness in *Othello*," *Women's Studies* 9: 157–76.

9. *Othello*, III.iii.91–92, *The Riverside Shakespeare*, ed. G. Blakemore Evans (Boston: Houghton-Mifflin, 1974). References to Shakespeare's plays throughout this essay are to this edition.

10. Edgar Snow analyzes with particular acuteness the sexual pathology of the patriarchal order as manifest in *Othello* in "Sexual Anxiety and the Male Order of Things in *Othello*," *English Literary Renaissance* 10 (Autumn 1980): 384–412.

11. Hélène Cixous, who emphasizes the ritualistic and sacrificial aspects of the play comments: "César aimait Brutus, et Brutus César. Et Brutus a tué César au moment même où il l'aimait le plus. Il a tué César par double et ironique amour," *Les Langues Modernes* 61 (1967): 53–55.

12. Joel Fineman argues that in Shakespeare's universe, sex differences are supported by violence. His understanding of the Shakespearean hero's difficulty establishing his masculinity is based on a concept of primary femininity: "For if the male's first sense of self is implicated in femininity, his masculinity is then conditional upon establishing a self distanced from its first sense of self. Women, on the other hand, because their gender is founded on a bedrock identification with maternality, have a kind of immediate gender reference to which they can refer their sense of self. In contrast to Freud, then, alienation from the object of desire is the preliminary condition both for male self-consciousness and for masculine desire." See "Fratricide and Cuckoldry: Shakespeare's Doubles," in *Representing Shakespeare*, pp. 70–109, especially p. 103.

13. Various critics have seen Volumnia's power over her son as darkly destructive. Janet Adelman states that "the cannibalistic mother who denies food and yet feeds on the victories of her sweet son stands

at the darkest center of the play, where Coriolanus' oral vulnerability is fully defined." See "Anger's My Meat," p. 140. Richard Wheeler refers to the "deep maternal antagonism toward the son who becomes the man such a mother longs herself to be herself," in "Since first we were dissevered," p. 159. Robert Stoller is more explicit in his portrayal of Volumnia as demanding the death of her son: "He knows his master's voice, and for the last time obeys, as always, her command, this time that he be killed." See "Shakespearean Tragedy: *Coriolanus*," *Psychoanalytic Quarterly* 35 (1966): 263–74, especially p. 273. Finally, D. W. Harding, in "Women's Fantasy of Manhood: A Shakespearean Theme," states "the proud Roman matron passes on triumphantly while the son, having performed his last act to the greater glory of his mother, goes to the death which she herself has made inevitable," *Shakespeare Quarterly* 20 (1969): 253.

14. I am taking the phrase "disidentification" from Ralph Greenson, who, like Robert Stoller, assumes an original symbiotic relationship between mother and infant, necessitating on the part of the boy a "disidentification" from the mother in order to achieve a sense of maleness. See "Dis-Identifying from Mother: Its Special Importance for the Boy," *International Journal of Psychoanalysis* 49 (1968): 370–73.

15. Coriolanus' uneasy relationship to rhetoric has drawn much commentary. Leonard Tennenhouse sees "his abhorrence of public speech and his distrust of words" as "functions of his obsessive quest for personal integrity which can only be correctly realized in physical action," quoted from "Coriolanus: History and the Crisis of Semantic Order," *Comparative Drama* 10 (1976): 334. James Calderwood, in "*Coriolanus:* Wordless Meanings and Meaningless Words," sees the inflexibility of Coriolanus' speech as an index of "a general insensitivity of feeling and a lack of discrimination in matters of human worth," *Studies in English Literature* 6 (1966): 216. In Stanley Fish's speech-act analysis, Coriolanus is "always doing things (with words) to set himself apart," "Speech-Act Theory, Literary Criticism and *Coriolanus*," *Centrum* 3 (1975): 107. For Lawrence Danson, "Coriolanus is not only the least eloquent of Shakespeare's tragic figures but one who (as we shall see) specifically rejects that humanizing speech sought by Titus or Hamlet." See *Tragic Alphabet: Shakespeare's Drama of Language* (New Haven: Yale Univ. Press, 1974), p. 142. For all of these critics, Coriolanus' distrust of words diminishes him in stature.

16. I have argued this point more extensively in "'All that is spoke is marred': Language and Consciousness in *Othello*." My understanding is that complex speech, as manifest in the use of lies, riddles, puns, and the condition of disguise, is largely attributed to women in the

Annihilating Intimacy in Coriolanus

comedies. As the issue of feminine betrayal becomes more prominent in the tragedies, ambiguous or complex speech also becomes more suspect. Like Othello who says that he is rude in speech, or Macbeth, who tries to subvert speech altogether by collapsing thoughts into actions, the hero in his attempt to establish his "honest" masculinity also expresses uneasiness about the instability of language.

17. One of the chief objections to the stage expressed in the antitheatrical tracts of Shakespeare's time concerns the practice of cross-dressing, which is seen as dangerously effeminate, subversive of both heterosexuality and male dominance. See in particular Stephen Gosson, *The School of Abuse* (London: for Thomas Woodcocke, 1579); William Prynne, *Histrio-Mastix* (London: E.A. and W.J. for Michael Sparke, 1633); John Rainoldes, *The Overthrow of Stage-Playes* (Middleburg: R. Schilders, 1599); and Phillip Stubbes, *Anatomy of Abuses in England* (1593), ed. Frederick J. Furnivall, *New Shakespeare Society* (London: N. Trubner and Co., 1877). For a discussion of Elizabethan reactions to transvestism on the stage see J.W. Binns "Women as Transvestites on the Elizabethan Stage?: An Oxford Controversy," *Sixteenth Century Journal* 5 (1974): 95–120. For commentary on Stephen Gosson's objections to the stage, in particular his assumption of the prurient appeal of plays see Stephen Hilliard, "Stephen Gosson and the Elizabethan Distrust of the Effects of Drama," *English Literary Renaissance* 9 (1979): 225–39. For a comprehensive discussion of the anti-theatrical tracts see Jonas Barish, *The Antitheatrical Prejudice* (Berkeley: Univ. of California Press, 1981). Though not strictly contemporary, William Prynne's association between the practise of cross-dressing (for men) and pagan worship of Venus is suggestive. Transvestism, in his words, "is not only an imitation of effeminate idolatrous Priests and Pagans, who arrayed themselves in woman's apparell when they sacrificed to their idols, and their Venus, and celebrated Playes unto them ... but a manifest approbation and renewall of this their idolatrous practice." See *Histrio-Mastix*, p. 207. Recently, Lisa Jardine has argued for the specifically homoerotic appeal of Shakespeare's use of boy actors. See *Still Harping on Daughters* (Totowa, NJ: Barnes and Nobles Books, 1983).

18. Charles Hofling and Ralph Berry both comment on the connotations of effeminacy contained in the word "boy." See Hofling's, "An Interpretation of Shakespeare's *Coriolanus*," *American Imago* 14 (1957): 407–35, and Berry's "Sexual Imagery in *Coriolanus*," *Studies in English Literature* 13 (1973): 301–16.

19. Janet Adelman says succinctly "there is no one here to love." See "Anger's My Meat," p. 144.

20. It is easy to dislike Volumnia, who draws severe criticism from many readers of the play. Charles Hofling, for instance, sees her as "an extremely unfeminine, non-maternal person" ("An Interpretation of Shakespeare's *Coriolanus*," p. 415). For D. W. Harding, she "provides Shakespeare's most blood-chilling study of the destructive consequences of a woman's living out at someone else's expense her fantasy of what manhood should be ("Woman's Fantasy of Manhood," p. 252). In Rufus Putney's words she is "a most repulsive mother" ("Coriolanus and his Mother," *Psychoanalytic Quarterly* 31 [1962]: 364–81, 377).

21. C.L. Barber sees in the image of Lear with the dead Cordelia in his arms a "pieta with the roles reversed, not Holy Mother with her dead Son, but father with his dead daughter." See "The Family in Shakespeare's Development: Tragedy and Sacredness," *Representing Shakespeare*, p. 200.

22. For an overview of the archeological evidence concerning the prevalence of goddess worship in prehistoric and early historic periods see Merlin Stone *When God Was A Woman* (New York: Dial Press, 1976). Stone summarizes the work of writers such a J.J. Bachofen, Sir James Frazer, Robert Graves, and others concerning myths of goddess worship and relates it to the contemporary scholarship that grounds such speculation in archeological investigation.

23. Stanley Cavel, in an extremely interesting reading of this play, argues that *Coriolanus* fails to achieve the conditions of tragedy because its hero fails to attain the status of the kind of sacrificial victim (like Christ) who could renew his society. "'Who does the wolf love?' Reading *Coriolanus*," *Representations* 3 (1983): 1–20. In focussing on the drama of Christian ritual, however, Cavel misses the intimations of pre-Christian ritual in the image of a mother mourning the death of her son. Part of the disturbing power of this image, I believe, derives from its seeming subversion of patriarchal order.

24. *The Standard Edition of the Complete Works of Sigmund Freud*, trans. James Strachey, vol. 18 (London: Hogarth Press, 1955). The death instinct, for Freud, represents "the most universal endeavor of all living substance—namely to return to the quiescence of the inorganic world" p. 62.

Coriolanus's Stage Imagery on Stage, 1754–1901

John Ripley

The growing contemporary interest in Shakespeare's visual effects, that "large body of images that is not part of the spoken words of the text, but directly presented in the theatre,"[1] offers a healthy corrective to the longstanding scholarly obsession with the plays' verbal content. While visual features such as entrances and exits, groupings, individual movements and gestures, costumes and properties—whether stipulated, implied, or hinted at in stage directions or dialogue—have always been integral components of Shakespeare's dramaturgy, only recently have they begun to receive the same kind of scholarly attention given to the poetry.[2] Evidence of the dramatist's visual intentions, although more plentiful than might be imagined, varies considerably in quality. Sometimes only verbal cues for stage images survive, as in Polonius's confident conclusion to his diagnosis of Hamlet's ills: "Take this from this, if this be otherwise" (II.ii.156). Clearly Shakespeare envisions a particular gesture at this point; Theobald conjectured it to be "*Pointing to his head and shoulder*," but its precise nature is now irrecoverable.[3] On other occasions, however, the playwright's instructions are gratifyingly specific. In *Coriolanus*, for example, the plunder carried off by the Roman soldiery at Corioli is identified by Martius as precisely as if cited from a property-plot: "Cushions, leaden spoons,/Irons of a doit, doublets that hangmen would/ Bury with those that wore them" (I.v.5–7).[4]

To read the plays with an eye for visual effects is to realize not only how many clues there are, but how economically Shakespeare achieves his ends: one telling costume or property, one carefully arranged entrance or exit, one slight change in grouping, or a single gesture strategically placed within an otherwise static sequence can speak with devastating eloquence. More interesting yet is Alan Dessen's observation that key stage images in any given play appear to be repeated with variations in a series of visual analogues that gain in meaning as the action progresses.[5]

While close reading can reveal much about the theoretical nature and function of Shakespeare's presentational images, their working dynamics are, one assumes, best demonstrated on stage. It is a sorry historical fact, however, that until this century the playhouse showed as little respect for Shakespeare's non-verbal artistry as it did for his text; indeed, any account of the visual treatment of the plays in the eighteenth- and nineteenth-century theatre must be largely a recital of mutilations and distortions dictated by audience taste, managerial ambition, actorial ego, and financial exigency. Study of the stage history of Shakespeare's visual effects is nevertheless profitable; for to place the original stage images, as nearly as we can reconstruct them, alongside their neo-classic, Romantic, and Victorian avatars, is to appreciate their subtle minimalist dynamic more richly than is allowed by an unassisted reading of the text. One comes to realize the significance not only of the raw material of the image—that is, who does what or wears what—but also of its spatial and temporal context. The preparation for an image, its stage location, the interplay of foreground and background, the orchestration of static and kinetic features, its timing and duration, and the overall rhythm of the pictorial sequence in which particular units appear, often reveal profound significance when their aesthetic function is violated onstage.

An apt subject for an historical approach to Shakespeare's stage imagery is offered by *Coriolanus*, a drama featuring a dour, laconic, unimaginative hero whose tale unfolds in a correspondingly bleak pictorial style. Its visual effects, carefully calculated to produce maximum impact with minimum means, consist primarily of telling entrances, small but meaningful stage groupings, eloquent individual movements and gestures, evocative sounds (vital ingredients of Shakespeare's presentational images), and severely expressive costumes. Moreover, these stark stage images appear to be patterned as visual analogues to achieve a cumulative thrust.

Eighteenth- and nineteenth-century actor-managers reckoned the play's grim characters and unromantic action to be box-office poison,[6] yet found themselves irresistibly drawn by the pyrotechnic highlights of the title role; and for the chance to strut in the Pleading and Assassination sequences, they taxed ingenuity to the limit in their attempts to render the drama's granite grandeur, if not quite alluring, then at least less repellent to audiences. Not surprisingly, the text was hacked into more genial shape, and actors did what they could to mellow the characterization of the protagonist. A further, and less predictable, strategy was the manipulation of the play's stage imagery to endow Coriolanus with charisma and his drama's bleak temper with color and sentiment, or, failing that, to befuddle the audience's sensibilities with visual distraction.

In the course of this essay, I shall attempt to reconstruct three of *Coriolanus*'s central stage image sequences as they may have appeared to Elizabethan audiences, and to compare their subsequent treatment in eighteenth- and nineteenth-century theatres. The first moments of Coriolanus's triumphal return from the wars (II.i.156–71), the opening of the Pleading Scene (V.iii.19–52), and Coriolanus's assassination (V.vi.48–154) all offer relatively firm clues to Shakespeare's intentions,[7] and also appear to be visual analogues. In trying to recreate Shakespeare's stagecraft, I have relied as much as possible upon the stage directions of the First Folio and performance hints contained in the dialogue. Where I have been forced to resort to conjecture, I hope, with Professor Charney, that I have "avoided trying to piece out this evidence with literary and fictional staging not clearly demanded by the play."[8] Details of the eighteenth- and nineteenth-century mounting of these sequences are drawn primarily from records of productions by Thomas Sheridan (Covent Garden, 1754), John Philip Kemble (Covent Garden, 1811), William Charles Macready (Covent Garden, 1838), Samuel Phelps (Sadler's Wells, 1850, 1857, 1860), Edwin Forrest

(Broadway, 1855; Niblo's Garden, 1863), and Henry Irving (Lyceum, 1901).[9]

1. Coriolanus's Triumphal Return

Coriolanus's entrance (II.i.156-71), carefully prepared for by Shakespeare and blocked with some precision, is of pivotal importance dramatically and is echoed visually at key points in the play thereafter. One of the first features to catch our attention is the rate at which the image unfolds. In the earlier part of the scene, the pace is frenetic: Volumnia's reiterated "let's go" (II.i.100,133), the ladies' staccato, monosyllabic outbursts—"Nay, 'tis true" (II.i.107), "O no, no, no" (II.i.120), "Yes, yes, yes" (II.i.133), "True? pow, waw" (II.i.142)—and the frequent contractions in the speech of all parties suggest impulsive forward movement (probably downstage in a deep curve toward center) as they gravitate towards the opposite exit in high excitement. The language is informal prose, naturalistically phrased. With Menenius and the women well downstage near center, and Sicinius and Brutus a little apart (*"Aside"*), most conveniently down left, *"A showt, and flourish"* fractures the scene's lighthearted rhythm. Menenius's monitory "Hark, the trumpets" (II.i.156-57) directs the attention of actors and spectators upstage for Coriolanus's entrance. Volumnia abruptly moves to highly poetic, almost incantatory, diction, a verbal fanfare that can hardly be heard without a shiver:

> These are the ushers of Martius; before him
> He carries noise, and behind him he leaves tears:
> Death, that dark spirit, in's nervy arm doth lie,
> Which, being advanc'd, declines, and then men die.
> (II.i.158-61)

Then, in a final crescendo of anticipation, *"A Sennet. Trumpets sound."* The entire sequence of visual and auditory effects from the first trumpet notes until this point is carefully calculated, using the simplest of means, to suggest less a civil ceremony than a supernatural visitation.

The ritual mood established prior to the entry is reinforced by the entry itself. The Folio direction runs "*Enter Cominius the Generall, and Titus Latius* [sic]: *betweene them Coriolanus, crown'd with an Oaken Garland, with Captaines and Souldiers, and a Herauld.*" Cominius enters first, followed by Coriolanus, with Titus Lartius bringing up the rear. To facilitate the entrance of the captains and soldiers, they must move slightly behind. Shakespeare is unspecific about the number of military supers, but we have no reason to assume that there was more than a token contingent designed to lend a touch of martial ambience. The Herald now steps forward to speak his highly stylized lines; and the speech, although brief, freezes the action for a sufficient time to allow the audience to grasp visually the drama's major forces.

Upstage, somewhere near center, stands Coriolanus, shoulder to shoulder with comrades and honored by an oak-leaf wreath (a simple effect that sets him off from the other military figures), supported by some degree of martial display, hailed by all, and as nearly at peace with himself as he ever manages to be. Well downstage, at a considerable distance (otherwise, why would he fail to notice his mother?), are grouped Volumnia, Virgilia, Valeria, and Menenius, representative of domestic ties; and to one side of them lurk the tribunes, a graphic reminder of the popular will. Throughout the Herald's speech Coriolanus is pictorially part of a formally structured background, while his family occupies the foreground. Here, as elsewhere in the play, small groups isolated from each other by large amounts of space are a feature of Shakespeare's stage composition. Individual gestures within each group thus enjoy stronger focus, and movements from one group to another acquire heightened force. Shakespeare's intention to keep the stage uncluttered is underlined by the fact that no mention is made of the presence of commoners; only after the procession exits does Brutus remark upon Coriolanus's offstage reception by the general public (II.i.204–21).

Coriolanus's impatient "No more of this" (II.i.168) breaks the spell, and as Volumnia is pointed out to him, he crosses down to her and kneels. It is significant that the victorious general moves to his mother while she and her party remain motionless. This willingness on the part of Coriolanus to yield pride of place to Volumnia immediately strengthens her visual and moral position in the eyes of the audience. The speed at which the blocking pattern is altered is also worth noting: only eleven words intervene between the son's recognition of his mother and the act of kneeling to her, and some of these words may be spoken as he kneels. Coriolanus's long, swift cross has the effect of bringing him from the military background into the domestic foreground, with the attendant reaffirmation of familial bonds the new grouping implies. The severe formality with which the scene unfolds endows the action with an almost sculpturesque quality, within which Coriolanus's act of kneeling, unattended by visual distraction, potently prefigures his fatal submission in the Pleading Scene, where the pictorial pattern of this sequence is reiterated with eloquent variations.

From the productions of Thomas Sheridan until World War I, Shakespeare's apt minimalist design for this episode was denied to theatregoers. For eighteenth- and nineteenth-century actor-managers, Martius's triumphal return was less a moment for highlighting the play's central issues than an occasion for spectacle, historical reconstruction, and heroic image-making.

In his conflation of Thomson's and Shakespeare's versions of the play, staged at Covent Garden in 1754,[10] Sheridan seized the opportunity to create a Roman ovation designed simultaneously to glamorize Coriolanus, titillate antiquarians, and delight spectacle-lovers. The preliminary excited chatter among Menenius, Volumnia, and Virgilia was left standing, but Volumnia's verbal trumpetry prior to Coriolanus's entry was reduced to two lines ("These are the ushers of Marcius; before him he carries noise, and behind him he leaves tears"). Further, the speech, far from heralding Coriolanus's arrival, served merely as an exit cue for Volumnia and her party. Not long after, they were back, as part of a civil procession, to begin a fresh scene. The civil parade, Sheridan tells us, consisted of "Priests, Flamens, Choiristers, Senators, Tribunes, Virgins, Matrons, and the Mother, Wife, and Child of *Coriolanus*. These walked to the sound of flutes and soft instruments, and lined the way to behold the military entry, and congratulate the victor."[11] For Volumnia and her companions to enter formally in procession is not at all the same thing as to be overtaken naturalistically by Coriolanus while *en route* to meet him. Worse still, to allow space for the ovation, soon to follow, the civil procession was marshalled in the downstage area; consequently, the statuesque image of Coriolanus's family and the tribunes isolated and immobile in the foreground was sacrificed to irrelevant clutter and bustle.

The ovation took place to the sound of drums, fifes, and trumpets, which accompanied Coriolanus's entry, rather than serving as an auditory preparation for it. And the complex instrumental sound texture had not at all the pure simplicity of the sennet Shakespeare calls for. The procession included lictors, incense-bearers, musicians, standard-bearers, and miscellaneous groups of soldiers. Highlights of the affair were "Four Captive Generals in Chains" and a series of groups of soldiers bearing biers loaded with spoils. According to Sheridan, "In the military Procession alone, independent of the Civil, there were an hundred and eighteen persons."[12] Unlike Shakespeare's plan, in which Coriolanus enters almost at once and takes up a position between his fellow generals, Sheridan has him arrive almost at the end of the parade, following two consuls and followed in turn by standard-bearers and soldiers.

Sheridan's arrangement of this sequence aptly illustrates the difference between a stage picture, contrived for its own sake, and a stage image devised as an integral part of a play's design. In contrast to Shakespeare's swift, severe, and businesslike entry, Sheridan's parade delays Coriolanus's appearance intolerably and operates as a visual interruption in the rhythm of the scene. Moreover, both the visual content of the episode and its timing evoke an air of colorful expansiveness quite out of keeping with the play's bleak spirit. The Herald's speech (somewhat shortened) still serves to freeze the stage image, but the audience sees only a gratuitous spectacle. Coriolanus's "No more of this," it may be noted, must have rung somewhat hollowly after his willing participation in pageantry on such a scale. The cross to his mother also loses its force and resonance, since she no longer stands isolated with her small family group but revels in civic splendor.

Kemble, in productions staged from 1789 to 1817,[13] retained Sheridan's version of the preliminaries to the triumphal entry: Volumnia and her party continued to exit after her "These are the ushers of Marcius" lines. Kemble restored the flourish of trumpets and shouts, but his fidelity to Shakespeare did not go much further. The new scene opened with the discovery of "A triumphal Arch in Rome," through which passed an ovation numbering some 240 persons. Sheridan's two processions—civic and military—were replaced with one gargantuan spectacle arranged in four divisions. Two divisions were military,[14] one division was religious, and a fourth division featured musicians and choristers singing "See the Conquering Hero Comes." At the end of the pageant walked twenty-eight senators, twenty-seven ladies, four Roman matrons, Valeria, Servilia, Virgilia, Volumnia, Menenius and Cominius, and, finally, Coriolanus, followed by the Chief Eagle.

Almost every element of Shakespeare's visual design is here distorted beyond recognition. Mrs. Siddons's Volumnia, "with flashing eyes and proudest smile, and head erect, and hands pressed firmly against her bosom . . . towered above all around her, and rolled, and, almost, reeled across the stage," we are told.[15] This effervescent matron, however admired by her audiences, was not Shakespeare's stationary and austere dowager. Coriolanus on his entry does not stand between his fellow generals, but remains, in full actor-managerial majesty, by himself. Sicinius and Brutus enter, curiously enough, as part of the procession. Kemble cuts the Herald's lines altogether, and the "freeze" effect disappears with them, although a *"Flourish of Trumpets—Three Shouts &c. when Corio. stops"* serve to create a momentary pause. The kneeling sequence is once more robbed of its force: the excision of the Herald's speech so speeds up the action that Volumnia, who enters just before Coriolanus, has hardly grouped herself and her party with proper picturesqueness against a colorful military display when she finds her son kneeling. As a result, she loses the visual weight that accrues to her in Shakespeare's blocking, and which is the product of a small group on a virtually empty stage, the static position that Volumnia is obliged to hold for a substantial period of time, and the considerable space between her and her son that Martius has to cross to show his filial duty.

Macready not only continued to make the scene a theatrical circus, but further crowded the stage with citizens who come to view the spectacle, despite Shakespeare's decision to have the commoners' reception of Coriolanus, described by Brutus, as offstage action. "The stage," noted the *John Bull* critic (18 March 1838), "gives a marvelous picture of a Roman holyday. It is filled with crowds of all classes with laurel boughs in their upraised hands; the walls and battlements are lined with spectators." In all, according to the *Sunday Times* (18 March 1838), some 300 persons took part.

Phelps, lacking in his 1850 production enough supers to stage a procession, offered audiences a discovery-tableau. When the curtain went up, theatregoers witnessed Coriolanus "standing in War Chariot," the promptbook tells us. In front of him were grouped "4 Boys with incense," flanked by "4 Volscian Prisoners R & L of chariot." Further to the sides were "Trophies &c.," and framing the picture were "12 Roman Lictors ranged across at back" with twenty troops and four officers placed to right and left. Once the tableau had been admired, "Vol. Virg X 6 Ladies enter," and as they cross the stage Cominius remarks, "Look, sir, your mother." Volumnia halts as Coriolanus approaches her, and the latter kneels. Phelps seems to suggest that Volumnia is almost casually passing, and that Coriolanus seizes the opportunity to pay his respects.

Phelps's neglect of this episode's visual design inadvertently underscores two key features of Shakespeare's image-making craft. First, a static discovery-tableau, suddenly revealed in its entirety, has an aesthetic impact quite different from that of a dynamic stage image that takes shape by degrees before the audience's eyes. The techniques are not interchangeable. Shakespeare clearly distinguishes between them and uses each for specific purposes. Second, and equally significant, is the interplay of static-dynamic elements at any moment. Shakespeare clearly intends Volumnia to remain motionless and obliges Coriolanus to move to her, with the dramatic result noted earlier. Phelps's decision to place both figures in motion means that the visual point made by the dramatist, and reiterated with such force in the Pleading Scene, is vitiated.

Forrest's treatment of this sequence was less insensitive to the visual demands of the text than downright indifferent. The procession entered on a scene that occupied "The whole extent of the stage, including paint Room. The Capitol of Rome on paint frame [on the back wall of the paint room at extreme upstage]." The streets leading to the Capitol were lined with three-dimensional houses from the windows of which citizens threw wreaths. The parade comprised no less than five divisions. Towards its end, Volumnia, Valeria, and Virgilia entered, walking in front of Coriolanus's chariot, which was drawn, with consummate incongruity, by a throng of citizens. Well might the *New York Times* critic protest, "The idea of Coriolanus permitting the greasy plebeians to make an exhibition of him!" (24 April 1855). In a further piece of mindless nonsense, Coriolanus descends to a flourish on "No more of this," and as Cominius says, "Look, sir, your mother," he kneels to honor the lady he had allowed to trudge before his chariot all along.

Henry Irving reverted to Phelps's discovery-tableau to permit him to incorporate into the scene a massive golden chariot and four cream-colored horses.[16] The Coriolanus who descends grandly from a gilded car to kneel to his mother strikes the eye quite differently from the one limned by Shakespeare. But subtlety of characterization, or indeed, mother-son relationships counted little with Irving when weighed against the pictorial charms of first-class horseflesh. The sequence was finally stripped of its meretricious trappings—animal and human—only with the Old Vic production of 1920.

2. The Pleading Scene

Shakespeare's design for the opening of the Pleading Scene (V.iii.19–52) strongly recalls the visual pattern of Coriolanus's triumphal return. Both sequences depict family reunions, both feature the formal entry of one party watched by the other, and both culminate in Coriolanus kneeling to his mother. But

Shakespeare now rings the changes on his earlier scheme with breathtaking effect.

After the exit of the Watch and the crestfallen Menenius, the Folio direction reads "*Enter Coriolanus and Auffidius,*" obviously from one of the stage doors, and, ideally, the one through which the triumphal entrance was made earlier. They have only about twenty lines to speak, so there seems no pressing reason for them to move far downstage. It is more likely that they remain upstage in the same spot where Coriolanus stood during his victory celebration. Their conversation is interrupted by a "*Shout within,*" announcing the arrival of the matrons. The earlier dialogue between Volumnia and Menenius, it will be recalled, was similarly checked by "*A Showt, and flourish,*" heralding Coriolanus's triumphal entry. This time the preliminaries to the entry are quite different; there is no shift to formal poetic diction (Coriolanus remarks simply, "Shall I be tempted to infringe my vow/In the same time 'tis made? I will not" [V.iii.20–21]), no trumpet fanfare, no military trappings, and no herald.

The women and their attendants enter in silence by the stage door opposite the one where Coriolanus stands. Shakespeare is careful, as he was earlier, to specify key features of the procession. The stage direction—"*Enter Virgilia, Volumnia, Valeria, yong Martius, with Attendants*"—identifies the group's membership, and Coriolanus's commentary makes clear the order of entry of the main figures:

> My wife comes foremost; then, the honor'd mould
> Wherein this trunk was fram'd, and in her hand
> The grandchild to her blood. (V.iii.22–24)

He now needs no Cominius to call his attention to the presence of his family; he sees them, to his distress, only too well. Since he speaks of the matrons as if they were at some distance, they probably move down the stage rather than across it, perhaps with poignant effect following the route of Volumnia's ecstatic quest for her son in the earlier scene. Visually the static-dynamic relationships of the major figures in the Triumphal Return sequence are now reversed: Volumnia and her party make the formal entrance as Coriolanus watches; and this procession, in contrast to the male, military spruceness of the former one, is predominantly female, physically debilitated, and shabbily dressed. Later Volumnia calls Coriolanus's attention to both "our raiment" and "state of bodies" as indicators of "what life/We have led since thy exile" (V.iii.94–96). The down-at-heel troop enters with stately formality, as did the earlier procession, but the mood is now one of grief rather than celebration. Two or three attendants, whatever number might be appropriate to a trio of poverty-stricken aristocrats, serve only to underline the wretchedness of war's victims. If the matrons were to stop precisely in the position from which Volumnia, Virgilia, and Valeria had formerly watched the Triumphal Return, visual analogue would render the world's "slippery turns" devastatingly self-evident.

Coriolanus's commentary spells out the business of the actors once the procession halts. Virgilia curtsies while looking directly at her husband, since he notes not only "that curtsy" but "those doves' eyes." Volumnia "bows," and Young Martius is described as having "an aspect of intercession." The isolation of the two small groups, distanced physically by an expanse of bare stage and emotionally by pride and fear, creates an almost palpable visual tension. Every movement, no matter how ordinary, assumes an extraordinary importance. After the bow and curtsy, Volumnia's party remains silent and transfixed as Coriolanus speaks:

> Let the Volsces
> Plough Rome and harrow Italy, I'll never
> Be such a gosling to obey instinct, but stand
> As if a man were author of himself,
> And knew no other kin. (V.iii.33–37)

These five lines, like those of the Herald in II.i, once more freeze the action while the audience observes the operative forces in the scene, and, consciously or subconsciously, collates this image with its happier predecessor. Coriolanus now stands where he stood in the victory pageant as a Roman hero, flanked then by friends and colleagues, crowned with an oaken garland, and hailed as his country's savior with trumpets and shouts. He now stands alone, accompanied only by his mortal enemy, and branded by his countrymen as a traitor. He still wears military uniform, but in the service of Rome's enemy. His family, earlier gathered in prosperity to laud his success, now assembles in poverty to denounce him as author of their ruin.

As the scene gains momentum, Shakespeare plots major movements with some care. As earlier, in the midst of national glory, Coriolanus was reminded of his family ties by Cominius's "Look, sir, your mother," now, in national disgrace, he is once more recalled to the claims of kinship by Virgilia's "My lord and husband!" (V.iii.37). In contrast to the swift genuflection with which he once greeted his mother, he now stands motionless to speak the line "These eyes are not the same I wore in Rome" (V.iii.38). That he waits an additional four lines before he stirs betrays his awareness of the threat posed to his survival by the spontaneous affectionate relationships he enjoys with his family. When he does move, it is toward Virgilia; and their kiss, a rarity in Shakespeare, occurring on an empty stage within a sequence otherwise almost bereft of action, has an electrifying impact. Virgilia's influence upon her husband, despite the "gracious silence" she evinces most of the time, is profound. Only after the kiss (twelve lines after Virgilia first addresses him) does Coriolanus kneel to his mother, the other, ostensibly stronger claimant to his loyalty. The fact that Volumnia remains stationary, and that Coriolanus crosses to her is again significant; nevertheless, an audience cannot fail to recognize how altered are the conditions under which he now manifests his affection and respect, or how much longer than formerly it takes him to make the deferential gesture. Is it an indication of Coriolanus's subconscious resistance to his mother's baneful influence that he postpones the moment of symbolic submission as long as he can? In any case, the battle lines between mother and son are finally drawn, and the scene moves inevitably to the conclusion this stage image prefigures.

The austere visual strength of this sequence was largely unknown to playgoers from the mid-eighteenth century until after World War I. The traditional staging took its inspiration from a production of James Thomson's *Coriolanus*, mounted by James Quin at Covent Garden in 1749, in which the scene was staged in part as a discovery. *"The scene discovers the camp,"* we are told,

> *a croud of* Volscian *officers with files of soldiers drawn up.* . . .
> *The* Roman *ladies advance slowly from the depth of the stage, with* Veturia [Shakespeare's Volumnia] *the mother of* Coriolanus *and* Volumnia [Shakespeare's Virgilia] *his wife at their head, all clad in habits of mourning.* Coriolanus *stands at the head of the* Volsci, *surrounded by his lictors.* . . .[17]

The eloquent visual starkness of Shakespeare's Pleading Scene held no attraction for Thomson. His version of the episode demands a formally magnificent setting, against which Volumnia and her son pose grandly and declaim with style. As the direction suggests, the *mise-en-scène* features a military tableau of considerable splendor. Officers and soldiers, symmetrically arranged on either side of the stage, function as living scenery, while Coriolanus is neatly disposed at center stage with lictors to his right and left. The matrons then process in ceremonial solemnity from as far upstage as possible. It should be noted that Young Martius was banned from the event: the presence of a child was deemed inimical to classic decorum.

An engraving, presumably inspired to some degree by this production and published in the *Universal Magazine* of 1749, shows the matrons accompanied by eight attendants, and the artist implies that there are more just behind those illustrated. The women are gowned in gracefully designed classical drapery, and some, including Veturia, have their heads covered. The visual effect implies tasteful simplicity rather than hardship. In the background military figures are grouped before a camp, while the Capitol looms in the distance. A martial display, an abundance of painted scenery, and a lengthy parade of mourning matrons remained fixtures of the Pleading Scene for well over a century and a half.

Sheridan, in his turn, provides the following direction for the opening of this scene:

> SCENE *a Camp with* Volscian *Soldiers.* . . . *Enter* CORIOLANUS, TULLUS, GALESUS, VOLUSIUS; *The* Roman *Ladies advance slowly with* VETURIA *and* VOLUMNA, *all clad in mourning.* CORIOLANUS *sits on his tribunal; but seeing them, advances, and goes hastily to embrace his mother.*

As in Thomson's drama, the scene opens with the discovery of the Volscian camp, before which is once more arranged a military tableau; this time, however, Coriolanus is not part of it. He enters with several companions shortly after the shutters are withdrawn and seats himself regally on a dais, with Tullus at his side, to watch the progress of the funereal train. Genteel sobriety, as opposed to charmless penury, characterizes the women's wardrobe. "The plain Neatness of Veturia's Dress, and the other Roman Matrons," noted one theatregoer, "were admirably suited to the Simplicity of those Times."[18] Since Sheridan played Thomson's text of the Pleading episode, his stagecraft for the rest of the scene is of little consequence. What does matter, however, is the fact that John Philip Kemble grafted Sheridan's Volscian Camp setting, martial tableau, and parade of grieving females upon his largely Shakespearean text, and thus consecrated the freakish result to theatrical posterity.

Kemble's version places all the play's action from the Pleading sequence onwards in one long scene designated as Act V. The promptbook orders "Everybody for last Act," so presumably the 240 persons who graced the ovation either were part of Volumnia's entourage or were picturesquely arranged to receive her. According to the promptbook, the *mise-en-scène* was again "The Volscian Camp," against which were massed "Senators, Officers, Soldiers, & Banners." Somewhere upstage of center were placed two throne chairs, near which Coriolanus and Tullus stand as the shutters are removed to a "Flourish of Drums and Trumpets." Shakespeare's preliminary conversation between the generals is replaced by three lines from Thomson:

> *Cor.* Here, noble Tullus, sit, and judge my conduct;
> Nor spare to check me, if I act amiss.
> *Auf.* Marcius, the Volscian fate is in thy hand.

The men occupy the throne chairs as in Sheridan's version.

In lieu of Shakespeare's silent entry, Kemble's matrons are heralded by "Soft Musick R. at first distant—nearer by degrees." The women appear as usual in well-cut *"mourning habits,"* and no mention is made by Volumnia of the toll war has levied on their bodies and dress. To continued instrumental music, the lengthy line of black-garbed suppliants (with Young Martius happily restored) passes diagonally through the civil and military ranks from R.U.E. (right upper entrance) to down left—but more a study in frigid majesty than domestic pathos, to judge from contemporary accounts. The inordinate time required for the company to cross the stage and compose itself elegantly retards Coriolanus's introductory commentary ("My wife comes foremost...") and utterly disrupts the brusque rhythm of Shakespeare's design. One is hard put to imagine a greater visual contrast than that between Shakespeare's monochrome image of two small grim parties isolated on an empty stage where every word and gesture counts and Kemble's technicolor extravaganza which from moment to moment threatens to swamp the main action, and tempts the principals into falseness and excess. In order to have her presence noticed against the competing background, Virgilia "Advances a step" towards Coriolanus as she says, "My lord and husband," and the static-dynamic tension so crucial to Shakespeare's stage image vanishes. The immobile stance and stern reserve as Coriolanus replies, "These eyes are not the same I wore in Rome" (V.iii.38) were also judged insufficiently flamboyant. The line was cut, and the exclamation "I melt, and am not/Of stronger earth than others" (V.iii.28–29) was transposed from elsewhere and delivered as Coriolanus unhesitatingly "Runs down to her." Kemble's Coriolanus eventually kneels to his mother using Shakespeare's words and on Shakespeare's cue, but the simple strength of the gesture must have gone for little in the welter of scenic display and spectacular movement that preceded and surrounded it.

Macready generally adopted Kemble's notion of this scene, but managed to outdo his mentor in the way of show. Indeed, Macready's version seems to have lost all sight of the purpose of this episode in a fascination with visual gigantism. "The city frowns in the distance," wrote one observer, "begirt with the lofty wall of *Servius*.... The Volscian army literally fills the stage with its dense files" (*John Bull*, 18 March 1838). The arrival of Volumnia's embassy, "stretching obliquely across the stage in the midst of these brilliant warrior-files, one long, dreary, sable line of monotonous misery," seemed to divide "as with a black thread the red masses of the Volscian army," wrote another (*Spectator*, 17 March 1838). Here the elaboration of archaeological and picturesque detail reduces the status of the scene's central image to something like an afterthought.

Phelps, who often mended the errors of his predecessors, this time was content to maintain the Kemble-Macready tradition. Forrest, with wonted vulgarity, added four Roman ambassadors with gold staffs to the procession, thus undermining the vulnerable femininity of the image. In Henry Irving's production, the matrons' costumes drew more attention than their wearers. "Leading out the ladies of Rome to sue for mercy in one of the camp scenes of Hawes Craven's wondrous designing," related a typical reviewer, "she [Volumnia] and they wear white girdled chitons of crêpe de Chine, with their heads bowed and draped in large togas of black crêpe de Chine" (*Daily Express*, 16 April 1901). With Irving's revival, however, it became apparent that the usefulness of the sequence as a vehicle for stage spectacle was waning. "When Volumnia comes to intercede for Rome," urged the *Pall Mall Gazette* critic (16 April 1901), "she should not be accompanied by so large a train of symmetrically-attired ladies. No doubt these ladies balance the assembled Volscians in the stage picture, but one could very well give them up too." Both Volscian tableau and mourning matrons disappeared with the Old Vic revival of 1920, and the episode was at last allowed its intrinsic austere grandeur.

3. Coriolanus's Assassination

The visual pattern of Coriolanus's assassination (V.vi.48–154), like that of the Pleading Scene, bears strong resemblance to the design for the Triumphal Return episode. A series of cues for sound, blocking, and business recall an earlier, happier image, while the ugliest of variations continuously and irrevocably deface it.

Prior to Coriolanus's appearance (V.vi.70), two groups are gathered onstage, as for his triumphal entry; there seems no obvious reason why Aufidius and the conspirators should not assume the space taken previously by Sicinius and Brutus, while the Lords (probably only three) occupy the area once tenanted by Volumnia, Virgilia, and their party. An audience could scarcely fail to notice the sad fact that the family group, once gathered to laud Coriolanus's conquests, is now replaced by strangers who compass his ruin. Again, as in the original episode, the noise of Coriolanus's approach interrupts a conversation, this time between Aufidius and the conspirators: *"Drummes and Trumpets sounds, with great showts of the people"* runs the Folio direction. As if to focus the audience's recollection upon the earlier scene, with Volumnia's proud assertion "before him he carries noise" (II.i.158–59) and the reiterated "Welcome to Rome, renowned Coriolanus" (II.i.166–67), the First Conspirator reminds Aufidius:

> Your native town you enter'd like a post,
> And had no welcome home, but he returns
> Splitting the air with noise. (V.vi.49–51)

Coriolanus, to preserve the visual analogue, must enter by the same door used for his triumphal entry. The nature of the present homecoming contrasts tellingly with the one the audience recalls. The Folio direction reads *"Enter Coriolanus marching with Drumme, and Colours. The Commoners being with him."* State ritual now is lacking; the comradely support of members of his own class is missing too; and the military effect of drums and colors seems a touch unapt for a meeting with civil powers. Stranger still, his companions are now commoners, a group rigorously excluded from the earlier entry. The imprecise phrasing of the direction *"The Commoners being with him"* may imply a disorganized presence, rather than an orderly arrangement, another striking variation on the Roman scene. Strangest of all, at the point in the action where the Herald formerly hailed Coriolanus's accomplishments, the man who shrank from hearing his "nothings monster'd" now blatantly hymns his own exploits.

On the phrase "and we here deliver" (V.vi.80), Coriolanus comes down to the Lords to hand them the armistice document, a movement that echoes visually the cross to his family who occupied the same stage space earlier. Now, however, he is met, not with assertions of kinship and affection, but with Aufidius's cry of "Traitor." The episode ends not with the warm re-establishment of family ties but with the Conspirators' "Kill, kill, kill, kill, kill him" (V.vi.130).

Shakespeare does not provide detailed blocking for the Assassination Scene, but indicates, as usual, key effects: *"Draw* both the Conspirators, and kils Martius, who falles, Auffidius stands on him." The action seems meant to be furtive and swift. Martius drops quickly, without resistance, and, in a moment of instinctive animality, Aufidius leaps upon the body. The inglorious end of Rome's erstwhile savior could hardly be more potently realized. The stage is by no means crowded: Aufidius and a few soldiers, a knot of commoners, three or four conspirators, and perhaps three lords witness Coriolanus's final moments. An alien, he dies by treachery among strangers without a word of enlightenment or insight, and, as a bizarre finale, his corpse is mistreated. His eulogy is spoken by a triumphant enemy, who grudgingly arranges a funeral procession and serves as pallbearer. The final direction, "*Exeunt bearing the Body of Martius. A dead March Sounded*," signals a cortège of only impromptu formality. The man whose life was heralded by trumpets leaves the stage to the beat of muffled drums; and as he does so, one is poignantly reminded of the matching exit in the Triumphal Return Scene with Cominius's upbeat "On to the Capitol" (II.i.204), the "*Flourish. Cornets*," and Coriolanus, his wife and mother holding either hand, departing "*in State, as before.*"

Shakespeare's dingy and muted dénouement held little allure for eighteenth- and nineteenth-century playgoers. A hero, especially a military one, should die heroically and be mourned with style. In an effort to mitigate the play's downbeat conclusion, managers gilded Shakespeare's stark imagery with abandon. Any visual analogy with the Triumphal Return Scene emerged entirely by accident.

Sheridan's Assassination sequence was drawn primarily from Thomson's play, with the addition of some Shakespearean lines. After the Roman matrons withdrew, the martial legions remained onstage to hear Tullus offer Coriolanus a safe return to Rome. When the latter insisted on justifying his behavior before the Council, Tullus called for Volusius. Volusius and the Conspirators entered "*with their swords drawn*," and were ordered by Tullus to "Seize and secure the traitor." Coriolanus resists, grandly "*Laying his hand on his sword*," and insisting, "Who dares/Approach me, dies!" Volusius shouts, "Die thou," and "*As CORIOLANUS draws his sword, VOLUSIUS and the rest rush upon him and stab him.* TULLUS *stands, without drawing."* Coriolanus goes down resisting nobly to the last. He is even given a line or two to expire by:

> Off!—Villains. [*Endeavours to free himself, falls.*
> Oh murdering slaves! assassinating cowards. [*Dies.*

Then "*Enter GALESUS, the Volscian states, officers and friends of CORIOLANUS, and TITUS, with a large band of soldiers, &c.*" Against an artfully posed mass of colorful living scenery, the statesman Galesus condemns the act and speaks a political homily. Tullus makes no attempt to stand on the corpse; and there is no procession and no dead march. The shutters simply close on the lavish tableau. Shakespeare's visual design for the episode could hardly have counted for less.

In Kemble's production, as in Sheridan's, the civil and military pageant remained in place after the matrons departed at the end of the Pleading sequence. Since Coriolanus was already on stage, there was no question of his entry with commoners or of any parallel with the opening of the Triumphal Return Scene. After Coriolanus refuses Tullus's offer of permission to return to Rome, again following Sheridan's version, the quarrel ensues more or less in Shakespeare's idiom, viewed, however, by an audience of some 200 souls. Volusius speaks Aufidius's "Insolent villain!" and "VOLUSIUS *and other Volscian Officers draw, and kill* CORIOLANUS." An assassination by Volscian officers is not at all the same thing, one should note, as death at the hands of anonymous conspirators. The sequence was at least shorn of the Thomson-Sheridan struggle, and the death itself, as performed by Kemble, must have been close to Shakespeare's concept. When the Volscian assassins ran Martius through, Sir Walter Scott recalls, "there was no precaution, no support; in the midst of the exclamation against Tullus Aufidius, he dropped as dead and as flat on the stage as if the swords had really met in his body."[19] As Coriolanus falls, "The Senators start up R," presumably in fright. The Lords do not intervene; their speeches are cut. Aufidius's lines are combined into one continuous address, from which his offer to be a pallbearer is omitted. On the order, "Beat, beat the drum that it speak mournfully" (V.vi.149), Kemble perversely calls for "Trump[ts] & muffled

Drum," thus altering the sound texture of the sequence. As the cortège moves off, the military figures are ordered to "Lower Ensigns & arms." Shakespeare's few but expressive trailing pikes were judged insufficiently eye-catching. Kemble does appreciate the dynamic effect of the processional exit, however, even if its impact is diminished by pictorial extravagance and neglect of crucial authorial detail.

Macready played something close to the Kemble text, and died in the Kemble manner. "He . . . is magnificently murdered by the onslaught of a dozen Volscians, who transfix him at once with their swords," one eyewitness noted (*Morning Post*, 13 March 1838). "The scene was disfigured by no physical struggles," recorded another; "the actor fell at once, as though that excess of vitality was only capable of instantaneous extinction" (*Morning Chronicle*, 13 March 1838). Macready also employed the Kemble processional exit, but augmented it further with scenic display. "In the last scene 200 soldiers of the Guards were employed as supernumeraries, to represent the Volscian army," we are told (*Theatrical Observer*, 13 March 1838). On "Bear from hence his body" (V.vi.141), a reviewer reported that "the warriors around lift up the dead body of the conqueror on their shields, hang round it the splendidest trophies of war, and trailing their steel pikes in sorrow, move with it slowly up the stage to the sound of mournful music as the curtain falls" (*The Examiner*, 18 March 1838). Shakespeare's *ad hoc*, almost grudging, cortège now becomes a highly formal farewell to an honored comrade. The pathos of Shakespeare's minimalistic staging is inundated by a tidal wave of Victorian grandeur.

As a final example of theatrical insensitivity to Shakespeare's visual directions, one must point to Forrest's handling of the assassination, probably the grossest manipulation of the play's stage imagery in its history. Like his predecessors, Forrest ignored Shakespeare's preliminaries to the murder, and, of course, any relationship to the Triumphal Return episode. On Coriolanus's "To use my lawful sword!" (V.vi.129), Forrest's promptbook offers the following instructions:

> Aufidius—Volusius and all the officers surround Coriolanus, draw their swords, & stab him. Same time they are speaking. As the officers advance the soldiers come down on R & L and close in double lines with backs to audience.... When Coriolanus falls dead. Officers and soldiers separate R & L and his body is discovered lying on stage. The senators on RH rise in astonishment.

Whether Forrest hid the murder out of squeamishness or the conviction that sudden disclosure of the body would be more dramatic than a stabbing, the effect was the same: the audience missed the transcendent instant when the lonely dragon passes from titanic rage to dispassionate death. As one theatregoer put it, "The crowd rush upon him, cover him from the view of the audience, and in the melee he is slain, but the manner of his death is left to the imagination." (*Morning Post*, New York, 28 April 1855). A spontaneous death by an enraged military, although a sure-fire way to elicit audience sympathy, is not at all the same thing as Aufidius's treacherous and premeditated murder. But there was worse to come. After Coriolanus had been carried off in processional panoply by military supers (some 150 in the 1863 revival) a new scene was added in which the curtain rose on

> a closely shaded Grove. Night. Stage dark—A Pyre discovered in C. 4G. [Centre. 4th Groove] with the body of Coriolanus on raised trap platform behind pyre to sink gradually when fire is burning during the Dirge.

With soldiers, senators, Roman ladies, Volumnia, Virgilia, and Young Martius kneeling at the sides of the stage, Coriolanus's corpse was cremated while a chorus of male and female citizens intoned a dirge, and a phoenix mounted heavenward from the flames!

Such flagrant abuse of Shakespeare's stage imagery is happily less common today; but visual philistinism remains far from unknown. And the root cause lies, as in earlier centuries, in an unwillingness on the part of theatre artists to trust the dramatist's minimalist design to speak for itself. Where Shakespeare's stagecraft is concerned, less is often more.

NOTES

This paper, in slightly altered form, was originally presented at the *Stage Images in Shakespeare* seminar during the World Shakespeare Congress (West Berlin, April 1986).

1. Maurice Charney, *Shakespeare's Roman Plays: The Function of Imagery in the Drama* (Cambridge, MA: Harvard Univ. Press, 1961).

2. Useful explorations of Shakespeare's stage imagery, in addition to Professor Charney's study cited above, include R.A. Foakes, "Suggestions for a New Approach to Shakespeare's Imagery," *Shakespeare Survey*, 5 (1952), 81–92; Alan C. Dessen, *Elizabethan Drama and the Viewer's Eye* (Chapel Hill: Univ. of North Carolina Press, 1977); Philip C. McGuire and David A. Samuelson, eds., *Shakespeare: The Theatrical Dimension* (New York: AMS Press, 1979); Sidney Homan, ed., *Shakespeare's "More Than Words Can Witness"* (Lewisburg: Bucknell Univ. Press, 1980); Ann Pasternak Slater, *Shakespeare the Director* (Brighton: Harvester Press, 1982); David Bevington, *Action is Eloquence* (Cambridge, MA: Harvard Univ. Press, 1984); Alan C. Dessen, *Elizabethan Stage Conventions and Modern Interpreters* (Cambridge: Cambridge Univ. Press, 1984); and James R. Siemon, *Shakespearean Iconoclasm* (Berkeley: Univ. of California Press, 1985).

3. See Maurice Charney, "Hamlet without Words," *Shakespeare's "More Than Words Can Witness,"* p. 24.

4. Unless otherwise noted, all *Coriolanus* quotations are taken from *The Riverside Shakespeare*, ed. G. Blakemore Evans (Boston: Houghton Mifflin, 1974). Stage directions, as noted, are from the Folio.

5. *Shakespeare and the Viewer's Eye*, pp. 55–70.

6. A major flaw in the play was judged to be the titular hero's want of sentimental appeal. This view is epitomized by the drama critic for the *National Advocate* (New York, 11 September 1818): "Coriolanus never seizes upon the heart, or awakens sentiment. Petulant and irascible, a soldier bred to the rough usages of the camp, filled with pride and tinged with ambition, he moves through the piece without any of those soft and touching qualities calculated to excite great interest, or awaken feelings of commiseration for the misfortune of a hero."

7. Although Shakespeare's production intentions are merely matter for speculation in many of the plays, his directorial hand is apparent in *Coriolanus* to a marked degree. Properties and costumes are spelled out (I.i.242; II.iii.40; II.iii.139–41; V.iii.94–96); movement and

speech instructions are provided for actors (I.i.255; I.iv.58–60; I.ix.91; Iv.i.19–20; III.i.188–89; IV.ii.52–53); and business is noted and carefully cued (I.vi.29–30; I.vi.73–75; II.iii.98–100; III.iii.133–35; IV.v.95–96; IV.v.109–10). These, and a multitude of similar examples, cumulatively suggest Shakespeare's concern for a simple, statuesque, uncluttered visual style for the play.

    8. *Shakespeare's Roman Plays: The Function of Imagery in the Drama*, p. 206.

    9. Production information, unless otherwise noted, is drawn from Sheridan's acting edition of the play, titled *Coriolanus: or, the Roman Matron* (1755) (Cornmarket Press reprint, 1969); Kemble's promptbook for the 1811 production at Covent Garden in *John Philip Kemble's Promptbooks*, ed. Charles H. Shattuck (Charlottesville: Univ. Press of Virginia, 1974); *The Shakespeare Promptbooks*, ed. Charles H. Shattuck (Urbana and London: Univ. of Illinois Press, 1965), *Coriolanus*, Samuel Phelps's promptbook (item 13), and Edwin Forrest's promptbook (item 22); and Henry Irving's promptbook, recently acquired by the British Library. I am grateful to the Folger Shakespeare Library and the British Library for permission to quote from unpublished promptbooks.

    10. Sheridan staged a number of *Coriolanus* revivals, the first of which was at the Smock Alley Theatre, Dublin, 29 February 1752; but the 1754 production at Covent Garden seems to be been his most successful effort. See Esther K. Sheldon, *Thomas Sheridan of Smock-Alley* (Princeton: Princeton Univ. Press, 1967) and her invaluable essay, "Sheridan's *Coriolanus:* An Eighteenth-Century Compromise," *Shakespeare Quarterly*, 14 (1963).

    11. "Advertisement," *Coriolanus: or, the Roman Matron*, n.p.

    12. Sheridan, "Advertisement," *Coriolanus*, n.p.

    13. Several Kemble promptbooks survive (see Charles H. Shattuck, *The Shakespeare Promptbooks*, cited in note 9). I have cited from the Wister copy with the Ovation addendum, published by Charles H. Shattuck in *John Philip Kemble's Promptbooks* (also cited in note 9), to enable the reader more easily to consult the book for himself or herself. The Wister promptbook, representing the production as it stood in 1811, does not differ materially in any of the directions I cite from the official Covent Garden promptbook (Shattuck, *Coriolanus*, 2) in the Folger Shakespeare Library.

    14. According to Thomas Goodwin (*Sketches and Impressions*, ed. R. Osgood, 1887), "The military part of the spectacle was 'by permission,' composed of a portion of . . . the Life Guards. They were a magnificent set of men, every one of whom was over six feet in height. . . . In a stage

procession a hundred or more such men with their natural military bearing, clad in the costumes and bearing the arms and armor of Roman soldiers . . . could hardly fail to make a grand and imposing feature" (pp. 34–35).

15. Julian Charles Young, *A Memoir of Charles Mayne Young* (London and New York: Macmillan and Co., 1871), I, 63.

16. Sheridan, in the "Advertisement" to his acting edition of 1755, emphasized that historically an ovation differed from a triumph in that a sheep was sacrificed instead of a bull; moreover, "in the Ovation all marched on foot, but in the triumph the victor was carried in a chariot drawn by horses." As early as 1799, however, a performance at New York's Park Theatre advertised as a feature of its ovation "Six Virgins strewing flowers before a Triumphal Car, *Two White Horses*" (*Daily Advertiser*, New York, 3 June 1799). John McCullough also used horses at the Grand Opera House in 1878 to the annoyance of the *New York Daily Tribune*. "The real horses distract attention from the serious business of the play," wrote their critic. "We need not enter a theatre to behold a horse." Undoubtedly the greatest display of livestock in the play's history was provided by Drury Lane for a 1837 production starring Pierce Butler, sometime husband of Fanny Kemble. The menagerie featured in the spectacular *Caractarus* seems to have been pressed into service. An advertisement reads in part: "Beasts for Sacrifice, richly decorated! (Furnished from the Zoological Gardens) . . . Wain, containing Spoils, drawn by Horses. . . . Riches borne upon a Camel (Furnished from the Zoological Gardens). . . . The Emperor's Car! drawn by Horses three-a-breast, followed by Elephants richly Caparisoned, bearing various Crowns and Sceptres tributary to Rome" (*Theatrical Observer*, 6 November 1837).

17. *Coriolanus, The Works of James Thomson* (London: W. Bowyer, W. Strahan, J. Rivington, et al., 1773), IV, 268.

18. Letter to the *Public Advertiser*, 13 December 1754.

19. James Boaden, "Memoirs of the Life of John Philip Kemble," *The Quarterly Review*, 36 (1826), 224.

Reprinted by permission from John Ripley, "Coriolanus's Stage Imagery on Stage, 1754–1901," Shakespeare Quarterly 38 (1987), 338–50. Copyright 1987 by The Folger Library.

Coriolanus: Body Politic and Private Parts

Zvi Jagendorf

Political thinking and, consequently, writing about politics have traditionally made use of certain master tropes that remain constant in principle even when the nature and content of political discourse change. At the foundation of Western political thought, for instance, is the trope of the dialectical relationship between man in the state of nature (that is, man fending for himself and caring for the propagation of his species) and man in the domain of culture (that is, man in the embrace of community, of *polis,* of an organism that, ideally, is himself writ large, but that also dominates him, subjecting him to a necessity beyond the easily graspable one of his own needs and instincts).

Among the archetypal scenes of politics are those that reveal the reverberation between these poles of unity and fragmentation, wholeness and separation. Achilles sulking in his tent, the tribes of Israel retreating after the death of Solomon, the Roman plebs leaving the city for the Mons Sacra in the time of Coriolanus, the secession to the tennis court in prerevolutionary France: we recognize in such historical and fictional scenes ur-configurations of political intercourse. An organism purporting to be a whole (a kingdom, a republic, a military expedition, an assembly) splits into parts, revealing itself to be an uneasy association of warlords, a hierarchy of classes, or a tenuous alliance of tribes. Politics is about division more than it is about unity. But the discourse of politics (as opposed to the history of political action), a discourse that occupies a rhetorical space between the opposing poles of fragmentation and wholeness, exploits the resources of both extremes, deriving as much energy from images of wholeness and totality as it does from the language of dismemberment and fission.

Political writings that attempt to analyze and describe the phenomena of the great wealth-creating and labor-exploiting industrial cities of the nineteenth century inevitably grapple with a spectacle of pervasive division. The city (London, Manchester, Paris) is a mass of people living in close proximity, but the people are separated from each other by great barriers of money and class. In *Capital* Marx quotes a London newspaper that describes not a riot or a rebellion but quotidian urban life during a severe economic depression in 1867:

> A frightful spectacle was to be seen yesterday in one part of the metropolis.... Next door to the most enormous accumulation of wealth the world ever saw, cheek by jowl with this are 40,000 helpless, starving people.[1]

The property-respecting, bourgeois newspaper that Marx quotes uses figures of proximity ("next door," "cheek by jowl") to convey the shame aroused in even the most passive observer by such glaring inequality. Marx himself uses the syntax of opposition to lay bare the workings of an industrial economy that accumulates wealth for the capitalist at the expense of the worker:

> The object of all development of the productiveness of labour, within the limits of capitalist production, is to shorten that part of the working-day during which the workman must labour for his own benefit, and by that very shortening, to lengthen the other part of the day, during which he is at liberty to work gratis for the capitalist. (p. 321)

"Shorten" is here paired with "lengthen" to mark the assertion that the increased effort of the laborer produces only the increased profit of the owner. Both Marx and the anonymous journalist who describes the London slums imagine a social space (city, factory) in which economic laws divide the hungry from the sated with the finality of God the Father separating the saved from the damned on the Day of Judgment. But whereas in

Coriolanus: *Body Politic and Private Parts*

the divine order Heaven and Hell are separate and independent, in the economic order the heaven of one class is made out of the hell suffered by the other. Plenty is then a function of dearth, and Marx's keen, quantifying intellect exposes the engineering of a fragmented society in which the division of the laborer's time into part for his wage and part for the owner's own profit deepens the worker's poverty as it increases the owner's wealth.

Most political writing has imagined society simultaneously as a whole, a complete organism, and as divided, fragmented. Even when the analysis emphasizes division, as Marx's does, the analysis could not function without the enabling metaphor or framing idea of a complete body: division is meaningless without a grounding wholeness. The concept of "the whole" may be quasi-scientific when it uses a measure such as "the market," but the discourse of totality in politics tends to be neither scientific nor pragmatic. When articulated in energetic, ambitious ways, it tends to be utopian, looking forward (or backward) to an ideal state of affairs such as the Rule of the Saints or communism, ideal states in which contradictions disappear and society, cured of division, becomes a whole body, a perfect community.

In Act 2 of *The Tempest*, Gonzalo's dream of a paradisal commonwealth envisions the disappearance of all distinction and division:

> Letters should not be known; riches, poverty
> And use of service, none; contract, succession,
> Bourn, bound of land, tilth, vineyard, none. (2.1.156–58)[2]

Even work would disappear, its place filled by the mellifluous music of laziness: ". . . all men idle, all" (l. 160).

Gonzalo's commonwealth is a version of a utopian state made possible by the discovery of the New World; he imagines European man beginning again. But Shakespeare's aristocrat/warrior of the history plays, rooted in the feudal relations of an old world undergoing drastic change, also has his dream of wholeness. John of Gaunt on his deathbed in *Richard II* magisterially summons up the memory of a self-enclosed world within a world: "This earth of majesty . . ./This happy breed of men, this little world . . ." (2.1.41,45). Gaunt's authoritative "This," like Gonzalo's confident "all," points to a political entity understood to be a perfect symbiosis between a motherland and a ruling caste. "This England" (l. 50), apparently such a confident, defining phrase, derives its strength, but also its weakness, from what it leaves out. For Gaunt the integrity of the ruling caste means the integrity of the kingdom. But already the monarch is busy "farm[ing] out" the "royal realm" (1.4.44), and the future holds out a spectacle of "these Englands" that is the fragmentation of the English into warring parties, pressed soldiers, bands of robbers—in other words, mortal men competing for a name or wealth or power or whatever goal they might use to justify their aggressions.

I

The opposing discourses of wholeness and fragmentation are present throughout Shakespeare's political theatre, both English and Roman. Rome is Shakespeare's well-equipped, sharply lit laboratory for research into the nature of politics. Not being England, the Roman political system lends itself to the kind of cold, unsentimental analysis that could not be practiced on one's own system. Rome is no demi-paradise. It boasts no hereditary monarchs; indeed, its founding acts include rebellion and regicide. Most important of all, Rome's land bears no mystery; metaphors of wholeness and sanctity are not "natural" here as they are in England. Rome is a city of men and women, a cultural construct suggesting a lucid, often geometric architecture of forum, street, villa, gate, and battlefield. In this setting a political drama is played out subordinating all other interests to itself. Its major features are oratory, debate, parades, public assemblies, and scenes of persuasion. In *Coriolanus* the factor that outweighs the others is the hatred between ruling class and common people in a city at war.

Although Coriolanus may be one of Shakespeare's most politically naive characters, he is the protagonist of a play that is hugely, indeed grotesquely, political. It starts in Rome with a riot over bread and ends in Antium with the assassination of a general in the middle of a parade. The action gains much of its driving force from the twin motives of class hatred and war.

Coriolanus: *Body Politic and Private Parts*

Indeed, war in this play may be seen as Rome's only non-political activity. War, for Rome, is a kind of relief, in the form of fighting others, from the obsessive rigors of internal strife.

My question of the play is not what makes Coriolanus run (or, electorally speaking, what makes it so hard for him to run)—although this is a fascinating question and one put by Plutarch when he draws attention to Coriolanus' lack of a father and therefore of a model of reason and restraint.[3] However, as psycho-history it is only tangentially related to my major question, which is "Why is the presence of the body and the impression of the body's language so prominent in this play?" The physical is inescapable in this most unerotic of plays; everywhere we encounter legs, arms, tongues, scabs, scratches, wounds, mouths, teeth, voices, bellies, and toes together with such actions as eating, vomiting, starving, beating, scratching, wrestling, piercing, and undressing.

One answer would be: War. The body language of battle is the language of body counts, the description of wounds, and the naming of limbs. Ever since the *Iliad*, the poetry of war has included catalogues of the physique and the wounds of the dying and of the victors. But the body language of *Coriolanus* is so insistent, especially in scenes of political controversy, that an argument for this language as merely another example of this poetic convention is insufficient. More is going on than the natural flow of language from blows on the field to insults in the forum. Indeed, the language of body is so vivid in the play that one might be drawn to understand it in the terms of a carnivalesque kind of physicality emanating from the people. That grotesque richness of expression was certainly available to Shakespeare. Bakhtin finds it in Rabelais and describes memorably the grotesque body as a body

> never finished, never completed; it is continually built, created, and builds and creates another body. Moreover, the body swallows the world and is itself swallowed by the world.[4]

In Bakhtin's drama of the grotesque body, lines that normally divide are blurred; sex and mouth, anus and belly exist in a fluid continuum. This is an optimistic, populist body that makes even insult serve abundance. Dismemberment is here a means of multiplication.

In *Coriolanus* a low language of cursing, insult, and scorn also obsessively dismembers the body, separating arms, legs, mouths, eyes, and belly in a recurring synecdochal pattern. But the political economy of this play is characterized by hunger and dearth rather than by Rabelaisian abundance. The tropes of dismemberment (synecdoche) in a context of class hatred and of competition for power based on a shortage of food speak of a body politic at war with itself. The play's rhetoric makes us see the body politic as chopped up into grotesquely independent limbs and organs that refuse to become a complete body even though political orthodoxy says that this is what they must do. In the light of the insistent synecdoche, or naming of parts, the foundations of the traditional trope of the whole, healthy body appear shaky. The trope may be seen in this play to be a rhetorical construct promoted by the rulers to keep the hungry plebs subservient and to persuade them to accept the inevitability of their hunger and powerlessness.[5]

The play is unique in Shakespeare's *oeuvre* in opening with a violent crowd scene, a bread riot that historical research has shown would not have been unfamiliar to Shakespeare's audience. But I do not want to make an issue of context; rather I want to show how the language of the rebellious citizen in the first long speech of the play sets out the terms of the dialectic by means of which the topic of the fragmented body may be interpreted:

> SECOND CITIZEN One word, good citizens.
> FIRST CITIZEN We are accounted poor citizens, the patricians good. What authority surfeits on would relieve us. If they would yield us but the superfluity while it were wholesome we might guess they relieved us humanely, but they think we are too dear. The leanness that afflicts us, the object of our misery, is as an inventory to particularize their abundance; our sufferance is a gain to them. Let us revenge this with our pikes ere we become rakes.... (I.1.13–22)

Division—the division of food and that of class—controls this surprisingly articulate, even elegant speech. As is common in highly political argument, the most familiar and conventional phrases become charged with the polarities of controversy. "Good citizens" is thus unsayable because the facts of hunger have redistributed the conventional adjectives. The First Citizen's speech sets out, both in its imagery of fat and thin bodies and in its antithetical syntax, the quite horrifying economics of the famine. As in Marx's analysis of the workshop, the abundance enjoyed by one class is measured by the hunger of the other (if not directly created by it). So at the very start of the play, the First Citizen makes clear the reality underlying the body-politic trope. The fat and the thin are indeed interdependent, but they are tied to each other by the cruelty of the market and not by bonds of community. The body trope is therefore closer to cannibalism ("if the wars eat us not up, they will" [ll. 83–84]) than it is to the mystique of a healthy, natural system.

A traditionalist critic of the play would have it that metaphors of the body politic keep reminding us that "the great natural order is realized in a whole of which the single man is only a part."[6] This is wishful thinking, for there is no place for the "great natural order" in the politically circumscribed cultural order of this play, in which the metaphor of the body politic becomes a trope of fragmentation. The body images are grotesque (*pace* Bakhtin) precisely because they *lack* any foundation in a valid concept of wholeness and are therefore split into unruly shapes and forms.

Menenius' well-known parable of the limbs' rebellion against the belly for holding the food and doing no work (ll. 93–153) could be read as a test case. Here an aristocrat who has the common touch argues for the absurdity of rebellion and for the interdependence of the several members of the body politic. Parable is a form of speech that can seduce an audience with a set of figures and tropes that entertain yet lead to a predetermined conclusion. Menenius' parable has a strange fate: it invites skepticism both because of its obvious *parti-pris* and because of its clear failure to achieve its goal of convincing a hungry crowd to go home. There is nothing so naked as failed rhetoric, and Menenius' picture of the altruistically digesting belly sending out nourishment to the carnal economy, leaving itself only the bran, verges on the grotesque, as detailed body tropes tend to do. The aristocrat wants to have it both ways—to talk a gross, popular language and to make his audience accept his view of the body as a map of benevolently authoritarian politics.[7]

The citizen who answers Menenius has his own gravely phrased lexicon of politico-corporeal metaphors—"... the arm our soldier,/Our steed the leg, the tongue our trumpeter" (ll. 114–15)—and they lay claim to a different interpretation of the body, an interpretation that stresses function rather than subservience, action rather than dependence, and, instead of Menenius' horizontal topography of storehouses, rivers, and offices centered on the belly, it posits a vertical model in which head, eye, heart, tongue, and leg cooperate in a common enterprise, restrained only by the guts at the bottom "Who is the sink o'th'body" (l. 119).

Each side in this argument makes metaphors out of limbs, and the result is a foregrounding of the fragment at the expense of the whole. But the aristocrat does this most aggressively: "What do you think,/You, the great toe of this assembly?" (ll. 152–53) asks Menenius of the First Citizen, setting the keynote for the body tropes in the whole play. The organic metaphor of body, reduced to the small change of this grotesque and demeaning synecdoche, cannot retain its cohesive force. If we could, because of the humor, entertain the fable of the smiling and negotiating belly, we cannot take seriously a thinking toe. The figure has become quickly cancerous, proliferating, and out of control. Too many signifiers are chasing too few signifieds, and that is a sure sign of economic trouble.

St. Paul's classic deployment of the body/member topos in 1 Corinthians 11 and 12 is instructive as a comparison of how the tropes of division are handled when the community is called *ecclesia* rather than *polis*.[8] The question of hierarchy is settled in the first several verses of Chapter 11—"But I would have you knowe, that the head of euery man is Christ: and the head of the woman is the man, and the head of Christ is God"—yet there are certain things in common between the state of Shakespeare's Rome and Paul's Corinth. "Schism" and "division" are recurring words in Paul's letter. The community is an unruly one: "For first of all when yee come together in the Church, I heare that there be diuisions among you" (11:18). Strangely enough, this division is marked most strongly in the ritual of the Lord's Supper. Instead of a decorous ceremony, there is pushing and shoving: "For in eating, euery one taketh before the other, his owne supper: one is hungry, and an other is drunken" (11:21). But unlike the real hunger of Shakespeare's crowd, there is no famine in Corinth. Hunger can be satisfied at home. Eat at home, says Paul, so that the Lord's Supper may be an orderly ceremony. Yet that benign solution cannot do away with the underlying cause of division among the faithful. The subtext of these chapters is the question of equality in the community. Not all are equal; some have spiritual gifts, other do not. Some prophesy, speak in tongues, work miracles; others do not. So Paul marshals the body trope in Chapter 12, making use of all its grotesque power to put jealousy and envy in their place:

> For the body is not one member, but many.... And if the eare shall say, Because I am not the eye, I am not of the body: is it therefore not of the body: If the whole body were an eye, where were the hearing: If the whole were hearing, where were the smelling.... (14, 16–17)

Christian commentators have pointed out that, unlike Menenius' fable in Rome, this is not about food. There is no belly in Paul's rhetoric. But the nutritional basis of his argument is still undeniable. The logic for the believer's acceptance of inequality in the division of gifts is set out in Chapter 11:

> ... the Lord Jesus, the same night in which he was betrayed, tooke bread: And when he had giuen thanks, he brake it, and sayd, Take, eate, this is my body, which is broken for you. (23–24)

The original division then is of Christ's body, a body that provides a store of never-depleted nourishment. On the basis of this division, which is the source of an infinite treasure of gifts, Paul can confidently risk the polemic of fragments.[9] Eye, foot, hand, and ear are ultimately restrained not by the logic and need of the human organism but, paradoxically, by the broken *soma Christou*.

Yet while inequality of distribution is not glossed over, and Paul maintains that the body's lower (sexual?) parts be given due honor, this remains the weak link in his argument. He writes that

> ... those members of the bodie, which seeme to bee more feeble, are necessary. And those members of the bodie, which wee thinke to bee lesse honourable, upon these we bestow more abundant honour, and our uncomely parts haue more abundant comelinesse. For our comely parts haue no need: but God hath tempered the bodie together, hauing giuen more abundant honour to that part which lacked. (12:22–24)

But how *has* God given honor to those parts of the body that lack it? *Is* such compensation visible in how we treat and dress the body? *Do* our "uncomely parts" have "more abundant comelinesse?" The answer may well lie in the primitive Christianity of pagan Lear when he contemplates the shelter offered him by the Fool: "The art of our necessities is strange,/And can make vile things precious" (3.2.70–71). But Paul, writing to the young church of Corinth, was more interested in organization than in revolution; order was more important to him than the exaltation of humility.

II

To continue my argument: I would like to distinguish between two focuses on the body in *Coriolanus*. One is the body of the people, the other the body of the hero. Much depends on how we interpret their interaction. Both are prominent features of the play's spectacle. The crowd—the citizens in the street and marketplace, the common soldiers on the battlefield—is a constant feature of the action. We hear their shouts on and offstage. We are encouraged to imagine them jostling for space in the victory parades, and we both see and hear them in the mob scenes of the expulsion and the assassination. Their rhythmic shouting, both in Rome and in Antium ("It shall be so, it shall be so," "He killed my son! My daughter!") accompanies the violent action like the heavily accented rhythms of the people at the climactic moments of the Bach Passions. They are the many-headed multitude, a babble of voices, a mass of limbs, monstrous in their multiplication.

Ranged against this common body in the economy of the play is the single, isolated, discrete body of the man who stands alone, the man who would claim to be all of one piece and even author of himself: Coriolanus. Wholeness is an aristocratic, not just a royal, fantasy. The absolute monarch says *"L'état c'est moi,"* making the wholeness of his body the ground for the totality and health of the state. But absoluteness is not only for kings. The aristocrat, as the observed of all observers, moves in an orbit of perfection, whether it is perfection of beauty, manners, military prowess, or dress. Distinction and excellence are truly aristocratic traits insofar as they are innate, coming with the blood rather than with individual effort. The aristocrat is a narcissist by class, although, unlike Narcissus, he imagines himself complete and self-sufficient. Coriolanus is positioned between an aristocratic fantasy of wholeness and the despised, fragmented carnality of the mass. The people are, in his words, shreds, fragments, scabs. Their breath stinks and they gather junk on the battlefield: "Cushions, leaden spoons,/Irons of a doit" (1.6.5–6). Metonymy and synecdoche are employed in his rhetoric to express an aristocratic contempt for contingency and dependence, indeed for desire, be it desire for food, for spoils, for a voice, or for a vote.

Set opposite the base ranks of those who want *things* is the man whose fantasy it is to be dependent on nothing, to be simply a sign of what he is, a kind of tautology.[10] Cominius knows this, and so addresses him before the victorious Roman army: "Therefore, I beseech you—/In sign of what you are, not to reward/What you have done—before our army hear me" (1.10.25–27). Ideally he is a verb with no object, a model of intransitive action. The emblem of this self-sufficiency is Coriolanus fighting alone in the enemy city with its gates shut behind him and his own army outside. As a trope this is the opposite of plebeian synecdoche. The kind of synecdoche we have seen foregrounds a grotesquely isolated part of the body; here, the solitary hero makes the entire enemy city a part of himself. He takes its name (Corioli), he engages it in a language of blows—"He is himself alone/To answer all the city" (1.5.22–23)—and he can presumably say, when it is all over, "*La ville c'est moi.*"

The people are empty while Coriolanus is full. This is both a statement about stomachs at the beginning of the play and a generalization about the difference between aristocrat and plebs. Because they are empty, they act in order to appease their hunger for food, for spoils, for a voice. Because he is full or, in more speculative language, because he is created essentially by means of a rhetoric of self-sufficiency and self-sustainment, his actions, military and civil, call for scrutiny. What are they for? What makes him work? Looked at from an economic point of view, the language of labor and its reward gives us contradictory answers. On the one hand, Coriolanus' labor, his military prowess, is self-rewarding. As the First Citizen says of him in the first scene, "he pays himself with being proud" (l. 31). This evokes an economic absurdity, though perfect for an aristocrat. It suggests a form of self-employment, a self-supporting activity in which pride is an inexhaustible form of wealth, both capital and wages. On the other hand, in Volumnia's eyes Coriolanus' work is far from self-rewarding. For her, in a shocking image, the intrepid soldier becomes the lowest kind of agricultural laborer, a wage slave. She imagines Coriolanus on the battlefield:

> His bloody brow
> With his mailed hand then wiping, forth he goes,
> Like to a harvest-man that's tasked to mow
> Or all or lose his hire. (1.3.36–39)

This soldier-mower is employed by a very hard taskmaster, and he is subjected to the cruelest of wage conditions, which reduce the heroic challenge of all or nothing (victory or death) to a slave's choice between exhaustion and hunger. Volumnia cannot entertain the possibility that her son may fail. The hero's birthright is to take all. But the possibility of "nothing" may not be ignored, especially when that absurdity, the aristocrat-laborer, must receive his hire and salary from that political oddity, the plebeian employer.

Two kinds of metaphor are used to describe Coriolanus in the play. Often he is imagined in a symbolism of wholeness ("A carbuncle entire, as big as thou art,/Were not so rich a jewel" [1.5.26–27]); at other times he is imagined as an instrument. At a key moment in the play, for example, he is likened to a sword (1.7.76[11]). Remembering the prevalence of synecdoche, we might take this as a demeaning image, another "part" in a play overloaded with fragments and lacking a body. But the killing instrument, stiff, sharp, and bearing no burden of consciousness, is appropriate as a figure for that aspect of Coriolanus' labor in which heroic action is its own end and contingent on nothing. "O' me alone, make you a sword of me?" (l. 76) is Coriolanus' cry to the massed soldiers, following the Folio stage direction *"They . . . take him vp in their Armes and cast vp their Caps."* Because metamorphosis into sword serves the impossible ideal of an absolute instrumentality that is innocent of consciousness, it makes possible the kind of activity that is its own end. As Cominius, the man who knows him best, says about Coriolanus the soldier, he "rewards/His deeds with doing them, and is content/To spend the time to end it" (2.2.127–29). Other soldiers pick up spoils on the field of battle; Coriolanus, disdaining any reward outside the deed itself, is the hero of a one-man economy that boldly distinguishes itself from the market and the getting, spending, exchanging of ordinary men.

But the political pressures of this play will not allow Coriolanus to avoid the market.[12] Doing is not *per se* in a world of rewards, honors, and contests for office. The aristocrat may desire to be simply a sign of what he is, but the logic of action in the world subjects him to the hated commercial practice of tit for tat or reward for what you have *done* rather than for what you are.

Coriolanus is surprisingly like the narcissistic young man addressed in the first group of Shakespeare's sonnets. "You shall not be/The grave of your deserving" (1.10.19–20), says Cominius, echoing the experienced voice in the sonnets that advises the young man to exploit his aristocratic gifts and invest in offspring instead of consuming himself in miserly isolation. To follow this advice, the young man in the sonnets must take a wife and accept the fact of his carnality as a shared nakedness; he must subject himself to the laws of economic and sexual exchange. Coriolanus, too, is urged toward subjection and investment. His hatred of politics, and of the common people who make it clear that politics is a form of exchange, is related to the play's fixation on the body. The weak link in Coriolanus' fantasy of separateness is a physical one, his body marked and scarred in battle for Rome.

Wounds are counters in the play in a grotesque way that mirrors the fragment imagery of Menenius' body metaphor. Coriolanus' wounds, like the belly and the limbs in the opening fable, have life in them: "they smart/To hear themselves remembered" (ll. 28–29); they might "fester 'gainst ingratitude" (l. 30); they are active and decorate the hero's body like some tribal tatoo. Above all, they are numbered counters of exchange in the political market:

> MENENIUS Where is he wounded?
> VOLUMNIA I'th' shoulder and i'th' left arm. There will be large cicatrices to show the people when he shall stand for his place. He received in the repulse of Tarquin seven hurts i'th'body.
> MENENIUS One i'th' neck and two i'th'thigh—there's nine that I know.
> VOLUMNIA He had before this last expedition twenty-five wounds upon him.
> MENENIUS Now it's twenty-seven. Every gash was an enemy's grave. (2.1.143–53)

Again like the young man of the sonnets, Coriolanus is a pre-economic man. He fears and hates the market. Just as the young man prefers to hoard his blood instead of investing it in "seed capital," so Coriolanus is disgusted by the system of exchange that would convert his deeds in battle into rewards, praise, and, worst of all, votes/voices of the common people. As an aristocrat whose motto is "Alone" and who will share neither corn nor power with the people, he is embarrassed by his wounds because, paradoxically, they mark his dependence on the people. Wounds are signs not of what he *is* but of what he has *done*. They tell stories and are interpretable. They are currency in a political/economic exchange that breeds votes in return for a certain amount of nakedness and verbal display in the marketplace. The Third Citizen puts the carnality of this exchange bluntly: ". . . If he show us his wounds and tell us his deeds, we are to put our tongues into those wounds and speak for them" (2.3.5–7). Coriolanus clearly cannot undergo the mouth-to-wound intimacy of such an exchange. He cannot bring himself to trade bits of his body ("Of wounds two dozen odd" [l. 128]) for bits of commoners' bodies, their voices.

In a memorable article D.J. Gordon has clarified both the Elizabethan relevance and intellectual significance of the term "voice."[13] In Elizabethan parliamentary politics electors meeting at the county court were asked to shout for their man: voting was indeed giving voice to one's choice. But Gordon goes on to show that in the classical literature about fame and glory there is unease about the way heroic reputation is dependent on the fickle opinions and voices of men. The appearance in 2 *Henry IV* of Rumour "painted full of tongues" underlines the connection between fame and the irresponsible, undiscriminating noise made by "the still-discordant wav'ring multitude" (Induction, l. 19). *Vox*, then, is both a responsible political act, a vote, and air blown generally through the people's pipe. Coriolanus, standing in the forum to undergo the ritual of candidacy, speaks in a savage parody of market language when he proposes the exchange of heroic deeds for despised votes:

> Here come more voices.
> Your voices! For your voices I have fought,
> Watched for your voices, for your voices bear
> Of wounds two dozen odd; battles thrice six
> I have seen and heard of for your voices, have
> Done many things, some less, some more. Your voices!
> Indeed I would be consul! (2.3.125–31)

In this play, shouts, flourishes, and soldiers' cries are characteristic of the triumph scenes. This is indistinct noise and Coriolanus can live with it. But to the hero who would be a guarantor of his own worth and whose military language is self-explanatory, the political voice by means of which *you* individually speak for *me* is intolerable. The play does not allow us to hear "voice" simply as "vote." It is inextricably entangled in body, in the common mouth and throat, in animal howling ("You common cry of curs" [3.3.124]), in teeth and tongues. Yet this stinking breath is, in Rome, capable of being counted and is decisive in conferring or revoking titles. Voice is thus both absurd and powerful. As a synecdoche of the common body, it is nothing when placed in relation to a wound signifying heroic deeds. But as a metaphor for a political act, it not only counts, it is counted. As fame it is a traditional goal for heroic endeavor. Coriolanus, refusing his assent to the metaphor, stays with the demeaning synecdoche.

By talking sarcastically of himself as a beggar troubling the poor (2.3.67–70), Coriolanus would like to see the transaction in the forum as a kind of absurd charity, as anything but trade, which is what the citizens understand it to be:

> THIRD CITIZEN You must think if we give you anything we hope to gain by you.
> CORIOLANUS Well then, I pray, your price o'th'consulship? (ll.71–73)

The hated ritual of showing wounds and asking for votes is simultaneously public and intimate. Every citizen may exercise his right to speak to the hero directly and to question him in return for the citizen's vote. The physicality of the encounter is insisted on by the language of the tongue, mouth, teeth, and scar, and by the spectacle of the hero dressed in the *toga humilis*, subjecting himself to the crowd's gaze. But this 'Nakedness" leads to no consummation. The display of wounds is promised, but they are never actually shown. Coriolanus' "strip" is a "tease," and the customers have a right to feel cheated because they were tricked into committing their voices in return for the *promise* of a show of wounds.

The aristocrat, then, brought to the edge of the market to exchange wounds for voices, balks and saves his nakedness from becoming currency. He would rather starve, he says, "Than crave the hire which first we do deserve" (l. 114). Strange language, because both starvation and hire are features of plebeian rather than aristocratic life. But as Volumnia's simile of the farm laborer-hero has already suggested, labor and its reward or the denial of reward is a problem for this representative of the ruling class, who will serve Rome only as a form of self-service. Coriolanus, as the man alone, can only pay himself with his own pride or consume his own actions in an economy of one, an economy that denies exchange. The kind of exchange he *can* contemplate is primitive and pre-commercial,

Coriolanus: *Body Politic and Private Parts*

the kind that allows for a magical transformation of one whole self into another. So he says of Aufidius, the enemy, though his equal and mirror: "I sin in envying his nobility,/And were I anything but what I am,/I would wish me only he" (1.1.230–32). In this exchange, which the plot proceeds to carry out, there is no surrender of parts, no tit for tat. Instead "I am I" becomes "I am he" because he and I are of a kind.

Coriolanus is imaginable only by means of a discourse of the whole. Indeed, he is a criticism of such a rhetoric. To his solipsism, number itself is anathema because it is more than *one*, and the only number he can tolerate is the replication of himself in his class. His inability to exist outside this discourse of the whole underlies his horror of playing a part (the part of a politic or "pleasant" man) in front of the people in the marketplace. The self-fragmentation of acting, like the making of commodities out of wounds, goes against the very grain of his nature: "To th' market-place./You have put me now to such a part which never/I shall discharge to th' life" (3.2.104–6). Unlike a whole gallery of Shakespeare's two-faced politicians, this soldier cannot teach his body deceiving gestures because (like the anti-theatrical Plato) he is afraid that the false action will infect the mind:

> I will not do't,
> Lest I surcease to honour mine own truth,
> And by my body's action teach my mind
> A most inherent baseness. (ll. 120–23)

The primacy of body in this formulation of the body/mind relation should not be unexpected in this play. It is a version of the body-politic analogy of the first scene. In Menenius' fable the body is by nature politic, being a system built around a belly. But in the marketplace Coriolanus' body resists becoming politic because that would mean possession by a lie and the surrender by each organ of its true nature:

> Away, my disposition; and possess me
> Some harlot's spirit! My throat of war be turned,
> Which choired with my drum, into a pipe
> Small as an eunuch or the virgin voice
> That babies lull asleep! The smiles of knaves

Tent in my cheeks, and schoolboys' tears take up
The glasses of my sight! (ll. 111–17)

If Menenius' political body flourishes by way of a fake ideology of give and take between the belly and the other limbs and organs, Coriolanus' unpolitic body cannot tolerate any division into parts. As Aufidius says, "Not to be other than one thing" (4.7.42) is his fate. It is also the fantasy of an unpolitical ruler. His enemy, Sicinius, the people's tribune, puts it well: "Where is this viper/That would depopulate the city and /Be every man himself?" (3.1.263–65). The logic of being only *one thing* is totalitarian but absurdly so, for it makes rule possible only in a city made a desert.

Our impossible hero dies, so the text tells us, in the "market-place" (5.6.3) of a city that mirrors his own, but it is a flat mirror uncharacterized by details of politics or class. The marketplace in which he dies is the twin of the arena in Rome where he failed to trade his wounds for voices and turn his reputation into liquid assets. What is more, the man so characterized by his effort to be "not . . . other than one thing" is stabbed to death as the people shout "Tear him to pieces!" (l. 121). In the economy of the play, pieces are the base currency that makes exchange possible. The shout of the Volscians, "Tear him to pieces!" is not just a cry of revenge; it represents the triumph of number over singularity, of the limbs over the belly, of the spread of power over its concentration.

Unable to accept the laws of *exchange,* Coriolanus chooses *change,* and that is what the closing action of the play examines. The change of exile and the choice of Antium are not as drastic as they seem. Rome and Antium are not opposites like Rome and Egypt. Aufidius is no Cleopatra. By "servanting" himself to the Volscians, who apparently have no plebeians with stinking breaths and no trade unions, Coriolanus can make a paradoxical and absurd gesture of autonomy. Servant to his mirror/opposite, Aufidius, he can create the illusion of another self even more alone than the first because denuded of all customary, natural ties. Here is a man with no past, no family, no country, no name. "He was a kind of nothing, titleless" (5.1.13), says Cominius after seeing him in the enemy camp. Shakespeare recalls the terrible music of Tamburlaine's inhuman consistency when Coriolanus' former commander describes the hero's immobility and his statuesque, locked-in power as he sits in wait for the fall of Rome: "I tell you he does sit in gold, his eye/Red as 'twould burn Rome, and his injury/The jailer to his pity" (ll. 63–65). But Tamburlaine had no mother to deal with. He was more truly than Coriolanus a self-made man, more convincingly an author of himself. Tamburlaine kills his son and surely would have killed his mother had she stood in the way of his consistency. But the thematics of that play are not political.

Any attempt at a politically weighted analysis of *Coriolanus* must admit its limits when asked to contemplate the spectacle of a son claiming to be author of himself and denying instinct as his mother bows down before him. Coriolanus, we know, was made not by himself, not by his class or economic laws, but was framed in a womb. The claim that his body has changed since he left his home—"These eyes are not the same I wore in Rome" (5.3.38)—is revealed, in a telling metaphor, as false: "Like a dull actor now/I have forgot my part, and I am out/Even to a full disgrace" (ll. 40–42). In Rome's market he could not force his body to act a part; part itself was anathema. Here in the camp outside the city, he cannot *maintain* the part of the self-authored man. To admit that the self-authored man is "a part" is an absurdity. He must be a whole; both maker and made, writer and thing written, seamless. The play is an enactment of the failure of this ideology as the hubris of a class and the nemesis of a man.

III

This essay began with a consideration of division in the body politic, of the rending of the cloak of society and its tearing into fragments. It ends with the spectacle of an absurdly unpolitical man inviting the crowd of his former victims and present masters to destroy him, saying, "Cut me to pieces" (5.6.112). The drama of the fragmented body haunts this play in ways that clarify the difference between the concerns of tragedy and those of political theatre. The torn body of the hero is a powerful tragic emblem. It is a violent yet therapeutic spectacle, like sacrifice. In the rituals of sacrifice, the animal is often split into pieces before the offering, as Abram in Genesis 15 tears apart the heifer, goat, and ram before composing himself to await God's sign in the darkness. I take the sacrificial tearing, both of the tragic hero and the animal, to be a successful working through of violence, both our own and that we attribute to the gods. The torn victim's body spread out before God or the gods is, in real or symbolic terms, food that will nourish the society that makes this ritual part of its history. Hippolytus becomes the source of a cult; the God who ordered Abram to prepare the sacrifice promises his seed a land to inherit. Thus the bloody fragments of sacrifice are transformed into a comforting whole, a coherent tradition of cult or community.

In *Coriolanus* the thematics of politics overshadow those of tragedy, and the body cut to pieces remains an obstinately secular final image. No nourishment can issue from these fragments, and no promise of any coherence that outlives the body is inscribed in them. The hunger of the people for bread, which was so blatantly the opening motif of the play, may have been sated in terms of plot, but it has been replaced by the protagonist's unappeased hunger for revenge, which, in turn, is finally transmuted into a hunger for self-destruction. That such a hunger is satisfied at the end affords the spectator no comfort, only food for thought.

NOTES

1. *Capital*, ed. F. Engels, 3 vols. (Moscow: Foreign Languages Publishing House, 1957–1960), Vol. I, 670.

2. All citations from Shakespeare are to *William Shakespeare: The Complete Works*, Stanley Wells and Gary Taylor, eds. (Oxford: Oxford Univ. Press, 1986).

3. *Plutarch's Lives*, 10 vols., trans. Bernadette Perrin (New York: Putnam's Sons, 1914), Vol. 4. Plutarch writes of the dangers of a lack of

Coriolanus: *Body Politic and Private Parts* 249

discipline to a generous and noble nature and compares the results to a "rich soil deprived of the husbandman's culture" (p. 119).

4. *Rabelais and His World*, trans. Helene Iswolsky (Cambridge, Mass: M.I.T. Press, 1968), p. 317.

5. In "Lenten butchery: legitimation crisis in *Coriolanus*" (*Shakespeare Reproduced: The Text in History and Ideology*, Jean E. Howard and Marion F. O'Connor, eds. [New York and London: Methuen, 1987], pp. 207–24) Michael D. Bristol argues for a plebs-centered reading of the play's dominant trope. Criticizing views that, mesmerized by Coriolanus, focus narrowly on his strengths or weaknesses as a leader and thus ignore the people's political culture, Bristol suggests that the body's language is a major vehicle for expressing the people's politics. The crowd and its speech are taken to represent an authentic political and social tradition that exists independently of the autocratic, martial model embodied in Coriolanus and refuses to be marginalized by it. Certainly the plebeians have a politics going back to the origins of republican Rome and are not the childish, malleable rabble shown so often on the stage. However, the major significance of the body trope, I would say, is less to characterize the plebeian political and social alternative than to generalize the state of social fragmentation enacted in a specific case on the stage and to isolate the lonely figure whose withheld body is the subject of so much attention (and would be so, I think, even in the most determinedly Brechtian production).

6. Reuben A. Brower, *Hero and Saint: Shakespeare and the Graeco-Roman Heroic Tradition* (Oxford: Oxford Univ. Press, 1971), p. 371.

7. Marx cites Menenius' fable as a prophecy of the fractionalization of work in the machine shop that turns the worker into a fragment of his own body (p. 360). He sees Menenius' rhetoric of fragments not as an argument for hierarchy but as an indication of how specific limbs become isolated and exploited in the interests of efficient production (cf. Chaplin's hands in the assembly-line sequences of *Modern Times*).

8. All biblical quotations refer to the *King James Bible* (London: Imprinted by Robert Barker, 1611).

9. Bristol cites Paul as an example of propaganda for an organic view of society (p. 213), but his concern is not with the vitality of the fragments in this rhetoric or with how it is kept in check in political or religious discourse.

10. See Janet Adelman, "'Anger's My Meat': Feeding, Dependency, and Aggression in *Coriolanus*," in *Representing Shakespeare: New Psychoanalytic Essays*, Murray M. Schwartz and Coppélia Kahn, eds.

(Baltimore and London: Johns Hopkins Univ. Press, 1980), pp. 129–49. I am indebted to Adelman's analysis of Coriolanus' horror of dependence. My attempt here is to look at that pattern of behavior in the light of economics and politics rather than that of gender and psychoanalysis.

11. In most editions the reference is 1.6.76.

12. Jean-Christophe Agnew's remarkable study of relations between the theatre and the market, *Worlds Apart: The Market and the Theater in Anglo-American Thought, 1550–1750* (Cambridge: Cambridge Univ. Press, 1986), traces the connections between new forms of liquidity in monetary transactions and the secular theatre with its emphasis on the transitory nature of personality and its delight in shifting shapes (pp. 11–12). Agnew contrasts the medieval marketplace, an actual location where goods were displayed and exchanged, with the seventeenth-century model, less a location than an expression of the fluidity of the cash economy. Coriolanus, I would add, is odd man out in all markets, the later one for reasons that I give in my essay, the earlier one because even the simpler forms of exchange are incompatible with his more primitive need to live in an economy of one. For other comments on Coriolanus and the market, see Terry Eagleton, *William Shakespeare* (Oxford: Basil Blackwell, 1986), pp. 72–74. Eagleton sees a conflict between Coriolanus' ideology of self and the framework of exchange that dominates the culture of Shakespeare's audience. For Eagleton, Coriolanus, the type of the bourgeois individualist par excellence, is ahead of rather than behind the times. I see him more as a dinosaur than a Henry Ford prototype.

13. "Name and Fame: Shakespeare's *Coriolanus*" in *The Renaissance Imagination: Essays and Lectures by D. J. Gordon*, ed. Stephen Orgel (Berkeley: Univ. of California Press, 1975), pp. 203–19.

Reprinted by permission from Zvi Jagendorf, "Coriolanus: Body Politic and Private Parts," Shakespeare Quarterly 41 (1990), 455–69. Copyright, 1990 by The Folger Library.

Drama, Politics, and the Hero: *Coriolanus*, Brecht, and Grass

Martin Scofield

I want to look at Brecht's adaptation and criticism of Shakespeare's *Coriolanus*[1] and at Günter Grass' creative response to these in his play *The Plebeians Rehearse the Uprising* (*Die Plebejer proben den Aufstand*);[2] furthermore, I want to raise some questions about the role of the hero in all three plays. Brecht's attitude to the cult of the hero in "bourgeois" drama is well known: it was his contention that the emphasis on the hero, particularly in Shakespeare, was a large part of what was wrong with current drama both socially and aesthetically. The conventional way of seeing the hero led in his view to an over-romanticizing, an exaggerated stress on audience identification with the hero, and a resulting lack of critical detachment. From a political point of view, this in turn had dangerous affinities with the cult of hero worship and led in the direction of fascism. What I want to suggest by looking at Brecht's version of *Coriolanus* is that, in addition to more obvious psychological dimensions which Brecht was expressly content to omit, there are important *political* dimensions of the play which the Brechtian version cannot accommodate—and that some of these are illuminated with striking wit and subtlety in Grass' play.

Behind my discussion there also lie questions concerning the conflicting claims of adaptation and interpretation of Shakespeare. By the term "adaptation" I mean the substantial changing of Shakespeare's text, amounting virtually to a new play, which takes place in Brecht's *Coriolan,* and by "interpretation" I mean the critical or directional drawing out of implication, or the stressing of one aspect of a play, which nevertheless respects the play's wholeness. There is, I think, in current criticism (or, in any case, in critical theory) a tendency to blur the distinction between the two: theories of deconstruction or ideas like Roland Barthes' "readerly text" put a premium on the reader's or critic's power to re-create the text, to collaborate with the author to the extent of realizing a work which may not only go beyond what the author might have conceived of it but may even run counter to his likely intentions. This is what happens, legitimately enough, in Brecht's adaptation. But it would be a pity, I think, if in reading, watching, or performing Shakespeare's plays themselves we lost the idea of "the play itself" or "the spirit of the play" or "what the author was trying to do." Indeed, if we do lose this entirely, we lose Shakespeare as an independent creator, writing in another time and with a unique power of dramatic creation and insight, against whom we may to some degree measure our own contemporary creations and our own sense of life. So there is, in my view, a point in comparing Brecht's and Shakespeare's two plays—not with the predictable aim of arguing Shakespeare's general superiority (though I confess that from time to time that note may creep in) but in the hope of bringing out the strengths and differences of both and also of suggesting a political dilemma about leadership which is at the heart of Shakespeare's play and which Brecht's play tries to resolve in a way rather different from Shakespeare's.

I

As a starting point, I will examine some of the things that Brecht had to say about Shakespeare in his critical writings in order to set the scene for his adaptation of the play and see with what kind of assumptions he was working. In such an approach, I think, one will find in his general criticisms a slightly wider and more accommodating sense of Shakespeare than one might assume the author of the German *Coriolan* to possess. At the

Drama, Politics, and the Hero

same time one will find a healthy corrective to uncritical or overly romantic views of the Shakespearean hero.

The more accommodating sense that I have in mind is that expressed in Brecht's view of Shakespeare as "pure material":

> With Shakespeare the spectator does the constructing. Shakespeare never bends the course of a human destiny in the second act to make a fifth act possible. With him everything takes its natural course. In the lack of connection between his acts we see the lack of connection in a human destiny, when it is recounted by someone with no interest in tidying it up so as to provide an idea (which can only be a prejudice) with an argument not taken from life. There's nothing more stupid than to perform Shakespeare so that he's clear. He's by his very nature unclear. He's pure material.[3]

I shall suggest later that in his version of *Coriolanus* making Shakespeare "clear" seems to be precisely what Brecht is concerned with—and that (to go further) "an idea (which can only be a prejudice)" has been imposed on the material to make a didactic point. In short, Brecht "tidies up" Shakespeare's play. The spectator cannot indeed do so much constructing because more is done for him. On the other hand, Brecht is salutary in his indictments of a kind of "traditional style of performance" which loses "the classics' original freshness, the element of surprise": "where the classics are full of a fighting spirit here [in traditional theater in Germany] the lessons taught the audience are tame and cosy and fail to grip."[4]

In his view of the Shakespearean hero, Brecht is both a mentor to be heeded and at times an object lesson. There *is* a problem of "empathy" in our relations with the Shakespearean hero; our tendency to identify with the hero, which Shakespearean dramatic style partly encourages, can make us blind to his faults and abrogate the critical attitude to the drama which, Brecht urges, should be our proper attitude as readers or audience. For Brecht, empathy in Shakespeare's theater was "a contradictory, complicated intermittent operation" whereas now it is overstressed. As Margot Heinemann has pointed out, there is a "politics" in this too: Brecht's antipathy to *Einfühlung* or emotional identification (literally "feeling with" or "feeling into") arose partly from what he described as "Fascism's grotesque emphasis on the emotions."[5] The fascist leader's appeal to the people is seen to be based on a theatrical identification of this kind: "The Führer personalizes his fight, his enemies, flies into a rage with them and so on, and the intensity of his feelings carries his hearers along with him."[6] (Incidentally, one might note how *dis*similar this handling of emotion is to the case of Coriolanus, and how it casts doubt on any interpretation of Coriolanus as a fascist leader of the Hitler type: Hitler would never publicly have expressed contempt for the people, whereas Coriolanus could not be less like a demagogue.)

When one remembers, say, Bradley's "empathy" with Othello or Coleridge's with Hamlet or Lamb's with King Lear, one feels that Brecht is making an important point about the need for an element of critical detachment. But there are points at which Brecht (or perhaps merely his followers) would seem to go too far. Heinemann quotes Brecht on the bourgeois emphasis on the naked individualism of the tragic hero:

> The great individuals were the material that produced the form of this drama.... Through four acts Shakespeare drives the great individual, Lear, Othello, Macbeth, out of all his connections with family and state out onto the heath, into total isolation, where he must show himself great in his ruin.... [T]he object of the exercise is the great individual experience. Later times will call this drama a drama for cannibals.[7]

It is a drama for cannibals presumably because we witness, as it were, the ritual dismemberment of the hero and perhaps because we become mere "consumers" of the spectacle of his suffering. The two points are very different, of course: if Brecht meant simply the latter we can readily agree that the practice is decadent. But to witness the "dismemberment" of the hero (like that of the god) may touch a deeper note which is not so easily dismissed. There is a further point arising out of Margot Heinemann's comment on this passage: "Thus performed, Shakespeare is of little or even negative value to modern spectators, who unlike Lear or Hamlet are small people, whose destinies are controlled not by fate or their own personal characters or actions but by the behaviour of collectives, large masses, social classes."[8] To which one might reply: "Well, yes, small people if you like: but surely even a Marxist might these days be bothered by that sweeping denial of free will and personal character and action"—and take away the idea that the tragic hero is in some way representative, and you do not have much left. Brecht himself would not seem to go along with this sweeping determinism, as Heinemann implicitly recognizes when she paraphrases Brecht thus: "The laws of causality in history . . . are . . . not of absolute causality determining the behaviour of each individual"; or again, in a direct quotation: "There are certain laws that apply to class, . . . i.e., not absolutely."[9]

But whatever Brecht's precise attitude (and clearly it changed over time), we can see that the hero is always a problem for him. With Coriolanus Brecht was not in favor of diminishing the hero entirely. In Brecht's dialogue on the first scene he is asked why he wanted Ernst Busch, a great "people's actor," to play Coriolanus, and if it was because he needed someone who would not make the hero too likeable. He replied: "Not too likeable, and likeable enough. If we want to generate appreciation of his tragedy we must put Busch's mind and personality at the hero's disposal. He'll lend his own value to the hero, and he'll be able to understand him, both the greatness and the cost of him."[10] As for *dialogue* in general, it is notable that Brecht here is much more concerned with exploring the ways the play can be put on as it stands—without adaptation. Later in life he considered rewriting his version of *Coriolanus* to bring it closer to Shakespeare and commented in his *Arbeitsjournal*: "When the feeling for history is more strongly developed, and when the masses have more self-confidence, everything can be left more or less as it is."[11] This, it seems to me, is a striking admission which leads one to wonder whether we may by now be ready for Shakespeare's *Coriolanus*: indeed, Brecht himself gives the answer in the same passage when he says, "In West Germany the piece could be performed just as it is." (If he had been writing today he would doubtless have included the former East Germany!) It also prompts the question: Isn't the earlier attitude in fact rather patronizing towards "the masses"? Might it not always have been salutary for them, or us—whoever "the masses" are supposed to be—to grapple with the play as it is?

II

Ronald Hayman, in his biography of Brecht, declares that "Unlike Brecht's variation on *Measure for Measure*, *Coriolan* stays respectfully close to its original."[12] However, I think it is clear that Brecht's adaptation is aiming at something other than respectful closeness, and I want now to survey his general changes. Rather than try to do this chronologically, I shall emphasize his main shifts in order of increasing importance. First, Brecht increases slightly, but not much, the aggressiveness of Coriolanus and the other patricians towards the plebeians. In I.i, for example, Coriolanus enters with a band of armed men *before* the end of Menenius' fable about the belly—a change which gives an added pretext for Menenius' concluding threats: "But make you ready for your stiff bats and clubs;/Rome and her rats are at the point of battle" (ll. 160–61). Again, changes are made in the scene equivalent to Shakespeare's III.i to make the question of the distribution of corn a *present* issue rather than something referred to in the past: corn has just arrived from Antium, and Coriolanus is asked what he will do with it if made Consul. His spurning of the idea of a free distribution is therefore not merely a past issue but a present provocation with immediate practical consequences. In fact, it is this, in Brecht, rather than manipulation by the Tribunes as in Shakespeare that leads the citizens to withdraw their support from him. As for the patricians, Brecht makes them not only class enemies of the plebeians but also ultimately traitors to Rome by making the Tribunes accuse them, without being contradicted, of abandoning Rome to its fate and taking refuge on their estates.

In his presentation of the Tribunes generally, Brecht adds to their dignity and integrity. He omits Shakespeare's episode of some hundred odd lines (II.iii.153–261) in which the Tribunes persuade the plebeians to change their minds after giving Coriolanus their "voices." Later, in the scene equivalent to Shakespeare's III.iii Brecht omits the Tribunes' coaching of the plebeians (ll. 1–29) in what to say at the hearing of Coriolanus before the Senate ("If I say fine, cry 'Fine,' if death, cry 'Death'," etc.). In V.i, when the Romans are lamenting Coriolanus' defection and news is brought that he is marching on Rome, Brecht's Tribunes are much more authoritative and less querulous than Shakespeare's. Whereas Shakespeare's Menenius reproaches them with a bitter joke about bringing down the price of coal through the burning of Rome, his taunt in Brecht is capped by Brutus' reply: "Whereas you are expert/At bringing down the price of Rome." In Brecht's V.iii, he eliminates all reference to one of the Tribunes being ignominiously "hale[d] up and down" (Shakespeare, V.iv.36–40).

Correspondingly, the plebeians in Brecht gain (as one would expect) in dignity and good sense, though Brecht does not omit their comic side entirely nor does he present them as unified among themselves. In I.i, for example, Brecht adds "*a man with a child*" to the group of rebellious plebeians: the man also carries a bundle and is ready to leave Rome should the uprising fail. This gives rise to an argument with the First Citizen, who calls him a "cowardly dog." Brecht also adds a shoemaker who is accused of giving Coriolanus his voice because a policy of war will keep up the price of shoes. On the other hand, Brecht also adds a dignified and articulate gardener who has a speech (in verse) which is a direct paraphrase of the gardener's speech in Shakespeare's *Richard II* III.iv.55–60:

> My garden, sir, that little realm
> Of flowerbeds and turnip patches, has taught me
> That even the noble rose of Corinth must
> Be pruned of undue pride of growth, or else
> It cannot thrive. (Brecht, II.iii)

In his Act IV, Brecht rewrites Shakespeare's Scene iii, the exchange between a Roman (Nicanor) and a Volscian (Adrian) who discuss the banishment of Coriolanus and the prospect of war. In Shakespeare the class of the two men is perhaps not fully clear, but they seem more like patricians. The Roman is a defector who reports that the patricians "are in a ripe aptness to take all power from the people, and to pluck from them their tribunes for ever" (ll. 23–25). Brecht makes them tradesmen talking of more everyday matters as well as of the historic events. And, perhaps surprisingly, he omits the report of growing patrician repressiveness. On the other hand, he would not have wanted, one presumes, to present a plebeian defector. The scene, in addition to conveying basic information as in Shakespeare's play, becomes a chance to glimpse "ordinary life" going on beneath the surface of patrician history.

Nevertheless, Brecht cuts in his Act IV, Scene ii, the memorable comic *volte-face* between Aufidius' servants after Coriolanus has been welcomed by the Volscian general:

> *First Serv.* Nay, I knew by his face that there was something in him. He had, sir, a kind of face, methought— I cannot tell how to term it.
> *Second Serv.* He had so, looking as it were—would I were hanged, but I thought there was more in him than I could think. (Shakespeare, IV.v.157–62).

It is surprising, as Willett and Manheim imply, that Brecht gave up this sharp bit of comedy, especially since he has an eye for it elsewhere.[13] Could his reason have been that he did not want to present the common man at this point in too unideal a light? In the remainder of Act IV Brecht does not give the plebeians any expressions of regret for banishing Coriolanus. Whereas Shakespeare in IV.vi.140–46 has the First Citizen say, "For mine own part,/When I said banish him, I said 'twas pity," and the second and third citizens agree (". . . though we willingly consented to his banishment, yet it was against our will"), Brecht simply finishes his scene thus:

> *Second Cit.*   Was it wise
> To banish him?
> *Sic.* Yes. (*The citizens go out slowly*)
> [or] . . . To the Capitol!

One issue that Brecht brings particularly to the fore—an issue that indeed is not really raised in Shakespeare at all—is the question of whether society really needs heroes, which leads to the further question of whether or not Coriolanus is "indispensable." In II.iii Brecht adds to the opening dialogue of the citizens a discussion of this matter:

> *First Cit.* . . . if he shows us his wounds and tells us his noble exploits, we've got to show a certain amount of appreciation. He's indispensable.
> *Second Cit.* Like a neck with a goiter.
> *First Cit.* What do you mean by that?
> *Second Cit.* The neck is indispensable even if it has a goiter. The goiter is his pride.

But by V.iii, Brecht's Tribunes have taught the plebeians to know better. It is the plebeians who will defend Rome. "[W]e," says Brutus, "whom Rome has lived off up to now, will defend it"—adding, with a nice touch, "Why shouldn't masons defend their walls?" And at the end of the scene Brutus sums up the moral in heavy-footed committee language (and presumably deliberate irony on Brecht's part would be out of place here); indeed the moral theme warning-light is flashing relentlessly:

> Mir scheint, und manchem, wie ich hör, dies Rom
> Ein besserer Platz, seit dieser Mensch nicht mehr
> In seinen Mauern geht, wert zu verteidigen
> Vielleicht zum ersten Mal, seit es gegrundet.

> I have the feeling, shared, I'm told, by many
> Others, that Rome's a better place
> With that man gone, a city worth defending
> Perhaps for the first time since it was founded.

Brecht's most extensive changes to Shakespeare come in V.iv of *Coriolan*, where Volumnia, Virgilia, Valeria, and Coriolanus' son plead with him. Brecht includes versions of the supplications of Virgilia, Valeria, and young Martius and a paraphrase of Volumnia's first long speech (at Shakespeare's V.iii.94ff) beginning "Should we be silent and not speak. . . ." But Volumnia's second speech he changes radically. In Shakespeare she first of all pleads that she is not asking him to destroy the Volsci but to gain honor from making peace instead of gaining "such a name/Whose reputation will be dogg'd with curses" (ll. 143–44). In this crucial last speech she appeals again to his honor, the motive force of his life—with a bitter dramatic irony when we remember her attempt to persuade him to compromise that honor earlier in the play. Then she turns to the wife—"Daughter, speak you"—then to the son. Finally, in a fine Shakespearean mixture of comic self-mockery and comic self-pity, she turns on him the full force of maternal emotional blackmail:

> There's no man in the world
> More bound to's mother, yet here he lets me prate
> Like one i'th'stocks. Thou hast never in thy life
> Show'd thy dear mother any courtesy,
> When she, poor hen, fond of no second brood,
> Has cluck'd thee to the wars, and safely home,
> Loaden with honour. (V.iii.158–64)

Thereafter she bids all the "ladies" to kneel, and when he still does not reply she rises:

> Come, let us go:
> This fellow had a Volscian to his mother;
> His wife is in Corioles, and his child
> Like him by chance. Yet give us our dispatch:
> I am husht until our city be afire,
> And then I'll speak a little. (V.iii.177–82)

After this superb threat come of course the famous stage direction *"Holds her by the hand, silent"* and Coriolanus' powerful speech:

> O mother, mother!
> What have you done? Behold, the heavens do ope,
> The gods look down, and this unnatural scene
> They laugh at. . . . (V.iii.182–85)

Most of this disappears in Brecht. Instead, for Volumnia's crowning speech we have the following:

> Enough of
> Your childish sentiment. I've something else
> To say. The Rome you will be marching on
> Is very different from the Rome you left.
> You are no longer indispensable
> Merely a deadly threat to all. Don't expect
> To see submissive smoke.

(In Brecht, Aufidius reported in IV.iv that Coriolanus has sent word to Rome to send up smoke signals if they surrender.)

> If you see smoke
> It will be rising from the smithies forging

Drama, Politics, and the Hero

>   Weapons to fight you who, to subject your
>   Own people, have submitted to your enemy.
>   And we, the proud nobility of Rome
>   Must owe the rabble our salvation from the
>   Volscians, or owe the Volscians our
>   Salvation from the rabble. Come, we'll go now.
>   The fellow had a Volscian for a mother,
>   His wife is in Corioli, and this child
>   Resembles him by chance.
>   *(The women go out)*
>   *Cor.* O mother, mother! What have you done?

Thus ends the scene.

As for the rest of the play: Brecht eliminates the short scene where the ladies return in triumph and replaces it with an even shorter one (four lines) in which Brutus says: "The stone has moved. The people takes/Up weapons, and the old earth shakes." And whereas Shakespeare's last scene ends with the murder of Coriolanus and the brief tribute from Aufidius, Brecht concludes with a short scene in the Senate. The consul announces that a motion for the Tribunes to restore lands taken from the inhabitants of Corioli is enacted into law. Another motion is put forward for the building of a new aqueduct. A messenger brings the news of the assassination of Coriolanus. Menenius proposes that his name be inscribed in the Capitol, but Brutus moves that the Senate proceed to other business. The consul raises a question: Coriolanus' family has petitioned that as stipulated in the law of Numa Pompilius its women may be allowed to wear mourning for ten months. "Abgeschlagen," Brutus snaps, and the stage direction thereafter indicates: *"The Senate resumes its deliberations."*

III

Now Brecht's version of Shakespeare's *Coriolanus* is clearly an adaptation, not merely an interpretation, and it would be foolish to criticize it as if it were the latter. It is an adaptation designed to carry Brecht's particular concerns—with the power of the working class, with the destructive nature of bourgeois heroism, with the way war can both weaken the working class movement (by causing it to align itself with the upper classes in the cause of national unity, as at the beginning of Shakespeare's play) and strengthen it in other causes (as at the end of Brecht's play, when it is the plebeians who show greatest firmness against Coriolanus). Brecht's version also, of course, adapts Shakespeare's text in German, the verbal power of which I am unable fully to judge. For those portions taken directly from Shakespeare—portions which are still substantial—Brecht used a revised version of Dorothea Tieck's early nineteenth-century translation. His own additions are written in a similar kind of verse and in prose. (The English translation by Ralph Manheim has sensibly alternated in the Shakespearean parts between straight Shakespeare and a kind of revised version *via* the German.)

The difficulty of a critical judgment of the German play is not insurmountable, however, and there is after all some point in drawing a comparison between Brecht's play and Shakespeare's. The question "Which is the better play?" will be dismissed by many with a wave of the hand—"But there is no comparison!"— and by others with the counter-question "Better for what?" Brecht was writing his *Coriolan* in 1951–52 in the German Democratic Republic, the East Germany of Pieck, Grotewohl, and Ulbricht. Economic and political conditions had already led to the exodus of a large number of refugees to West Germany since the founding of the DDR in 1949. It was a situation in which, one might say, East German Communism needed considerable moral support. It is fair to say—and I intend the point to be made without, for the moment, any evaluative implication—that Brecht was writing a deliberately partisan play, intended like many if not most of his plays to educate "the workers" in the nature of genuine socialism. It could be argued that Brecht's version was what was needed for that time and place—and that different versions (or interpretations) will be needed at others. In the production of *Coriolanus* at the National Theatre in 1984, for example, there seemed to be some kind of attempt to relate the play to "Thatcher's Britain" by using modern dress and having a section of the audience on the stage to help make up the crowd of plebeians. This alone did not seem

Drama, Politics, and the Hero

quite enough to achieve the desired effect, which was also blurred by having Coriolanus played as a kind of flamboyant, white-suited Italian film star who metamorphosed inexplicably in the battle scenes into a leather-clad warrior of a familiar theatrical type. It seemed to me here that any attempt at "relevance" was trite and shallow. Brecht's version, at the very least, achieves a considerable didactic irony and power.

But what I want to suggest is that while adaptations like Brecht's have often been made in the past and will no doubt be made in the future for perfectly valid reasons, there is a point in holding on to the importance of Shakespeare's play and its interpretation, and that interpretation as opposed to adaptation involves a different kind of discipline and responsibility. There is, therefore, a point in comparing Shakespeare's play and Brecht's if one understands oneself to be comparing two separate plays on the same subject and which use the same sources. One will be comparing on one hand, a play which in itself seems to present no clear political "line" but offers something else of value and, on the other, one which openly incorporates a political message.

IV

Apart from its incomparable poetic power, what Shakespeare's play clearly offers is the tragedy of an *individual*, and this is what Brecht's deliberately avoids as much as possible. Brecht's treatment subordinates the relationship of Coriolanus to Volumnia, and as a result the psychological dimension of the play largely disappears—which is, of course, consistent with Brecht's general theories of "epic theater." Brecht said that there was no need in his version "to play down the tragedy of pride," and perhaps much of this is still there. (I take it that the "tragedy of pride" involves the way in which pride is both a good and a bad thing: it is part of Coriolanus' integrity and refusal to compromise, but it is also part of his unjustifiable contempt of the plebeians.) But what is not fully there is the tragedy of kinship, the tragedy of a man who tries to cut himself off from his family and society and to live "as if a man were author of himself/And knew no other kin" (a line that Brecht does not retain). Hence this tragedy has political as well as individual implications. Brecht's Coriolan does say to Aufidius in V.iv, before the arrival of his mother and wife:

> The
> Volscians can plow up Rome and harrow Italy
> Before you'll see me bow to nature or
> Grovel before my instinct.

But the way that Brecht changes Volumnia's speeches and Coriolanus' capitulation means that it is less the power of filial instinct and the natural bonds of family which we see overcoming the hero—and more the realization that he is caught in the absurd predicament of fighting his own class. As a result one of Shakespeare's central political points—that the sense of being part of a society begins with the experience of personal relationships—is lost.[14]

According to Willett and Manheim, Brecht, cutting and changing Volumnia's speeches because he could not take them seriously, contended that Shakespeare had purposely made them unconvincing.[15] As we have seen, Volumnia's crowning argument in Brecht is rooted in class politics: Coriolanus put his family and the patricians in a position that

> ... we, the proud nobility of Rome
> Must owe the rabble our salvation from the
> Volscians, or owe the Volscians our
> Salvation from the rabble (Brecht, V.iv.)

whereas in Shakespeare Volumnia appeals to Coriolanus' honor and filial feeling. But it seems unlikely that Coriolanus, in either play, would believe that the plebeians stood much chance against the might of his and Aufidius' army or that he would regret saving the patricians from the plebeians with the use of Volscian allies. Brecht has also been led into an equivocal position on the question of what will happen to Coriolanus' family and the patricians in general. Brecht's Volumnia suggests here (though not elsewhere) that if Coriolan wins she and the nobility will be saved. This implication, of course, strengthens Brecht's presentation of the issue as a class struggle. Her first speech of pleading assumes that Coriolanus' wife and children

Drama, Politics, and the Hero

will perish, but her second speech assumes that they will be saved. Above all, Brecht changes Volumnia's final appeal so that there is no kneeling by wife and son, no silent appeal from the son which Shakespeare's Volumnia points to:

> Nay, behold's,
> This boy that cannot tell what he would have,
> But kneels, and holds up hands for fellowship,
> Does reason our petition with more strength
> Than thou hast to deny't. (V.iii.173–77)

This appeal of silence in a play which has so much in it about the relative powers of silence and of speech is of course immensely telling. It is the climax of that silent love represented by Virgilia—love which appeals beneath and beyond words or mere "voices."

Now there is a great deal in Brecht's version that is memorable—and memorable in its surprising and often ironic contrast to Shakespeare. There is the terse, crisp ending, for example, with its brisk political realism and curt rejection of sentiment at the final meeting of the Senate as Brutus rejects a request for public mourning from Coriolanus' family. And even in the pleading scene there is a certain pleasurable shock of surprise at being brought up short with Coriolanus' truncated reply, the single line "O mother, mother! What have you done?" But I hope it is not just the unregenerate bourgeois in me that feels in the end that something valuable has been lost here. In focusing more exclusively on the class struggle, Brecht has not only lost the full dimensions of the individual tragedy which he is presumably content to lose but also a political dimension. What is important to Brecht is the collective dilemma, the tragedy of a people that has a hero against it, as he puts it. But the further stage of my argument will be that first, of course, Brecht's play is not a tragedy for the people of Rome but a triumph, and that, second and more substantially, the political dimension which Brecht loses is crucially important to the question of leadership and political authority. And in trying to encompass this idea, I shall bring to bear Grass' *The Plebeians Rehearse the Uprising*.

V

The dimensions that Brecht's adaptation leaves out are dimensions which can speak to any audience or reader. I have in mind two in particular: the dimension of psychological tragedy, the tragedy of son and mother, of the "boy of tears"; and the dimension of the exceptional man or leader. They are related to each other, and both are political as well as personal. The "psychological" tragedy I shall deal with quite briefly. It consists of a failure of independence in a man who is otherwise outstanding in personal courage and integrity. Coriolanus has been taught his high ideals of military honor by his mother. At a critical moment in his career, as he stands for Consul, she persuades him to compromise his integrity and play a part in which he does not believe: that is his crucial failure of independence. The failure leads him to a wild over-reaction—the repudiation of his country and his family. There is a slight problem here, since after his banishment we see him bidding farewell to his wife and mother, and promising that they will get news of him and "never of me aught/But what is like me formerly" (IV.i.52–53). But I think this can be seen as only a softening of the blow: the damage has already been done. He will join Aufidius; but, confronted again with his mother and the bonds of his deepest attachments, he capitulates to her. The central tragic irony here is that this is from the point of view of the soldier—i.e., the independent man—a weakness; but our view of it is radically ambiguous, and we must also see it as a strength of humanity. So when Aufidius taunts Coriolanus with the stinging insult "boy of tears," it has a painful validity but is all the more painful because we know it is also deeply unjust.

Brecht does retain a large part of the Coriolanus-Volumnia relationship: the early scene with Volumnia and Virgilia talking of Coriolanus' heroism, Volumnia's persuasion with regard to the consulship, the final confrontation. But as we have seen, he plays down much of the personal force of the pleading scene. He also loses, earlier, some of the more acute revelations of the way in which Volumnia's maternal tenderness is subdued to her "militant enthusiasm," her zeal for her son's soldiership—for instance, her extraordinarily perverse and vivid comparison:

> The breasts of Hecuba
> When she did suckle Hector, look'd not lovelier
> Than Hector's forehead when it spit forth blood
> At Grecian sword contemning. (I.iii.40–43)

And what he loses here is, I think, not only a personal dimension but also a political one as well. For there is a way in which we feel that Coriolanus' hatred and contempt of the plebeians is partly a function of his psychological formation. There is insufficient space here to do more than to suggest this; but it can be shown, I think, that his antipathy to the people is closely related to his contempt of them as merely sensual beings—in particular mere mouths that clamor for food. His extreme and one-sided relationship with his mother in which she takes on the more usually paternal role of encouraging his martial valor leads, one can say, to a hypertrophy of martial spirit and a contempt for the satisfactions of peace and ordinary life. But there is the sense in Shakespeare that Coriolanus' relation with his family is simply the most intimate aspect of his bond with his society as a whole, the very center of all his relations with others, and that when this is broken he breaks with humanity in general, aspiring to be like a god but becoming like a machine (Menenius' image for him). By playing down the relationship with Volumnia, Brecht loses this central political perception.

The other dimension is that of "the tragedy of the exceptional man." A central element in Brecht's adaptation is that Coriolanus is shown to be not indispensable, that society does not need heroes. The question of his dispensability or indispensability is added by Brecht at several points, most notably by the First Citizen in the first scene and in Volumnia's final speech. The idea that the loss of Coriolanus may be a loss to Rome does not enter Brecht's reading; and the tragic feeling of pity for Coriolanus is almost entirely removed by the omission of such moments as his speech of capitulation after Volumnia's plea or the sorrow and tribute of Aufidius at the end of the play—and here and there by small but significant cuts such as the omission of that moment in Shakespeare's verse where Coriolanus is allowed an imaginative flight, a touch of the sublime, at the instant when Volumnia kneels:

> What's this?
> Your knees to me? to your corrected son?
> Then let the pebbles on the hungry beach
> Fillip the stars. Then let the mutinous winds
> Strike the proud cedars 'gainst the fiery sun,
> Murd'ring impossibility, to make
> What cannot be, slight work! (V.iii.56–62)

There is also a significant omission in Cominius' set speech of eulogy on the Capitol in II.ii after Coriolanus has returned victorious from the wars. Shakespeare's Cominius says near the beginning of his speech:

> It is held
> That valour is the chiefest virtue and
> Most dignifies the haver: if it be,
> The man I speak of cannot in the world
> Be singly counter-pois'd. (II.ii.83–87)

Shakespeare follows Plutarch's observations about "valiantness" or "virtue" here, and this is surely of great importance: Coriolanus is not only an outstanding soldier, but he is pre-eminent in the quality which his society reveres above all others.

It is this dimension of the exceptional man which Günter Grass makes wittily and subtly central in his play *The Plebeians Rehearse the Uprising*, first published in 1966. Brecht, designated in the play as "the Boss," ("Der Chef"), is rehearsing his version of *Coriolanus* in East Berlin in June 1953, the time of the uprising against the government which was finally put down with the help of Russian tanks. As he rehearses, a group of workers enter the theater with the news of the uprising and ask the Boss to write a statement in support of their movement. The Boss' feelings are pulled in two directions, but he finally refuses because he feels the uprising is misconceived. In the course of the play he is at one point almost lynched by angry workers. After the uprising is over, he writes a statement or "obituary" in which he both criticizes the state and finally affirms solidarity with it. But his colleagues point out that until all his papers are published after his death, only the paragraph of solidarity will be published.

The wit of Grass' play resides mainly in the fact that a parallel develops between the Boss and Coriolanus. Both are—in

Drama, Politics, and the Hero

different ways—proud; both are critical of the workers or plebeians; and above all both are loth to compromise their integrity or what they believe is right by submitting themselves to the judgment of the workers. The actress who plays Volumnia in the Boss' production taunts him with being a mere aesthete and tries to persuade him to write something for the uprising. In Act IV, after the uprising fails and is judged "counter-revolutionary" by the party theorist Kozanka, Volumnia urges the Boss to write something supporting the views of the State; in response the Boss exclaims with amusement that first she had accused him of being like Coriolanus in his criticism of the workers, and now she wants him to be like Coriolanus in siding with the enemy. The workers in turn accuse him of wanting to remain in favor with the authorities simply to save his theater. The Boss tries on his side to involve the rebellious workers in his production, to help them see what went wrong with theirs. For the Boss, integrity resides in sticking to the artifice of his production rather than in trying to play a part in the real uprising. Confronted by the accusations of the workers, the Boss begins to act Coriolanus' part: "'Like a dull actor now/I have forgot my part/And I am out . . .'/Give me the book. What does he say next?" (I.viii). The ironies and ambiguities of "playing a part" or of "acting a role" in the revolution become even more marked in this play than they do in Shakespeare's.

The point that Grass makes about Brecht—and incidentally about Brecht's Coriolan—is that as leaders or "exceptional men" they are necessarily involved in a potentially tragic paradox in relation to politics. They are part of a larger community in which, as an entity, they both passionately believe. And yet their real qualities—Brecht's artist's insight and Coriolanus' "valour"—set them at odds with the ordinary worker or plebeian. Grass' play focuses on Brecht's dilemma, but he subtitles it *A German Tragedy* (*Ein deutsches Trauerspiel*) presumably because he sees this problematic relation between leader and people (whether political or intellectual) at the heart of Germany's problem. But the focus is on Brecht because it is in him that we see the problem most acutely and consciously felt and understood. Brecht is representative of society as a whole because he focuses this problem of relation between the outstanding and the ordinary man: the play is, if not the Boss' tragedy, then his dilemma. Coriolanus thus is representative of the dilemma of politics—the dilemma that politics inevitably involves compromise. By taking some of the spotlight off the hero in his *Coriolan* Brecht loses something of this central dilemma. Brecht said that Shakespeare's play showed "the tragedy of a people that had a hero against it," but his own play is precisely not a tragedy for the people because they are simply seen as triumphing politically—and there is no sense of tragic loss at the end of the play. This might be said by some to be merely a contrast between the tragedy of "bourgeois individualism" and a modern drama of political struggle. But Günter Grass' play helps us to see, I think, that the tragedy of the individual is also a political tragedy, a tragedy for the state. For just as the society in Grass' play fails to appreciate the role of one of its leading figures, so Shakespeare's Rome loses the man who represents its highest ideal of valor, "the chiefest virtue" which "most dignifies the haver."

To sum up and return to some of my opening questions. What Brecht's adaptation does is to change the play cleverly in a particular direction. Perhaps this was timely, and perhaps there will be room for other adaptations of *Coriolanus* at other times. A strongly "loaded" interpretation might also have a similar effect, but it would also keep the whole of the play "in play." A Royal Shakespeare Company production in 1967 brought out, for instance, the extraordinary emphasis on martial valor, the almost Spartan cult of soldiership in early Republican Rome, the physical asceticism of Coriolanus. Another R.S.C. production in 1973, noticeably influenced by Brecht, made one see better exactly how much weight Shakespeare gives to many of the citizens' views—what good sense there is in them. But the rest of Shakespeare's play was there too so that one could note which parts were left in the shadow. Finally, what does one stress in the seminar room? Again the possibilities are various and will depend on the individual disputants. But I suggest that in the end one will also want to stress the extraordinary even-handedness of the play, not only its openness to different interpretations but also its broad rootedness and balanced wisdom. We live in an age of critical intervention and polemical utilization of Shakespeare. At such a time it is perhaps all the more important to try to keep fresh the meaning and rightness of the dog-eared and sometimes derided phrase of Coleridge when he wrote in relation to *Coriolanus* of the "wonderful philosophic impartiality in Shakespeare's politics."[16]

NOTES

1. Bertolt Brecht, *Coriolan*, in *Gesammelte Werke* (Frankfurt: Suhrkamp, 1967), VI, 2396–2497; in most instances, however, I quote from the English translation by Ralph Manheim in Bertolt Brecht, *Collected Plays*, ed. Ralph Manheim and John Willett (New York: Random House, 1972), IX, 57–146. Quotations from Shakespeare's *Coriolanus* are from the Arden edition, ed. Philip Brockbank (1976; rpt. London: Methuen, 1980).

2. *The Plebeians Rehearse the Uprising*, trans. Ralph Manheim (Harmondsworth: Penguin, 1972); for the German text, see Günter Grass, *Theaterspiele* (Neuwied and Berlin: Luchterhand, 1970), pp. 233–321. The play was first performed in Berlin in 1966 and caused an outraged reaction among Brecht's supporters, who saw it as an attack on Brecht.

3. *Gesammelte Werke*, XV, 119, as quoted in translation by Margot Heinemann, "How Brecht Read Shakespeare," in *Political Shakespeare*, ed. Jonathan Dollimore and Alan Sinfield (Manchester: Manchester Univ. Press, 1985), p. 206.

4. *Brecht on Theatre*, ed. and trans. John Willett (New York: Hill and Wang, 1964), p. 272.

5. Heinemann, p. 214, quoting Brecht, *Gesammelte Werke*, XV, 242.

6. Heinemann, p. 215.

7. Brecht, *Gesammelte Werke*, XV, 149, as quoted in translation by Heinemann, p. 205.

8. Heinemann, p. 205.

9. Ibid., p. 208, citing Bertolt Brecht, *Messingkauf Dialogues*, trans. John Willett (London: Methuen, 1977), p. 80.

10. *Brecht on Theatre*, ed. and trans. Willett, p. 263.

11. *Arbeitsjournal*, ed. Werner Hecht (Frankfurt: Suhrkamp, 1973), II, 1002, as quoted in translation by Heinemann, p. 222.

12. Ronald Hayman, *Brecht: A Biography* (London: Weidenfeld and Nicolson, 1983), p. 356.

13. Brecht, *Collected plays*, ed. Willett and Manheim, IX, 399.

14. It is also interesting to note, however, that when the Berliner Ensemble produced *Coriolan* on the stage in 1964, working from Brecht's draft, they restored "most of the lines cut from the play's private scenes" and "tried to develop the relationship between Marcius and his mother as both a personal and a political one" (John Rouse, "Shakespeare and Brecht: The Perils and Pleasures of Inheritance," *Comparative Drama* 17 [1983], 277). Rouse also points us to Peter Brook's judgment of the production that the scene between Coriolanus and his mother failed because it was still rewritten and changed. Coriolanus' recognition that the smoke rising from Rome is from the forges of the people's armories, the recognition that they can fight without him—that he is not indispensable—is made the central motive for his submission. "Without the clash of the two protagonists in its most intense form, the story remains castrated" (Peter Brook, *The Empty Space* [1968; rpt. London: Macgibbon and Kee, 1977], p. 82).

15. Brecht, *Collected Plays*, ed. Willett and Manheim, p. xvi.

16. Samuel Taylor Coleridge, *Shakespearean Criticism*, ed. Thomas Middleton Raysor (1960; rpt. London: Dent, 1964), I, 79.

Reprinted by permission from Martin Scofield, "Drama, Politics, and the Hero: Coriolanus, Brecht, and Grass," Comparative Drama 24 (Winter 1990–91), 322–41. Copyright 1990 by Comparative Drama.

To Their Own Purpose: The Treatment of *Coriolanus* in the Restoration and Eighteenth Century

David Wheeler

Reconstructing a play's (especially a Shakespeare play's) stage history is always useful. Through such a reconstruction, we can assess a playwright's reputation, an audience's taste, an era's prevailing dramatic values. Now and then we are able to gain real insight into a historical period or into a play. With Shakespeare's *Coriolanus*, it seems to me, two such periods stand out with regard to the play's production history, and they stand out because of the play's political content. In the twentieth century *Coriolanus* has seen the stage with more frequency than in the past, as directors have used the play's politics to address the phenomena of fascism and its strong-man rule, and socialism, with its emphasis on class struggle. As various countries have experimented with these forms of government, *Coriolanus* has assumed a rich poignancy. And in Restoration and early eighteenth-century England, an England torn by the competing forces of monarchical and parliamentary rule, *Coriolanus* became a political weapon.

Coriolanus was not particularly popular during the Restoration and eighteenth century, however. In his two-volume survey of eighteenth-century staging of Shakespeare, Charles Hogan ranks the play's thirteen performances between 1701 and 1750, twenty-eighth in popularity among the thirty-four Shakespearean plays produced during the half century. The only ones less popular were *The Comedy of Errors, Troilus and Cressida, Pericles,* and the three parts of *Henry VI. (Antony and Cleopatra, Love's Labour's Lost,* and *The Two Gentlemen of Verona* were not staged at all.)[1]

But the stage history of *Coriolanus,* between 1660 and 1800, is more complicated than any list of statistics might suggest. The play was produced not only in its original Shakespearean form (or as close to that form as possible, given the period's time limitations; the free, conjectural hand of eighteenth-century editors; and the desire of actor-managers to cater to the contemporary taste of playgoers), but also in four distinct adaptations. Importantly, the adapters were not literary hacks, seeking merely to cash in on Shakespeare's general popularity; on the contrary, the adapters were Nahum Tate, who produced *The Ingratitude of a Common-Wealth* in December 1681; John Dennis, whose *The Invader of His Country,* was produced in 1718–19; James Thomson, whose *Coriolanus* was produced posthumously in 1749; and Thomas Sheridan, whose version was first performed in Dublin in 1752. (I use the terms "adaptation" and "adapter" inclusively: Tate's and Dennis's versions are technically adaptations; however, Thomson's is more properly a new play, and Sheridan's is a combination of Shakespeare and Thomson.) How do we explain four major writers at the height of their careers rewriting one of Shakespeare's least popular plays?

One way to begin answering this question is to examine one of the earliest pieces of criticism of *Coriolanus*—Charles Gildon's brief essay, which, with his other "Remarks on the Plays of Shakespear" was included in volume 7 of Nicholas Rowe's edition of Shakespeare (1709). After summarizing the plot, Gildon moves to a discussion of the title character, where, in attempting to account for Coriolanus's "Modesty" and "Aversion to Praise," traits he cannot locate in the Plutarchan source, he comments:

> Our Poet seems fond to lay the blame on the People, and everywhere is representing the Inconstancy of the People, but this is contrary to Truth; for the People have never discover'd that Changeableness which Princes have done.... And any one that will look over the *Roman*

> History will find such Inconstancy, and such a perpetual
> Changeableness in the Emperors, as cannot be paralleled
> in the People of any Time or Country. What the *Greeks* or
> *Romans* have ever done against any of their fortunate or
> great Generals, is easily vindicated from a guilty
> Inconstancy, and Ingratitude.[2]

While it is rare to find such interpretive comments in eighteenth-century Shakespeare criticism, most of which is related more to genre, language, sources, or prosody, *Coriolanus*, too, is a rarity. It is clear that Gildon regards the play politically—that he sees its central issue as power. Curiously, he views the contest for political power not as a class struggle—aristocrats versus plebeians, as we in the twentieth century generally do—but as a momentous competition between the individual prince or military commander and a comprehensive political entity Gildon calls (almost reverently) "the people." Though Gildon might share Shakespeare's contempt for the apron-wearing, garlic-eating working class, he, a staunch Whig, holds elected government in high esteem. And so when he observes, as he does in *Coriolanus*, conflict between those born to govern and those elected to govern, he reformulates that conflict into Restoration and early eighteenth-century England's central political struggle—whether the Civil War of the 1640s, the 1688 Revolution, or the party conflict in the final years of Queen Anne's reign—that between monarch and Parliament. By the end of the eighteenth century that conflict was over, and John Philip Kemble could stage a politically neutered *Coriolanus* as a historical spectacle—a "Roman piece"; but, during the preceding eighty years, the play, in its varied forms, offered a vivid, thinly veiled representation of a Stuart monarch (either reigning or exiled), wrestling for control of the state with members of an elected government. The political complexity of Shakespeare's play renders it particularly appropriate to resurface, modified to suit a party or personal agenda, at moments of political crisis.

Also notable in the quotation above is Gildon's assumption that drama is mimetic, that it depicts an external reality that he can, with enviable confidence, call "truth." Shakespeare's failure to portray that truth accurately, Gildon ascribes to the playwright's conservative bias. Furthermore, as he comments on the issue of blame, he alludes, with the use of the term "ingratitude," to another conservative playwright closer to his own generation: Nahum Tate. Like Shakespeare's "blaming" the people, Tate, in *The Ingratitude of a Common-Wealth*, imputes the ingratitude to the people who banished the victorious Coriolanus from Rome. Tate, whose play was a court propaganda piece designed to support the claims of James, Duke of York (later James II) against Parliamentary attempts to bar his succession with the Exclusion Bills (being debated in Parliament when Tate's play was produced), analogously charges the people with ingratitude for turning against James, despite his personal sacrifice and military achievement. Gildon, whose Whig party was founded on the issue of the Exclusion Crisis, sees another truth.

I stated earlier that interpretive criticism is rare in the Restoration and eighteenth century; interpretation (or "reading") is uncommon, because with their conception of poetry—both what it is and how it functions—critics of the period simply did not share our preoccupation with "meaning." That Gildon's remarks on the meaning or message of *Coriolanus* are exclusively political, however, conforms to the prevailing poetic. Responding to Ronald Paulson's assertion that the eighteenth century lacked a poetic of satire, Jane Tompkins observes that "Paulson's judgment that the Augustans had no theory of the genre at which they excelled is based, of course, on a particular notion of what poetry is. If the poem is thought to be an 'organic system of relationships,' then it is true that eighteenth-century critics have nothing to say on the matter. But if the poetry is thought of as a weapon to be hurled against an opponent, as a partisan activity whose purpose is to advance individual and factional interests, then its social function and the motives of its users inevitably occupy the center of critical discussion."[3] Certainly, not all Restoration and eighteenth-century drama is satiric, yet, as the most public of literary forms—performed as it is in public space licensed during the period as a state monopoly—drama is, I believe, frequently subject to Tompkins's definition as "partisan activity," sometimes serving a personal interest, sometimes a political one. Surely, Gildon sees Shakespeare in this light; in representing "the people" as an unruly, anarchic mob that threatens political and social stability in *Coriolanus* and other plays, Shakespeare is serving the interests of his royal and aristocratic patrons who regulate his workplace and supply his livelihood. With his allusion to Tate's "ingratitude," Gildon acknowledges the only other English version of the play and acknowledges its politics, transferring the charge of ingratitude to the other side. While the production history of *Coriolanus* reveals that, in its nearly 400-year history, the play is occasionally performed as just such a partisan activity, the period 1660–1760 is unique in English stage history, in that *Coriolanus* was reconfigured so that it can always be viewed as a political event.

Tate's *Ingratitude of a Common-Wealth* was produced in 1681, on the heels of Titus Oates and the Popish Plot and at the height of the Exclusion Bill crisis. The conflict between Stuart monarch and Parliament was at once ideological—focused on hereditary versus elected authority, Catholicism versus Protestantism, and the influence of foreign powers (particularly France)—and personal—Charles's interest in preserving the throne for his brother James versus the ruling ambitions of Shaftesbury and Monmouth, who enjoyed considerable Parliamentary support. As the crisis unfolded, Exclusionist (Whig) drama was officially censored and effectively banned from the stage. In Tate's version, the people are again presented as a threatening mob, and his play serves to promote order and the status quo.

Dennis began writing *The Invader of his Country* in 1711 but completed and revised the play for 1718–19 production. The intervening years witnessed the failed 1715 rebellion by the Stuart Pretender and permitted Dennis to appropriate the political climate. With the Stuarts now exiled, outsiders, Dennis's opposition to the Pretender also constitutes an articulation of order and the status quo. Thomson's *Coriolanus* was written in the aftermath of the dashing Charles Stuart's invasion of England from Scotland in 1745. Thomson was both an "Opposition Whig" party writer and a Scot, a combination that, I believe, results in political ambiguity in his play. Thomson's revisions of Shakespeare are thus, necessarily, more extensive than those of his predecessors; he employs, as sources, versions of the Coriolanus story by Livy and Dionysius rather than the life by Plutarch solely used by Shakespeare, Tate, and Dennis, allowing an alteration of the prevailing politics. Thomas Sheridan's *Coriolanus*, an amalgam of Shakespeare and Thomson, is appreciably less political, and, as a piece written by an actor and stage manager, is more a vehicle for spectacle and star performers: a transition to what we might call "more traditional productions." What's notable here is that in the three most political versions, the prevailing power structure is essentially upheld, despite the changes to those structures over this seventy-year history. With the changing fortunes of the Stuarts, the dramatists could favor the appropriate side of the people/tribunes versus aristocracy/Coriolanus conflict to support the power in place. And with official stage licensing and censorship, the state dictated that the status quo would be maintained in stage productions: there was simply little opportunity for revolutionary drama.

Many twentieth-century critics have attempted to explain the Restoration and eighteenth-century practice of "improving" Shakespeare, of adapting the plays to suit a different social and literary milieu. Dryden, Rymer, Dennis, and other drama critics introduced Aristotelian methodology and French neoclassicism to focus discussions of the drama on a play's formal elements. When scrutinized in such a way, Shakespeare's loosely structured plays did not fare well. Even the briefest comparison between *Antony and Cleopatra* and Dryden's *All for Love*, for example, will easily show the formal effects of combining Shakespearean material and Restoration concerns with structure. Shakespearean commentators from Dryden to Johnson also display an emphasis on morality, in the moral effect of a play on its audience, that Shakespeare could not have foreseen. The principle of poetic justice, for instance, encouraged many adapters to alter Shakespeare's endings. Additionally, the differences in staging and in the physical theatre prompted changing the original versions. Restoration theatres had smaller stages, employed moveable sets that slid in grooves, and used artificial lighting. Moreover, plays were usually performed as part of a whole program of entertainment and, thus, were subject to stricter time limitations. The Restoration theatre also witnessed performances by actresses for the first time, and female parts were frequently expanded to accommodate demands by leading female performers. All of these factors contributed, no doubt, to the desire (perhaps the need) to adapt Shakespeare to the times.

With regard to *Coriolanus*, however, I think the first three adaptations were so political in their intent as to render the *Coriolanus* adaptations worthy of examining exclusively in this light. In his dedication to *The Ingratitude of a Common-Wealth*, Nahum Tate, the first of these adapters, is candid in expressing his aim:

> Much of what is offered here, is Fruit that grew in the Richness of his [Shakespeare's] Soil; and what ever the Superstructure prove, it was my good fortune to build upon a Rock. Upon a close view of this Story, there appear'd in some Passages, no small Resemblance with the busie *Faction* of our own time. And I confess, I chose rather to set the *Parallel* nearer to Sight, than to throw it off at further Distance.[4]

While this declaration may sound radical to twentieth-century purists, it is typical of the dramatic impulses during the 1680s. Matthew H. Wikander maintains that

> Far from being a process of improving Shakespeare by means of clarification and purification of language, prompted by "zeal for dramatic economy," as Hazelton Spencer argued, the adaptation of Shakespeare to the Restoration stage in the 1680s was primarily a political activity.... the agenda was conservative in its politics, involving as it does the portrayal of all civil unrest as butchery; and was spectacular in its means, shaped by a continuing attachment to traditional iconographic ways of seeing that found expression in the new possibilities for spectacle on the Restoration stage.... All draw specific analogies between the unrest they depict, contemporary events in the 1680s, and the events of the 1640s that led to the outbreak of civil war.[5]

Nahum Tate, probably the most notorious of the Restoration adapters of Shakespeare, applied his pen to three of Shakespeare's plays: *King Lear* and *Richard II*, in addition to *Coriolanus*. All three plays were written and performed in 1680 and 1681. Though working first on *Lear*, Tate brought his *Richard II* play, initially entitled *The Sicilian Usurper* (performed on 11 December 1680 at the Theatre Royal, Drury Lane), to the stage first "in order to," as Ruth McGugan speculates, "take advantage of the current interest in political tensions."[6] While hoping to feed London's political appetite, Tate no doubt shifted the play's action to Sicily in order to distance it from actual events in England. Nevertheless, in this politically tumultuous time, *The Sicilian Usurper* met ill success on the stage: the government suppressed the play only three days after its first performance. Tate's King, like Shakespeare's Richard, is portrayed tragically, victim to his advisors and a popular, ambitious usurper. Late seventeenth-century audiences would have identified Richard with their own century's martyr-king, Charles I; thus, the government could have perceived the play as sympathizing with the besieged monarch and opposing insurrection. Other aspects of *Richard II*, however, are more troubling. Richard, like Charles II, was isolated from his people, depending on a close circle of confidants and on the support of foreign interests; more significant, perhaps, are parallels between the confident, dashing Bolingbroke and the equally popular Monmouth, Charles's bastard son. Shakespeare gives Bolingbroke—regardless of what we think of his arrogance or his political manipulations—a righteous cause, and history gives him success. With the potential of being seen as a pro-Monmouth work, *The Sicilian Usurper* had to be banned.

As Timothy J. Viator points out, the suppression of Tate's *Richard II* was an important event in theatre history:

> In light of the political difficulties and Charles II's programme to stop antimonarchical propaganda, Arlington [the Lord Chamberlain] wanted to demonstrate to the theatres that the Court planned to prohibit controversial plays. To this end, the Lord Chamberlain closed Drury Lane for ten days, an unprecedented decision. With only one exception, in the previous twenty

years the Court had closed the theatres only for the Plague in June 1665 and for mourning royal deaths, such as the Queen Mother's death on September 3, 1669. . . . Indirectly, therefore, the banning [of *The Sicilian Usurper*] accelerated the King's Company's declining fortunes, resulting in the final closure of Drury Lane in April 1682 and the union with the Duke's Company the following November. Moreover, Charles's campaign to control the theatres proved effective. Fearing further sanctions, the King's Company must have avoided plays which appeared to attack or satirize Charles, his Court, its Roman faction, and in general the monarchy. And although one cannot conclude with any certainty, because *The London Stage* performance records are incomplete, both companies seemed to have avoided (with few exceptions) "Whig" plays and began to stage after early 1681 only "Tory" plays.[7]

That Tate was able to publish the text of his play (with new character names and the title, *The History of King Richard II*), the following year provides an indication of the particularly inflammatory potential of the stage; the same censorship was simply not applied to printed texts. With his text, Tate included a letter defending his play, claiming to have deliberately rewritten the play in order to provide "an Active, Prudent Prince, Preferring the Good of his Subjects to his own private Pleasure," and "to engage the pitty of the Audience for him in his Distresses."[8] In short, Tate claims to have written a pro-Charles play, a Tory play.

Anyone who has ever studied either Shakespeare adaptations or *King Lear*, knows about Tate's *Lear*; it is the happy-ending *Lear* that dominated London stages for well over a hundred years, the best-known of the Restoration Shakespeare adaptations. The play was first staged at Dorset Garden in March 1681, with its Edgar-Cordelia romantic plot and Cordelia crowned queen at its conclusion. Lear makes his mistakes, but order—rightful, hereditary order—is reestablished.

In selecting *Richard II*, *King Lear*, and *Coriolanus* for adaptation, Tate chose plays where the tragic figure is problematic; Richard, Lear, and Coriolanus are not exemplary. And, as Wikander maintains, Tate's three adaptations "show contradictory impulses: critique of Charles's court collides with fear of change and horrified recollection of civil war.... Tate's selection of these plays reveals his interest in the issues raised by the Exclusion Crisis: insurrection, abdication, succession, and the dangers of mob rule are issues which Tate finds in the Shakespeare plays and emphasizes in his redactions."[9]

Tate's procedure for modifying *Coriolanus* was similar to those employed on the earlier efforts. His first task was to shorten the play by cutting characters, scenes, and lines that he felt were unnecessary. By McGugan's count, Tate cut 2130 lines from Shakespeare's play, leaving 1274; of these remaining lines (which constitute 60 percent of *The Ingratitude of a Common-Wealth*), Tate left 470 intact and revised the other 804.[10]

Most of Tate's original lines can be found in the final act, which takes place after the successful pleas of Volumnia for her son to spare Rome, and his plot-changes here are both substantial and radical. Tate expands the role of Aufidius's right-hand man, Nigridius (unnamed in Shakespeare's version) and villainizes these two characters almost indescribably. Tate extends Aufidius's rivalry with Coriolanus from one of military valor and political power, to the sexual, by adding an element of violent lust for Virgilia, Coriolanus's wife. Nigridius, a Roman who had been left in charge of the captured Corioli by Coriolanus, is humiliated and banished by Coriolanus for treason, and while pursuing his own vengeance against Coriolanus serves also to goad Aufidius in the pursuit of his. Because of the prominence of these two characters, we have a strong sense of conspiracy against Coriolanus, who is portrayed more nobly and innocently than his Shakespearean counterpart. The chaste Virgilia summarizes the action:

> False *Nigridius*,
> (Disbanded for his Villany by *Martius* [Coriolanus])
> Is busy for Revenge; and hourly plots
> Against his precious life: The industry
> Of good *Menenius* sends this information;
> Whilst *Martius*, confident in Innocence,
> Is obstinately blind to all his dangers. (V.i.72–77)[11]

The women hurry to Corioli to warn Coriolanus, where they are taken prisoner; Aufidius charges Coriolanus in the Volscian

Senate with betraying their cause to the despised Romans; and all major characters are slaughtered in a bloodbath that leaves no one standing to tell the tale. Significantly, outside the palace walls, soldiers who had followed Coriolanus battle in the streets of Corioli against those loyal to Aufidius in civil war.

McGugan makes a persuasive case that the combined characters of Aufidius and Negridius suggest Shaftesbury, the chief architect of the Exclusion Bill and primary opponent to Charles and his brother James. She also draws convincing parallels between Coriolanus and James—both were heroic defenders of their nations, now exiled; both assumed their claims to power were legitimate; and both were too proud to submit to even the customary forms demanded by the "people."[12] While I grant that most of the plot changes made by Tate were implemented for political reasons, I think it is the overall effect of the play that is more important politically than a possible allegorical or parallel reading. Many of the changes—those involving the brutality of rape and mutilation, which are narrated rather than represented—result from the current stage's interest in "affective tragedy" that Otway was practicing at the same time. The purpose was to tear at the audience's emotions, generating not only the customary pity, but also fear and revulsion. Consequently, the effect is to demonstrate graphically and horrifically, the dangers of political instability, with its factions, rivalries, and power struggles: to illustrate that, once legitimate rule is challenged and abandoned, the chaos of civil war is the inevitable result.

In some of the earlier acts, Tate changes speeches in order to lend to them a contemporary and distinctive anti-Whig flavor, such as in this one by Coriolanus to the tribunes:

>   You, Faction-Mongers,
> That wear your formal Beards, and Plotting Heads,
> By the Valor of the Men you Persecute;
> Canting Caballer, that in smoaky Cells,
> Amongst Crop-ear'd Mechanicks, wast the Night
> In Villanous Harrangues against the State.
> There may Your Worship's Pride be seen t'embrace
> A smutty Tinker, and in extasy
> Of Treason, shake a Cobler by the Wax't Thumb. (III.i.64–72)

This hostility toward the tribunes suggests that, in banishing Coriolanus, the instability is perpetuated rather than resolved, and what we see in Tate's final act is a reenactment, much more violently, of the same kind of power rivalry. With the stage littered with corpses—of heroes, women, children—and civil war in the streets, *The Ingratitude of a Common-Wealth* gives us a bleak view of the current political situation, much in the same vein as Otway's *Venice Preserv'd*, which was performed during the same London theatre season. As Parliament debated the Exclusion Bill, Monmouth, at Shaftesbury's urging, was touring the west of England, testing his popular support; if he found it, he'd make a play for the throne. I think Tate is issuing a warning, showing his audience the only possible conclusion of such an attempt. In doing so, he is offering a pro-monarchy, status-quo play, but a work much less sure in its stance than is Dryden's *Absolom and Achitophel* of the same year, where the poet urges the monarch to take stronger action against the conspirators. We must note, however, that Tate's support of Charles (and, by implication, of his brother James) was regarded as sufficient for Dryden to elicit his assistance in composing the second part of *Absolom and Achitophel*.

Written as it was for these turbulent times, Tate's *Coriolanus*, unsurprisingly, more overtly addresses contemporary politics than the other adaptations. When we turn our attention to John Dennis's adaptation, moreover, the picture is made more complicated for two important reasons: (1) Dennis was known better in his own day (and known almost exclusively in ours) as a critic; consequently, he has, in addition to political motivations, critical motivations that prompted his revision of Shakespeare. (Since I have discussed Dennis's theoretical concerns with regard to his Shakespeare adaptations elsewhere,[13] I will take them up here only where they relate to his political concerns.) (2) Dennis began writing *The Invader of His Country*, in 1710 or 1711 but continued to revise it until its first performance in late 1718. The years during which Dennis was working on *The Invader of His Country* witnessed several significant political changes: the end of the War of Spanish Succession and the fall from favor of the Whig Duke of Marlborough; the Death of Queen Anne and the succession of George I in 1714; the transfer of political power

To Their Own Purpose 285

from the Tories to the Whigs upon her death; the failed Jacobite Rebellion of 1715; and the rise of Robert Walpole as Britain's first real prime minister. Because of all of these events, the singularity of political purpose that we can identify in Tate's version, directed as it is against the Exclusion Bill and in favor of lawful, hereditary succession, is much more difficult to ascribe to Dennis's play.

Dennis began his critical career as a defender of the stage, and, in defending the stage, Dennis defines precisely its political function. One of dozens of direct replies to Jeremy Collier's *A Short View of the Immorality and Profaneness of the English Stage* (1698), Dennis's *The Usefulness of the Stage, To the Happiness of Mankind, To Government, and To Religion*, published the same year, argues that, in addition to providing individual pleasure, tragedy is useful to the state (to both the governor and the governed) in depicting examples of pride leading to falls and examples of misguided rebellions. Tragedy, Dennis asserts, "reminds men of their Duty, and perpetually instructs them, either by its Fable, or by its Sentences, and shows them the ill and the fatal consequences of irregular Administration."[14] Believing that tragedies ideally demonstrate by example the general principles of good government, *Invader*, as we shall see, points out the divisive dangers of party politics and of strongman rule, suggesting, in traditional English fashion, a middle course between anarchy and tyranny.

Another important element of Dennis's dramatic poetic is the concept of poetic justice, an issue he debated hotly and at length with Joseph Addison. In his *Essay on the Genius and Writings of Shakespear* (1712), Dennis states flatly,

> The Good must never fail to prosper, and the Bad must be always punish'd: Otherwise the Incidents, and particularly the Catastrophe which is the grand Incident, are liable to be imputted rather to Chance, than to Almighty Conduct and to Sovereign Justice. The Want of this impartial Distribution of Justice makes the *Coriolanus* of *Shakespeare* to be without Moral.[15]

We can attribute many of the changes Dennis incorporates to this critical principle, particularly at the end of the play; Aufidius, portrayed as a cowardly conspirator, is killed (as in Tate's version) by Coriolanus; the villainous tribunes, manipulating the people against Coriolanus out of their own jealousy and party interests, are executed by the common people, who realize their proper allegiance too late; and of course, Coriolanus, who has betrayed (and invaded) his country must die also.

When we begin to gauge Dennis's political position in the play, we might first look at the *Essay on Shakespear*, which is related by time of composition and (as illustrated by the example of *Coriolanus* quoted from it above), by its subject matter to the *Coriolanus* project. The *Essay* was dedicated to George Granville, (Lord Lansdowne), who was both a frequent patron to Dennis and himself an adapter of Shakespeare; his *Jew of Venice* was produced in 1701. Of more significance politically, Granville in 1712 was British Secretary at War and the chief negotiator for the controversial Treaty of Utrecht, which brought conclusion to the War of Spanish Succession. The treaty was opposed by Whigs, who were led by the Duke of Marlborough, the British general conducting the campaign on the Continent. Anne's desire to end the war brought about the dismissal of Whig ministers and their replacement by Tories opposing the war. To achieve a favorable majority in the House of Lords, Anne packed the House with newly-created Tory lords, one of whom was Granville. Not coincidentally, Alexander Pope's most overtly political poem, *Windsor Forest*, a pro-peace, pro-Tory poem, was also dedicated to Granville in 1714.

I find it interesting to speculate that Dennis's original intention with the project was to figure Coriolanus as Marlborough, a successful, brilliant general with rash political ambitions and (like Bolingbroke and Monmouth before him) a potentially dangerous popular following. While Marlborough was abroad, government policy was greatly influenced by his wife, Sarah Churchill, who enjoyed at least the Queen's ear during most of the century's first decade. If she reminds us of the politically powerful Volumnia, then the Churchill estate, Blenheim Palace, given to the family by the Queen in honor of Marlborough's great victory over the French at Blenheim, suggests the honorific title Coriolanus gains for his victory at Corioli.

But in 1718, when *The Invader of His Country* was finally accepted for the stage, Marlborough and the Treaty were old news. Dennis, in his dedication, blamed Drury Lane's Richard Steele for the delay, complaining bitterly, "Thus did they [the Drury Lane managers] take occasion to exercise a real Barbarity upon an old Acquaintance to whom they and their stage are more oblig'd than to any Writer in England." It is possible, of course, that Steele, often a Whig party writer, held up the play for political reasons. At any rate, in its final version *The Invader of His Country* focuses its political attention on the Stuart Pretender and his invasion of England, a topic more suitable to Steele's views.

Shakespeare's *Coriolanus* revolves around two threats to Rome's political stability, one domestic and one foreign. Dennis, in his version of the play, adapts both of these threats to the current British political situation, but his balancing of the two requires far greater emphasis on the foreign threat than is present in Tate's play, which, appropriately, focuses more on domestic strife and personal rivalries. England's great fear in 1715 is of a French-Jacobite alliance, that France would actually send troops to accompany the Pretender in his invasion. *The Invader of His Country*, consequently, contains not only anti-French sentiment but also the kind of invective frequently used in England to fuel anti-Catholic hysteria:

> *Cor.* Our Gods are like to be finely help'd up, by Sempronius's bringing young Tarquin in. Sempronius and he have been travelling; . . . they have been in Aegypt together, and now we must exchange our own for Aegyptian Gods; Apollo must give place to a Leek, Mercury to an Onion, and Jove himself to a Clove of Garlick. Blessed Gods are these Aegyptian Divinities! which they who worship devour.[16]

Adopting the France-Egypt analogue employed earlier by Dryden in *Absolom and Achitophel*, Dennis attacks the Catholic doctrine of transubstantiation and, playing upon contemporary anxieties, inserts a strong religious element into the political conflict. Those familiar with Dennis's critical works should perhaps expect a religious presence in his play. Dennis maintained that religion is essential for the sublime and for moving the passions, both of which are required in true tragedy. Thus, Coriolanus's invasion poses a threat, not only to Rome's political stability and legal government, but also to the true religion. This alteration of Shakespeare is consistent with the English political climate, where the conflict was as much between Catholic and Protestant as it was between monarchy and Parliament.

If Dennis intensifies the religious and foreign nature of the political threat, he also provides a plausible domestic explanation for how that threat became a real one. Political parties were new in Tate's England. But a couple of generations later, by the time Dennis treats *Coriolanus*, they were in full force, factionalizing politicians, neighbors, families, and writers. The personal correspondence of authors such as Swift, Addison, and Pope records the intensity of party politics and the difficulty of writing anything that would not be interpreted as a party piece. Pope's ironic *A Key to the Lock* (1715), for instance, offers a joking political reading of *The Rape of the Lock*, in an attempt to disarm party poetics. Almost naturally then, Dennis introduces formal political parties to Coriolanus's Rome and blames party hatred for Coriolanus's banishment and the foreign invasion. Coriolanus becomes a kind of dupe to the manipulations of both foreign and domestic political figures. Nevertheless, Coriolanus's betrayal of his country is unforgivable, as the good and patriotic Cominius concludes the play with an overt moral lesson:

> But they who thro' Ambition, or Revenge,
> Or impious Int'rest, join with foreign Foes,
> T' invade or to betray their Native country,
> Shall find, like Coriolanus, soon or late,
> From their perfidious Foreign Friends their Fate. (p. 79)

The Invader of His Country, then, is a clear call for support of the constitutionally balanced monarchy, a suspension of party strife for the good of the country, a plea for the true Protestant religion, and a nationalistic protest against French meddling in internal English politics and French territorial designs. Though the political situation has changed dramatically, Dennis's play, like Tate's, is a voice for the status quo.

The author of the next adaptation, James Thomson, presents us with a bit of a curiosity. While his *Coriolanus* is less obviously partisan than either Tate's or Dennis's, Thomson spent most of his career as a party writer; indeed, as Christine Gerrard reminds us, "the popularity of *The Seasons* should not disguise the fact that Thomson was, first and foremost, a political poet."[17] After the remarkable success of *The Seasons* (1726), Thomson aligned himself with writers such as Pope, Fielding, David Mallet, and Aaron Hill and political figures like Bolingbroke, George Lyttelton, and the Prince of Wales in opposition to Robert Walpole's administration. His poems *Liberty* and *The Castle of Indolence*, have consistently been assigned to the "Whig Opposition" (a group of Whigs who joined forces with Tories in opposing Walpole in the mid and late 1730s) camp, and his first three tragedies, as John Loftis maintains, "include, with varying levels of emphasis, themes that may be interpreted as critical of Walpole."[18] Loftis characterizes Thomson's and other opposition drama as plays in which "opposition to encroachments on constitutional rights by a powerful political or military force animates dialogue and conditions dramatic action."[19] In the 1730s, Thomson and his friends Aaron Hill and David Mallet were virtually in the employ of opposition politicians, but by the time of Thomson's *Coriolanus*, Walpole had long been out of power and, in fact, died in 1745, the year Thomson probably completed his play.

For an insight on Thomson's changes (and Thomson's version is much closer to being a new play than either Tate's or Dennis's), one need only look at the opening scene:

VOLUSIUS

WHENCE is it, TULLUS, that our Arms are stopt
Here on the Borders of the *Roman* State?
Why sleeps that Spirit, whose Heroic Ardour
Urg'd you to break the Truce, and pour'd our Host,
From all th'united Cantons of the *Volsci*,
On their unguarded Frontier? Such Designs
Brook rot [*sic*?] an Hour's Delay; their whole Success
Depends on instant vigorous Execution.

TULLUS [Aufidius]

VOLUSIUS, I approve thy brave Impatience;
And will to thee, in Confidence of Friendship,
Disclose my secret Soul.[20]

Even in this short passage, several things are noticeable at once. First, Thomson has considerably condensed the action of the play, which begins with the second Volscian uprising. Gone are the battle of Corioli, Coriolanus's military heroism, and Shakespeare's interest in the class competition in Rome: Thomson's play begins after Coriolanus's banishment. Secondly, placing the first few scenes in the Volscian camp, Thomson elevates Aufidius—whom he, (following Dionysius rather than Plutarch) calls Tullus—into a prominence rivaling that of Coriolanus. And, finally, though Tullus does, at last, "disclose his soul" to Volusius, it takes him a couple of pages to do so. Such dialogue characterizes the style of Thomson's talky, declamatory, inactive play. Seemingly, Thomson is more interested in assigning psychological motivation than in depicting dramatic action. The rivalry between Tullus and Coriolanus exists less on the battlefield than in the mind of Tullus, who is jealous of the Roman's reputation, political power, and popularity with the troops. Consequently, his envy, continually inflamed by his followers, rather than any true patriotic zeal, leads Tullus first to try to banish Coriolanus from the Volscians and then to have him killed. Likewise, Coriolanus's mother, called Veturia by Thomson, after his sources, makes a personal appeal—to filial love—rather than to patriotism:

> It is in vain we try to melt a Breast,
> That, to the best Affections Nature gives us,
> Prefers the worst—Hear me, proud Man! I have
> A Heart as stout as thine. I came not hither,
> To be sent back rejected, baffled, sham'd,
> Hateful to *Rome*, because I am Thy Mother:
> A *Roman* Matron knows, in such Extremes,
> What Part to take—And thus I came provided.
>   [*Drawing from under her Robe a Dagger.*
> Go! barbarous Son! go! double Parricide!
> Rush o'er my Corse to thy belov'd Revenge!
> Tread on the bleeding Breast of her, to whom
> Thou ow'st thy Life!—Lo, thy first Victim! (54)

The dramatic sentimentality of this scene is typical of mid-century tragedy, and the personal, familial nature of Veturia's plea shows how Thomson goes about deemphasizing the play's politics.

In general, Thomson gives us, in Coriolanus, a sympathetic hero wrongfully exiled and bent on revenge. Thomson's political interest seems to be the one he emphasized in *Tancred and Sigismunda*—that of dynastic rivalry. And in this important theme, Thomson points to the current 1745 rebellion. While we might sympathize with Coriolanus's rivalry with, and hatred for, the ruling government in Rome, we cannot condone warfare against his own family and country. Thomson's closing speech, given by Coriolanus's friend Galesus, underscores the playwright's essential loyalty:

> This Man was once the Glory of his Age,
> Disinterested, just, with every Virtue
> Of civil Life adorn'd, in Arms unequall'd.
> His only Blot was this; That, much provok'd,
> He rais'd his vengeful Arm against his Country.
> And, lo! the righteous Gods have now chastis'd him,
> Even by the Hands of those for whom he fought. (61)

In toning down Coriolanus's pride and his class arrogance and by focusing attention on the single action of the invasion of Rome, Thomson portrays a hero about whom we feel ambivalent.

In her biography, *James Thomson, Anglo-Scot*, Mary Jane Scott wraps biographical details around her central idea of the sometimes-competing nationalistic impulses Thomson feels for Scotland and England. For instance, Scott claims that in *Liberty*, "Thomson takes great pains to dissociate himself from any taint of Jacobitism" and later asserts that Thomson probably contributed to Fielding's *True Patriot*, advocating tolerance toward loyal Scots during the Jacobite uprising of 1745.[21] Concerning *Coriolanus*, Scott points out that

> much of Thomson's play is set in the Volscians' camp and his plot is presented more from their viewpoint. Again, the pattern seen in *Sophonisba*, of Thomson's ambivalence toward Roman values and of a degree of sympathy for the integrity of the smaller nation, emerges: are the Romans

models of social virtue, or are they oppressors? Heroes or tyrants? Thomson seems never to have resolved this dilemma to his own satisfaction but, corresponding to his own British and Scottish conflicts, his ambivalence appears to generate a certain creativity, a "negative capability," in his handling of the themes of nationalism and patriotism in the dramas.[22]

She continues, "the history of Coriolanus—a noble, rebellious leader camping outside his own capital, then withdrawing—closely parallels the Jacobites' abortive London campaign. *Coriolanus* probably celebrates the Whig poet Thomson's relief as well as gratification at this turn of events."[23] The anti-rebellion sentiment in Thomson's play prompts Loftis to proclaim, "he closed his dramatic career in a spirit of loyalty to the government that would be typical of the drama performed in London for the rest of the century."[24]

Politically, the crucial thing about Thomson's play is its timing. Probably written during, or just after the Jacobite Rebellion, Thomson's *Coriolanus*, like those of Tate and Dennis, uses the Roman story to figure the conflict between Stuart monarch/pretender and the English government. And, importantly, just as the Old '45 is the Stuarts' last gasp, so too is Thomson's—the last of the century's overtly political representations of *Coriolanus*; with Sheridan, we begin the transition into the next century of *Coriolanus* stage history.

Thomas Sheridan, playwright, actor, and theatre manager, is a figure intimately linked with Shakespeare during the mid-eighteenth century. As Esther K. Sheldon observes, "Even more than Garrick in England, he worked tirelessly as Dublin stage manager to repopularize his favorite playwright. During one season (1749–50), for example, 43 performances out of 145 at his Smock Alley Theatre were of Shakespeare's plays—almost one-third of the total."[25] Though the *Coriolanus* was published anonymously and there is no actual proof that Sheridan wrote it, Sheridan produced and played the title role in the February 1752 premiere; moreover, since, as Sheldon notes (154), the style of the Preface to the published version is "very much like Sheridan's prose style," his authorship has long been assumed.

Sheridan's *Coriolanus* is also closely related to Thomson's play. In the spring of 1749, Sheldon reports, "Sheridan had planned to stage Thomson's version of the Coriolanus tragedy and had in fact brought the piece almost to production, deferring it once and then postponing it till next season 'because of an Indisposition of a principal Player.' But the next season nothing was heard of the play, which had been a failure at Covent Garden."[26] Sheridan's version ran five nights in 1752 and was revived briefly during the next season; in 1755 Sheridan took it to London's Covent Garden, where it ran opposite Garrick's revival of the original Shakespearean *Coriolanus* at Drury Lane. The two versions are humorously contrasted by contemporary drama critic Paul Hiffernan, who had frequently attacked Sheridan's work in Dublin:

> The original Coriolanus as played at *Drury Lane* Theatre, is the most mobbing, huzzaing, shewy, boasting, drummy, fighting, trumpeting Tragedy I ever saw.... As exhibited in *Covent-Garden* it is the divine but nodding, Shakespear, put into his Night-Gown by Messire Thomson; and humm'd to Sleep by *Don Torpedo* [Sheridan], infamous for the Mezentian Art of joining his *Dead* to the *Living*: For which he is most justly damned.
>
> The Roman Mother of one House, the Gentleman declare for; the Ladies for that of the other: And the Generality of Spectators in behalf of the young Warrior.[27]

Sheridan's play is an amalgam: the first two acts are largely Shakespearean, the final three taken primarily from Thomson. Sheldon remarks that "in general, he tried to achieve a more 'regular,' more classical plot (closer to Thomson's) and still keep Shakespeare's colorful 'romantic' characterization."[28] But Sheridan does alter Shakespeare's characterization. The tribunes are even more villainous than in Shakespeare, and Coriolanus himself is more heroic. Perhaps these changes are due to Sheridan's wishing to further elevate Coriolanus's character, since he was playing the hero's role himself, and to provide a more positive motive for Coriolanus's contempt for the people than mere pride or class hatred.

While Sheridan diminished the play's political dimension and, particularly, its relation to contemporary political events, he added greatly to its spectacle and enhanced the character of Coriolanus's mother (Veturia, in Sheridan's play), most obviously, by opening the play with a lengthy speech by her and adding the subtitle, "Or the Roman Matron." Sheridan had, in his company, the famous actress Peg Woffington, and no doubt changed the role to take advantage of her talents and box-office appeal. Though Sheridan's stage direction to Coriolanus's triumphant return to Rome following his victories over the Volscians (I.iii; p.8 in Sheridan's play) seems ordinary enough ("*Trumpets sound, enter* Cominius *the General, and* Minucius; *behind them* Coriolanus, *crown'd with an oaken garland, with* Captains *and* Soldiers, *and a* Herald."), the "Advertisement" preceding the printed play lists the "order of the ovation" which totals 118 people! Surely this kind of stage spectacle contributed to the play's success throughout the rest of the century, and its emphasis on principal actors (Sheridan and Woffington) signals the treatment of *Coriolanus* hereafter, as well.

No history of *Coriolanus* in the eighteenth century would be complete without at least a mention of John Philip Kemble, who adopted Coriolanus as his trademark role. As Sheldon asserts, Kemble used Sheridan's "play as the basis of his own acting version, first played and published in 1789—a year after Sheridan's death."[29] In order to get a proper idea of how Kemble performed this, his most famous role, David Rostron studied Kemble's promptbooks in detail for both *Coriolanus* and *Julius Caesar*. Rostron makes a claim for their value:

> By using these prompt copies in association with the remarkably detailed contemporary accounts of the great moments in Kemble's production of *Coriolanus* and *Julius Caesar*, it would be possible to mount a very accurate reproduction of almost every move and climax in these plays. Even the most cursory examination reveals Kemble's attempt to supply pageantry, his enormous patience and skill in the planning and organisation of crowd scenes, his meticulous marking of all "calls," his fondness for musical effects, his concentration on those sections of the plays in which he himself appeared, the general freedom of response and interpretation which he permitted to his colleagues and the fact that he occasionally changed his mind.[30]

As Odell reminds us in his still useful encyclopedic history of Shakespearean production, "Coriolanus has come down in theatrical history as that part in Shakespeare which most exactly fitted the style and personality of John Kemble,"[31] and, as we know, the late eighteenth and all of the nineteenth century were known for their leading actors. (Indeed, Odell's second volume has, as its section headings, "The Age of Kemble," "The Age of Macready," "The Age of Phelps and Kean," "The Age of Irving.")

Coriolanus's potential for spectacle and its leading role as a vehicle for virtuoso performances account for its relative popularity during the late eighteenth and early nineteenth centuries. But the audience's interest in these productions is of a far different sort than that of the spectators who witnessed the staging of Tate's or Dennis's plays, charged, as they were, with contemporary politics. As we move from Tate's *Ingratitude* to Kemble's *Coriolanus*, we move from the work of the political author to that of the brilliant performer; Shakespeare provides the raw materials but for quite variant purposes. As the political situation in early modern Britain stabilized, the theatre became a different place, and plays assumed different values. Equally important is the change in poetics; by the mid-eighteenth century, poetry and drama were far less likely to be employed as partisan weapons. Political literature gives way to a poetry based on individual human experience and to the novel with its often-sweeping views of human society. The treatment of *Coriolanus* in the eighteenth century, decreasing in its political content from Tate to Kemble, offers an insightful mirror of these larger changes.

Notes

1. Charles B. Hogan, *Shakespeare in the Theatre, 1701–1800*, 2 vols. (Oxford: Oxford Univ. Press, 1952–57), I, 460.

2. Charles Gildon, *Remarks on the Plays of Shakespear* in *The Works of Mr William Shakespear*, ed. Nicholas Rowe (London: E. Curll, 1710), VII, 362.

3. Jane P. Tompkins, "The Reader in History: The Changing Shape of Literary Response," in *Reader-Response Criticism from Formalism to Post Structuralism*, ed. Jane P. Tompkins (Baltimore: Johns Hopkins Univ. Press, 1980), p. 211.

4. Nahum Tate, Dedication to *The Ingratitude of a Common-Wealth* (London: Printed by T.M. for Joseph Hindmarsh, 1682).

5. Matthew H. Wikander, "The Spitted Infant: Scenic Emblem and Exclusionist Politics in Restoration Adaptations of Shakespeare," *Shakespeare Quarterly* 37 (1986), 341.

6. Ruth E. McGugan, *Nahum Tate and the Coriolanus Tradition in English Drama, with a Critical Edition of Tate's* The Ingratitude of a Common-Wealth (New York: Garland, 1987), xxxiii.

7. Timothy J. Viator, "Nahum Tate's *Richard II*," *Theatre Notebook* 42 (1988), 114.

8. Quoted in McGugan, p. xxxiv.

9. Wikander, p. 351.

10. McGugan, p. lxi.

11. I use as a text for *Ingratitude*, the one provided by McGugan.

12. McGugan, lxix-lxxi.

13. David Wheeler, "Eighteenth-Century Adaptations of Shakespeare and the Example of John Dennis," *Shakespeare Quarterly* 36 (Winter 1985), 438-49.

14. John Dennis, *The Usefulness of the Stage* in *The Critical Works of John Dennis*, 2 vols., ed. Edward Niles Hooker (Baltimore: Johns Hopkins Univ. Press, 1939, 1943), I, 164.

15. Hooker, II, 6.

16. John Dennis, *The Invader of His Country: Or, the Fatal Resentment* (London: J. Pemberton, 1720), p. 24.

17. Christine Gerrard, "*The Castle of Indolence* and the Opposition to Walpole," *Review of English Studies*, n.s., 41 (1990), 47.

18. John Loftis, "Thomson's *Tancred and Sigismunda* and the Demise of the Drama of Political Opposition," in George Winchester Stone, Jr., ed., *The Stage and the Page: London's "Whole Show" in the Eighteenth-Century Theatre* (Berkeley: Univ. of California Press, 1981), p. 35.

19. Loftis, p. 37.

20. James Thomson, *Coriolanus. A Tragedy* (London: A. Millar, 1749), p. 1.

21. Mary Jane W. Scott, *James Thomson, Anglo-Scot* (Athens: Univ. of Georgia Press, 1988), pp. 219, 232–33.

22. Scott, p. 238.

23. Ibid.

24. Loftis, p. 52.

25. Esther K. Sheldon, "Sheridan's *Coriolanus:* an 18th-Century Compromise," *Shakespeare Quarterly* 14 (1963), 153.

26. Esther Sheldon, *Thomas Sheridan of Smock-Alley* (Princeton: Princeton Univ. Press, 1967), p. 177.

27. Quoted from *The Tuner* (1754–55) in Charles Gray, *Theatrical Criticism in London to 1795* (New York: Columbia Univ. Press, 1931; rpt., New York: Benjamin Blom, 1964), p. 155.

28. Sheldon, "Sheridan's *Coriolanus* . . . ," p. 155.

29. Sheldon, p. 160.

30. David Rostron, "John Philip Kemble's *Coriolanus* and *Julius Caesar*: An Examination of the Prompt Copies," *Theatre Notebook* 23 (1968), 33.

31. George C.D. Odell, *Shakespeare—From Betterton to Irving*, 2 vols. (1920; rpt., New York: Benjamin Blom, 1963), II, 104.

Shifting Masks, Roles, and Satiric Personae: Suggestions for Exploring the Edge of Genre in *Coriolanus*

Karen Aubrey

It is curious that, in spite of general critical acclaim that *Coriolanus* does not adequately fulfill the expectations of a text representative of the genre of tragedy, very few critics have been willing to deviate from the notion of reading the play as just that—a failed piece of tragedy. And though the critical history of *Coriolanus* includes much debate over its merits as a tragedy, the bulk of expended critical effort has been to reveal the play's weaknesses when viewed in light of its very ascribed genre. Barring its easeful fitting into this genre, then, a handful of critics debated whether or not *Coriolanus* was, indeed, a tragedy, and put forth the suggestion that perhaps *Coriolanus* was "something else" and thus began expanding the genre boundaries by which the play is encompassed. Though, undoubtably, there is much of the tragic genre in the play, *Coriolanus* should be viewed in the similar light shed on other of Shakepeare's "tragedies," especially *Timon of Athens* and *Hamlet*. This light reveals the common linking of Shakespearean tragedy with satiric impulse. *Coriolanus* continues this linking of the tragic and the satiric. In fact, the tragic in the play often enlivens and intensifies the satiric. And, if meaning follows form, as Bakhtin asserts, then we have a vast opening up of meaning. When viewed with this broadened generic perspective, much critical circumspection, especially that centering on the notion of the Self as related to

Coriolanus, is more easily reconciled and much more satisfying. How, then, can we read *Coriolanus*? If not a satisfying tragedy, then perhaps we should pay heed to the minority of critics who have referred to the play as satiric.

Perhaps one reason the play is so closely associated with the tragic mode is that *Coriolanus* uses the vehicle of tragedy both to mask the satire and to simultaneously intensify it once it is recognized. In discussing the satiric overtones of the play, critics, such as James Holstun, have pointed out these meta-generic satiric qualities. Holstun purports that "*Coriolanus* satirizes tragedy and the tragic affiliations of the body politic by placing a tragic king-figure within a satiric plot as its gull" (504). He calls the play an aristocratic satire in which the genre of tragedy itself is satirized and in which the tragic overtones are used as a mode of political rhetoric by which to show tragedy as repeatable. The masking of the satiric by the tragic is intensified by the apparent casting of Coriolanus in the role of tragic hero. Once we feel we have identified a "tragic hero," we are then tempted to view the structural entirety of the play as tragic. But time after time, for critic after critic, the play has resisted just such standards of judgment and classification. Stanley D. McKenzie, for instance, complains of "an overwhelming sense of unresolved paradox and uncertainty" (189) which complicates seeing the play as traditional tragedy. I hope to show that it is much more helpful to recognize that the "tragic" role and the "tragic" trappings are merely part of the rhetorical and political techniques which Coriolanus and Shakespeare adopt throughout the play to ease its satiric intent. In exploring this satiric intent, I wish to suggest alternatives to the play's interpretations as tragedy.

Through the use of paying rather strong homage to the tragic genre, Shakespeare masks a brilliant satire with Coriolanus as the figure of the satirist supreme in a politically chaotic world. Though critics acceptingly speak of Hamlet's satiric impulse, this impulse is not so widely recognized in Coriolanus. Donald Hedrick's article focuses on the satiric strain in *Hamlet*, but much of his article is equally relevant to *Coriolanus*. In calling Hamlet a "heroic satirist" (65), Hedrick could just as well be speaking of Coriolanus. When, at one point, Michael Goldman calls Coriolanus the hero who "seems simplest in inner consti-

Shifting Masks, Roles, and Satiric Personae 301

tution, a relatively narrow or immature self" (77), he has oversimplified, but when he adds that "he [Coriolanus] runs the risk of being interpreted as comic," (77) he hints at a beginning awareness of the satiric strains which run through Coriolanus' character. When speaking of Shakespearean tragedy, John Bligh asserts that "the hero is imperfectly understood by the people surrounding him" (259). But this statement is equally valid when applied to the role of the satirist, that figure who acts and speaks out of a sense of difference.

Through this complicated satire and satiric mask, Shakespeare is able to prudently express many opinions about his contemporary England. In addition to the subtle satiric layering which occurs in the play, though, *Coriolanus* is rife with the typical overt qualities of satiric text. We have the presence of a satirist, the all too expected satiric targets—war, looting, mass ignorance, doctors—in the recognizably comic sections of the play, the historic particulars on which the metaphoric satiric targets rest, and other such elements which are ever-present in a satire. One of the earlier critics to recognize the satiric possibilities of the play, O.J. Campbell, calls *Coriolanus* "Shakespeare's second and more successful experiment in tragical satire . . . perhaps the most successful of Shakespeare's satiric plays" (198–99). Donald K. Hedrick acknowledges the "special connection between the satiric and the heroic" as being compatible genres (62). So, I wish to join the argument that *Coriolanus* fails as a tragedy. But the play fails in critical assessment as tragedy because viewing it as such ignores the satiric impulse underlying its structure. *Coriolanus*, though admittedly full of the tragic, is also a satire, a satire firmly grounded in the roots of satiric tradition and satiric expectation. I will discuss the satiric influences on the structure of the play, especially the influence of Menippean satire; the identifiable elements which justify classifying the play as a satire; and the use of the satiric mask related to issues of Self in the character of Coriolanus.

Still debating, critics continue to seek an all-inclusive definition of satire. In the opening of his article "Rhetorics of Attack: Bakhtin and the Aesthetics of Satire," Craig Howes, after quoting definitions from critics such as Patricia Meyer Spacks, Alvin Kernan, Robert P. Elliott, Northrop Frye, and Freud, concludes his paragraph with "purposive content and a conditioned form are apparently essential terms for any discussion of satire or expressed aggression" (215). In order for satire to work, its "purposive content," which I take to be indicative of definite intentionality, must be recognizable. If we miss the underlying intent behind the meaning of the content, then we miss the satire. Much criticism on *Coriolanus* has done just this. We neglected to suspect Shakespeare's satiric critical intent and focused, instead, on the tragic. We just didn't get it. And, invariably, the "conditioned form" of satire is that of some pre-existing, readily identifiable genre. Satire, in a sense, then, is formless. It is parasitic in its occupation of a pre-existing, sometimes masking, form. Again, this accounts for some of the confusion in reading *Coriolanus*, a play which appears to be tragedy because the tragic genre is playing host to and obscuring the satire. Howes's definition is particularly enlightening to this play, then, because it emphasizes the two elements of satire which, I believe, the play exploits in masking its satiric intent—form (i.e., genre) and intent. These two elements seem to have caused the most confusion among critics as to how to regard the play. For the parameters of my discussion of *Coriolanus*, I assume that satire is an intentional attack through a parasitic form and is grounded in historical particulars while reaching into the allegorical or metaphorical. In the case of *Coriolanus*, the allegorical/metaphorical masks the particular satiric targets of contemporary England; the parasitic form further masks the satiric intent of the play.

Coriolanus presents a double edged paradox whereby the principal character fights for, and devotes his life to, a society whose governance he disagrees with and a people whom he despises, while fighting against a foe, Aufidius, whom he respects and seems to regard as a mirror of himself. Conversely, he later aligns with his enemies in Corioles to fight against his beloved/hated country. Yet even in his new alignment, Coriolanus is faced with the same fickle plebeians and is branded a "traitor" by both sides. Not surprisingly for a satiric work, this duality and ambiguity pervades nearly every element

Shifting Masks, Roles, and Satiric Personae

of the play in some respect. Kevin L. Cope notes that "the vocabulary of dualism yield[s] the basic language of satire" (176). Duality and multiplicity comprise the bulk of the play, and these oppositions are noted by the characters in the play, as well as by critics of the play. Coriolanus, in particular, is aware of such dualisms and, as satirist, often consciously sets them against one another to accomplish his satiric exposure. When Cope speaks of Butler's *Hudibras*, his statement is applicable to *Coriolanus* as well: "Like two hemispheres, the oppositions defined by the dualistic philosophy belong to a single whole, yet intersect at no point" (177). The satirist willfully places side by side the irreconcilables of "how things should be" and "how things are." These irreconcilables will be recognized even within the character of Coriolanus himself.

James Taylor divides Alvin Kernan's research on satire into three essential elements: "the satirist or critic, who is often seen as a hypocrite; the scene, which is always crowded; and the plot, which is static in that no essential change occurs" (374). At a quick glance, the play seems to immediately fit into Kernan's satiric parameters. The first of these elements explains the dual or split personality often attributed to Coriolanus. Coriolanus the satirist also becomes Coriolanus the hypocrite by the end of the play once he is revealed, through his own satire, as being one of the objects of the satiric attack. The scene is definitely crowded from the very outset of the play. Not just a crowd, but a crowd in uproar, in the midst of violence, sets the opening tone for the play. And, superficially, the static plot is realized in Coriolanus's final "boy" speech when it is apparent that he has returned to his opening air of "nobility" at the price of prudence, the vice which Coriolanus criticizes in rulers. Yet the underlying stasis of the play rests on the satiric truths which are revealed throughout. All roads truly lead to Rome once we realize that Aufidius' Corioles is no different from Coriolanus's Rome.

Section i, "Social Satire/Satire as Social," of Craig Howes's article provides an excellent summation of Bakhtin's system of locating satire on a spectrum which broadens our perception of what we might call "satiric." Because of critical reluctance to read *Coriolanus* as a satire, Bakhtin's work seems particularly helpful here. Howes points out that Bakhtin tells us in

"Discourse in Life and Discourse in Art (Concerning Sociological Poetics)" (1926) that:

> any locution actually said aloud or written down for intelligible communication (i.e. anything but words merely reposing in a dictionary) is the expression and product of the social interaction of three participants: the speaker (author), the listener (reader), and the topic (the who or what) of speech (the hero). (Howes 218)

Discourse can only take place, then, once this triptychal discourse community is established. According to Bakhtin, this discourse community involves "co-participants who know, understand, and evaluate the situation in like manner" (Bakhtin "Discourse in Life" 100). Let me here refer to the necessary recognized intent of satire which requires this co-participation in shared understanding. Bakhtin's observation is particularly relevant to the satiric mode which necessitates the shared recognition of author/reader, allowing intelligibility of the satiric intent. Satiric discourse is not merely dependent on this recognition, but the satiric stance accentuates the division and existence of the three elements which Bakhtin isolates. The satiric stance is one of distance from the object of attack, either through disassociation or through recognition of the characteristic within oneself. Even when the satirist recognizes the satiric target within him/herself, with that recognition comes the suggestion of separation, reform, and implied distance. Simultaneously, the satiric stance involves identification with the listener/reader, a joining through joint condemnation of the target, or through joint potential reform. So, these three elements are constantly changing their proximity to one another.

Bakhtin posits that the relationships between the author, reader, and hero (the topic of the text, or satiric target in *Coriolanus*'s case) determine the text's genre. "The most important stylistic components of the heroic epic, the tragedy, the ode, and so forth are determined precisely by the hierarchical status of the object of the utterance [hero/topic] with respect to the speaker [author]" (110). The importance of the distance maintained between these entities is paramount in impacting style/genre. Howes points out that the reader's proximity to the author thereby determines the reader's relationship to the topic.

Using Bakhtin's spectrum of exclusive, inclusive, Romantic, and conservative to radical satire (which I find impossible to summarize adequately here), Shakespeare's *Coriolanus* metamorphizes throughout the spectrum. Shakespeare attacks the "topic" (which shifts from society's rulers to the ruled), and aligns with the reader (for criticizing the rulers and the state of society), and attacks the reader (for sympathizing with the plebeian mob, and for being critical of Coriolanus for hating the mob). Shakespeare creates a tangle of contradictions—obviously inherent in the vast number of paradoxical elements within the play—which confuses the formal assumptions of the reader. At times, we feel on the defensive; at times we are the attackers. At times, we are unsure whom we are expected to side with.

Using Bakhtin's discussions on Menippean satire in *Problems of Dostoevsky's Poetics*, we can see that *Coriolanus*'s roots reach firmly into the satiric tradition. In this work, Bakhtin points to the continuing influence and development of the Menippea through modern literature. And in speaking of Menippean satire as being "extraordinarily flexible and as changeable as Proteus, capable of penetrating other genres" (113), Bakhtin's assessment reverberates that familiar idea of the parasitic formlessness of satire which often contributes to its misidentification. Though this article could dwell on delineating in *Coriolanus* the entire elements of Menippea outlined in Bakhtin, the more prominent features must suffice for argument.

Bakhtin privileges the characteristic of the carnivalesque in Menippea, a characteristic in which he seems to include such elements as the fantastic, liberation from the limitations of history, and the adventurous exploration of "truth." Certainly the deeds of Coriolanus qualify as "fantastic." He is seemingly superhuman in his valiant one-man efforts on the battlefield. Yet this feel of the carnivalesque surrounds not only the extraordinary events, but the day-to-day and custom-bound events as well. They have such an element of theatricality that they almost become parodic of themselves, reaching into the realm of the fantastic, the parausual. There is the grotesque feel of Roland Barthes's Spectacle permeating the mundane *cum* fantastic of Bakhtin's Menippea. The theatricality of the humility scene, for example, begins even before Coriolanus dons the ritual robes of humility to expose his wounds, much like Christ exposing his wounds acquired through his saving of others. In Volumnia's advice to her son about the rhetorical strategies he should rely upon in his role of the suppliant, she suggests ways to plead for the crowd's voices. Christina Luckyj refers to Volumnia's advice as a "rehearsal" (335), though she is paralleling this scene with Volumnia's later pleading for mercy on behalf of Rome. Luckyj points out that this pre-humility scene is fraught with the language of and references to acting, from Coriolanus's "I play / The man I am" (III.ii.15–16) to Volumnia's parody of Coriolanus's impending act of supplication through her exemplary performance (335). Once the reader gets to the actual humility scene, the implication is strong that Coriolanus is merely playing a role, or at least trying to. He has adopted one of his many masks. The tradition of asking for voices has become a "fantastic," other-than-normal event.

Through not just the deeds of the man, though, but through "the creation of extraordinary situations for the provoking and testing of a philosophical idea, a discourse, a truth, embodied in the image of a wise man, the seeker of this truth" (Bakhtin *Problems* 114), Coriolanus becomes both a particular person, and a simultaneous allegorical vehicle for testing the "truth" of the text's philosophical idea—namely, that rulers are faulted and that the governed shouldn't govern. We watch Coriolanus endure one exaggerated instance after another, much beyond the bounds of historical likelihood. As the heroes of Menippean satire "wander through unknown and fantastic lands, are placed in extraordinary life situations" (114), Coriolanus finds himself extraordinarily fighting for the enemy against the very Romans he has pledged his life to serve. (And, ironically, he has pledged his life to serve those very Romans whom he so deeply detests. He has fought to uphold a society whose rules of governance he no longer agrees with.) As in Menippea, the man embodying the idea "collides with worldly evil, depravity, baseness, and vulgarity in their most extreme expression" (115). We see these extremities in the actions of both the Roman and the Volscian plebeians, for example. One critic, James Holstun, has cited the ending of the play to be a most inglorious example of the baseness inherent in the play, a baseness which belies the play's erratic attempts at transforming into tragedy. With Aufidius trampling on the body of Coriolanus and the Volscians hurriedly getting on to the "administrative business of managing a city and a military campaign" (Holstun 505)—as we assume the Romans do also—the tragic overtones cheapen to insincere dissembling. Coriolanus plays through the entire spectrum of human experience, being a ruler, soldier, father, husband, son, servant, and so forth. Everywhere, Coriolanus meets the stripped-down "ultimate questions" (Bakhtin *Problems* 115) at the core of Menippea. The allegorical significance of the everyday is portrayed through this mixture of the fantastic and the mundane. Even the play's ruling metaphor of the body is "so vivid in the play that one might be drawn to understand it in the terms of a carnivalesque kind of physicality emanating from the people" (Jagendorf 458).

The play is "liberated from those limitations of history" (Bakhtin *Problems* 114) through its fantastic situations and deeds, but also through its allegorical potential. Allegorical readings abound. Coriolanus's situation is often referred to within the play as parallel to the wars with Tarquin, and likewise, Shakespeare's contemporary historical environment is surely being allegorized, as discussed in detail later in this paper, in relation to the historical particulars being satirized. Bakhtin reminds us "it is essential to emphasize once again that the issue is precisely the testing of an *idea*, or a *truth*, and not the testing of a particular human character.... The testing of a wise man is a test of his philosophical position in the world..." (114–115). Though bound to the particular, this allegorical realm gives the play its timeless quality, making the idea behind the text applicable to many time frames. Jarrett Walker's article "Voiceless Bodies and Bodiless Voices" speaks of the out of time quality of the play where the characters resist being placed or confined to any particular moment. Such timeless, allegorical qualities are perhaps easily distinguished in the concept of Coriolanus's wounds. Menenius regards the wounds as evidence of heroism: "every gash was an enemy's grave" (II.i.155–156). The wounds are the particular which evidence the abstraction of Coriolanus's identity as heroic in his actions and loyalty to Rome. This abstraction of one symbol for another, of one time for any time, is a necessary prerequisite for satire to effectively exist. Rather than an indictment of the actions of the characters in the play, *Coriolanus* is now in the realm of existence where its message can become applicable to those outside of the play's immediate scope of time and place. The play reaches into the allegorical, and into the realm of contemporary Elizabethan England.

Critics have debated much over Coriolanus's psychic state, centering on issues of identity and fragmentation. This concern over psychic state reflects another prominent satiric element of the Menippea which focuses on "moral-psychological experimentation" (116). Many have posited the apparent split personality of Coriolanus, his unruled passions, the Oedipal implications he shares with Volumnia, and his peculiar, perhaps sexual, relationship with Aufidius. This fragmentation is multiplied in the various roles which Coriolanus adopts throughout: that of ruler, humble suppliant, victim, soldier, father, husband, son, friend, and so on. The pointed discussion over what to "name" Coriolanus again calls to our attention the indecision over who he is. Characters in the play don't know what to call him. Volumnia has trouble in "placing" him as soldier, son, man, or hero: "Nay, my good soldier, up; / My gentle Martius, worthy Caius, and / By deed-achieving honor newly nam'd—/ What is it —Coriolanus . . ." (II.i.171–174). Menenius recognizes multiple roles when he says of Coriolanus "when he speaks not like a citizen, / You find him like a soldier (III.iii.53–54). Cominius comments on this when he says "Coriolanus / He would not answer to; forbade all names; / He was a kind of nothing, titleless" (V.i.11–13). And this confusion is recognized by Coriolanus himself: "I play the man I am" (III.ii 15–16). There is disagreement over "who" he is when, for example, Menenius refers to "The consul Coriolanus" (III.i.278) and the plebeians deny that identity: "No, no, no, no, no" (III.i.279). Even critics of the play are confused as to how to refer to him as they comment on the connotations of each chosen name.

The psychic destruction of a man's wholeness is persistently characterized in Menippea by a "diologic relationship to one's own self (fraught with the possibility of split personality)"

(Bakhtin *Problems* 117). If *Coriolanus* is, in part, a satire against those who govern poorly, then Coriolanus the satirist must satirize himself at some point. Part of Coriolanus's self-criticism is fulfilled through the character of Aufidius. In many ways, Aufidius embodies this fragmented part of Coriolanus against which he must satirize. Aufidius is the "traitor," the tyrannical politician figure which is also evident in Coriolanus's own being. At the beginning of the play, Coriolanus expresses his admiration for Aufidius in saying: "I sin in envying his nobility," (I.i.229) and "were I anything but what I am, / I would wish me only he" (I.i.230–231). This identification, for both men, continues throughout the play. By identifying so closely with Aufidius, by effecting a sort of transformation with him, Coriolanus calls attention to the shared qualities between the two men. He defines himself in terms of Aufidius, whether as the enemy or as the fellow noble soldier. And to further compound this issue of fragmentation, Bakhtin notes that soliloquy, a dialogue with oneself, is one of the staples of the Menippea, thereby again setting up a diologic relationship. This idea supports the criticism done on the shifting Selfs of Coriolanus, and also supports the idea of seeing Aufidius as a kind of *doeppelganger* of Coriolanus. We see a literal diologic relationship which metaphorically represents the relationship Coriolanus has with himself.

The idea of fragmentation and split personality is enhanced, again, when James Taylor reminds us that the Renaissance metaphor for the satiric figure was the monstrous half-human half-goat form of the satyr, whose speech was roughly crude (375–376). This image presents an interesting play on the notion of split personality for the satirist, joining the "vexed soul and the melancholic condition" (376) of satirists such as Hamlet. More than explaining the dual personalities of Coriolanus though, the scourge of the plebeians yet the melancholic—especially in the mercy scene with Volumnia begging for Rome—this duality is a wonderful metaphor for the dual satiric targets of the play, the rulers and the ruled.

This fragmented relationship with the Self also has historical grounding in the sixteenth-century conception of the "King's Two Bodies" in political theory. "This political theory, formulated initially to protect the continuity of the crown, distinguished the king's body natural from the body politic" (Miller 306). In the later 1649 execution of Charles I, justification was that the execution was of "solely the king's body natural without affecting seriously or doing irreparable harm to the King's body politic" (306). With this in mind, there is some historical basis for the plebeian uprisings not appearing solely reprehensible, which allows the reader to shift focus from the satirist's criticizing of the uprising masses to the criticizing of the ruler who could inspire such an uprising. The theory that political uprisings were at least partially justifiable facilitates enough empathy for the plebeians and their hardships to allow the criticism of the rulers. And perhaps this accounts for the somewhat schizophrenic tone of the ending with the raucous murder of Coriolanus followed immediately by the assertion of Coriolanus's "noble memory" (V.vi.153). Within a span of approximately thirty-five lines, Coriolanus is criticized, torn apart, then nobly elegized. The swiftness of the change in tone is disarming, but perhaps in this instance, the crowd is vengeful against the "enemy" Coriolanus who killed their sons, yet can still feel a degree of respect and awe for the "idea" of the man. The body is torn apart, yet the noble idea remains to be praised.

And the fragmentation which occurs throughout the play does not end with the being of Coriolanus. Fragmentation is a controlling metaphor throughout, affecting nearly every character, and affecting the play in a more universal way. The State itself is fragmented from the opening metaphor of the body's parts rebelling against each other. Menenius's metaphor implies an initial unity which has become unnaturally fragmented. And numerous comments are made throughout, identifying the State as torn apart, though still joined, as when Martius refers to the somewhat cohesive crowd as "you fragments" (I.i.222). We must remember, though, that Coriolanus, too, rebels against the body, not only in his joining the forces of Aufidius, but in his rebelling against a law he disagrees with, that of allotting power to the plebeians. In his refusals to follow custom in the humility scene, and in his constant undermining of the authority of the plebeians' tribunes, Coriolanus is just as guilty of furthering political chaos as is the rioting mob. There is truth to what Sicinius speaks of Coriolanus prior to his banishment from Rome:

> What you have seen him do, and heard him speak,
> Beating your officers, cursing yourselves,
> Opposing laws with strokes, and here defying
> Those whose great power must try him—even this
> So criminal, and in such capital kind,
> Deserves th' extremest death. (III.iii.77–82)

This Menippean element of fragmentation of the Self metaphorically mirrors the notion of the satiric mask. The satirist takes on other personae in order to facilitate the message of critique. By taking on the mask of the tragic hero, Coriolanus merely appears to be acting from the tragic impulse. Instead, he artfully combines this stance with that of the scourge. James Holstun interestingly argues this point of the tragic mask by quoting Francis Bacon's "Of Envy" in explaining the benefits of tragedy to the politician. A paraphrase of Bacon's passage states that great men, by lamenting the perils and hardships of attaining their honor, "abate the edge of envy" (496). Coriolanus refuses to do this, however, in the baring of his wounds in the humility scene, and in his general ungraceful acceptance of praise. "Coriolanus would rather encourage 'the cruelty and envy of the people'" (IV.v.75) ". . . and shrinks from a public performance that might bring him the ritual authority of tragedy" (Holstun 496), thereby falling short of proclaiming himself the tragic hero.

Coriolanus is a sort of truth-teller throughout the play. As satirist, he wishes to expose. Yet he simultaneously veils truths, truths about his own role and purpose. John Bligh points out one notable instance of this that occurs when Coriolanus announces to the Volscians that he has established peace with Rome:

> His carefully worded report on the campaign tells the truth but not the whole truth: "We have made peace / With no less honor to the Antiates /Than shame to th' Romans" (V.vi.78–80). What he does not say is that he could have destroyed Rome once and for all but spared it for his family's sake. (266–267)

He is, then, a teller of selective truths. He continually complains of being unable to dissemble or role play beyond his true nature while he, ironically, role-plays throughout the entire play. We see this explicitly in his conversation with Volumnia before he goes to beg for voices in the marketplace:

> Must I go show them my unbarb'd sconce? Must I
> With my base tongue give to my noble heart
> A lie that it must bear? Well, I will do't;
> Yet, were there but this single plot to lose,
> This mould of Martius, they to dust should grind it
> And throw't against the wind. To th' market-place!
> You have put me now to such a part which never
> I shall discharge to th' life. (III.ii.99–106)

Though he protests the dishonesty of it, time and again, Coriolanus will take on an "untruthful" role and consciously adopt a mask, in order to accomplish his goal of revealing *a* truth. As satirist within the play, Coriolanus recalls Kevin L. Cope's estimation of satire as it "openly esteems truth more than art [or dissembling]" (175). So, Coriolanus does and does not, reveal the truth. He reveals the satirist's truths, yet conceals truths, especially about himself and his roles which would interfere with the revelations of the satirist.

Through this false denial of dissembling, Coriolanus somewhat fulfills Bakhtin's roles of the rogue, clown, and fool which he delineates in *The Diologic Imagination*. Bakhtin speaks of the development in the Middle Ages of "forms that tended toward satire ... literature of the dregs of society" which featured the three literary types of the rogue, the clown, and the fool. Significantly, these types date back to classical antiquity (158), relevant since Shakespeare's setting is of classical antiquity. And Bakhtin connects these type roles with "the theatrical trappings of the public square, with the mask of the public spectacle" (159). Coriolanus certainly has a theatrical connection not only in his role playing, but in certain performance-oriented scenes, such as the humility scene. Bakhtin goes on to express that these characters are "connected with that highly specific, extremely important area of the square where the common people congregate; second ... the very being of these figures does not have a direct, but rather a metaphorical

Shifting Masks, Roles, and Satiric Personae 313

significance" (159). Coriolanus's fate is decided in that public square among the common people. His major actions either occur or are retold in that public square, primarily for the judgment of the people. The infamy connected to his public name could not exist without that square. And, as discussed in relation to the Menippea, Coriolanus's being has immense metaphorical significance for Shakespeare's contemporary England. So, because this type of character can view events from a different perspective, that "ultimate truth" of Menippean satire can be attained.

This type of character is also somewhat outside of the rules of society, a status which gives the character more freedom of action and expression:

> Essential to these three figures is a distinctive feature that is as well a privilege—the right to be "other" in this world, the right not to make common cause with any single one of the existing categories that life makes available; none of these categories quite suits them, they see the underside and the falseness of every situation. There they can exploit any position they choose, but only as a mask. (159)

Again, the relevance here is multiple. Coriolanus is continually depicted as "other"—in his superhuman feats, in his shifting roles of "outcast" from Corioles, then Rome, and then Corioles again, as enemy and traitor, and as "other" from himself in his multiple states of fragmentation. Coriolanus is literally set apart as "other" in the humility scene, where he is expected to adopt a new appearance, with a new significance in his wounds, and a new personality in his humility. And again he becomes "other" in his disguise as a beggar arriving at Aufidius's house. There is no sense of integration of Coriolanus into any society of the play, not even a sense of integration with his own family. As a result, he has the privilege of seeing situations from different perspectives, from different roles, and can more easily get to the "ultimate truth" of the Menippea. So, for example, when Coriolanus speaks in the role of the soldier, he possesses a certain freedom of expression which is not available to him in the role of the politician. This is a primary reason for the hatred of the citizens. Coriolanus has been accused of displaying a sort of simple-minded naivete in his reluctance to play the part of the politician. Zvi Jagendorf calls Coriolanus "one of Shakespeare's most politically naive characters" (457). But this naivete is purposeful. It is the false naivete of the Menippean technique of "not understanding." This rhetorical stance allows him freedom of expression and freedom of perspective which he would not otherwise possess in his various roles. For example, in the humility scene where he is told that acquiring consulship requires him "to ask it kindly" (II.iii.77), through a play on words, Coriolanus deliberately does "not understand" and replies with: "Kindly sir, I pray let me ha't" (II.iii.78), thereby retaining his ability to express disdain for the situation. Coriolanus confuses these roles, cannot fully metamorphize from one to the other. Menenius makes just this excuse for him at one point when he tries to calm the citizens by arguing:

> That when he speaks not like a citizen,
> You find him like a soldier; do not take
> His rougher [accents] for malicious sounds,
> But as I say, such as become a soldier
> Rather than envy you. (III.iii.53–57)

As Menenius points out to the people of Rome, the secret to understanding Coriolanus's behavior and rhetoric is in first discovering from which role he is acting. Again, if meaning follows form, this applies to the form of the role which Coriolanus has appropriated.

Bakhtin stresses the metaphorical role of the rogue/fool/clown character, and relates this allegorical nature to metamorphosis (*Problems* 161–162). And again, Coriolanus performs an incomplete metamorphosis when he dresses as a beggar and appears before Aufidius's house. Though initially unchallenged as Coriolanus, Aufidius remarks "thy face / Bears a command in't; though thy tackle's torn, / Thou show'st a noble vessel" (IV.v.60–62). And the servants note the same mixed identity:

> *First Serv.* Here's a strange alteration!
>
> *Second Serv.* By my hand, I had thought to have strooken him with a cudgel, and yet my mind gave me his clothes made a false report of him.

Second Serv. Nay, I knew by his face that there was something in him. He had, sir, a kind of face, methought— I cannot tell how to term it. (IV.v.148–156)

Not only do examples such as this denote the role playing which Coriolanus is privy to as a rogue/fool/clown type, but they also denote the issue of the allegorical which can be found in the constant state of metamorphosis in which Coriolanus seems to reside.

Bakhtin relates the rogue/fool/clown to a metamorphosis of a godlike figure, one of the roles which we have seen Coriolanus place himself in and be placed in by others. Coriolanus is referred to frequently as godlike, but in his transformed states, Coriolanus becomes the underside of the god image. He becomes humble, as in the humility scene, or seemingly powerless, as in his transformation to beggar. If as satirist, Coriolanus is intent on laying bare the underside of his satiric targets, these disguises allow him to "spy" on behavior, to see it from a perspective other than normal. He somehow takes on an aura of objectivity when in these roles, and we feel that those acting around him are acting out of their true natures, a confidence which the satirist intends to cultivate.

Both Castiglione and Erasmus heavily influenced Renaissance thinking to include that "just as noble temperament was considered fitting in a satirist, so satiric or ironic temperament was considered fitting in a prince" (Hedrick 65). Donald Hedrick points out that a typical theme in Renaissance satire concerns magnanimity: joining the self-assuredness of one's own rightful power with self-restraint in exercising that power. "Such a posture, with respect to power, one should notice, is fully compatible with aristocratic disdain" (95). Using this prevalent theme, Coriolanus again fits yet another aspect of the role of satirist. Coriolanus seems, in various instances, to be holding his actions in check while his tongue speaks his scathing opinions of the plebeians. In the humility scene, we see Coriolanus appearing to reign his self-assured sense of nobility in order to play the humble suppliant; as noted by all, however, his "aristocratic disdain" cannot be, or perhaps willfully is not, fully disguised. Hedrick notes many parallels between Diogenes and Hamlet which are viable for Coriolanus. For example, he cites an instance of Diogenes' claiming absolute power when seemingly powerless. "Shakespeare and his audience may have recalled the incident when Diogenes is captured and sold into slavery. To a prospective buyer, who asks him what he is good at, Diogenes responds curtly, 'I govern men'" (96). Such a trait is seen in Coriolanus's response to his banishment when he turns and shouts to the crowd:

> You common cry of curs, whose breath I hate
> As reek o' th' rotten fens, whose loves I prize
> As the dead carcasses of unburied men
> That do corrupt my air—I banish you! (III.iii.120–123)

He ends this speech by turning their intent of stripping him powerless and professes that they will be the ones powerless and fearful now that they have banished their chief defender. Like Diogenes, in his moment of potential weakness, Coriolanus empowers himself through speech. And Hedrick also notes the prevalence of sixteenth-century works which pair Diogenes with Alexander, establishing an "enantiomorphous relation between satirist and prince" (97). This would do much to explain the paradoxical depiction of Coriolanus as godly, kingly, noble, yet seemingly rash in his harshly critical attitude toward others. Like Hamlet, the princely Coriolanus slips into the role of satirist. This combining of roles is merely a beginning for seeing the myriad roles which Coriolanus will adopt.

The brutality of Coriolanus's revenge on Rome is satisfyingly justifiable only when it is seen as a punishment for the exposed folly of the Roman plebeians (just as the brutality of Coriolanus's own death is justifiable when he is viewed as an exposed faulty ruler). So, Coriolanus the satirist must first clearly expose the wrongdoings of the plebeians before he can punish. The uprising of the plebeians and the banishment of Coriolanus is entirely necessary to enable the exposure of this folly. Coriolanus is able to expose fully only while under disguise as "the victim/enemy" of the Roman people. Once this role is adopted, Coriolanus becomes an outsider who can comment on the society he has left. Coriolanus does this by allowing his actions to mirror the actions of the plebeians, establishing a parallel situation.

Shifting Masks, Roles, and Satiric Personae 317

Hedrick points out that in *Hamlet*, the mousetrap plan of the play "relies on a traditional [satiric] notion of the power of satire's 'mirror' (i.e., the imitation of personal vices) to make the conscience of the victim reveal his crimes" (70). Coriolanus uses just such a mousetrap device when he turns "traitor" to Rome. By refusing to bow to the law of Rome, to fulfill his duties of asking for voices in the humility scene, and by refusing to recognize the lawful power of the plebeians, he is challenging the governance of the State, rebelling against a wrong he feels has been committed, just as the plebeians had threatened rebellion against established law. Similarly, the plebeians, too, feel that a wrong has been committed by the alleged intentional withholding of corn by the nobility. Coriolanus, then, has adopted their role, mirrored their role as traitors, as rebels against ordered governance. Through his mirroring act of disobeying Roman law, the plebeians are forced to take punitive action against him, to recognize that Coriolanus is wrong in disobeying the law. Though the Roman people seem not to realize it, the reader sees here that the satirist Coriolanus has made the people condemn their own actions. If Coriolanus must be punished for disobeying the law, then too the plebeians must also be wrong and must be punished for doing the same. It is only when Coriolanus becomes, literally and openly, the scourge of Rome, through his siding with Aufidius's army, that the plebeians admit their mistake in banishing Coriolanus and are forced to recant not only the banishment, but the abuse of power which had taken place prior to that banishment. In addition, Coriolanus also creates a mirroring of the plebeians by imitating a false loyalty to Corioles when joining Aufidius. The plebeians had demonstrated just such a loyalty to Rome, one which is shown to be false once they threaten rebellion against the law.

In speaking of *Hamlet*, Hedrick concludes that the play ends with combining the heroic with the satiric, and that Hamlet "devote[s] his final energies to what on the one hand is a conventionally heroic action—keeping his loyal friend Horatio alive. But that same action serves a complementary satiric function in insuring that the villainy Hamlet has brought to light ... is universally published" (74). Coriolanus carries out a similar action at the end of the play. His last heroic act, which some critics identify as his negotiating peace, and some identify as his return to "nobility" in his final disdain for Aufidius, is, indeed, conventionally heroic. Yet this same act is satiric in that it reveals the same faults in the fickleness of the Volscian plebeians that the Roman plebeians have shown, and the same faults are revealed in Aufidius, a faulty ruler, which Coriolanus has also exemplified in his role of ruler. Coriolanus the satirist exposes the body politic as unstable and incapable of rule, yet exposes the existing ruling class, represented by Aufidius, as proud, manipulative, and unwise in its wielding of power.

To further this comparison between the criticisms of both Coriolanus and Aufidius, their two reputations as rulers suffer by the end of the play. Just as Coriolanus suffers through his exposure as a faulty leader and by being branded "traitor" in the end, Aufidius suffers from his "traitorous" alignment with the enemy of Corioles. His superhuman image is greatly diminished by the numerous comparisons the Volscians make between their ruler and Coriolanus. Servants speak of Coriolanus as "the rarest man i' th' world" who is seen as "the greater soldier" (IV.v.162, 167). And Aufidius's esteem is lowered in the eyes of his soldiers:

> Your soldiers use him as the grace 'fore meat,
> Their talk at table, and their thanks at end;
> And you are dark'ned in this action, sir,
> Even by your own. (V.vii.3–6)

And Aufidius himself admits to feeling like Coriolanus's "follower, not partner" (V.vi.38). Because of his desire for complete power, Aufidius has diminished his influence with his own people, and can be seen as—at least—ethically traitorous. If, as some critics have suggested, Aufidius is seen as the "traitorous" side of Coriolanus, the tyrannical ruler, then Coriolanus dies after revealing the faults within himself.

Another element of the Menippea which Bakhtin identifies, and which *Coriolanus* uses throughout, involves manipulation and frustration of customary language and actions. This element of the Menippea includes "scandal scenes, eccentric behavior, inappropriate speeches and performances, that is, all sorts of violations of the generally accepted and customary course of events and the established norms of behavior and

Shifting Masks, Roles, and Satiric Personae

etiquette, including manners of speech" (Bakhtin *Problems* 117). Of course, the very opening of the play sets the tone for the play's breaking of all sorts of customary behaviors. By opening with an angry mob scene, Shakespeare immediately exposes the reader to political chaos in the form of a carnivalesque spectacle, a crowd displaying scandalous and inappropriate behavior. And, as James Taylor asserts, "[t]he scene of satire is a crowded and teeming one, perhaps best perceived in the image of the carnival or fair—masses of people, loud, vulgar, dirty, milling aimlessly about" (375). Though this opening mass is not totally "aimless," the solidity of their convictions is immediately called into question by their lack of action. After all agree "No more talking on't; let it be done" (I.i.13), they begin discussion and procrastination which lasts throughout the play. So, if not aimless, their aim is certainly murky. The opening scene, in fact, sets the tone for the satiric impulse of the play. The mutinous mob becomes a metaphor for the satiric act. They are waving their weapons, and brandishing their words, opening the play with the combative tone of satire and the emphasis on the communicative act. And when Taylor comments that the "satirist . . . cannot help being infected by it [the diseased masses]" (375), we hear the echo of Menenius's complaint of being "infected" by listening to the masses.

Though an example of this element of Menippea could be provided from almost any scene in the play, the humility scene embodies its essence. Coriolanus's costume presents an incongruous image from the onset of the scene. He is playing a part which is foreign to his nature, setting appearance at odds with his spirit. Though this supplication for "voices" is customary, "Pray you go fit you to the custom, and / Take to you, as your predecessors have . . ." (II.ii.142–143), Coriolanus behaves inappropriately by making a mockery of this tradition. In action, his etiquette belies the solemnity of the occasion when he refuses to reveal the wounds for public view. And his manner of speech is sarcastic rather than suppliant:

> I will not seal your knowledge with showing them.
> I will make much of your voices, and so trouble you no farther. (II.iii.108–110)

to which the citizens respond: "Was not this mockery?" (II.iii.173). Scandal surrounds the decision of Coriolanus's banishment, both in the way it evolves and in its resultant alignment of Coriolanus with Aufidius. And the eventual death of Coriolanus is also scandalous in its lack of decorum and ethical efficacy.

The element of the language of the Menippea is particularly relevant to the prosodic criticism surrounding the play, especially that on Coriolanus's manner of speaking. Michael Goldman, in discussing the speech patterns of Coriolanus, points to one prevalent technique of verbal attack where "the sense of attack comes from the pursuit of the delayed idea, the buried trigger" (79), where the language progresses toward not just an accumulation of ideas, but a final invective point. His descriptions are of a rather unsettled and convoluted style of speaking. This manner of speaking offers both an overt attack, yet also generally carries a more covert and more damning statement with it. This very speech mannerism mirrors the role playing, or masking, in which Coriolanus participates throughout the play. The covert mask belies the more pointed criticism underneath.

As numerous critics have pointed out, Coriolanus, as well as others in the play, manipulates language and methods of rhetoric throughout. Yet as a rogue/clown/fool type, Coriolanus retains this privilege of "bluntness" granted in Menippea (Bakhtin *Problems* 161). We expect such manipulation and use of various types of rhetoric from a satirist. As asserted in the opening of this article, the play has been discussed in terms of its parody of the language of tragedy. And in the humility scene, Coriolanus speaks in the language of commerce, which Jagendorf refers to as a "parody of market language" (465):

> Here come more voices.
> Your voices! For your voices I have fought,
> Watched for your voices, for your voices bear
> Of wounds two dozen odd; battles thrice six
> I have seen and heard of for your voices, have
> Done many things, some less, some more. Your voices!
> Indeed I would be consul! (II.iii.125–31)

Coriolanus's thinly veiled contempt of this ritual implies the selling of loyalty and nobility, something he has previously rejected in turning down the spoils of war as payment for his duty. Heroism becomes cheapened when bought. His double parody here of the language of exchange and the language of praise both acknowledges his stooping to "buy" votes through his display of wounds and false act of humility, and implies that the plebeians stoop in allowing their votes to be "bought." Through this one act of rhetoric, Coriolanus exposes multiple targets to his satiric tongue. His heroic actions turn to self-serving bargaining chips; the plebeians are belittled, not only for this love of Spectacle, but for their acceptance of this marketing of loyalty. The praise rings false, undercutting Coriolanus's motives for his heroic deeds. And the entire process of election, of the power of the plebeians becomes a cheap market bargain. The process is debased as the involvement of the plebeians' power seems to cheapen the ideas of nobility and loyalty. This speech, then, criticizes both the debasement of government by the involvement of the masses, and criticizes the leadership of the nobility which would debase itself to such a degree. Both parties are satiric targets here.

Much of the criticism of the language and style used in the play has concluded that Coriolanus's rough manner of speaking is merely analogous to his rough mannerisms and violent attitudes toward the plebeians and what he views as unjust, that Coriolanus's rough speech corresponds to his abilities as a warrior and shortcomings as a politician. He is characterized as having a "thunder-like percussion of ... sounds" (I.iv.59). A more fully satisfying explanation of the roughness of the verse, though, should include notice that *Coriolanus* is exploiting the sixteenth-century satiric verse tradition of using just such rough speech. Through studying John Marston and others, James Taylor, in particular, links Marston's harshness of style and vehemence of expression to Shakespeare and *Hamlet*. Taylor concludes that the sixteenth-century satirist insists that he is "unskilled in the art of rhetoric and that his language will be direct and even crude" (374). Taylor points out the irony, however, that this claim shows itself to be false once the satirist's language proves itself to be highly rhetorical in its use of crudities. Coriolanus's language, then, fits in well with the rhetorical and stylistic expectations of a sixteenth-century satirist, seen as eloquently vehement in his scathing language while focusing on vile imagery in these attacks. Taylor asserts that the majority of satiric theories during this period "tend to support the notion that satire should be rough and bitter" perhaps leading the Elizabethans to mimic this satiric bent for "crudeness of language and fascination with vice" (375).

Perhaps this crudeness of language, the *slum naturalism* of Menippea, accounts for the number of vile images used throughout the play. Again, recalling the image of the satyr's animalism, this "monstrous" bent associated with satire could explain such things as Coriolanus's many references to the masses as being a diseased many-headed beast, and the prevalent, but typical, use of medical metaphor, "a staple of Renaissance satire" (Sitter 18), in the many body metaphors used throughout the play. Though the specific and more commonly used metaphor of progressing disease as reflective of progressive situational decay is not specifically used, Shakespeare has substituted the metaphors of starvation and cannibalism in his body metaphors. This substitution implicates issues of responsibility both on the part of the ruling class and the plebeians. It becomes an even more appropriate metaphor for *Coriolanus*, since none of the play's situations seems "fated" as implied by progressive disease metaphors. Implications of imposed starvation, cannibalism, or starvation resultant of behavior provide the satiric vehicle for which to criticize both parties.

Menippea is also full of "sharp contrasts and oxymoronic combinations ... the emperor who becomes a slave, moral downfalls and purifications, luxury and poverty.... The Menippea loves to play with abrupt transitions and shifts ... m'esalliances of all sorts" (Bakhtin *Problems* 118). Examples of such instances include the humility scene, Coriolanus's disguise as a beggar, his aligning with the enemies of Rome, his swift expulsion from the city of Rome, the fickleness of both the Roman and Volscian plebeians, the swift change of loyalties of the plebeians which leads to his murder, and his abrupt fall from "hero" to "traitor." The language Shakespeare uses in *Coriolanus* contributes greatly to the play's paradoxical feel. As McKenzie points out, *Coriolanus* reverberates with rhetorical figures of contrast and irony" (195). He cites examples such as "valiant ignorance" (IV.vi.104); lines such as "You have deserv'd nobly of your country, / and you have not deserv'd nobly" (II.iii.88–89), "crows to peck the eagles" (III.i.139), and emphasizes the pervasive tone of paradox in Coriolanus's first descriptive speech of the plebeians (I.i.168–84) (195). And though Derek Traversi views this speech as "one of the most disconcerting initial utterances ever put into the mouth of a tragic hero," (McKenzie 195) the resolution of paradox is more readily accessible when viewing Coriolanus as a satirist, one who is expected to dissemble, rather than as a tragic hero.

And then, finally, Bakhtin lists what he calls the "'journalistic' genre of antiquity, acutely echoing the ideological issues of the day" (*Problems* 118), which corresponds to the historical particulars at which satire aims its criticism. We see Shakespeare working through various sociological and ideological issues of his time in these particulars. Though the historical particulars of *Coriolanus* have been noted by numerous critics, Shannon Miller presents the play's use of these particulars in such a way as to reinforce our reading of the play as satire.

Necessary for the impetus of satiric intent in *Coriolanus*, are the particular satiric targets which motivate Shakespeare to attack. As Shannon Miller points out, "Jacobean parliamentary battles, the 1607 Midlands Insurrection, conceptions of a Renaissance soldier, and the theory of the body politic are some of the historical events and cultural ideas" (287) on which critics have traditionally focused in reading the play as topical. Her identification of these particulars is not new, but she carries her identification further by giving new perspective to the play's juxtapositions of these topical references. Not only do these widely accepted historical references provide satiric particulars on which to point, but Miller's assessment of the juxtaposition of these topical references in the play strengthens reading the play as satire and reveals some rather harsh criticisms of Shakespeare's for James and contemporary politics.

Miller reads parallels between Coriolanus and King James in the references to James's parliamentary battles, and to the simultaneous Midlands riots—a rebellion which James had to suppress. Yet, though she notes that previous critics had rejected such parallels once Coriolanus is branded a traitor—thereby retaining a conservative subtext of the play in Shakespeare's criticism of James—Miller departs from this viewpoint and maintains and provides evidence that this parallel with James continues to the end of the play, offering an image of King James as a traitor. Her reading, then, implies a harsh satiric thrust of *Coriolanus*, a thrust so pointed that it's no wonder Shakespeare buried it under layers of tragedy and paradox. Miller's reading of this continuing parallel may be, perhaps, reinforced by the earlier and persistently erratic portrayal of Coriolanus as tragic hero. If these particulars are presenting the ideology of the time, as in Menippean texts, then Coriolanus, and by implication, James, is seen as a man who is kingly in a time which wants or needs no absolute power of kingship, a character displaced in time. And though "allegory distances the terror of satire by generalizing its object" (Bruns 130), this would, indeed, become a harsh, though veiled, criticism of King James.

Through satire, the play becomes a critical response to the political issues of the day. Miller's article offers detailed analysis of the James/Coriolanus parallel, with many examples. But one element which is remarkably striking is that in 1598, James put himself above the law by asserting that "'the King is aboue the law, as both the author and giuer of strength thereto'" (289). Thus ensued a debate between James and the House of Commons as to the nature of kingship and power, and, more specifically relevant to the play, the parallel between the creation of the tribunes representing the Roman plebeians and the Renaissance supporters of Common Law (289). As with James, Coriolanus is accused of just such rising above the law. In several instances Miller quotes James, in fact, likening the Common Law supporters who challenged traditional authority, to the same type of Roman tribunes depicted in Shakespeare's play. Coriolanus attempts to rise above custom when he wishes to forsake the baring of the wounds for voices, and rise above the law when he refuses to recognize the power of the plebeians' tribunes. He actively rebels in the act of drawing his sword against the tribunes prior to his banishment and actively rebels in his disavowal to submit to the tribunes' legal power.

Miller also briefly mentions the debates of 18 November 1605 "concerning the crown's traditional right to purchase goods at lower than market values..." (289). Though she does not make the analogy, perhaps this incident may be hinted in the play's opening plebeian debates over the distribution of corn. These comments combine the issue of corn with metaphors of commerce:

> What authority surfeits [on] would relieve us. If they would yield us but the superfluity while it were wholesome, we might guess they reliev'd us humanely; but they think we are too dear. The leanness that afflicts us, the object of our misery, is as an inventory to particularize their abundance; our sufferance is a gain to them. (I.i.16–22)

> Suffer us to famish, and their storehouses cramm'd with grain; make edicts for usury, to support usurers; repeal daily any wholesome act establish'd against the rich, and provide more piercing statutes daily to chain up and restrain the poor. (I.i.80–84)

In the opening scene of the play, goods are linked to unfair commercial practices. Especially with the introduction of the notion of usury, the implication is made that the rich, the privileged, are provided with goods which the poor must purchase at a considerably higher price, if they are allowed access to these goods at all. This may be an oblique reference to the crown's privilege of purchasing goods at a reduced price, thereby causing the common price to smack of usury.

In regard to the debate over power and the nature of kingship, Miller notes two other parallels between James and Coriolanus. The first is that both the House of Commons and the Roman tribunes assert that they are a *traditional* source of authority, while, in fact, they are not. As in the case of the creation of power in the House of Commons, we see the creation of the plebeians' tribunes in *Coriolanus*, "but Brutus and Sicinius consistently emphasize the 'ancient' power they represent...

they believe they have 'shown' it as well as maintained the 'ancient strength' (IV.ii.3,7) of the people" (290). And power is, according to Donald Hedrick, "the object to which Elizabethan verse-satire dedicates itself" (64). The second parallel is in both James's and Coriolanus's absolute disdain for the voice of the people who support the "tribunes."

Miller also points out common personal traits of James and Coriolanus such as "their analogous disdains for the people and their repudiation of theatrical performance" (291). "Like James, Coriolanus views public performance as a burden" (292). Instances of this dislike can be found in almost any speech of Coriolanus to the people, and his dislike of theatricality is obvious in the humility scene, even though he hypocritically participates in this theatricality. Even Coriolanus's expression of revulsion for the populace, in terms of a diseased mass, can trace to James's own responses where James is quoted as using much the same imagery (292). Miller also notes that Shakespeare made many changes from his source for the play in Plutarch, such as omitting numerous justifications for the people's revolt which can be found in the original. By doing so, the citizenry "appear more like rebels" (298) linking them with English rioters, and it intensifies the satiric criticism of both the exercise of power in the hands of the unruly masses and having the poor judgment to grant such a mob power.

Miller states that *Coriolanus* articulates the sides of the Renaissance debate over balance of authority, but her conclusion is unclear when she states that the play does not posit an answer to whose authority is supreme, but then asserts that the play "exposes the dangers of insisting upon the prerogative of rulers" (302), and that the play ultimately supports limited monarchy rule. Again, I think the confusion over what to conclude at the end of the play resides in the double-edged nature of the satire in the play. The plebeians, perhaps, deserve the criticism and disdain they receive from Coriolanus, yet by insisting on inflexible rule, Coriolanus becomes a threat to the State and to order, equal to what the plebeians had been previously. Both sides are dangerous to the State. The play, then, is equally a critique of the English masses and a critique of James and seems to posit that should either side go too far, chaos will result.

Shifting Masks, Roles, and Satiric Personae

Apparently missing from *Coriolanus* are the religious/mystical overtones which occur in Menippean satire. James Holstun notes that the supernatural and mystic actions of gods are all but missing in the play. He does concede, however, that the "institution of display itself has the trappings of tragedy, for it aims to elevate a heroic figure through a public spectacle centered on his near-martyrdom" (494). Rather than reaffirming the play as a tragedy, though, I would argue that these larger-than-life spectacles move toward the satiric, falling under the mystical-religious element of the Menippea which is often combined with what Bakhtin calls "crude *slum naturalism*" (*Problems* 115). There is mention of a godlike presence, though, in the being of Coriolanus. He is often referred to in term of mystical reverence. Cominius compares him to an immortal "planet" (II.ii.113) sent to aid the mortal city; a messenger describes the nobles kneeling to Coriolanus "As to Jove's statue" (II.i.266); Brutus claims Coriolanus "will not spare to gird the gods" (I.i.256), then later accuses him of speaking "as if you were a god, to punish; not / A man of their infirmity" (III.i.81–82); and Cominius refers to Coriolanus by saying "He is their god; he leads them like a thing / Made by some other deity than Nature" (IV.vi.90–91). Coriolanus himself acknowledges this image of himself when he refers to Menenius as having "godded" him (V.ii.11). Such scenes as the humility scene carry multiple religio-mystic elements as the public spectacle, and the religious element with its ritualistic structure.

In relation to Coriolanus's shifting identity, Shakespeare uses the relatively minor mode of "character progress," often found in satire. As is usual of both a depiction in a character progress, and the depiction of the rogue type in Menippea, one's being coincides with one's actions. This is particularly relevant when we remember the number of generalized titles under which Coriolanus is identified. Even his attributed name "Coriolanus" is adapted from a deed which he has performed. "The character progress is the reduction of identity to career ... the career *becomes* the man" (Sitter 9).

According to John Sitter in *Arguments of Augustan Wit*, the character progress introduces the question of "inevitability" of one's actions. This is reminiscent of the many comments made in the play regarding the question of "nature" and Coriolanus's motivation for his behaviors. Menenius states that Coriolanus's "nature is too noble for the world" (III.i.254). Is it Coriolanus' nature to behave as he does, or is it poor judgment, as Aufidius will question toward the end of the play? As Sitter points out, within the protagonist's scheme of things, given his historical particulars of class, education, nurture, and such, the reader infers a degree of fatality in the realized prediction of the character progress (11). While this notion of fatality is expected in the tragic genre, the character progress, used most extensively in the early to mid-eighteenth century, became associated primarily with the satiric or didactic (if the two are separable). This question of inevitability of Coriolanus's outcome confuses our empathetic response to his character. His progress is dynamic, in that it is presented as sequential stages:

> At sixteen years,
> When Tarquin made a head for Rome, he fought
> Beyond the mark of others. Our then dictator,
> Whom with all praise I point at, saw him fight,
> When with his Amazonian [chin] he drove
> The bristled lips before him. He bestrid
> An o'erpress'd Roman, and i' th' consul's view
> Slew three opposers. Tarquin's self he met,
> And struck him on his knee. In that day's feats,
> When he might act the woman in the scene,
> He prov'd best man i' th' field, and for his meed
> Was brow-bound with the oak. His pupil age
> Man-ent'red thus, he waxed like a sea,
> And in the brunt of seventeen battles since
> He lurch'd all swords of the garland. For this last,
> Before and in Corioles, let me say,
> I cannot speak him home. He stopp'd the fliers,
> And by his rare example made the coward
> Turn terror into sport; as weeds before
> A vessel under sail, so men obey'd
> And fell below his stem. His sword, death's stamp,
> Where it did mark, it took; from face to foot
> He was a thing of blood, whose every motion
> Was tim'd with dying cries. Alone he ent'red
> The mortal gate of th' city, which he painted

With shunless destiny; aidless came off,
And with a sudden reinforcement struck
Corioles like a planet.... (II.ii.87–114)

Again, this particular progress records Coriolanus's growth into the soldier. Coriolanus is defined as an idea or role, implicating the idea/role as much as the particular character himself once the satiric exposure is complete. Defining Coriolanus in terms of an idea again appropriately supports the Menippean combining of the particular and the allegorical as discussed earlier:

> Like other forms of reduction, the character progress does not encourage identification with the subject as individual, offering only what Hans Robert Jauss would classify as "ironic identification." In its particular selectivity, the progress tends to present character as materially determined by class goals, economic relationships, and physical conditions; as a specialized form of satire, the progress shares the tendency Keith Fort identifies in satire generally to depict characters as "subservient to the laws of nature, society, and type when they pridefully think they are unique in their individual differences." [quoted from Keith Fort, "Satire and Gnosticism," *Religion and Literature*, 20.2 (Summer 1988), 1–18; p. 6.] (Sitter 46)

Fort uses three terms which are echoed frequently in the ideas and situations presented in *Coriolanus*: subservience, pride, and individual difference. In one of Aufidius's longer assessments of Coriolanus's character, Aufidius notes Coriolanus's shifting roles and raises questions about the motivation for Coriolanus's actions, in a sort of mirroring of Menenius's progress depiction of Coriolanus:

> First he was
> A noble servant to them, but he could not
> Carry his honors even. Whether ['twas] pride,
> Which out of daily fortune ever taints
> The happy man; whether [defect] of judgment,
> To fail in the disposing of those chances
> Which he was lord of; or whether nature,
> Not to be other than one thing, not moving
> From th' casque to th' cushion, but commanding peace
> Even with the same austerity and garb

> As he controll'd the war; but one of these
> (As he hath spices of them all, not all,
> For I dare so far free him) made him fear'd,
> So hated, and so banish'd; (IV.vii.35–48)

Confusion arises, not only for the reader, but for the characters within the play, about this question of inevitability of action. "Tragic and romantic characters have *fates;* comic and satiric characters have *parts*, social parts" (Sitter 14). Though Coriolanus continually decries belonging to the "whole" of the social group, and continually stands apart in his deeds and is regarded as "other," he is forced into playing these social roles throughout the play. He feels the tension of joining/disjoining, and this tension is recognized by all in the play. Sicinius and Brutus use this irreconcilability against him in invoking his anger during the humility scene. They realize Coriolanus's aversion to playing the social role of humble suppliant and force the issue into the public square. Menenius must constantly remind him of his social obligations. And the argument that finally wins his mercy on Rome in the end, after he has completely separated from the Romans, is one of social obligation to family and Self. This obligation resides heavily in preserving the "hero" status of his reputation so that society will remember him as such, rather than as a traitor of Rome. This simultaneous awareness and denial of social perceptions and expectations seem relevant to the play's satiric multiple targets of both affirming and criticizing the social status quo.

Perhaps the embodiment of this conflict is in the Aufidius/Coriolanus connection. In noting this attraction-repulsion relationship, the ironic link works as a wonderful metaphor for Coriolanus's struggle with being "a part of" and "apart from" others. Aufidius is the ultimate "other"; joining the Volscians is the most radical way Coriolanus disassociates himself from the Romans. Yet there is such similarity in Aufidius's relationship with the Corioles plebeians and their treatment of Coriolanus, it is almost as if Coriolanus has never left home. His acts of nonconformity, then, become less statements of individuality, and more expressions of learned roles. This becomes especially evident in his mother's speeches involving the appropriation of roles, and in her teaching of roles as if he were a child. Sitter frequently points out that fates in the character progress often are a result of just such social scripts (27). The tragic genre is invoked through such character progresses because of the fatalistic feel. Individual control and influence seem limited and deviation from the projected end appears impossible. But as "structures of foresight" (Sitter 31), progresses can serve as a warning to change, the social change desired by satire.

The character progress moves away from the tragic, though, and informs the satiric by changing the proximity of the relationship between the author, topic, and reader that Bakhtin speaks of. "[I]n presenting characters whose progress is mechanical, degenerative, and fatal, and in providing the real pleasure of predictability, the character progress automatically posits a higher ground, inhabited by author and viewer, where movement is less blind and more vital" (Sitter 19). Here we have the much used description of the satiric stance. We, experienced readers, anticipate the outcome. We recognize and perceive the errors and the outcome of these errors. In order to maintain the satiric tone though, we can't rely entirely on fate to achieve this outcome. That is why we have the passages implicating Coriolanus as using bad judgment, making the wrong choices. He and the other Romans must hold some degree of accountability for their demise.

By the end of the play, Coriolanus manages to alienate nearly everyone, including, to a great extent, the reader. In spite of being described as one of Shakespeare's most disliked characters, Coriolanus must, in order to function as a satirist in the text, evoke, to some degree, our empathy and our trust of his satiric revelations. Though at first glance, he seems to express nothing but disdain for all around him, this disdain is forgivable when we realize the purpose behind it. Though we dislike him throughout much of the play, we feel curiously sympathetic for him by the end. By then we've affirmed that the plebeian tribunes are manipulative and scheming, fickle and short-sighted. In short, the plebeians are, in fact, guilty of those things which Coriolanus finds so distasteful. So, it is not his censure of them which we cannot reconcile, it is his vehemence in delivering that censure. Once Coriolanus is recognized as a satirist, especially a sixteenth-century satirist, this vehemence is to be somewhat expected. We understand its harshness. And, by the end of the play, once the full extent of the plebeians' faults has been revealed by this satirist, we can almost share in that vehemence.

I think, however, that there is a more subtle reason why we can and do begin to empathize with Coriolanus, why we can even begin to like him toward the end of the play. The presentation of Coriolanus's character changes at various points in the play so that, at times, he is more accessible to us than at others. We see ourselves at various distances from Coriolanus in the Bakhtinian discourse triangle, so our interpretive ground continually shifts between identifying with and being critical of him. This shifting allows our simultaneous dislike of him and our sympathetic feelings toward him in the end. In short, he moves through various stages in his character development which alternately allows us to identify and distance ourselves from him. It is this degree of distance which will determine the degree to which we feel empathetic. This movement in proximity occurs with each fragmentation and shifting of character identity.

By seeing Coriolanus in a series of roles rather than as a real personality, we focus on his "titled" qualities, our expectations of his "role." We are allowed little chance to get to know the person behind the mask. Instead, we see a "titled" persona reacting to a series of events. As in most character progresses where "we do not see them debate or struggle over their choices" (Sitter 20), when viewing Coriolanus as a "role," we expect not to have to witness a debate over action. The action is programmed into the particular role he is occupying at the time, which, again, contributes to our feeling of inevitability. These questions of inevitability versus responsibility depend greatly on the role into which Coriolanus fits at any given moment. As depicted in the character progress, Coriolanus is not liable for his action, "the liberty of knowing their own thoughts is precisely what the characters of the progresses do not possess" (Sitter 20), thereby leading to a lack of self-recognition. It is at such times that we can feel some sympathy for Coriolanus. However, during moments when Coriolanus reveals himself to be in control of his destiny, to be consciously adopting personae for various purposes, we are capable of feeling revulsion for this man who is using disastrously poor judgment.

The issue of masks and personae is particularly relevant to this play, for the main character of Coriolanus resists critical location as a character, as well as being "fixed" by other characters within the play who, too, are attempting to understand him. Much criticism has been written on the nature of his Self, in trying to define, explain, and describe it. The difficulty in doing so, I believe, arises from the shifting nature of the masks which Coriolanus wears. Literally, we see him adopting many roles in the play, many outward Selfs, again, that of the soldier, the son, the father, the hero, the traitor, the statesman, the friend, the enemy, the lover, the beggar, and so forth. Some roles he fulfills more successfully and more fully than others, but importantly, we feel a sense of his search for the role into which he can comfortably fit—a role which he never really finds.

In *Mind in Action* Amelie Rorty includes the chapter "Characters, Persons, Selves, Individuals" in which she differentiates categories of being, and discusses "criteria for personal identity" (78). In her system, she describes a spectrum of being which begins with the "character" and moves through "figures," "persons," "selves," "individuals," "subjects," to "presences." This spectrum moves generally from the more allegorical or generalized, to the particular. The spectrum implies moving from determinism to free will, from a joining of mind/body to a separating of mind/body, from "acting is being" to the ownership of acting/thinking. Satire begins with a paradoxical existence of its elements, for it must be allegorical in its particularities; and in the Menippea, Coriolanus is seen to represent the generalized "acting is being" as well as the allegorical figure for the particularized James. It is within this spectrum that Coriolanus moves, and his position within the spectrum affects the distance maintained between him and the reader. The degree of distance then affects the reader's ability to identify or sympathize with Coriolanus.

Through much of the play, Coriolanus exists in the category of the "character," the state of most Greek tragic heroes—thus the pervasive feel of the genre of tragedy. The "character" is fixed, fated, by his parentage (hence the criticism on Volumnia's influence on his nature), and the "hero is known by his deeds: setting himself superhuman tasks, providing himself worthy of divine regard..." (Rorty 79). "Characters" tend to be constant, predictable, and their acts *are* their identity, as Coriolanus is frequently denoted. They act with a sort of "ruling passion," whereby their responses to situations are determined by their inflexible propensity of disposition. Rorty points out that valued "character" dispositions are relative and that "characters in time of great social change—are likely to be tragic" (80). We see Coriolanus living in a time of social and political change, not merely because of the raging wars, but internally, due to the rise of the plebeian class into the Roman political arena. So Coriolanus's ineptitude at political maneuvering causes him to be seen—by the plebeians, by his friends, by his family, and by the reader—as overly proud and inept in judgment. But this is a faulty evaluation of the "character" of Coriolanus. "Characters" do not choose their lot. Thus, Coriolanus is a victim of his "character" and we can, therefore, sympathize with him.

Once seen as a "character," though, the reader will realize that were Coriolanus in a different context, such as battle, he becomes a hero. Shakespeare overtly reveals this paradox to us by placing his "character" is such diverse situations. As a soldier, Coriolanus is praised by all within the play and is admired by the reader as heroic. In the political context, though, we despise him, fault him, as do those within the play. James Holstun makes a related assessment when he remarks that Coriolanus is the "'kingly crown'd head'" of Menenius's opening metaphor for the 'Renaissance body politic,' but that, tragically, Coriolanus is living in a time with no need, and, I would add, no tolerance, for a king (489). "Coriolanus is a ... tragic king-figure in a satiric drama that does not need a king. He is a tragic hero only insofar as he is tragically miscast" (489). Not only does this describe Coriolanus, but this category of being also seems to coincide with many of the requirements of the Menippean satirist.

Without moving through Rorty's entire spectrum, my point here is that Coriolanus undergoes a series of meta-

Shifting Masks, Roles, and Satiric Personae 335

morphoses throughout the play. At times we view him as a sort of type character fated by his parentage; and it is at these times that his surface appearance is most like the tragic hero we expect from a play labeled a "tragedy." However, it is also at these times when Coriolanus is actually the satirist, merely masked by the role of the heroic type character. And thus masked, Coriolanus is able to expose the faults of the plebeians with their newly acquired powers. It is during this role when we are allowed to like Coriolanus, to feel sorry for him, to feel he is a victim of the Roman and Volscian rabble. We see his "inappropriate," yet consistently savagely noble approaches to situations. Though we notice the inappropriateness of it, we also notice the crowd's reaction to him. We cannot chastise Coriolanus in this category because he is only acting as he was taught. He is not choosing to act this way. Therefore, we turn our censure toward the plebeians (and Elizabethan England commoners).

But once Coriolanus moves into the stage of "persons," the issue of liability for one's actions is introduced. Persons adopt masks or roles by which to act (Rorty 85). Here begins the realm in which Aufidius can justly wonder if Coriolanus acted out of bad judgment, where confusion arises over which role Coriolanus has chosen, where Menenius can hope that Coriolanus will willfully change his mask to that of politician when speaking to the citizens. Though the reasons for one's actions are still obscure, self-cognizance is introduced and, therefore, punitive judgment by the reader becomes possible. The "person" stage marks the turning point for the reader's censure of Coriolanus. When assuming we are reading about a "person," we begin to "search for the principles by which choices are to be made" (Rorty 86).

And this judgmental mode on the part of the reader continues through the stage of "individual." It is frequently tempting to see Coriolanus as an "individual." He protests throughout that he will follow his own conscience, submit to no social pressures. He seems to wish to remain outside of the social group and maintain himself as a loner. "Individuals" tend to fall outside of society in that they are "defined against existing and presumably corrupt societies" (89), and Coriolanus surely sees himself as not only apart from society, but somehow morally better. And "individuals" resist typing in their expression of uniquely particular Selves (90). When Coriolanus is in the category of the "individual," he can be identified as the particularized James, or the particularized universal notion of the faulty ruler. And particularly relevant to Coriolanus's scenes which involve issues of commerce and the language of commerce, individuals' "rights are not property; they cannot be exchanged, bartered. Their rights and their qualities are their very essence, inalienable" (90). Since Coriolanus's apparent motivation for hating the plebeians is that he feels their political participation will destroy society, it is tempting to see him in the act of being an "individual" at these moments. Again, judgment is proper here, but not when he is in the guise of a "character."

During these times when Coriolanus can be placed into realms of liability for his actions, when he has become a being responsible for making decisions which redirect his future and the future of those around him, we judge him rather than the plebeians. When Coriolanus is seen making his own choices, we assume poor judgment or assume that some willfully chosen character trait has gotten in the way of good decision-making. We listen to the plebeian arguments and see the irrationality of Coriolanus's judgment. Coriolanus (and James) is seen as the bad ruler. Coriolanus reaches these stages of liability so that he may indict himself, to show himself to be a Roman Aufidius. When Coriolanus is a "character" we see a victim; when he is an "individual" we see a man making grave mistakes.

As does Hamlet, Coriolanus both fulfills his role as satirist, exposing the vices and incorrect thinking of both common rule and royal tyranny, and suffers the fate of the tragic hero. As satirist, Coriolanus is imbued with the typical irreconcilable dual view. He retains an "inner vision of an ideal city of Rome which he has fashioned for himself on the basis of his mother's instruction" (Bligh 256). This ideal vision, as is the nature of ideal visions, will never be attained, and many of Coriolanus's behavioral struggles exemplify just this duality of ideal and the "practical" or, at least, the political. This idealism is recognized by the people, though not identified as such, when the tribunes debate Coriolanus's willingness to serve second to Cominius: "I do wonder / His insolence can brook to be commanded / Under Cominius" (I.i.261-263). Their assumption is that Coriolanus "is as crafty and self-seeking as they are" (Bligh 256-257). Rorty's state of the individual "begins with conscience and ends with consciousness" (89). In a satirist, we assume a conscience of some sort; Coriolanus wants to expose inadequacies to censure. Yet in the play's ending, Coriolanus does not seem to reach consciousness as a political figure. He reverts to his criticized Self, his inept role as ruler, his mirror image of Aufidius. His last act may be heroic, but it is undercut by the satiric stroke which not only neatly cuts off the head but dismembers the body standing underneath it.

WORKS CITED

Bakhtin, Mikhail. "Characteristics of Genre," *Problems of Dostoevsky's Poetics*. Trans. Caryl Emerson. Theory and History of Literature 8, Minneapolis: Univ. of Minnesota Press, 1984.

———. "Discourse in Life and Discourse in Art (Concerning Sociological Poetics)," *Freudianism: A Marxist Critique*. Trans. I.R. Titunik. New York: Academic Press, 1976. 93-116.

———. "Forms of Time and Chronotope in the Novel," *The Dialogic Imagination: Four Essays*. Trans. Caryl Emerson and Michael Holquist. Austin: Univ. of Texas Press, 1981. 158-167.

Bligh, John. "The Mind of Coriolanus," *English Studies in Canada* 3 (Sept. 1987), 256-270.

Bruns, Gerald L. "Allegory and Satire: A Rhetorical Meditation," *New Literary History* 11 (1979), 121-32.

Campbell, Oscar James. *Shakespeare's Satire*. London and New York: Oxford Univ. Press, 1943.

Cope, Kevin L. "Satire: The Conquest of Philosophy," Donald G. Marshall, ed., *Literature as Philosophy/Philosophy as Literature*. Iowa City: University of Iowa Press, 1987.

Goldman, Michael. "Characterizing Coriolanus," *Shakespeare Survey: An Annual Survey of Shakespeare Studies and Production* 34 (1981), 73–84.

Hedrick, Donald K. "'It is No Novelty for a Prince to be a Prince': An Enantiomorphous Hamlet," *Shakespeare Quarterly* 35.1 (Spring 1984), 62–76.

Holstun, James. "Tragic Superfluity in *Coriolanus*," *English Literary History* 50.3 (Fall 1983), 485–507.

Howes, Craig. "Rhetorics of Attack: Bakhtin and the Aesthetics of Satire," *Genre* 18 (Fall 1986), 215–243.

Jagendorf, Zvi. "*Coriolanus*: Body Politic and Private Parts," *Shakespeare Quarterly* 41.4 (Winter 1990), 455–469.

Luckyj, Christina. "Volumnia's Silence," *SEL: Studies in English Literature* 31.2 (Spring 1991), 327–341.

McKenzie, Stanley D. "'Unshout the Noise That Banish'd Martius': Structural Paradox and Dissembling in *Coriolanus*," *Shakespeare Studies* 18 (1986), 189–204.

Miller, Shannon. "Topicality and Subversion in William Shakespeare's *Coriolanus*," *SEL: Studies in English Literature, 1500–1900* 32.2 (Spring 1992), 287–310.

Rorty, Amelie. "Characters, Persons, Selves, Individuals," rpt. in *Mind in Action*. Beacon Press, 1988.

Shakespeare, William. *Coriolanus, The Riverside Shakespeare*. Boston: Houghton Mifflin Company, 1974.

Sitter, John. "The character progress as an Augustan phenomenon," *The Arguments of Augustan Wit*. Cambridge Univ. Press, 1991.

Taylor, James. "Hamlet's Debt to Sixteenth-Century Satire," *Forum for Modern Language Studies* 22.4 (Oct. 22 1986), 374–384.

Walker, Jarrett. "Voiceless Bodies and Bodiless Voices: The Drama of Human Perception in *Coriolanus*," *Shakespeare Quarterly* 43.2 (Summer 1992), 170–185.

"On Both Sides More Respect": A Very British *Coriolanus*

S.K. Bedford

It is now nearly ten years since the first "Lights Up" call on Sir Peter Hall's triumphantly unbiased production of *Coriolanus* at the National Theatre, but the ovation accorded its opening has been eclipsed by a growing swing toward more primal interpretations of Shakespearean tragedy. Emotional urgency has overridden intellectual debate as the dominant mode of expressing the chaos and the violence born of economic depression which characterise the 1990s. In 1984 we had time to applaud an exploration of political crisis which was fair to all sides; today it seems that an overabundance of sympathy for one's fellow man can endanger personal survival. We need a story with a through-line that sets us a problem, then clearly teaches us how to solve it. We need answers, not more questions, and we need those answers now. We are, ironically, in the same position as "The People" in the opening scenes of *Coriolanus*.

An audience entering the Olivier auditorium during the run of Hall's production was plunged into an atmosphere of instability and civil discord long before the house lights dimmed. Together, the director and the designer, John Bury, created a timeless amphitheatrical setting dominated by the central image of Rome gates, whose iron frame concealed a false wall that moved inwards to transform the set into the Volscian cities of Antium and Corioli. This imposing structure was flanked on either side by two banks of 'stone' benches, which seated the on-stage audience and provided a secondary acting area whenever its members were called upon to descend to the sandpit below—as they were in Act 1, scene 1.

A guard watched from his station atop Rome gates as the city's plebeians entered carrying union banner and placards, beckoning the promenade audience to swell their ranks in the fight for corn at their own rate. This exodus from the stands revealed old, discoloured "Vota DP" posters and "Danger" notices along the back wall and scaffolding, which united to reinforce the political aura encompassing the play, and evoked the sense of an ancient society in the last stages of deterioration and decay. The sound of shouts and intermittent bursts of gunfire issued from speakers strategically placed throughout the auditorium, as the citizens distributed a list of their demands, spray-painted political slogans across Rome gates, and addressed the audience in character, telling of the reasons for their revolt.

The actors portraying the militant plebeians were instructed to supply their costumes from their own wardrobes so that the garb would appear comfortable, lived in, and would blend seamlessly with the clothes worn by the on-stage audience. While this facet of Bury's design was in keeping with the overall visual eclecticism of the production, I felt strongly at the time that it ultimately served to weaken the case for the plebeians, for in no way could they be described as the physical embodiment of the starving poor. "Hunger" is a catchword of the rebellion, yet here it seemed to issue solely from the mouths, not from the souls and bodies, of the mutinous "rabble." In fact, the clothing worn by several of the citizens planted them firmly in the ranks of the middle class. Although it is certainly credible that such individuals would join the demonstration from the promptings of passionately held political beliefs, it diminished the sense of desperation inherent in the play-text, and dissipated the tension of an uprising staged "in hunger for bread, not in/thirst for revenge" (1.1.23–24).

Paying mere lip service to such issues as food-rationing, usurious interest rates, and a government which robs from the poor to give to the rich would never do in our current economic climate; yet on re-viewing the production with the objectivity of hindsight and placing it within its socio-historical context, perhaps Hall's portrayal of the citizenry was not as inappropriate as I first believed. His production was mounted during a period of economic growth and prosperity. True, it came at the tail end of the British miners' strike and on the cusp of a series of arts-grant cuts which would cripple the budgets of subsidised theatres throughout the country; but the poll tax riots, the collapse of Communism, the Gulf War, and the Bosnian/Somalian/Sudanese crises still lay unsuspected many years in the future. (Not to mention the Hezbollah, which led to the self-imposed exile of Salman Rushdie in almost parodic parallel to the story of Coriolanus.) We must not forget that in the geography of Shakespearean tragedy Italy stands as a metaphor for England, and Rome, its capital, is London. And the brief of any director mounting a show is to make it relevant to the time and place of production—once again London, 1984—when we did have the tendency to polemicise from a position of relative comfort. Looking back on a decade when the mantle of political correctness was adopted as the latest fashion, perhaps we were better dressed at our mass uprisings than we are today.

Certainly Bury's overall design for both set and costumes remains a highlight of *Coriolanus* as staged at the National Theatre. He instantly conjured a society which existed independently of time and space by clothing the plebeians in modern dress, the senators in classical robes thrown over twentieth-century jumpers, and the matriarchs of Rome in simple white gowns. This sartorial eclecticism was further explored on the battlefield, where the military uniforms had a futuristic feel, and the warring generals were seen to strip down to primitive loincloths for their gladiatorial combat in Act 1, scene 8. Far from proving a radical departure from Elizabethan stagecraft, this philosophy of design is basic to the original, for Shakespeare's company played in the open air with a minimum of scenery, and costumed its shows with the cross-section of articles available in stock. There was no unity of time or place, though the actors would have largely performed in modern—i.e. Renaissance—dress. Finally, the visual accessibility of Bury's design freed its audience to concentrate on the more complex demands of the play's text, to listen to the performers they were watching.

The greatest obstacle for a modern actor approaching Shakespeare's drama for the first time lies in his or her probable grounding in naturalistic performance. Frequent pauses, the stressing of off-beat words and, above all, the avoidance of falling into a regular vocal rhythm are standard methods of representing the inarticulateness of "real" speech, and are directly opposed to the stylized nature of Shakespeare's stagecraft. Any attempt to find a compromise between naturalistic delivery and Renaissance rhetoric can only result in a halfheartedly embarrassed performance; one must have confidence in the verse form and pursue those very rhythms which are alien to contemporary theatre, if the beauty and strength of the text are to be exploited to their full potential.

For this reason, Hall presented his cast with a set convention for vocalising the script at the very start of the rehearsal process. His years of intensive work on Shakespeare's plays had led him to conclude that there is a definite formula for the delivery of Renaissance verse, and that its structure must be strictly observed before the creative process of developing the character's psyche can effectively breathe life into the bare skeleton of correct speech. Far from imposing restrictions on the artistic invention of the role, Hall maintained that proper phrasing merely guides the actor to the correct interpretation of his or her lines, and therefore facilitates the playgoer's comprehension of both dialogue and characterisation.

Hall repeatedly insisted that the actor's task is not to create a unique pattern of inflection, but to build the overall shape of the role and its individual gear changes. *Coriolanus* was written by a man who *heard* his words as he wrote them down, and each of his scripts contains the complex orchestration of a symphonic score. Before the key note to one musical phrase ends, a new one begins. Indiscriminate use of pauses thus only serves to dissipate the audience's attention and brings the production to a standstill. Although Shakespeare himself offers no more concrete directorial advice than "suit the action to the word,/the word to the action" and never go over the top (*Hamlet*, 3.2.19–20), the structure and phrasing of the text itself are written as notes to the actors. Rhymes, ends of lines, cues, and monosyllables must be picked up, used, and emphasised in order to bring out the full meaning of the verse.

By using a compilation of the Arden edition and the First Folio for *Coriolanus*, Hall ensured that the text for his production was as close as possible to the original script (despite corruptions), so that his interpretation of its structure might be the more accurate. Not only did Shakespeare's words come under his scrutiny; punctuation was also held to provide an influential clue to analyzing the line. A full stop means a gear change, a shift in tone; it is the signal for variety in the coloration of a passage—a quality not shared by the semicolon or comma. The latter often tells the actor to take what Hall called a "sniff" at a certain rhythmic point in the speech; thus the first citizen says "Let us kill him, (sniff) and we'll have corn at our own/price" (1.1.9–10). The briefest of pauses after the comma draws attention to both movements, while placing particular emphasis on the plebeians' cause of action. This specific example reinforces Hall's general observation that the weight of meaning in Shakespeare resides in the second half of the line, whose end serves as a springboard to its successor. A rush of emotion may entitle the actor to run on to the next line but never into it, or the form will be lost and the result nonsense. The text of *Coriolanus* is so complex that clarity of speech must be the governing principle in performance if the audience is to follow the play's difficult language and dense imagery.

Clarification of archaic phraseology also proved a crucial factor in the director's decision to make textual cuts and emendations five weeks into the rehearsal process. At this time Hall staged a full run-through of the show, not only to check on the development of characterisation and general cohesion, but in order to determine which passages would be incomprehensible to an audience with no prior knowledge of the script. Wherever an illustrative gesture was felt to be theatrically worse than a cut, the line was lost. Yet this was but one consideration in abridging the work—the play was pruned on three counts: comprehension, repetition, and weakness in performance. The servant scene which follows and comments on the new-found alliance between Coriolanus and his old enemy Aufidius never found its proper rhythm in rehearsal; it slowed the action without injecting the necessary comic relief, and so was cut during previews. The lines expressing Coriolanus's scorn that the plebeians dare speak of

> side factions, and give out
> Conjectural marriages; making parties strong,
> And feebling such as stand not in their liking
> Below their cobbled shoes (1.1.192-95)

were deleted, as they add no further information to his prior claim that they

> presume to know
> What's done i'th'Capitol: who's like to rise,
> Who thrives, and who declines. (1.1.190-92)

Brutus's outrage at Coriolanus's popularity in the marketplace was likewise shortened by three lines:

> Seld-shown flamens
> Do press among the popular throngs, and puff
> To win a vulgar station. (2.1.211-13)

Hall felt that the antique religious image would prove inaccessible to a modern audience, yet the removal of this passage produced unexpected results. As James Hayes, the actor portraying Brutus, was the first to point out, the abridged speech has sexist implications, for the remaining examples held up to ridicule by the tribune—the "prattling nurse," "kitchen malkin," and "veil'd dames"—are all women.

In addition to such cuts, various amendments were made to the script in the interest of comprehension—"Corioles" was regularized to "Corioli," "Good den" to "Good e'en" and "lenity" to "leniency"—and several choric lines were divided and ascribed to individual citizens or tribunes. The most significant alteration to the text occurred in the rebel leader's response to the news of Coriolanus's impending attack on Rome. The Arden edition reads:

> That we did for the best,
> and though we willingly consented to his banish-
> ment, yet it was against our will. (4.6.144-46)

The dark humour of the pun lies in Shakespeare's ambiguous use of the word "will." Although the commoner is rebuking his

"On Both Sides More Respect"

parliamentary representatives for choosing to banish Coriolanus from the city rather than invoke the extreme sentence of death, his line can be read as a total and unjustified transference of guilt. And this becomes the sole interpretation registered by a twentieth-century audience, whose wholehearted laughter at the vacillations of the mob shattered the tension of the scene and transformed the proclamation of Apocalypse into a circus act. During previews, Hall exchanged "yet it was against our will" for "yet it was his death we wished for," thus reducing the double-edged clause to a single meaning and preserving the serious tone of the exchange. Although this emendation did clarify the people's intentions, it was regrettable that the line no longer scanned as in the original; seven syllables became eight, and that small addition ended the line with a weak preposition rather than a strong noun. In this instance, connotational embarrassment was exchanged for a structural defect. Generally speaking, however, the cuts and alterations introduced by Hall did serve to elucidate what remains an exceptionally difficult text, not only linguistically, but in its psychology and its politics, and kept the play moving at a brisk tempo that sustained the audience's interest throughout.

The director further tightened the pace of his production by editing minor props and furniture originally designed for inclusion in the show. The resulting visual minimalism not only intensified the set's emblematic power to evoke an atmosphere or hard political debate, but also had the practical effect of facilitating entrances and exits, and simplifying scene changes. By rapidly cross-cutting his lighting cues, Hall directed the audience's focus with the invisible dexterity of a master film editor. Only two blackouts interrupted the play's momentum: one at the interval, the other at curtain down.

Designed by John Bury, the lighting plot was comprised of general states, with two follow spots constantly trained on the principal players, so that they might move freely among the melee of nervous "extras" created whenever the stage audience was called upon to enhance their crowd scenes. Lights were hung upstage at a thirty degree angle to heighten features and basic shapes (rather than provide the more flattering illumination of a down-front positioning), and thus forged an austere luminary landscape for a work whose thrust is starkly antiromantic.

Not only did Bury's lighting design compensate for the presence of a promenade audience, it exploited this central facet of the director's vision. From the very top of the play, Bury incorporated the audience into his stage picture, in the first scene totally eradicating the traditional barrier between actor and spectator through the use of a preset wash. His first lighting cue came two minutes into the show, as a slow fade which gently lured the viewer into its action. The "reality" of shifting seats and rustling programs merged smoothly into the theatrical moment, without a word of dialogue being lost. The danger of the promenade audience intruding on the play's private scenes was avoided by the designer's ability to "lose" the stands by further dimming his peripheral lights, while retaining a hot spot on the sand centrestage. Transitions between scenes were seamless: before the matriarchs had completed their exit at the end of Act 1, scene 3, lights went down on the sandpit, and a spot hit the stage right scaffolding where Caius Martius stood perched for his opening line "Yonder comes news" (1.4.1). The spectator was instantly transported to the Roman camp outside Corioli, mentioned by Valeria only moments before. The dramatic "discovery" of the warrior above plunged us into the action *in medias res*, and established a quickening dynamic which was maintained throughout the battle sequences in Act 1.

The taking of Corioli proved to be of greater technical difficulty than most battle scenes in Shakespeare's canon, because of its dependence on strategic intelligence for success. Hall took great care to follow both stage directions and information given in individual lines, for this was clearly not a war to be won on the strength of brawn alone. At the same time, he warned his actors not to lose their sense of militaristic frenzy and pleasure in blood sport. He asked them to consider Shakespeare's attitude toward the kind of fighting men they were and the kind of war they were engaged in, then to push for the same critical response the play would have engendered in an audience indigenous to its time.

The fight director, Malcolm Ranson, also met with the logistical problem of having to choreograph the sequence with

"On Both Sides More Respect"

twelve actors for the Roman power, and only eleven for the Volscian side; of those eleven, two were women and four musicians, yet they must at first prove victors of the field. Thus it was decided to create a menacing tableau to set the scene. A rhythmic drumbeat and the emanation of smoke from behind Corioli walls drew the enemy army's attention to the upstage gates, on which two senators stood inviting them to battle. Suddenly, the gates flew open to reveal the Volscian soldiers in a haze of dry ice, illuminated from behind so that they appeared as faceless figures, their weapons gleaming in the light. The Romans stood amazed; this surprise tactic robbed them of the attack and led to their initial rout. The musicians remained well-camouflaged among the Volscian numbers, whose female contingent issued war cries as they chased the enemy round the perimeter of the circle, then vanished again into the city.

Despite the textual reference to ladders being used to besiege Corioli (1.4.22), Ranson opted against having the Roman soldiers scale the city walls. Such an image would have reduced Corioli to the small space represented by its gates, which had to form the focal, though not sole visual point of reference, if the element of spectacle were to work to its full potential. Likewise, the stage picture was felt to be dramatically weakened if the Volsces issued "forth their city" (1.4.23) while the Romans were perched above their heads. The moves of the fight had to be brief and remain a peripheral image to the gates and to Coriolanus himself, who stood at the centre of the stage, brandishing the Roman banner and cursing his men as they ran past in twos and threes in retreat to the trenches downstage centre. The gates then slowly opened inward, unleashing a hazy light and eerie chords of music to entice the warrior into their confines. Ironically, the same sense of supernatural danger, which proved so irresistible to Coriolanus, also accounted for his legion's lack of enthusiasm to follow him into battle. He is separated from his men by that ideal code which is the very essence of heroism, yet which remains incomprehensible to the ordinary footsoldier who follows orders rather than glory. Thus the second soldier's practical comment that the gates have shut him in "To th'pot" (1.4.47) exploded the emblem of heroism we had just witnessed, and revealed Coriolanus to be as isolated within the culture of the battlefield as he is in the beau monde of social life.

Act 2, scene 1 returned the audience to the Roman street which opened the play, thus heightening the visual juxtaposition between the city on the threshold of war and its response to the news of Coriolanus's victory. The Roman matriarchs entered through the main doors to bring certain news of Martius's success. The mingled joy and relief with which they greeted their old friend Menenius brought an added lift to the scene and quickened its tempo, as each capped the other's line, and Menenius posed question after question without waiting for an answer to the last. The glee with which he demanded "Is he not/wounded? He was wont to come home wounded" (2.1.117–18) and Volumnia's staunch "Oh, he is wounded; I thank the gods for't" (2.1.120) never failed to meet with hearty laughter from the post-Freudian audience, which found the image of this self-contained middle-aged mother, bloodthirstily revelling in the battle scars of her son, infinitely amusing. A trumpet fanfare interrupted their discourse to announce the approach of the conquering army, and their fast-paced prose suddenly moved into verse as Volumnia set the scene for her son's victorious entrance. Her lines

> Death, that dark spirit, in's nervy arm doth lie,
> Which, being advanc'd, declines, and then men die
> (2.1.159–60)

were chillingly counterpointed by the sound of a solo drumbeat, recalling the awesome force of Coriolanus's deeds on the battlefield, and establishing the tone for the triumphal ritual to follow.

A herald took his position above Rome gates as senators and nobles entered from various sides of the stage to assume a circular formation, with Volumnia, Virgilia, Valeria and Menenius at its centre. Hall wanted the ceremony to be "supremely vulgar," in order to heighten Coriolanus's disgust with the hollow trappings of social intercourse. Thus he originally blocked the scene with four red banners suspended from the flies, a red carpet issuing from Rome gates to run the length of the sand, and a rush of gold metallic confetti falling over Martius's position at the foot of the stairs, in visual allusion to our contemporary practise of hailing the conquering hero with a ticker-tape parade. Unfortunately, the use of confetti during previews was found to be impractical, for there was no opportunity to clear its remains from the sandpit before the interval, and its presence proved distracting during the interior domestic and senate scenes which followed; hence it was cut before opening night. Hall instead chose to incorporate four extra banners within the stage picture; two dropped into position near the wings, and one fell to either side of the nuntio above. They unfurled simultaneously with the company's mass entrance and the herald's announcement "Know, Rome, that all alone Martius did fight/ Within Corioli gates" (2.1.161–62).

Cued by the company, the stage audience stood and applauded rhythmically as Martius, accompanied by Cominius and Titus Lartius, made his way down the auditorium's central aisle, arriving at the foot of the stage on cue for the proclamation of his agnomen. Flags were waved to the sound of a trumpet fanfare, prompting his angry outburst "No more of this; it does offend my heart" (2.1.167), the first of the warrior's futile gestures to break through the offensive formality of public show. Cominius recalled him to the necessary performance of the triumphal rite with "Look, sir, your mother" (2.1.168), and Martius ascended the stage to kneel by her side, attempting to release his pent-up emotion within the bosom of his family, and thereby transform the public event into a private reunion. Yet this, Volumnia could not allow; she raised her son to his feet as she pronounced the name which he had won "By deed-achieving honour ... Coriolanus ..." (2.1.172–73).

Virgilia then stepped forward to silently greet her husband, who enfolded her within his cloak of victory and tenderly embraced her on "My gracious silence, hail" (2.1.174). The momentum of the scene became a whirlpool spinning in tighter and tighter circles, as Coriolanus greeted mother, wife, friend, and senators. It was discovered in rehearsal that a slow procession of one after the other to shake his hand, diminished the scene's rising dynamic; Valeria was therefore positioned right so that she could be easily seen by Coriolanus over Menenius's shoulder as he "clipped" his friend, before hastily moving to kiss her hand on "O my sweet lady, pardon" (2.1.179).

Volumnia's "I know not where to turn" (2.1.180) gave the cast its cue to spring into action to greet the three returning generals, and the stage was briefly overrun with a flurry of ecstatic handshakes and embraces. This visual confusion was resolved only with Menenius's enthusiastic pronouncement "You are three/That Rome should dote on" (2.1.185–86), as the military leaders turned to link arms and face him centrestage. Yet the well-meaning patrician could not resist a jibe at the people's tribunes who stood in isolation down left, and whose sour faces did indeed resemble "crabtrees ... that will not/Be grafted to" the general relish (2.1.187–88). The scene abruptly halted with the old man's faux pas, as the assembly turned in a body to observe the tribunes' confusion. Some found the remark silly, some offensive, but all found it eminently interesting. Coriolanus uttered a dark laugh, ironically agreeing "ever, ever" (2.1.191), while Cominius quickly signalled the herald to restore order with "Give way there, and go on" (2.1.192).

All might still have been well, had Volumnia quit the ceremony without publicly announcing her desire that Martius's military triumph also be crowned with the laurels of political office. Cominius again jumped into the breach to move the procession offstage, lest the explosive situation become irretrievable. Trumpets sounded and the stage audience applauded rhythmically as Coriolanus made his exit upstage centre, flanked by his wife and mother, and closely followed by the rest of the cast.

Volumnia's political ambitions for her son are, of course, realized before the end of the act, yet no sooner is Coriolanus elected consul than he is again summoned to appear before the people to answer charges of treason against the state. The trial in Act 3, scene 3 underwent massive revision during the production's week of previews. Hall's original staging saw the action played out with a dual focus on Coriolanus above right, and the tribunes above left; yet this led to something of a tennis match for the stage audience which had been brought down from the stands, as each side vied for its attention. In this initial version of the scene, Coriolanus delivered "Let them pronounce the steep Tarpeian death" (3.3.88) in a tone of easy contempt rather than violent anger. He had already decided to leave the city, and thus could afford to provoke the tribunes with ironic laughter and arm movements which demonstrated to the audience the absurdity of his predicament.

Coriolanus descended from the stands only with his climactic declaration of self-banishment, while seeking out specific faces in the crowd to whom he might address each line. It was a chilling moment because the insult was made personal, the more so as it was spoken in a tone of ironic knowledge, cool and detached, rather than in the heat of anger. Yet this gesture of upstaging the prosecution and taking control of the trial seemed more characteristic of the theatrically flamboyant Richard II during his deposition scene, than the irascible tenor of Coriolanus's single-minded return to the matters of the corn, the people's cowardice, and the necessity for patrician rule. Although playing irony as the dominant note of this sequence highlighted unexpected passages and called attention to the complexity of thoughts and images that had hitherto appeared straightforward, it also served to invest the role with a depth of interpretation not inherent in the text. There was too much of the English nobleman about him, and not enough military fighting-machine.

Shakespeare's Coriolanus acts and speaks from the simple strength of personal, passionately held beliefs. He can see but a single truth, and irony implies the ability to stand back and examine a situation from many different angles. Coriolanus is incapable of responding in such a detached manner—if he could, he would not be at the point of banishment in this scene. He is always a driving agent in the action, yet expresses his disposition not only out of stubborn pride, but a highly developed sense of integrity. Thus Hall and actor Ian McKellen wisely chose to reblock the sequence, with Coriolanus standing in stunned and contemptuous silence during his sentencing.

The staging as performed on opening night alluded to the decorum observed in a modern court of law. The tribunes representing the state took up their positions in the stands above left, while the defending patricians moved above right; citizen jurors seated themselves in a circular formation along the perimeter of the sandpit, with members of the stage audience standing behind, and the accused isolated in their midst. Sicinius delivered the sentence of banishment as though calmly reading a preestablished document, while the people's choruses of "It shall be so" (3.3.106) were not merely a mechanical echo of their leaders' earlier command, but the registering of independent votes, at first spoken by a lone citizen with gravity rather than hostility. After the ruling was made and assimilated, repetition of the phrase grew in intensity as other solo voices chimed in from either side of the circle, and culminated in a final choric utterance, during which the jurors unanimously raised their arms in a right-hand vote. Pronunciation was crisp, for impact and emphasis. Only the first citizen pointed to the Tarpeian rock (localized to the back top of the Olivier for continuity) on the earlier cry of "To th'rock, to th'rock with him" (3.3.75). His colleagues again voted silently by extending their hands in the air. This version of the trial sequence both preserved the integrity of the people's court, and ensured that its sentence came, not as the hysterical cry of a lynch mob, but as the affirmation of a judicial verdict.

The jury became emotional only with Brutus's stirring restatement of their decree:

> There's no more to be said but he is banish'd,
> As enemy to the people and his country.
> It shall be so! (3.3.117–19)

The citizens are accorded but two choruses of "It shall be so" at this point in the text (3.3.119), but Hall chose to include three additional repetitions of the phrase, as the people jumped to their feet and incited the promenade audience to join in their chant, thereby assuming an active role in banishing Coriolanus from the city. The stage was covered in a frenzy of vocal and physical movement, as the plebeians moved in on the still stationary central figure to invoke the penalty without delay.

Suddenly, the hero spoke for the first time since demanding sentence a full thirty lines earlier. His explosive words stopped the citizens dead in their tracks:

> You common cry of curs! whose breath I hate
> As reek o'th'rotten fens, whose loves I prize
> As the dead carcasses of unburied men
> That do corrupt my air: I banish you! (3.3.120–23)

As he cursed the people in vengeful terms which he himself was fated to enact, Coriolanus walked among their ranks and addressed each phrase to individuals in the crowd, causing them to look away and transforming their unbridled hysteria into an air of silent yet stubborn revolt. Delivering "Despising/For you the city, thus I turn my back" (3.3.133–34) from his position down left, he stood for a moment to survey the mob with a look of scathing contempt, then determinedly marched off into the wings. Yet even after his exit, Coriolanus's presence hung over the stage as his disembodied voice boomed across the auditorium: "There is a world elsewhere" (3.3. 135). It is his climactic statement of heroic isolation and invincibility; this Coriolanus could not rest without ensuring that he had the last word, even if it echoed from offstage.

The revised blocking of the trial sequence successfully heightened the image of organised chaos which dominates the third act of the play, where scenarios are constantly set up only to be blown apart, as Coriolanus finds his absolute nature swaying back and forth between a desire to please his mother by quelling Rome's civil discontent and his volcanic revulsion from dissimulation. In Act 3, scene 3, Hall translated this inner dichotomy into physical reality, as Coriolanus found himself literally caught between the opposing forces of senate and tribunes, and surrounded by a citizenry whom he despises, yet who act as masters of his fate. The tension was the greater for the unflinching integrity with which both people and tribunes were portrayed. This was no simple case of unjustified villainy persecuting an innocent hero, or indeed of a fascist tyrant persecuting an innocent nation—each side was painted, like Cromwell, with "warts and all." The momentum built to fever pitch with the climactic explosion of the hero's curse and subsequent celebration of the people's triumph, then abruptly dropped as the audience was invited to witness the devastation wrought by Coriolanus's banishment in the second half of his story.

Displaced by the politics of peacetime, Coriolanus instinctively reverts to the culture of the battlefield; Rome once more finds itself at war against the Volsces, and against the military genius of its own best general. The city's last recourse is to send its women to plead for mercy. In Hall's staging of the supplication scene, Coriolanus stood down front as his family mounted the stage right steps to take up their position at the centre of the sandpit. Despite his outward defection and his desperate resolution to stand "As if a man were author of himself/And knew no other kin" (5.3.36–37), the soldier repeatedly proved incapable of sustaining his independent mien. After affectionately acknowledging wife, mother, and friend, and blessing his son, young Martius, it obviously took a supreme effort of will for Coriolanus to realign himself with Aufidius stage right, as he refused to call off the Volscian attack on Rome.

As Volumnia began her argument of persuasion, Coriolanus seated himself with Aufidius at his shoulder, so that his ally might bear full witness to the scene. Perceiving that rhetoric would not sway him, Volumnia advanced to confront her son directly with her bared wrist, vowing to kill herself rather than see him destroy his native city:

> thou shalt no sooner
> March to assault thy country than to tread —
> Trust to't, thou shalt not—on thy mother's womb
> That brought thee to this world. (5.3.122–25)

Virgilia's and young Martius's affirmation of her oath overwhelmed the seemingly implacable warrior. He rose as though to physically brush away his debilitating leniency, and crossed with Aufidius further right. Volumnia then broke away from the Roman contingent to pursue her son and arrest his departure with "Nay, go not from us thus" (5.3.131), bowing before the Volscian commander to make her request for peaceful conciliation between the warring nations. She appealed to Coriolanus's sense of personal loyalty and integrity, to his name and fame, then abandoned all vocal persuasion for the creation of a more powerful visual emblem, as the Roman virgins prostrated themselves in the sand before his new position down left.

The women first dropped to their knees, then stretched out flat, Middle-Eastern fashion. It was initially a very slow, formal, and dignified action; their attitude of begging came only with the final obeisance. Perceiving that her strategy had once again proved fruitless, Volumnia cued the ladies to rise and make their exit stage right. She moved with them, then suddenly caught sight of her grandson mimicking their gesture of supplication, and called upon Coriolanus to witness this moving sight. He watched, expressionless, as Virgilia gathered up young Martius; and Volumnia beckoned the procession to advance before interrupting her exit a second time, for one final attack on her son. She crossed to confront him face-to-face, spitting out the words:

> This fellow had a Volscian to his mother;
> His wife is in Corioli, and his child
> Like him by chance. (5.3.178–80)

Throughout the scene, Coriolanus's invulnerability before Roman persuasion lay in his resolution to stand without kin; yet once the repercussions of that intent were articulated for him by Volumnia—that his real mother must be a Volscian and both he and his son bastards—his destruction became inevitable. Volumnia gazed coldly into his eyes, then turned away in a powerful image of maternal rejection. Coriolanus literally clutched at her retreating figure, to hold "her by the hand silent" (5.3.182). Still gazing opposite, Volumnia straightened her back, and her facial expression betrayed the knowledge of her triumph. The moment was electric. Then slowly she turned, and the two faced each other once more as Coriolanus uttered "O mother, mother!/What have you done?" (5.3.182–83) in the tone of an agonized child. There was no apology, just a moving statement of his realisation that in giving life to Rome, Volumnia has robbed him of his own:

> But for your son, believe it, O, believe it,
> Most dangerously you have with him prevail'd,
> If not most mortal to him. (5.3.187–89)

As he spoke, he pumped her arm in rhythm to the lines to drive the point home. He then abruptly broke away to cross right, expressing an active acceptance of his fate: "But let it come" (5.3.189). Coriolanus's movement away from his mother was played as a step toward death.

Volumnia's triumphal procession through her city provided a sombre contrast to the ticker-tape parade which celebrated Coriolanus's victories in Act 2, scene 1. The capitol's political representatives filled the stage as before, motioning the promenade audience to rise and applaud rhythmically as the women of Rome slowly made their way down the theatre's middle aisle. Yet this time, the perimeter around which the senators aligned themselves remained in semidarkness. Only the centre of the circle was brightly illuminated for Volumnia to receive the adoration of the multitude. A single drumbeat sounded as the first senator appeared atop Rome gates to announce:

> Behold our patroness, the life of Rome!
> Call all your tribes together, praise the gods,
> And make triumphal fires. Strew flowers before them;
> Unshout the noise that banish'd Martius;
> Repeal him with the welcome of his mother:
> Cry, "Welcome, ladies, welcome!" (5.5.1–6)

Volumnia's triumph was truly a stunning piece of stagecraft. Standing on the hotbed of the sand, surrounded by the townsmen she had saved, she spread her arms wide and fought back her tears as she turned to accept their expression of joy and thanksgiving. Her facial expression bore witness to the conflicting emotions of public jubilation and personal grief at war within her, providing a second climax to the persuasion scene of Act 5, scene 3. As she completed her turn, the stage audience was once again instructed to applaud rhythmically as the procession exited through the gates of Rome.

The triumphal image was given a third and final twist in the next scene, as Coriolanus returned to the city which had lent him its name. Followed by a single attendant, he ran through the auditorium carrying the Volscian standard, to be greeted by enthusiastic cheers and applause from the people who rushed to shake his hand. It was to prove an ironic moment, for his troubled past was soon to repeat itself at an accelerated tempo, with the warrior accused of treason against the state and publicly executed. The blocking of the assassination was yet another sequence which underwent fundamental revision in the week which preceded the show's first preview. Hall wanted above all to undercut any representation of romantic heroism, insisting that Coriolanus's end be ugly and very rapid. Fight director Malcolm Ranson, originally instructed the three conspirators to converge on the central figure from opposite sides of the playing area. The first cut him across the stomach, the second slashed him at waist height from behind, while the third slit the back of his throat. With his spinal column cut, Coriolanus's head fell forward and he collapsed like a broken puppet; there could be no "noble corse" after such an execution, just a bloody trunk. This, however, gave rise to the practical problem of cheating a run on a half-naked body (for Coriolanus had torn off his Volscian uniform earlier in the scene)—a piece of stage business which must appear artificial to the promenade audience which stood in close proximity to the action. Even though Coriolanus was positioned alone in the focal centre of the sandpit, it would have been discordant with his past military fame for three men to run at him from a distance and overpower him. Thus it became necessary to rethink the staging of his judicial murder.

Hall felt that the play's already well-established eclecticism justified the modernisation of this sequence. He therefore armed the conspirators with pistols and a rifle, positioning one man on the stage right ledge of Corioli gates, and the other two in the slips at opposite ends of the theatre. As Coriolanus made his ill-fated run on Aufidius, they gunned him down in a powerful emblematic explosion of the heroic myth. It was, however, unfortunate for the continuity of the production that no guns were seen earlier in its action, but the dilemma of how to stage these final moments arose too late in rehearsal to introduce modern weapons into previous scenes, and so prepare the audience for their use. The only concession possible was to include rifle fire in the sound tape employed to suggest the citizens' revolt in Act 1, scene 1.

Though something of an auditory shock, there were no visual horrors to this political execution. Because he was shot from such a great distance, no actor was physically close enough to transfer blood to the body of the hero; the use of pneumatic blowguns was likewise discounted because of their insufficient range of fire. The director's options were thus reduced to a choice between the impact of an unexpected explosion or a continuation of the visual theme of blood. Although I preferred the never performed knife-ambush on Coriolanus, I must concede that the assassination in its final version, with emphasis on aural rather than visual effect, presented a clear, stark dramatic moment. The image of the hero's corpse lying within the empty circle, bloodless though it was, movingly encapsulated the barbaric violence and impossible "absoluteness" which lie at the heart of the play. This final emblem of human and heroic waste was fully exhibited to the audience, as Coriolanus's body was ceremoniously lifted and carried in state around the outer perimeter of the circle, before disappearing forever behind the city walls. Piercing music and a high-pitched whine swelled to ear-shattering intensity, then fused with the thunderous percussion of Corioli gates slamming shut. The tragic cycle was complete.

Skilfully performed and stylishly produced, Sir Peter Hall's *Coriolanus* well deserved the critical and popular acclaim it enjoyed throughout its run at the National Theatre. The story was enacted with a simple directness that helped to make its archaic vocabulary intelligible to a modern audience. If anyone was unable to follow the logic of the verse, it was largely due to the acoustical problems within the theatre itself, rather than the actors' delivery of their lines. Hall's painstaking insistence that his company follow the natural rhythm of the text ensured that Renaissance poetry flowed with the ease of modern English; and it was this clarity of presentation which proved the fundamental strength of his production.

Effective, too, was his staging of the iconic tableaux which both stemmed from and further motivated the movement of the verse. Few who saw the show can have forgotten the emblems of childhood, maidenhood, matrimony and motherhood prostrating themselves in the sand before the husband/father/friend, the mingled triumph and despair of Volumnia's welcome back to Rome, or the solemn finality of Corioli gates swallowing the hero's corpse, the sandpit still littered with his discarded uniform as the only remnant of his towering, yet troubled existence. Hall also created a series of symbolic stage pictures where none were explicitly called for by the script, such as the emblem of Coriolanus as a "thing of blood" perched on his soldiers' shoulders with fist upraised and banner flying in Act 1, scene 6, and the image of the people's court trying the heroic defendant in Act 3, scene 3. These tableaux invariably worked hand in hand with the text to supplement the information conveyed through its dialogue; and when Renaissance images were translated into their modern equivalents, as in the aforementioned trial, or indeed the rapid gunfire which mockingly curtailed the hero's final demand for single combat, they remained faithful to the spirit and essence of the original. The transitions between stage pictures were also effected with seemingly effortless precision. Image flowed smoothly into image, and scene into scene, for the creation of a self-contained and harmonious whole.

My one serious criticism of the production paradoxically arose from this sense of integration—the show was almost too neatly packaged and slickly presented. It was, above all, a highly intellectual staging of the tragedy, and consciously so, yet it seemed that in adopting such a cerebral approach, much of the "blood and guts" of the drama were lost. *Coriolanus* is an earthy play about the confrontations between a nonthinking man of action and the illiterate masses, and between violent warriors on the field of battle, set in the primitive days before Rome became a republic. It is a play, too, in which every major transition within the hero occurs either offstage or during a moment of silence: Coriolanus literally makes his decision to join forces with the Volsces during the interval, and his final capitulation in sparing Rome is signalled by an impulsive clutching at his mother's retreating figure during the production's sole extended pause. Coriolanus takes action, then resigns himself to the consequences of that action; he cannot rationally explain his decision, for it is made on a purely emotional level. Nor can he camouflage the stubborn simplicity of his inner nature, even when his own survival is at stake. Coriolanus can perform but one role, "the man I am" (3.2.16)—a line cut from this production, and the only textual abridgement which I found detrimental to the play's thematic development. Yet even though Hall's production could have benefited from a touch more of our '90s aggression, its lasting significance for me lies in its prophetic rejection of this decade's desensitization to the other side of the story. Today, as ten years ago, I applaud Hall's commitment to the text and to his allowing Shakespeare's words to speak for themselves.

Source material taken from Kristina Bedford. Coriolanus at the National *(Selinsgrove: Susquehanna University Press/London and Toronto: Associated University Presses, 1992); by kind permission of Associated University Presses, Inc., 440 Forsgate Drive, Cranbury, NJ 08512, U.S.A.*

Illustrations

1. 1959 Royal Shakespeare Theatre Production, Stratford
from left: Virgilia (Mary Ure), Corolianus (Laurence Olivier),
Volumnia (Judith Evans).

Photography by Angus McBean.
Reproduced by permission of the Harvard Theatre Collection.

2. Full stage view of the Triumph Scene (2.1) in the 1984–85 National Theatre Production Director: Peter Hall; Designer: John Bury; Coriolanus (Ian McKellen).

Photography by John Haynes, London. Reproduced by permission.

3. Banishment Scene in the 1989 New York Shakespeare Festival Production
Director: Steven Berkoff; Coriolanus (Christopher Walken); Volumnia (Irene Worth).
Photography by Martha Swope. Reproduced by permission.

4. "Asking for Voices," the 1989 New York Shakespeare Festival Production
Director: Steve Berkoff; Coriolanus (Christopher Walken).
Photography by Martha Swope. Reproduced by permission.

5. Aquila Productions 1993 U.S. Tour Production
from left: Cominius (Robert Richmond), Menenius (Tim Frances), Coriolanus (Andrew Tansey)
Photography by Sam Appleby, London. Reproduced by permission.

6. Aquila Productions 1993 U.S. Tour Production *from left*: Aufidius (Tim Frances), Coriolanus (Andrew Tansey).
Photography by Sam Appleby, London. Reproduced by permission.

Reviews

1901 London Production of *Coriolanus* with Sir Henry Irving

Somewhat mistrustfully Sir Henry Irving has carried out a long-cherished purpose of producing Shakespeare's "Coriolanus." We say mistrustfully, since the changes that have been made in the disposition of the scenes amount to a virtual reconstruction of the play; and some of the characters, notably Volumnia, are much altered. In the case of Caius Marcius the omissions consist principally of scenes of action. The interrupted fight with Tullus Aufidius disappears, as does the scene in which, entering Corioli alone and having the gates shut on him, Caius Marcius earned his cognomen of Coriolanus. Against the banishment of these things nothing needs be urged. Their due presentation calls for a robust style, which is not always a desirable possession and has never been an attribute of Sir H. Irving. Stage fights other than those between dual combatants are by no means easy of presentation, and a man who has to assign verisimilitude to a combat of one against half a dozen or more must have a lightning-like rapidity of action and an impetuosity of attack not to be maintained when the encounter has to be bloodless. Rendered as "Coriolanus" now is, its interest is purely psychological. Caius Marcius hated the fierce democracy of Rome, and his character, as seen in Plutarch and in Shakespeare, has to be gathered from the expression of his loathing. No language which he, and after him Menenius, can use is strong enough to express his contempt for the plebeians and his resentment against the laws which placed power in their hands and those of the tribunes. When deprived of the one endowment of splendid bravery, which has now to be taken for granted, he is a turbulent, haughty, exacting, and wholly unmanageable being, such as subsequent history has scarcely given us, except perhaps in Charles the Bold. This being in the hands of Sir Henry is shown with exemplary fidelity, the feature most distinctly indicated being sardonic contempt. Until the tribunes proceed to deeds of active hostility, laying upon him violent hands, he scorns to recognize his antagonists, speaking of them to the aristocrats and not to themselves. The scorn which animated him when asking their votes penetrated their thick skins, and rendered inevitable his loss of the half-accorded office of consul and his banishment. The most effective scenes were those without and within the house of Aufidius, the latter being especially fine. No violence of speech or gesture marred a performance which was throughout self-contained and convincing. There was little effort, moreover, except perhaps to avoid the points in search of which his predecessors travelled far. The famous speech "I banish you," uttered by Coriolanus to those who are sending him into exile, was delivered without any form of emphasis. Miss Terry was not the Volumnia of our conception, but was a sweet and gracious creature, the influence of whose intercession might well be fatal, as it proved. Mr. Laurence Irving and Mr. Hearn were well contrasted as the tribunes, and Mr. J.H. Barnes rendered good service as Menenius Agrippa. Mr. Tyars made a strikingly martial and impressive figure of Cominius.

"Coriolanus" is not dramatically stirring, and, since the days of Kemble, it has been no great favourite with managers. Macready even, though Barry Cornwall in a rather inflated sonnet applied to his Coriolanus Shakespeare's line concerning Julius Caesar, "This is the noblest Roman of them all," does not seem to have been at ease in it. Sir H. Irving has won in it an honourable *succès d'estime*, which it may well be held is the utmost triumph now to be hoped. The scenery from Sir. L. Alma Tadema's designs is picturesque, though centuries later, we should suppose, than the alleged date of the action.

The Athenaeum, 20 April 1901.

1901 London Production of *Coriolanus* with Sir Henry Irving

Let it be taken as read that I have a profound admiration for the genius of Sir Henry Irving. My sentiment being what it is, and Sir Henry, alas! being seldom now at the Lyceum, I would rather see him there in a bad play that gave him a chance either of being himself or of making an effective impersonation than in a good play that was not so accommodating. That "Coriolanus" is a bad play we all agree. That it contains one fine and interesting part we all agree. Played by an appropriate actor, this part would justify to me the play's production—except during Sir Henry's tenancy of the Lyceum. No profundity or admiration can cheat me into the notion that of the appropriate actors Sir Henry is one. On the contrary, Love, ever acutely perspicacious through that bandage which has earned him a false epithet, reveals to me Sir Henry as an actor who cannot "touch" the part of Coriolanus, nay! as one who never could have "touched" it at any moment in his career. By the defects of those very qualities which I love would Sir Henry have always been debarred. It is no mere matter of age. It is not merely that Sir Henry's noble face and subtle voice are no longer the face and voice of a vigorous man in the prime of life. It is a question of innate temperament. Coriolanus, fine soldier, was a very stupid man. All the egomaniacal pride that obsessed him came directly from narrowness, from lack of imagination—from stupidity, in short. And, just as the soldier is the one type of man that never could have been reconciled by us with Sir Henry's outward bearing, so the one human quality with which Sir Henry never could have harmonised his soul is straight-forward stupidity. As a schemer (in the large sense of the word) Sir Henry, with his obviously active intellect, is seen at his best. As a passive, stubborn monster, with the strength and insentience of a rock, he is seen at his very worst; indeed, *he* is not seen at all; nor is the monster. I know two or three actors who could impersonate this monster quite admirably, declaiming its speeches for all they are worth. Sir Henry, to the best of my knowledge, never has been able to declaim. Beauty of diction he has often compassed, and he compasses it, now and again, as Coriolanus, but at the expense of the part's whole significance. To take the speeches of Coriolanus with a rush—to "spout" them—is the only legitimate method. To break them up, and to inject vocal subtleties into them, is to make them absurd. Coriolanus, as interpreted by Sir Henry, is a character wasted. And—this is to me a far more lamentable matter—Sir Henry, interpreting Coriolanus, wastes himself. Not the beauty of the whole production did one whit appease me for the loss. Nor, certainly, did the sight of Miss Ellen Terry as Volumnia. Indeed, Miss Terry was not less disastrously wasted than Sir Henry. She is always, whatever she do, the merry, bonny, English creature with the surface of Æstheticism—always reminds me of a Christmas-tree decorated by a Pre-Raphaelite. To see her thus when she ought to have been a typical ancient Roman matron, was rather more than I could bear.

The Saturday Review, London, 27 April 1901

1933 Paris Production

Shakespeare Irks French Deputies They Object to 'Coriolanus' at Comedie Francaise as Gibes at Democracy Are Cheered

Lansing Warren

Paris, Dec. 15.—Shakespeare is being accused of mixing into present-day French politics and several Deputies have announced they will question the government about it.

They do not dispute that Shakespeare put words of condemnation for representative government in the mouths of his players, but they do object to modern French audiences cheering these words, and they particularly wish to know how it came about that a national theatre, the Comédie Française, should have decided to produce Shakespeare's "Coriolanus" at this particular time.

The theatre's management protests its innocence and says that the trouble is due merely to the faculty classical drama possesses for suddenly coming up-to-date in its application to actual events. The management had not thought the play had any special modern significance at all until spectators this week began wildly applauding passages in the play in which Galus Marcius excoriates the fatuousness of the Roman mob and rails against the stupidities of democracy.

Minister of Fine Arts Anatole de Monzie himself was present in the government box when "Coriolanus" in a newly translated French version was first produced this week and was as much surprised as any one to hear the enthusiasm of the audience at a speech that translators rendered:

"Whenever the wisdom of rank and nobility finds its decisions depending upon the imbecilic mob, weakness and disorder reign, the interests of the nation are neglected and nothing can be done at the proper time."

Again there was cheering at such utterances as "You delegates of the people are good for nothing" and "Senators and patricians, is your love for Rome great enough to preserve it if necessary by supporting a great change?"

The Deputies present at this opening performance resented this enthusiasm as directed against themselves since it comes at a time when the parliamentary régime in France has been under severe criticism.

The theatre, however, has gone to great expense to create a splendid production of Shakespeare's play and is loath to remove it from the boards. The management points out that audiences have taken to demonstrating at similar speeches with political applications in other plays in its répertoire, notably Alfred de Musset's "A Caprice," when applause regularly greets the statement beginning, "Shall we have another Ministry tonight?"

Reprinted by permission. Copyright 1933 by The New York Times Company.

1954 New York Production

Theater

Harold Clurman

The American theater, almost wholly given to journalistic realism, hankers for more color, dream, and poetry than can find their way into this narrow mold. Efforts to break through are chiefly made off Broadway. The result is that while one is always anxious to hail these efforts with grateful enthusiasm, one is embarrassed because they rarely achieve that degree of professional polish which would make it easy to greet them as true rivals of the more conventional product. . . .

We should also thank John Houseman and the Phoenix Theater for bringing us one of Shakespeare's neglected plays, "Coriolanus." The play was written rather late in the dramatist's career, when, it seems, he was becoming possessed by a pessimistic view of the world. In a certain way "Coriolanus" constitutes a corollary to "King Lear." For if the theme of "Lear" is the emptiness of power—and with it most of the goods, institutions, and trappings of social life—the theme of "Coriolanus" is the hoax and folly of political life.

During the period preceding the formation of the Popular Front in France (around 1934), when "Coriolanus" was produced at the Comédie Française, the fascist-minded greeted it as a propaganda piece illustrating the meanness of the *canaille* (the riffraff—the masses—or, as they are called in the play, "the mutable, rank-scented many"). The Communist-minded made counter-demonstrations against the fascists and thus indirectly against the play.

The truth, I believe, is that Shakespeare in "Coriolanus" was not merely crying, "A plague o' both your houses," but "A plague on all your houses." In the later years of his life Shakespeare was—as most artists and poets tend to be—a compassionate anarchist. None of the political factions are treated kindly in "Coriolanus." The surface techniques of all politics had become for Shakespeare a disheartening, almost a paltry business: he believed only in human affection, in the individual's capacity for love. When a man feels this, the play infers, he is on perilous ground. When Coriolanus proves himself a man, instead of a seeker or manipulator of power, he is politically liquidated.

The Phoenix production of "Coriolanus" makes the plot and most of the words entirely intelligible. That is its chief—and I am inclined to say its only—merit. But that is not trivial. Most of Shakespeare on our stage, for one reason or another, remains opaque. When a concise production—story and line clean—is made of a Shakespeare play, we are so delighted that we forget that very little has been created. It is easy to forget, since Shakespeare gives so much through sheer language.

Coriolanus is described: ". . . when he walks he moves like an engine, and the ground shrinks before his treading; he is able to pierce a corselet with his eye, talks like a knell, and his hum is a battery." It is not Robert Ryan's fault if he does not answer to this description. The cast has many able, even excellent actors—though only a few are equipped in voice and diction for Shakespeare—but that is not enough for a drama of this kind. What is required is an over-all artistic conception as a basis for a visual, emotional, "musical"—that is, a truly integrated theatrical articulation of the play's meaning. This entails more than understanding the play's lines, ordering the crowd scenes neatly, adding a few good-looking costumes, and editing the text sensibly. But, let us remember, to produce Shakespeare well with pick-up companies in four weeks is an almost insuperable task. We are still thankful for "Coriolanus."

Reprinted from *The Nation*, February 6, 1954, by permission. Copyright 1954, The Nation Company Inc.

1954 New York Production

Robert Ryan Heads the Cast in One of the Rarest of Shakespeare's Plays

Brooks Atkinson

Unless life starts improving enormously, New York is not likely to see for many years a performance of "Coriolanus" as good as the one that opened last evening at the Phoenix Theatre. Many better plays by Shakespeare are less well acted on the stage. For "Coriolanus" is not in the first rank of the tragedies, either in poetry or craftsmanship. Doubtless that is the reason why it has been played in New York only once since 1885.

Now John Houseman has given the text a good shaking up and staged a terse, fiery performance. Probably it is quite different from what you may have been expecting. Although Robert Ryan's Coriolanus is an egotist, snob and chucklehead, he is personable in his own way. He lacks the fatuousness that is generally assumed to be the vulnerable point in the character.

* * *

He is as valiant a soldier as his mother thinks he is. He is modest personally. His hatred of the mob is hardly more than the one blind point in an authentic military hero. Played in this key, the story of "Coriolanus" is not the routine destruction of a tiresome boor, but the tragedy of a very human being with a mind that has never been stirred out of the commonplace. Mr. Ryan's pleasant, irrational Coriolanus who has more heart than head is an admirable piece of acting and the key to a mettlesome performance.

Mr. Houseman is an enormously able director of Shakespeare, well remembered here for the "King Lear" he staged a few seasons ago. Without straining either the text or the actors, he has molded a performance that has pace and coherence, stormy mob scenes, tender domestic scenes, a flourish or two of battle warfare and a general impression of excitement and headlong logic. In his beautiful though simple stage scenery, Donald Oenslager, at the top of his form, has designed a notable production that surrenders detail to action. Shakespeare did not write for a stage of this kind. But Mr. Houseman and Mr. Oenslager have collaborated on a stage form that preserves the fluidity of the playwriting and perhaps adds a little variety that it is difficult to find in the text.

* * *

The actors play with remarkable insight into the contrasting natures of the people. Alan Napier's tall, gracious, good-humored Menenius has both vitality and distinction. As the lion-hearted mother to Coriolanus, Mildred Natwick, who is not a very rugged lady, nevertheless gives an extraordinary impression of courage, strength and forthright honor. When John Emery gets settled in the part of Aufidius in the second act, he, too, breaks through the conventionality of the writing and acts a warlord of some weight and stature.

Unfortunately, there is not time enough at the moment to discuss adequately the acting of Joseph Holland, as Cominius; Will Geer and John Randolph, as rabble-rousers; Paula Laurence, as a woman of sophistication, and Lori March, as a wife of loyalty and silences; Jack Bittner, as a tempestuous citizen, or Lou Polan as an amiable Roman general.

In Shakespeare's abundant career, "Coriolanus" comes toward the end of that royal succession of tragedies that included "Hamlet," "Macbeth," "Julius Caesar," and "King Lear." Presumably he was exhausted by the fury of all that creation. "Coriolanus" is a tamer play; the narrative is pedestrian, the characters are not drawn with much passion and the poetry is something less than inspired. Custom and usage in the theatre have sorted out the most kingly of the Shakespeare plays. "Coriolanus" is not one of them.

But you would hardly suspect that from the enkindling performance at the Phoenix. Under Mr. Houseman's direction, "Coriolanus" seems to be a tragedy of great pith and moment. It looks like its betters.

Reprinted from the *New York Times*, January 20, 1954, by permission. Copyright 1954 by The New York Times Company.

1954 New York Production

Rare Shakespeare Play Put On Admirably

Brooks Atkinson

In its second production, Shakespeare's "Coriolanus," the new Phoenix Theatre in Second Avenue is doing something useful for the town. It is offering a trenchant performance of a classical play new to most New Yorkers. In 1938 "Coriolanus" was acted here for six performances by the Federal Theatre. Previous to that it had not been done professionally since 1885.

To people who are curious about every detail of Shakespeare's career, any production of "Coriolanus" would be an event of consequence. But the Phoenix Theatre production is a notable piece of theatrical work. John Houseman's sentient staging gets to the heart of the drama more cogently, perhaps, than Shakespeare did. On an uncluttered stage it drives straight into the clash of personalities and political forces that Shakespeare copied out of Plutarch. It is simple, vehement and powerful—free of the platitudes of Shakespearean producing, absorbed in its own theme and characterizations.

Mr. Houseman was associated with the Orson Welles "Julius Caesar" in 1937, as well as the Negro "Macbeth" of the year before. He staged the excellent production of "King Lear" in which Louis Calhern acted in 1950, and he produced the current motion picture version of "Julius Caesar." Although Mr. Houseman is now more closely associated with Hollywood than Broadway, his command of Shakespeare is eminently theatrical. Since we are woefully backward in our ability to put on Shakespeare in this country, Mr. Houseman is a very comforting man to have in this neighborhood. Some day he may be lucky enough to direct a company that cannot only act but speak verse intelligently and beautifully, although that is only an idle dream.

Egotism and Stupidity

"Coriolanus" is the tragedy of a martial hero and patrician who hates the common people of Rome and cannot help antagonizing them. When they banish him, after he has rudely insulted them, he goes over to the Volscians, who are the enemy, and leads them against Rome. Having betrayed Rome to the Volscians, he in turn is betrayed by them. In sum, that is the story of Shakespeare's play.

From the intellectual point of view, Coriolanus is a stuffy, dull-minded egotist. The natural instinct would be to play him like a pompous ass—glorious on the battlefield, stupid in the forum. But Robert Ryan plays him like an attractive, well-bred son of the upper classes who despises the people more out of intellectual sluggishness than malice. As Aufidius describes him in the last scene, he is a boy, incapable of mature thought; and he blunders into treason out of pique. Nothing much goes on inside the handsome head supported by his uncommonly stiff neck.

This is a refreshing interpretation of the massive personality of Coriolanus. Mr. Ryan plays it with warmth, candor, grace and a kind of artless sincerity. It sets the mood for a tumultuous performance in which there are some other admirable pieces of acting. Alan Napier's genial, sagacious and lucidly spoken Menenius, the gossip and counselor (Polonius without imbecility); John Emery's Aufidius, the opportunist with an impulsive attitude toward Coriolanus; Mildred Natwick's heroic-minded mother of Coriolanus, full of pride but uncompromising in her devotion to honor—these well-articulated characterizations compose an unhackneyed background for Mr. Ryan's portrait of Coriolanus.

Long Cast

The cast is a long one, but Mr. Houseman has succeeded in rallying it out of the dreary cant that overwhelms the back rows of most Shakespearean assemblies. Donald Oenslager's practicable yet glowing scenery, Alvin Colt's Roman costumes in variegated colors and Alex North's background music that keeps the clamor of warfare hovering over the play contribute toward a general impression of liveliness and professionalism.

If "Coriolanus" is seldom played, it is because theatregoers have long since separated the great Shakespeare dramas from the second-rate. It came at the time in Shakespeare's life when he had exploited his tragic formula to the point when he was not really stirred by it.

Everyone likes to discover hidden profundities in Shakespeare's dramas. Students occasionally try to match "Coriolanus" against the political ideas of today. If you rationalize furiously enough, you can interpret "Coriolanus" as the tragedy of a public idol who resists democracy. But that would be putting modern ideas into Shakespeare's mind. He did not love the common people any more than Coriolanus does. For Coriolanus' disgust with their sweat and sour breath turns up in other Shakespeare dramas and probably expresses the mind of the author as much as the disdain of the character.

If Shakespeare had lived on into the time of Milton, he would have been compelled to choose sides in the political warfare of the seventeenth century when Milton became the pamphleteer of freedom. But Shakespeare did not have to bother with such things. Under Elizabeth and in the early stages of James' reign, the masses were not a critical problem. Shakespeare was a conservative man who believed in the sanctity of the throne, the power of the upper classes and the solid delights of investing money profitably and going to the law to preserve his property. The common people amused him with their chop-logic and exuberance. But he was no crusader. He was upsetting no apple-carts. The apples looked very delicious to him.

"Coriolanus" has to be accepted, not as a tract, but as a merchantable piece of drama that deals in the vendible goods of tensions, crises and disasters. We owe the Phoenix Theatre thanks for rescuing from obscurity one of Shakespeare's least familiar texts, and thanks also to Mr. Houseman for staging it with so much dash and clarity.

Reprinted from the *New York Times*, January 24, 1954, by permission. Copyright 1954 by The New York Times Company.

1959 Stratford Production

Olivier Performs Coriolanus Role
Stars in Stratford-on-Avon Production—
Last Played Part 22 Years Ago

W.A. Darlington

Tonight at the Shakespeare Memorial Theatre expectation ran high for Laurence Olivier's appearance in this centenary season as "Coriolanus." It is a part for which he is equipped beyond most actors and in which he has not appeared for twenty-two years.

Coriolanus is the least likable of all of Shakespeare's tragic heroes, because the sin by which he falls is a fierce, intolerant personal pride. He is that most difficult character—a man undeniably great who is yet not great enough to be humble. No modern audience in this age, which prefers its great men to be regular fellows when not on show, can readily take to such a man.

It is up to the actor, then, to give him an inner quality of nobility that can make him command the respect of the audience in spite of his obstinate hatred of the common people and his flat refusal to accept democratic institutions.

This Olivier achieves in the first part of the play by the very outrageousness of his behavior. You cannot help admiring a man so completely sure of himself even when you think him completely wrong-headed. Up to the point of his banishment from Rome two-thirds through the play, the actor is triumphantly successful.

Later, when Coriolanus leads an enemy army against Rome merely to gratify his private grudge against the city, our belief in his fundamental nobility becomes more difficult to sustain.

Here the actor's performance loses some of its authority.

Peter Hall has directed with vigor—perhaps with too much vigor in some places, since the scene of fury before Coriolanus' banishment dissolves into a shouting match. In contrast to this, Edith Evans' playing of Volumnia, Coriolanus' mother, is dignified and restful.

Reprinted from the *New York Times*, July 8, 1959, by permission. Copyright 1959 by The New York Times Company.

1965 New York Production

Robert Burr Impresses as Angry Patrician

Howard Taubman

The most impressive aspect of the New York Shakespeare Festival's "Coriolanus," which opened officially on Tuesday night at the Delacorte Theater in Central Park, is Coriolanus himself. Robert Burr makes of him a proud, impulsive, foolish, uncompromising figure with whom any of us can identify.

Mr. Burr is the actor who stepped into the breach last summer to save a Central Park "Hamlet." He is a performer of virile power and smashing intensity, and these are the qualities Coriolanus must have. He begins the role in full cry, and one fears that neither his voice nor his energy will hold out for later scenes. But they do—admirably.

There is the scene in which Coriolanus puts on the gown of humility and sets out to appeal for the "voices" or votes of the plebeians. But the words stick in his gorge. He cannot conceal his contempt for the rabble; he cannot bear to pretend; he is by his hot-blooded nature the very antithesis of the soft-soaping politician.

*

Mr. Burr makes this Coriolanus utterly credible. He is all restlessness and impatience, as if his nerve ends rebelled at opportunism. His roaring at the crowd is a cry of wrath at himself, the anger of a man who should have known better than to let himself be talked into a try for the consulship.

Mr. Burr manages to intensify the fury in Coriolanus where it needs to be intensified. In the climactic scene when he confronts the people in the market place, he is a man clinging desperately to a determination to be calm, as he has promised his wife and patrician friends. But when one of the tribunes questions his patriotism, he bursts out in a towering rage. Mr. Burr is here a tragic figure, for he knows that he is compounding his troubles.

At the end, even when the ferocity of the vengeful Coriolanus has been tamed by the pleas of his mother, wife and little son, Mr. Burr does not let us forget the tempestuous nature of the man. One sympathizes fully with Coriolanus's predicament. He emerges as a protagonist in a tragedy instead of an arrogant, truculent snob, and that is not only Shakespeare's doing but also Mr. Burr's.

*

Gladys Vaughan's staging in Ming Cho Lee's evocative set has probably helped Mr. Burr to achieve stature as Coriolanus. She has approached the play with turbulent vigor. In the early scenes of the fighting and the rushing about of the people, the production tries too hard for momentum. Some of the action, indeed, is unintentionally comic. But in the best passages the performance builds with power and tension.

The cast is variable, like nearly all the Shakespearean groupings we get in this country. Staats Cotsworth brings warmth and dignity to old Menenius. Jane White is a passionate and eloquent Volumnia. James Earl Jones is a crafty and dominant demagogue as a tribune, very much in contemporary terms. Mitchell Ryan's Aufidius is a little soft for a warrior.

As the young Marcius, "the poor epitome" of Coriolanus, there is Robert Ross Burr, 7-year-old son of Mr. Burr, and touching, too, in the bit part. As if to make sure that young Marcius in this production will always be the real thing, the festival has another Burr boy, Edward Britton, as Robert Ross's understudy. Quite an acting family, the Burrs.

Reprinted from the *New York Times*, July 15, 1965, by permission. Copyright 1965 The New York Times Company.

1965 New York Production

The New York Shakespeare Festival 1965

Alice Griffin

For the 1965 summer season at the open-air Delacorte Theatre, the New York Shakespeare Festival bravely—and successfully—presented three of Shakespeare's less popular plays: *Love's Labour's Lost*, *Coriolanus*, and *Troilus and Cressida*. Admission is free to the Central Park productions, whose audience is a varied one as to age and social and economic strata. As has been true of the Festival since its inception, the season was better as a whole than in its parts. The complex technical production has steadily improved until it is now almost perfect. A necessary evil of the outdoor stage is amplification by microphones hidden in small blocks jutting up at the edge of the hexagonal stage, but the quality of reproduction is good.

To the credit of Joseph Papp, the producer, the Festival since the beginning has always approached Shakespeare with great honesty, letting the merits of the play speak clearly for themselves, rather than overlarding the play with such tricks as changes of period, devices which call attention to themselves rather than to the action and dialogue, and the general "hoking up" which modern productions often employ. There is always an atmosphere of excitement about a production at the Delacorte, partly because the producers realize that Shakespeare is exciting theater and partly because productions on the excellent permanent open stage designed by Eldon Elder by their very use of that stage generate such an atmosphere. Clarity always has been the keynote of the Festival productions: action and dialogue are assisted by gesture and stage business to explain lines that might be difficult, and the decor and spectacle serve the play, rather than the other way around.

Like every other American Shakespeare production, the festival plays are weakest where a Shakespeare play should be strongest, in the acting. A Shakespeare play makes three demands upon the actor, which only isolated actors in these productions have been able to fulfill: to grasp and convey larger-than-life emotions in a way that is realistic and convincing; to render both the meaning and the poetry of the lines; to look and move as if one is the character portrayed, and not an actor masquerading as that character. Except for an occasional genius—like George C. Scott, whose Richard III and Shylock remain the Festival's high points of acting—actors must be trained to play Shakespeare. Mr. Papp has asked for foundation assistance for such training during the winter, and surely no cause in the performing arts is more deserving or more urgent. Until such training of American actors is undertaken by a professional of the caliber of Michel St. Denis, who heads the actors workshop for the Royal Shakespeare Theatre of Stratford-upon-Avon, American productions of Shakespeare, whether in Central Park, Minnesota, Stratford, or California always will be uneven and unsatisfying.

Because the performers were not up to the demands of the play, *Love's Labour's Lost* (June 9-July 3), which is almost entirely dependent on style in acting and delivery, was the least satisfying of the three 1965 productions; *Coriolanus* (July 7-31), dominated by the good performance of one actor, Robert Burr, was the best; *Troilus and Cressida* (Aug. 4-28) was somewhere in between....

For *Coriolanus* the unit setting consisted of three sections of arches suggestive of Roman triumphal architecture, with upper and lower sections. In the storming of Corioli, the upper stage became the walls of the city, while the city gates were represented by the lower middle section, through which Coriolanus rushed when the city was attacked, after which the gates slid together ominously behind him. For his victory procession, the set became a triumphal arch, and it served as well for indoor scenes, with the addition of curtains or a taper.

Gladys Vaughan, the director, noted in the program that *Coriolanus* was "a play of powerful forces not only in conflict with each other, but with inner turmoil as well," and this was the note the production struck, with clarity and effectiveness. She approached both factions objectively, and brought out the rights (and wrongs) of the aristocrats and the common people. The two Tribunes she cast as a negro and a Puerto Rican, to lend a local as well as general timeliness to the production. James Earl Jones, the Othello of last year's Festival, was an outstanding Junius Brutus, blending the aggressiveness and the humanity of this Tribune, who enjoys wielding power over the people he represents and for whom he is fighting the power of others. Morris Erby and Leonard Jackson made significant contributions as members of the mob, whose scenes Miss Vaughan staged with an almost frightening realism.

Robert Burr had both the voice and physical presence for Coriolanus, and his interpretation was credible as well as impressive, presenting Coriolanus as a modest, courageous hero (or anti-hero) who wants public office but abhors public contact. Both his interpretation and Miss Vaughan's staging brought out the timeliness of the play and our "heightened . . . awareness of the interaction between a single man's personality structure and the pressure of the historical moment," as the director stated in a program note. Unfortunately, many of the supporting roles were inadequately played, and in the important part of Volumnia, Jane White was so excessive as to be unbelievable.

Reprinted from *Shakespeare Quarterly* 16 (1965), 335–39, by permission. Copyright 1965 The Folger Library.

1965 New York Production

Mugging the Bard in Central Park

John Simon

Shakespeare has had a hard time of it in America. Not only is there no Shakespearean acting tradition and adequate schooling available, but also what theatrical method has prevailed here is the exact opposite of the style, or stylization, Shakespeare requires. Thus the Bard has fallen into the hands of either academicians and their student productions, or culture-mongering socialites banding together with the backwash of Broadway to Theatre-Guild the lily. Typically, the American Shakespeare Festival at Stratford, Connecticut, wallows in both errors: a representative production there is a "Measure for Measure" done as a Strauss operetta in Old Vienna, with a company full of Broadway has-beens or mincing eunuchs, and directed either by a cast-off director of the Old Vic with his wonderfully Edwardian ideas, or by an ex-college professor with no stageworthy idea whatever.

But my concern here is with the New York Shakespeare Festival, to be had in Central Park every summer, and singled out for every kind of praise by every kind of reviewer. Night after night it sells out—not its seats, which are gratis, but its artistic standards, which, if any, are gratuitous.

Two things should be noted right away about Joseph Papp, the man who conceived and produces the Festival. He is passionately dedicated, and he was able to get the project going over all manners of opposition and, what is worse, indifference. He raised the money, and, God knows, it's easier to find sermons in stones than to squeeze blood, or money out of them. But though Papp is a gifted money-raiser, that does not yet make him a theatrical producer of quality—and certainly not a valid artistic, let alone stage, director. He has undeniable talents for getting things started, and no idea where to stop.

As I look back on many summers of Central Park theatregoing, I see few things to recall with genuine pleasure. Perhaps no more than three: Philip Bosco's Angelo, Penny Fuller's Celia, and John Morris's music for "Love's Labour's Lost" (or, as the Pappians in their non-U way spelled it, "Love's Labor's Lost"). Even there I cannot be quite sure about how much additional dignity Bosco gained by the cloddishness of Marianne Hartley's Isabella, how much Penny Fuller's stature was raised by the total collapse of Paula Prentiss's Rosalind, and how much Morris's unpretentious melodiousness profited by contrast with the customary claptrap of David Amram. In any case, what are these few bright spots as against that army of Rorschachian blots spreading across Mr. Papp's scutcheon?

What, for example, of Frank Silvera's Lear, a vapidly self-pitying whiner from beginning to end; of Nan Martin's Beatrice, all leaden cutenesses; of Colleen Dewhurst's and Michael Higgins's turning "Antony and Cleopatra" into the humdrum affair of an Irish washerwoman with an Irish cop, complete with brogues? What of Julie Harris's baby-talking Ophelia; of Papp's staging of "The Merchant of Venice" so that Shylock emerges the undisputed hero; of Gerald Freedman's directing "The Tempest" as a series of vaudeville acts bristling with sight-gags and stage tricks further obscuring the already mumbled and uneasily rattled-off poetry? And what of the repeated casting of performers like Betty Henritze, who has only to appear on stage for the aesthetic eye to boggle; or Jane White, who has only to open her mouth for the civilized ear to revolt? Or take the current directional trio, Gladys Vaughan, Gerald Freedman, and Papp himself; individually, I dare say, they could be matched, but I defy anyone to adduce a threesome as monumentally untalented.

Consider the most recent Park production I have seen, Mrs. Vaughan's "Coriolanus." Here were crowd and battle scenes of which a third-rate discotheque would have been ashamed; swordsmanship that looked like a bunch of tourists in Chinatown insistent upon using chopsticks; blocking that had, for example, Coriolanus bidding farewell to his wife from clear across the stage; low comedy involving the Volscian servants lingered over with much more gusto (though no more taste) than any of the tragedy surrounding the protagonist; a Valeria interpreted not as a noble Roman matron but as an Eve Arden-style comic-relief *hausfrau;* and an entire cast mispronouncing the Volsces as "the Volskis"—shades of the Russkis, perhaps?

The individual performances, with the exception of Robert Burr's manly and personable, though hardly great and tragic, Coriolanus, were foul to middling; of these the most hauntingly horrible were the tribunes of Alan Ansara and James Earl Jones, the Virgilia of Kate Sullivan, and—hysterically cheered by reviewers and audiences alike—the Volumnia of Jane White. Jones sounded like a one-stringed double bass with a faintly Calypso accent, and rolled about like a huge barrel set in motion by a homunculus within. As for Miss White, her every look, gesture, and move is that of a fishwife suffering in equal measure from neurasthenia and megalomania. But the supreme giveaway is her voice, inflating every sound, blowing up every syllable into an egomaniacal balloon, until her entire hypertrophic ego is wafted heavenward on bloated, unnatural vocables.

Proper Musicality

Both Miss White and Mr. Jones are Negroes, which brings me to yet another trouble with Papp's productions. Out of a laudable integrationist zeal, Mr. Papp has seen fit to populate his Shakespeare with a high percentage of Negro performers. But the sad fact is that, through no fault of their own, Negro actors often lack even the rudiments of Standard American speech—itself well behind British English in musicality and appropriateness to Shakespearean verse; moreover, they have been unjustly deprived of sufficient training and experience in even the standard American repertoire, such as it is. As a result, desegregation will take even longer on the poetical than on the political plane.

But is not only aurally that Negro actors present a problem; they do not look right in parts that historically demand white performers. As the painter Larry Rivers—neither a highbrow nor a square, but possessed of an acute visual sense—remarked during a recent symposium, "I don't think putting Negro actors in white parts is possible—I don't see how you can keep life out of the stage." Thus a black Henry V runs counter to the lifelikeness of the play—all the more so when, as always happens, his brother is played by a white actor. With Mrs. Vaughan's Roman citizenry about four-fifths Negro, Rome became, clearly, the capital of Abyssinia, the few whites presumably accountable for as missionaries. The trouble with this sort of thing is that it cannot help setting off wrong responses, so that it is scarcely surprising to find the innocent who passes for *Cue* magazine's drama critic commenting that "the bitter clashes are sometimes startlingly suggestive of Bogalusa or Selma." Fine, except that, unfortunately, that is not remotely what the play is about.

The critical evaluations of Papp's enterprise have been consistently and thoroughly misleading—whether because of the assumption that something free of charge and for the people must be evaluated along democratic, not dramatic, lines, or simply because of the popular reviewers' abysmal lack of discrimination, it would be difficult to say. What, for instance, is one to conclude from Judith Crist's review of "Coriolanus" in the *Herald Tribune*, which reads in part: "Whenever the play bogs down in talk or scene change—and the play does—director Gladys Vaughan has set a citizen to scrambling about, a flag to waving and a lackey to pratfalling. None of this is excessive, all of it is part of the excitement generated by this handsomely dressed, fast-flowing production." The conclusion, I suppose, is either that Shakespeare at the height of his creative powers was a bungler happily rescued by Mrs. Gladys Vaughan, or that Miss Crist, at the height of her critical powers, is beyond rescue.

What justification is there for feeding audiences no Shakespeare but pap—whether with one or two p's? Some twenty-five years ago, arguing for the movies as they then were, the playwright Gerhart Hauptmann wrote: "One does not drag down 'Peer Gynt' when one makes a film of it; but one may, perhaps, raise an audience consisting of decent chambermaids, hansom cab-drivers, or even of all kinds of uncontrollable elements, up to its level." Rather than the Germany of 1920, this is the democratic America of 1965 with hardly any chambermaids or hansom cabbies left (though a few of the latter survive, precisely along the perimeter of Central Park), but Papp's Shakespeare today is very much what a 1920 silent-film version of "Peer Gynt" might have been. No doubt there are those—drama reviewers included—who enjoy, of a sticky New York evening, going into the summery Park for an uplifting sermon against Governor Wallace, but those whose concern is with Shakespeare, with theatre, with art will find little or nothing of value in it.

Mr. Papp is not really interested in art, let alone poetry, about which he manifestly knows nothing. To him, Shakespeare is the friend of the common man, the spokesman for the underdog, the social, or socialist, Messiah. But Shakespeare was no such thing, and in the attempt to wrench him into that, his true magnificence is irretrievably lost.

The New York Shakespeare Festival had best be considered as an act of charity for underprivileged New Yorkers, and should, as such, be reviewed by those reporters whom the papers regularly send out to cover charity balls and bazaars. Or is that whom they have been sending all along?

(Mr. Simon, who here contributes a guest column, is drama critic for the *Hudson Review*.)

Reprinted from *Commonweal*, September 3, 1965, by permission. Copyright 1965 by Commonweal Publishing Co.

1979 New York Production

"Some Thanks for Most Sweet Voices"

Eileen Blumenthal

Joe Papp's black and Hispanic Shakespeare company has taken a quantum leap forward. Its *Julius Caesar* was an object lesson in dull, inept Shakespeare; the new *Coriolanus*, however, features some of the company's most gifted performers and though its concept is not especially inspired, the production is exciting.

Coriolanus is about a military hero who, banished from Rome for his anti-republican pronouncements, joins Rome's enemies, the Volscians, to lead a mortal attack on his homeland. Coriolanus's tragic flaw, unlike most, is precisely the quality that makes him great—a fanatic, egomaniacal need to win without compromise. The play contrasts his brutal dynamism with the semi-effectual grace of Rome's civilian leaders and the moronic manipulability of the common people.

At the center of this production are three fine performances. Morgan Freeman's portrayal of Coriolanus is as intelligent as it is electric. Anti-civilized, with his hair napped together, his face and body scarred, he combines commanding dignity with the alertness of a lean, angry dog. Without undercutting Coriolanus's stature, Freeman makes clear from the first moments that this hero is suited for authority only in battle and is unwilling to be curbed by anything. Robert Christian, as Coriolanus's Volscian arch-rival, is of the same taut breed—but with the bitter vulnerability of one who is second best; audiences who have seen Christian's lyrical work in Fugard's plays will be the more impressed by his steeliness here. And Gloria Foster, though occasionally a bit ponderous, captures the brutality, authority, and intelligence of Coriolanus's mother.

These three performances are so strong that they compensate for a few real deficiencies in the production. While much of the supporting cast is at least competent, some of the acting is plain inept. The roles of the civic leaders—Coriolanus's friend Menenius and, especially, the two tribunes who represent the common people—are not only weakly performed but misconceived. Director Michael Langham has followed the standard critical line that the tribunes are conniving, narrow-sighted fools, whose championing of the rabble's cause nearly plunges Rome into ruin. But Shakespeare's script is more subtle. Coriolanus really *is* an enemy to the common people, and the banishment the tribunes engineer backfires not because it was inherently unwise, but because they underestimated their adversary's fanaticism. The interplay of their civilized moderation with Coriolanus's amoral brilliance is central to the play, and it is trivialized when the tribunes are too lighthandedly dismissed.

The production also fiddles excessively with the text. The heavy surgery seems to me judicious (the show is nearly three hours long even with cuts). But I am uneasy with the extensive modernization of Shakespeare's language. In some instances subtleties of meaning have been sacrificed (for example, Coriolanus's "I had rather be their servant in my way/Than sway with them in theirs" changed to "... rule with them in theirs"); elsewhere, the verse is fractured by word changes ("[I] attach thee as a traitorous innovator" rendered as "[I] arrest you as a traitorous revolutionary"). Shakespeare's poetic rhythms generally are ignored even by the leads, and the distinction between prose and verse passages is lost completely. The implication seems to be that minority Shakespeare must be simplified Shakespeare. And I find that awfully patronizing.

Which brings me to the inevitable question: Why a black and Hispanic Shakespeare company in the first place? Papp's commitment to minorities in mainstream theatre, as both creators and spectators, is longstanding and vigorous—and for years he has been casting blacks and Hispanics in major Shakespeare roles. But the rationale for this new company is

"Some Thanks for Most Sweet Voices"

unclear. If Papp feels that a minority company can open up elements in the plays that are unrealized in mixed-cast productions, that a black rather than white sensibility (whatever that means) should be given a chance to dominate, why use a white director? Both *Julius Caesar* and *Coriolanus* have been utterly traditional in their directional concepts. If he simply feels that despite his and other producers' efforts, minorities still do not get their share of classical roles (and this is no doubt true), why not intensify the commitment to cast them rather than create a solely black and Hispanic company? That solution would preclude the false impression that Morgan Freeman, Robert Christian, and Gloria Foster are big fish only in a small, dark pond, and the larger pool of actors would mean that these first-rate performers would be able to play with colleagues more consistently their artistic peers.

Reprinted from *The Village Voice*, March 26, 1979, by permission of the author and *The Village Voice*. Copyright 1979 *The Village Voice*.

1979 New York Production

Public Theatre, New York, 1979

John Simon

To have a group of black and Hispanic actors, almost totally untrained in Shakespearean acting, do *Julius Caesar* (at the Public Theater) was rashness and folly; to have them do *Coriolanus* ranks as advanced dementia. *Coriolanus,* a vastly superior play, is also incomparably harder to carry off. Moreover, its theme is the undoing of its aristocratic hero by his excess of upper-class antipopulist fastidiousness. The consummate, uncompromising patrician is a figure far removed from the ken of most white Americans; to black and Hispanic Americans, actors or otherwise, he is through historical and economic circumstance, even more remote and inconceivable. Morgan Freeman, who plays Coriolanus, cannot even approximate the part in sound, look, or demeanor; but, for one reason or another, no one in the company begins to approach what is required of them.

Shakespeare, to begin with, is poetry as well as drama. To speak poetry demands a whole separate technique anterior to the technique of acting: The flow of poetry must be maintained under, and to some extent uninfluenced by, the histrionic operation. Of this, no one in the current production is capable, and hardly anyone even aware. As Volumnia, Gloria Foster does some powerful vocalizing, but it has very little connection with Shakespeare's rhythms and, often, even his meanings. Furthermore, she forces her mighty instrument into a range so low that it frequently sounds needlessly unnatural and grating. Maurice Woods has some stature as Menenius, and Michele Shay is pretty as Virgilia. The entire production, under Michael Langham's direction (though not necessarily through any fault of his), looks beggarly, and Erik Fredricksen has staged some of the worst fighting sequences I have ever seen, the shape and size of the theater being an additional handicap. I left at the interval, which I thought would never come.

Reprinted from *New York* magazine, April 2, 1979, by permission. Copyright 1979 K-III Magazine Corporation. All rights reserved.

1985 London Production

The Grand Style: In London, three great actors go for broke

Jack Kroll

Ian McKellen, his near-naked body streaming with blood, whirls his sword and launches Shakespeare's words like cannon fire in *Coriolanus*. Maggie Smith tosses her gold curls, flutters her gold fan and swings her gold furbelows as she warbles the comic ironies of Congreve in *The Way of the World*. Glenda Jackson, her mouth a red wound of passion, pours out a confession of incestuous love to her stepson in Racine's *Phedra*. These stunning performances by three of England's greatest actors highlight the London theater season—and raise questions about the future of the grand style in a world of diminishing grandeur.

Coriolanus is the most unlovable of Shakespeare's tragic figures, an arrogant hero who saves Rome on the battlefield but despises the Roman masses and their representatives. Peter Hall's brilliant production at the National Theatre has a sharp political edge. Reflecting the ideological tension between left and right in today's Britain and America, he stages the play in a time warp between the ancient and modern worlds. Coriolanus is alternatively a fierce, naked warrior and a dandy in a white suit reminiscent of Tom Wolfe—and who, like Wolfe, mocks the "radical chic" of his time.

McKellen's Coriolanus is a titanic study in arrogance. He's a beautiful animal in war, but in peacetime his body contorts into a neurotic ballet when he must court the favor of the people. When his mother, Volumnia (played with tremendous power by

Irene Worth), urges him to butter up the plebeians, McKellen squirms and writhes in a gigantic petulance, toying with his sword like a scolded child. When his enemy, Aufidius, calls him "boy," McKellen repeats the word with apoplectic wrath. "Boy" sticks in his throat with a terrifying gurgle, the death rattle of his overweening pride. His assassination comes not face to face with Roman swords, but at long distance with the stuttering fire of automatic weapons—the impersonal instrument of modern terrorism. At the end we hear from the dark a rising roar, the sound of nuclear death. McKellen's Coriolanus is a hero who poisons his heroism with his lack of human contact. Such heroes leave a vacuum into which the final inhuman disaster may rush.

Reprinted from *Newsweek*, January 7, 1985, by permission. Copyright 1985, Newsweek, Inc. All rights reserved.

1985 London Production

A "Coriolanus" That Mixes Modernism and Tradition

Benedict Nightingale

It's an encounter easier to imagine occurring on the modern Via Veneto or outside some fashion house in Milan than in the narrow streets of ancient Rome. In comes Ian McKellen's Coriolanus, exquisitely accoutered in white overcoat, white suit, white shoes and blue tie and shirt, to confront several dozen members of the National Theater audience who have been specially corralled onstage. "What would you have, you curs?" he asks this ad hoc lynch mob, which the night I was there included a young lady with a Gucci handbag, a beaming professorial type in tweed, and some puzzled-looking Japanese tourists; and answer comes there none.

Peter Hall is the director of this "Coriolanus," as he is of the National itself, a theater that has been making much public noise of late about its financial problems. Was this improbable Roman rabble, one wondered, actually his demonstration to the powers-that-be that he couldn't afford even a scattering of walk-ons, let alone the multitudes recorded by critics and historians of the past? In one 19th-century production of Shakespeare's play, for instance, no less than 200 plebeians "fluctuated to and fro as their violent assent or dissent impelled them, with a loud and overwhelming suddenness and one-minded ponderosity, truly fearful to think of encountering."

Mr. Hall's counterparts spent the evening in forlorn transit between the stage, where they milled sheepishly about, and some specially erected benches at its sides and back, from which they wanly bleated "it shall be so" to Coriolanus's banishment from Rome. You'd find more violent dissent, suddenness and ponderosity among the shoppers at a bargain counter.

But there's more to the production than this pointed reminder of the National's penury, or gesture toward "audience participation," or whatever it may be. There is, above all, Ian McKellen, that brilliant yet exasperating actor. With him, classical style can sometimes become classical affectation. He abandons straight, standard English for a strange regional accent in which stretched-out vowels melodiously throb, then soar or swoop into little cadenzas all their own. The mere word "boy" can become almost an aria in itself, a long euphonious whinny of "boohaya-heeah." It's true that Coriolanus is a pretty narcissistic character, and therefore that some degree of vocal preciosity can be justified, perhaps especially here. You wouldn't expect him to react with brusque monosyllables when his great enemy has just provoked him to a suicidal display of hubris and rage. All the same, "boohay" would surely be sufficient.

*

Happily, the musical decoration can't conceal that the performance has a tune, and one that's strong and true. Coriolanus, you'll probably recall, is a disconcerting blend of romantic thug and heroic brat. His exploits in war win him a popular acclaim he despises; he's exiled for his mandarin politics and personal arrogance; and Rome and the Roman plebs are saved from his vengeance only by the intercession of his mother Volumnia, the one human creature who awes him. On the face of it, the part wouldn't seem altogether suited to Mr. McKellen, an actor not noted for martial machismo. Yet he's surprisingly effective even as a killing-machine, with his blood-streaked torso and grim relish for the fray. And when it comes to expressing pride, disdain and contempt, he verges on the astonishing. Is there another living actor who can sneer quite like him?

It is done in the most relaxed way. He saunters across the stage, one hand in a pocket and the other casually holding the sword he likes to keep poised on his shoulder, and he smiles, always he smiles. Up go his lips, almost to the sides of his nose, in a fastidious smirk; then out they spread in a big, knowing, dangerous grin; and from between them there pours something it would be absurdly inadequate to describe as sarcasm. Call it rather emotional acid, burning and biting even when lightly applied. Is there another living actor paradoxical enough to give us so much fussy mannerism one moment—and so much forceful matter the next?

Mr. Hall has been paradoxical, too. At any rate, he has played odd Einsteinian games with Rome's space-time continuum, presenting us with a place where weapons of war are sometimes broadswords and sometimes bullets, and command is exercised by men in pin-striped suits, men in togas, and (for variety) men in pin-striped suits *and* togas. And the quality of supporting performance is as unpredictable as the costume department, extending from the barely adequate to the very good, a category most memorably filled by Irene Worth's majestically unruffled Volumnia, a lady with the kind of absolute confidence that inspires absolute meekness in others. For a moment in her final encounter with her son it looks as if she may not get her way, and you can sense her hurt, pique and sheer bafflement; but of course it passes. There is a long, long pause, and Mr. McKellen stretches out his hand to her, with a helpless gurgle of "Mother, mother, what have you done?" Formidable fellow though he is, he never stood a chance with Miss Worth.

Reprinted from the *New York Times,* January 6, 1985, by permission. Copyright 1985 by The New York Times Company.

1988 New York Production

The Public Theatre *Coriolanus*

William Over

Under the direction of Steven Berkoff, *Coriolanus*, the sixth production in the "Shakespeare marathon" of plays presented by the New York Shakespeare Festival Public Theatre, managed to qualify for that rarest of categories: a creative "modern-dress" Shakespeare production. During the performance, which I attended 11 January 1989, I overheard an audience member say to a friend, "Isn't it marvelous when they can put the unpopular Shakespeare plays into contemporary terms and have them come out alive?" After the opening moments of the first scene, audience members were drawn in by the contemporaneity of this production as well as by its ensemble stylization and blocking. The mixture of contemporary characterization with individual and ensemble stylization gave the Berkoff production a rich texture.

The fast tempo of this production was established in the first scene of Act I, where a tight crowd of citizens kept up a cacophony of repeated sounds suggested by Shakespeare's repetitions of the same words: "Speak, speak," "Resolv'd, resolv'd," "We know't, we know't." Although the effect was to demonstrate the fickleness of the Roman citizenry, a manifestation of the irrational forces that shape public opinion, the movement of the acting ensemble in this scene was precisely choreographed, as in a Greek tragedy. Instead of tunics, however, the actors wore black leather pants, black buttoned-up shirts, and pointed leather shoes. The citizens seemed a hybrid of

American mafioso and urban homeless. Their combination of emotional stridency and well-synchronized ensemble movement was striking and effective. This was indeed Shakespeare's unruly and unwashed mob, a dangerous and unpredictable lot, accurately described by Marcius (Coriolanus) himself as "no surer . . . /Than is the coal of fire upon the ice,/Or hailstone in the sun" (I.i.171–73).

Christopher Walken's Marcius was a modern urbanite. Well-dressed in 1980s high fashion, he wore a long, black leather overcoat, black silk shirt, and black trousers. The dress was not so much mafioso, however, as the latest Italian fashion from the pages of *GQ*. Walken's movements were also rhythmic and stylized. His walk even suggested elements of rap-singers' movements, with elbows bent and hands folded into fists. The impression was one of street-smart bravado and male exuberance. Clearly, Coriolanus in this production displayed a refined and fashionable presence together with the not-incompatible ethos of a street bully. This combination of refined elegance and snobbery with vaulting, athletic egotism expressed an intended irony in Berkoff's production. Marcius sees himself as at once both the aristocrat, whose superior virtues automatically entitle him to the consulship of Rome, and as the gang leader, set upon maintaining his turf in a bleak world of brute force. The production's statement was clear: aristocratic and martial values common to modern-day nationalism derive from primitive political structures.

That Shakespeare intended such an interpretation is, perhaps, debatable; however, Berkoff's production felt unified, able to maintain these tensive realities within its two hours' traffic. Walken's performance worked because he was able to sustain the tension between these contradictory elements within the role. His acting was low-key, with a Roman *gravitas* that made his occasional outbursts all the more compelling. As the play's central focus, Walken's Marcius strutted in rhythm with the percussive score, which combined martial music with a new-wave urban sound. While his walk was not the rolling "pimp walk" found in urban ghettos, it did suggest a certain *Saturday Night Fever* aesthetic that revealed the character's egocentric stylishness. Walken's speech was also generally low-key, ranging from extended monotonic mumblings of disdain to sudden loud bursts of outrage. The dialect he hinted at was urban Italian-American—a choice that reminded the audience of the play's setting in the Rome of the Italic wars—a setting also evoked by the mafioso dress of many of the Roman officers. Walken's face remained deadpan throughout, except for moments of emotional breakdown, when his facial features resembled a crying-Janus face-mask, displaying open mouth and stretched muscles, a visual emblem suggesting Rome once again.

The complexity of Walken's portrayal was impressive, and his character strong and compelling. The audience felt an affinity with this Marcius despite his social snobbery and stiff rejection of almost everyone in his life. When Sicinius, one of the conniving tribunes, sneeringly advised him that he needed a "gentler spirit" to be a consul (III.i.55), the audience remained in sympathy with Coriolanus. The Berkoff/Walken interpretation avoided turning him into an aristocratic lout by making him the only character in the play with a sense of humor—it was an understated, gestural humor for the most part, but well timed and, in Walken's hands, expertly employed. Only a few of Shakespeare's lines were thrown away in an attempt at glibness, moments in the play when the audience felt slightly embarrassed by the flippancy of his modern readings.

Shakespeare seems to have attempted to portray the people and their elected tribunes as unreliable in their public loyalties and feeble in their powers of rational judgment. He went further in this direction than did his source, Plutarch. Shakespeare underemphasized the legitimate needs of the Roman citizenry during the Volscian Wars and chose instead to focus on their demands and common prejudices. Berkoff's production developed this perspective fully, giving the mob a stridency and coercive conformism in their synchronized choral movements and staccato bellowing of stichomythic dialogue, which at times brutally evoked the shadow side of public opinion. The ensemble members played multiple roles as Volscian warriors and Roman soldiers, their inhumanity articulated by the military stiffness of their bodies and the repeated formation of single lines on the same stage plane. Only occasionally did anachronistic awkwardness creep into their finely tuned performance, for example, when as Volscians they mimed pulling out pistols and automatic weapons in reaction to Coriolanus's sudden appearance before them. Such techniques in this production generally worked quite well, however, and were used in ironic counterpoint to the historical setting. The appearance of the Volscian senate members in the black shirts of Italian fascists, for instance, pressed the theme of the villainy and commonality of war.

With a set design by Loren Sherman that complemented Martin Pakledinaz's costumes, the black-and-white theme of a too-rigidly-understood moral perspective was reinforced. The open stage was interrupted only by slender classical columns upstage that framed a straight row of identical black chairs. The rigidity and austerity of the Roman state—and of the modern American cityscape—was communicated in the look of the stage.

Irene Worth's Volumnia was deep-voiced and as headstrong as her son, but her character seemed more willing to smile at the contingencies of Roman political fortune, a quality lacking in Marcius. Volumnia's anger can be quick and enduring onstage, but her softness and more developed sensibility were evident here, most clearly in her first appearance, I.iii, when her rather bloodthirsty lines managed to come off sounding like the hyperboles of a proud mother. Worth's interpretation relied on a chemistry between her and her son that departed from many earlier stage versions. Her softer qualities served to place Walken's Marcius in sustained focus during their confrontation of V.iii. The effect of a strong Marcius and a relatively suppliant Volumnia kept the direction of the play away from the mother-son relationship and on the developing relationship between Marcius and Aufidius.

Keith David's portrayal of the Volscian general was intelligent and reflective, in spite of his warlike posturing; this interpretation was necessary, since Aufidius is capable of making insightful comments about Marcius, even as he struggles with intense feelings of rivalry (see, for example, his comment at IV.vii.42–45). His stronger character balanced the less assertive, more sensitive interpretation of Volumnia in this production. The effect was to concentrate more attention on the jealous Aufidius's motivation for his betrayal of Marcius in Act V.

Accordingly, the tragedy of male competitive passions remained in focus to the end of the play, even though the supplication scene with the three women in V.iii became the central emotional crisis for Marcius.

The particularly harsh diction and violent imagery of Shakespeare's language in this play has long been recognized. Actually, it is confined to descriptions of Marcius's military activities, to the violent roughness of the Roman crowds, and to the language Marcius himself uses throughout the play. This language would tend to keep him at a distance from us, but Berkoff and Walken turned the hard cadences of the play into a lighter, at times even whimsical, interpretation of Marcius and his warriors. This was due, to a great extent, to the sensitive integration of the percussive music with the rhythms of the actors' movements. What also served to mellow Marcius was the astute translation of Shakespeare's spoken sounds into the street sounds of modern urban America. Walken in this respect must be praised for keeping his speech patterns just on this side of a marble-mouthed Brooklynese dialect that would have lowered his tragic stature and seriously compromised the interpersonal and class tensions within the play.

Richard Venture's Menenius embodied the norm of Roman justice and respect for law and family. He came closest to being the *raisonneur*, commenting succinctly on Marcius's character, for instance, in III.i: "his nature is too noble for the world." Venture's reflections were rendered with an equanimity and mildness that contrasted with the attitudes of the other male characters in the production. The tribunes, Sicinius and Junius Brutus, were urban hustlers who confidently sported fashionable walking sticks, *à la* 1890s, when it seemed apparent that Marcius had lost his bid for power against them.

In the final scene the envelope containing the terms for peace between Rome and Volsces was refused and silently returned to the briefcase in which it was delivered. War would continue, as would the irrational forces that shape such conflicts, with or without proud and unresponsive leaders like Marcius. His life was given a wider perspective in this final, silent moment with the envelope, a perspective in which neither his guilt nor our affection really figured. Peace is finally out of

Marcius's hands, carried instead by the unseen and unspoken forces that have controlled people and events throughout history.

Reprinted from *Shakespeare Quarterly* 41 (1990), 365–68., by permission. Copyright 1990 The Folger Library.

1988 New York Production

Kid Coriolanus

Robert Brustein

Although Shakespeare rarely displays affection for what he called the "beast with a thousand heads," his scorn for people's power is nowhere more evident than in *Coriolanus*. Bernard Shaw once defined democracy as substituting government by the incompetent many for rule by the corrupt few. Shakespeare's few are more arrogant than corrupt, but his many are not only incompetent but mindless and vicious. Representing the nobility they would curb, Caius Marcius (awarded the name of Coriolanus after his victory at Corioli) is a Roman general whose dauntless courage in battle against the Volsces qualifies him for election as a Consul. But he is too proud to pretend respect for the "voices" required to endorse his election or to grovel before this "common cry of curs." As a result, through the machinations of some jealous politicians, he earns the hatred of the masses and banishment from the country he helped to save. The timeliness of the play is almost too obvious to mention. Imagine Coriolanus equipped with a couple of media experts, some well-placed sound bites, and a thousand points of light.

Steven Berkoff's muscular, energized New York Public Theater production never apologizes for the play's anti-majoritarian bias. Quite the contrary, it demonstrates how thin a line exists between populism and fascism, between democracy and demagoguery. In this radical adaptation, we are in a police state where an "ensemble" of citizens costumed in torn jackets and wielding baseball bats—they also treble as senators and soldiers—rants, screams, threatens, and shouts whenever its collective will is thwarted. It is during the scenes between Marcius and the citizens that the production gathers the most steam. Advised by his mother and his friends to boast of his exploits and show his battle scars, Marcius responds by bidding the people to "wash their faces. And keep their teeth clean." Christopher Walken adds an "Ugh." Walken turns Marcius's pretended humility into farce. Appalled at having to occupy the same space with these "stinking breaths," he mocks their power over him ("May I change these garments?"), supplicating in accents heavy with irony: "I pray, let me ha' it; I have *wooounds* to show you."

Walken is not the most patrician Coriolanus in memory. His manner often resembles that of the rabble he detests, and this makes it hard to believe that he and his mother Volumnia, elegantly played by Irene Worth, come from the same family (they were better matched as Chance Wayne and the Princess Kosmonopolis in *Sweet Bird of Youth*). He rages against "the tongues of the common mouth," but his own gritty urban dialect marks him as a member of a similar class. Walken, furthermore, does not seem particularly comfortable inside Berkoff's highly choreographed production, which has him—and the rest of the cast—running, marching, riding, and fighting in a frenetic ballet (even the women sew in unison). Walken, a gifted dancer, sometimes seems purposely out of step, as if protesting the rigid boundaries of the concept. Still, what he lacks in nobility he more than compensates for in command and charisma. He is one of our most daring, unpredictable, and dangerous actors, and for most of the evening he is fascinating.

Walken plays Coriolanus less like a soldier than like a prize-fighter. His hips in constant motion, he shambles, spars, feints, wriggles, and chops as if he were replaying his part in *Kid Champion*. Using imaginary weapons against the enemy, he slaps and kicks his own soldiers. With the rebellious plebeians he uses his fists, punching them out with well-placed cuts to the face and body. In a fury from his first entrance, he stalks the stage like a sullen hood in a black leather long coat. Always at top energy, he rasps, roars, yells, and snarls, then just as quickly lapses into a soft, ironic smile. With his mother he is less the obedient child

Kid Coriolanus

than the silken wooer. Worth, lipping and tasting Volumnia's verse, comes on like a slightly dotty Madame Arcati in *Blithe Spirit*; Walken courts her like a lover, even leading her into a brief little dance. "There's no man in the world more bound to his mother," Volumnia tells us—and in the climactic scene Aufidius drives him into a fatal rage by calling Coriolanus a "boy of tears": "I flutter'd your Volscians in Corioli," he replies, "Alone I did it. 'Boy!'" But Walken seems parentless. Among his "faults in surplus" one cannot count filial dependency.

Still, the performance is tumultuous and so is the production (sometimes to cover a little shallowness). On a black marbleized floor, decorated with 12 straight-back chairs (also black), the show moves forward with manic energy, punctuated by loud percussive music. The interracial "ensemble" of actors, in constant motion, change roles so fast that it's sometimes hard to identify them. They are in black too; so is most of the cast. Tullus Aufidius, costumed in a synthetic black jumpsuit, Sam Browne belt, studded gloves, and jackboots, is played by Keith David as a mature and commanding African dictator, his spine arched with military stiffness, always standing at parade rest. Larry Bryggman and André Braugher as the scheming Roman tribunes wear the pin-striped suits and black slouch hats of Mafia henchmen (Braugher's shaved head and granny glasses also give him a marked resemblance to Malcolm X). Playing the Roman generals, Moses Gunn, stolid and saturnine as Cominius, and Thomas Kopache, wily and hooded as Titus Lartius, are friendly accomplices. And Paul Hecht plays Coriolanus's elder friend, Menenius, as a dapper wit in a fur-collared overcoat and homburg, cogently speaking his "pretty tale" of the body's revolt against the head.

Nevertheless, this Rome is in a parlous political condition; even the graciousness of the three ladies, Volumnia, Virgilia, and Valeria, cannot redeem its overwhelming masculine brutalism. In Berkoff's production, it has been brought to this state by the lures and traps of democratic rule. "With every minute you do change a mind," snarls Coriolanus to the mob, "And call him noble what was now your hate,/Him vile that was your garland"—which is a pretty fair description of the media-soaked, poll-dominated electorate. Were Coriolanus chosen, he would hardly have been a judicious leader, but he was the only hope for peace. By the end of the play, the one possibility for political resolution—a Roman-Volscian treaty negotiated by Coriolanus after his mother prostrated herself before him—is abandoned on stage, a useless envelope lying inside a tattered briefcase.

Reprinted from *The New Republic,* January 2, 1989, 26–27, by permission. Copyright 1989 *The New Republic.*

1988 New York Production

Coriolanus Without Rome

Garry Wills

The *gressus* of a well-born Roman male must have been one of the great sights of antiquity. Those destined for public life were trained to a macho swagger not tolerated in their inferiors. Cicero said this walk should borrow more from the wrestler's moves than from the dancer's.[1] And Peter Brown has shown that a demonstrative virility was still required in the second century of the Common Era.[2] Movies about the Roman Empire often give us senators mincing about in togas. Actually, Rome's leaders—roving the city with their gangs of clients and armed dependents—probably carried themselves more like "home boys" on MTV. A man who forswore such an entourage, like Cato of Utica, was more than once cudgeled in public and was constantly threatened with violence. *Gravitas* meant something more like throwing your weight around than like having a steady ballast.

Shakespeare shows, in his Roman plays, that he had read Plutarch well enough to know the atmosphere of Roman streets (which was not far from the jostling factions in his Verona). Plutarch says (21) that not even exile from Rome made Coriolanus lose his haughty *badisma* (Greek for *gressus*). Shakespeare read this passage in Thomas North's translation: Coriolanus "neither in his countenaunce, nor his gate [gait], dyd ever showe him selfe abashed."[3] So Steven Berkoff, directing *Coriolanus* in Joseph Papp's marathon series of all the Shakespeare plays, is closer to the truth than might be supposed when he makes Coriolanus (Christopher Walken) a bike-gang leader, bopping about with bristly challenge, keeping his followers in line, aching for a rumble with the rival gang leader, Tullus Aufidius. When Walken moves to battle (wielding invisible weapons) it is with a boxer's shuffle and leer, dipping his left shoulder, drawing his right arm back.[4] He was bred as a fighter, and his managers (Volumnia his mother and Menenius Agrippa his mentor) treat him as a valuable property, one that can mow down all challengers. His mother exults:

> Death, that dark spirit, in's nervy arm doth lie,
> Which being advanced, declines; and then men die.
> II.i.157–58 (The Oxford Shakespeare, 1986)

Berkoff stages with great insight Volumnia's opening scene with Virgilia, her son's wife. Virgilia sits in the middle of a bright square of light, miming a dutiful and worried sewing (setting up later references to her as Penelope), while Volumnia treads the outer edges of the square, gracefully plucking roses (in mime), restlessly pushing at the enclosure of the women's space, while she rhapsodically describes her son's exploits on the field. Irene Worth plays Volumnia with an uncanny blend of maternal calculation about her son's political future and delirious identification with his present martial exploits. Ashley Crow, as Virgilia, shrinking into herself at the center of this lethal stalking, conveys almost wordlessly her dread of her mother-in-law and her concern for her husband.

The minor roles—Roman mob, Roman Senate, Volscian army—are all played by the same black-jacketed "gang" members. This allows for some spectacularly choreographed movements, to the inventive percussion score-and-performance of Larry Spivak. The battle scenes (enacted without visible weapons, sometimes in slow motion) inevitably look like the rumbles in *West Side Story;* but there are some magical moments—as when the Romans "ride" toward the Volscians using Agnes De Mille "dressage" movements. The anonymity and interchangeability of the actors is also good at suggesting the quality that the "mob" is named for—mobility. There is an almost Keystone quality to this mob's quick changes of direction, as its loyalties flit from Coriolanus to the tribunes and back again. Shakespeare reflects Plutarch's critical attitude toward mobs in all his Roman plays.

But this anonymity of the followers undermines the very thing Berkoff is trying to accomplish. He told *The New York Times* that he resents, on political grounds, the idea of "spear carriers" standing unobtrusively around the star players. He wants a social equality of parts: "My conception was to take all the small parts of this play and organize them as a union."[5] By the promiscuous use of identical figures as Roman patricians and paupers, as Roman soldiers and Volscian soldiers, Berkoff presents a nihilistic vision of war and political scrambling as purposeless, with robotlike participants acting on senseless urges. They are *all* reduced to interchangeable "spear carriers," in a union of non-producers.

There is, admittedly, a jolt of bitter cynicism in the play; but Shakespeare's political insights are complicated, and depend on the marked differences between (and within) the classes in Rome, as well as between Rome and Rome's adversaries. *Coriolanus* is Shakespeare's most complex political play, though it is usually presented as his simplest. Jan Kott calls it a two-character play, Coriolanus against the people.[6] Even Bertolt Brecht's analysis of the first scene, which is famous for sketching the many levels of political activity in the play's opening situation, considerably simplifies that situation.[7] For one thing, Brecht thinks the populace introduced in the first lines is leading the main revolutionary assault on Rome's patrician government. He worries, for instance, whether they are sufficiently armed to encounter the legionaries. Actually, we learn later in the scene that the main body of the popular party has been elsewhere, wrestling real concessions from the patricians—five tribunes of the people added to the constitution. The Roman general Caius Martius (given the surname Coriolanus after his capture of the Volscian town of Corioles) has been a spectator, not a participant, at those events, and he comes in reeling with anger at them.

What, then, are the people we first see trying to do? They plan to assassinate Martius. They make up, in fact, the kind of private conspiracy that succeeds in assassinating Martius at the end of the play, where Volscians are the conspirators. The Roman people, though they are presented as shopkeepers and "mechanics," are not a single "character." They include the looters who run from battle with spoils (a scene Berkoff omits) as well as loyal soldiers who admire Martius. They include the spies who make the Romans superior to Volscians in intelligence (there is a scene where a Volscian spy meets a Roman spy and they compare intelligence notes like characters from a John Le Carré novel—another scene omitted in this production). Martius, the military aristocrat, passes most of the popular hurdles on his way to the consulship, and only a mounting scene of popular unrest, where the tribunes manipulate the people and the patricians back Martius with misgivings, leads to the exile of Martius. (Berkoff presents only one side of this conflict. Where Shakespeare has a superior force of patricians protect Martius and drive the people off, Berkoff leaves only the mob facing Martius, and he mows them all down with his fists!)

If the Romans are differentiated in their shifting positions around Martius, the Volscians to whom he deserts after he is banished are an even more distinct body of people in the play. We hear nothing of shopkeepers or mechanics among them—or of spies who are any good at their craft. The Volsces are a purely martial society, in which Martius is accepted enthusiastically, despite all he has done against them in the past. The Volscians never, as a people, reject Martius—that is why their former leader, Tullus Aufidius, has to organize a conspiracy to assassinate him. The many absurdities of Berkoff's production reach their climax when the assassins become the only Volscians in the last scene of the play, leaving no one to speak the lines of the Volscian nobles who are shocked at the murder. So Berkoff brings in a Roman, Titus Lartius, to preside over this Volscian scene. It makes political nonsense of the entire play.

Martius himself has the swagger the mob cannot aspire to—but everyone walks the same way in Berkoff's world, Roman or Volsce, noble or ill-born. Plutarch says that Martius, being orphaned of his father, did not have the upbringing (*poideia,* 2) of a political father. Menenius, who was Martius's general when he first went to war, is his grandfather's age, and a representative,

Coriolanus Without Rome

like his mother, of outmoded values. The orator's walk and eye and voice, all praised by Cicero, are evident in Martius:

> When he walks, he moves like an engine, and the ground shrinks before his treading. He is able to pierce a corslet with his eye, talks like a knell, and his "hmh!" is a battery. (V.iv.18–21)

But Martius lacks the civil and suasive discourse that was supposed to crown the orator's supremacy in public life. Words bewilder and madden him. The tribunes, knowing his "provocability" (what Plutarch calls his *philoneikia*, 3), taunt him with words that invade his mind and buzz there—"shall," "traitor," "boy"—as he tries to shake them out in frenzy.

Martius is really a Volscian in attitude, the natural leader of a simple society, and he thinks he sees in the Volscian leader, Aufidius, the last worthy opponent of a heroic age:

> And were I anything but what I am,
> I would wish me only he . . .
> Were half to half the world by th'ears and he
> Upon my party, I'd revolt to make
> Only my wars with him. He is a lion
> That I am proud to hunt. (I.i.231–36)

Later, when he learns that Aufidius is at Antium, he says,

> I wish I had a cause to seek him there. (III.i.20)

Martius spares one of the citizens of Corioles, the town he has just captured, for observing the hospitable code of the heroic days. Named for his enemies, he is like them in ways that prepare for his desertion to them.

One of the many ironies of the play is that Aufidius is as displaced in his own society as Coriolanus is in Rome. Coriolanus is a Volsce by temperament; the crafty Aufidius might well be a Roman amid duller warriors. He rails against the Volscians' inferior intelligence operations, and admits he cannot beat Coriolanus without the help of the kind of craft Romans accept in war:

> I would I were a Roman, for I cannot,
> Being a Volsce, be that I am. (I.xi.4–5)

Thus, though the two heroes embrace in a lustful alliance, Martius's friend Menenius Agrippa, who knows they are polar opposites, not mirror images, speaks a three-word Aeschylean line about them:

> He and Aufidius can no more atone
> Than violent'st contrariety. (IV.vi.75–76)

As Berkoff has flattened and erased the complex domestic politics that drive Coriolanus from Rome (where his mother counsels dishonor, providing a morbid *paideia* to match with her unnatural bellicosity), so he omits all the complex diplomacy of the second half of the play. His Coriolanus marches vengefully on Rome; but the character as Shakespeare wrote it is also sending terms for surrender, giving Menenius a letter to confirm earlier offers to the Romans, asking the Volscians what they want in tribute—all matters omitted here.

When his mother leads an embassy to make Coriolanus relent, Miss Worth plays the scene magnificently, though Berkoff puts her under the restriction of appealing to a character not present in his production (Martius's son) and makes her famous attempt to make anyone speak—Martius, his wife, even his son—look like appeals to Martius alone. He also deprives of its force her most powerful plea, the one in which she composes a lengthy epitaph for Coriolanus, describing how his name will be held in perpetual dishonor. We miss the point of this tremendous argument because Berkoff has omitted all but slight hints of the first embassy to Coriolanus, about which the general Cominius reports:

> "Coriolanus"
> He would not answer to, forbade all names.
> He was a kind of nothing, titleless,
> Till he had forged himself a name o' th' fire
> Of burning Rome. (V.i.11–15)

Martius won the name Coriolanus by capturing Corioles—it was the only special spoil he would take from that victory, and he said he would wear it with honor. What name will he receive if he conquers Rome? *Romanus*—by the unnatural repatriation of a son who has destroyed his mother city. It is the unholiness of this ambition that Volumnia spells out in her elaborate dwelling on the epitaph. Coriolanus does not yield simply to her will, as if he were the "boy" Aufidius calls him, but to a shocked recognition of the unnatural errand he has undertaken. And even this cannot be understood unless we see that his desire to burn Rome went beyond the Volscian war plan spelled out in the diplomacy we are deprived of.

Christopher Walken, though he looks sometimes like an Elvis impersonator, does what he can with the snippets of Coriolanus's lines Berkoff has left him. The great central soliloquy of his three—the one where he ponders the interchangeability of love and hate, speaking of dream obsessions in language that Aufidius immediately echoes when they meet—is simply cut. More astonishing and disturbing, Walken omits the last word of his role, the climactic "Boy!" that, in answer to Aufidius's taunt, turns Martius's last boast into an agony. On opening night, I thought Walken might just have run out of breath in the soaring phrase Shakespeare gives him. But I returned, to a matinee, and he left it out again, though with breath to spare for it. (He also missed an entrance at that performance, and had to be covered by the man playing Aufidius.) Several reviewers have called the sixth in Papp's Shakespeare series the best. Having seen one better (*King John* last summer), I wonder how any of the others can have been worse.

NOTES

1. *De Oratore* III.vix.220, developed by Quintilian, *Institutio Oratoria* I.xi.18–19.

2. *The Body and Society: Men, Women, and Sexual Renunciation in Early Christianity* (Columbia University Press, 1988), p. 11. Statius praises a young man for excelling all others of his age in haughtiness of expression and stride (*vultu gressugue superbo*), *Silvae* II.1.108.

3. North's text in Geoffrey Bullough, *Narrative and Dramatic Sources of Shakespeare*, Vol. 5 (Columbia University Press, 1964), p. 525.

This passage gives extra warrant to IV.v.127 of the disputed Folio text, where war is called "sprightly walking."

4. Though Shakespeare has Coriolanus do most damage with a sword in his play, Plutarch said the hero preferred engaging his foes in hand-to-hand grapplings, making his muscles his only armor and weaponry (2, cf. North in Bullough, p. 506).

5. Merwyn Rothstein, "Trims and New Twists to Clarify *Coriolanus*," *The New York Times*, November 30, 1988.

6. Jan Kott, *Shakespeare Our Contemporary*, translated by Boleslaw Taborski (Doubleday/Anchor, 1966), p. 190.

7. Bertolt Brecht, *The Collected Plays*, edited by Ralph Manheim and John Willett (Pantheon, 1972), pp. 378–94.

Reprinted from *The New York Review of Books*, January 19, 1989, by permission. Copyright 1989 Nyrev, Inc.

1988 New York Production

Theater

Thomas M. Disch

Coriolanus is the sixth production of the Shakespeare canon to be presented by Joseph Papp at the Public Theater, and I liked it as little as last season's *Julius Caesar*, though I must credit the director, Steven Berkoff, with erring for the sake of an idea, or at least of a style. He choreographs as much as directs, having the mob move and speak in choral unison and requiring stylized movements of the stars even in their big scenes. Irene Worth as Volumnia must pantomime picking the roses from an entire hedge during her first big scene, while Ashley Crow as Virgilia contends with a compulsion mechanism that appears to derive from the art of weaving, a traditional activity of classical wives. The battle scenes, which can be the glory, even the raison d'être, of a proper *Coriolanus*, were the pits. In the first, the ensemble members fight invisible foes—and look like a bunch of kids playing cowboys and Indians. Then they kill each other serially and seemingly at random—in slow motion. Then Christopher Walken in the title role deals with the lot of them with a few effortless uppercuts to the empty air as the actors obligingly take a fall. Walken acts as though he were, indeed, Coriolanus, and not yet persuaded to accommodate, by acting, the base requirements of the stinking mob. Not that he was regal; only disdainful.

The set design by Loren Sherman and the costumes by Martin Pakledinaz were in keeping with the star's approach—to call it muted would be to overstate the matter. Some light shone from the darkness. Paul Hecht delivered his lines as Menenius Agrippa so well that one regretted Walken could not more often have been onstage to hear them: He needs lessons in delivering Shakespearean diction. Also, the two tribunes, played by Larry Bryggman and Andre Braugher, acted with some vigor. I confess I didn't stay for the end. That's one of the nice things about Shakespeare: There'll usually be another chance.

Reprinted from *The Nation*, December 19, 1988, by permission. Copyright 1988 The Nation Company, Inc.